MODERN JEWISH RELIGIOUS MOVEMENTS

A History of Emancipation and Adjustment

Revised Edition

by

David Rudavsky

BEHRMAN HOUSE, Inc.

Publishers   *New York*

Publishing history: The First Edition was published by
Diplomatic Press, Inc., New York, and Living Book Ltd.,
London, and was entitled *Emancipation and Adjustment:
Contemporary Jewish Religious Movements, Their History and Thought.* The Second (paperback) Edition was
published by Behrman House, Inc., New York. This
Third (revised) Edition contains many emendations and
interpolations of new material, bringing statistics and
trends up to date and incorporating recent research and
thought.

Published by:
Behrman House, Inc.
1261 Broadway
New York, N.Y. 10001

NEWLY REVISED THIRD EDITION

Library of Congress Cataloging in Publication Data

Rudavsky, David.
 Modern Jewish religious movements.

 Published in 1967 under title: Emancipation and adjustment.
 Bibliography: p. 435
 Includes index.
 1. Judaism—History—Modern period, 1750-
I. Title.
BM190.R8 1979   296.8'3   79-11266
ISBN 0-87441-286-2

MANUFACTURED IN THE UNITED STATES OF AMERICA

To the sacred memory

of my dearly beloved wife

SARAH RUDAVSKY

שרה בת ר׳ יצחק הכהן ז״ל

A princess in Israel . . .

ACKNOWLEDGMENTS

The author and the publishers gratefully acknowledge the permission granted by the following publishers to use quotations from their publications: Abelard Schuman (*Point of View* by Dr. Israel H. Levinthal); American Jewish Committee (*American Jewish Year Book*); Burning Bush Press (*Seminary Addresses* by Solomon Schechter); Funk and Wagnalls (*Nineteen Letters of Ben Uziel* by Samson Raphael Hirsch, translated by Bernard Drachman); Harper and Row (*The American Jew*, edited by Oscar Janowsky; *Two Types of Faith* by Martin Buber; "Religion and Ethics" in *Eclipse of God*, by Martin Buber, translated by Maurice S. Friedman *et al.*); Horizon Press (*Hassidism and Modern Man*, edited by Maurice Friedman); Jewish Frontier Association ("Martin Buber" by Ernest Simon, in *Jewish Frontier*, Feb. 1948); Jewish Publication Society of America (*Solomon Schechter*, by Norman Bentwich; *Students, Scholars and Saints*, by Louis Ginzberg; *Studies in Judaism*, by Solomon Schechter); Jewish Reconstructionist Foundation (publishers of the *The Reconstructionist*); The Jewish Reconstructionist Press (*Judaism As A Civilization* by Mordecai M. Kaplan); Philipp Feldheim, Inc. (*Fundamentals of Judaism*, by Jacob Breuer); Philosophical Library (*Hassidism* by Martin Buber); Oxford University Press ("Major Aspects of Judaism" by Leo Jung, in *Judaism in a Changing World*); Rabbinical Assembly of America (holders of copyright to *Tradition and Change*, edited by Mordecai Waxman); Schocken Books, Inc. ("The Faith of Judaism" by Martin Buber, in *Israel and the World*); Simon and Schuster, Inc. (*The Rise and Fall of the Third Reich* by William L. Shirer); Soncino Press (*Judaism Eternal*, Vol. I & II by Samson Raphael Hirsch, translated by L. Grunfeld; *Horeb* by Samson Raphael Hirsch, translated by L. Grunfeld); University of Chicago Press (*The Life of Dialogue* by Martin Buber, translated by Maurice Friedman).

CONTENTS

FOREWORD by ABRAHAM I. KATSH   9

PREFACE   11

PART ONE: BACKGROUNDS

PRELUDE   17

1 IN GOD'S NAME

    I. *Terror and Libel*   19
    II. *The Medieval Jewish Community*   24
    III. *The Ghetto*   27

2 THE ROAD TO EMANCIPATION

    I. *Introductory*   34
    II. *The Intellectual Revolt*   35
    III. *Renaissance and Hebrew Learning*   37
    IV. *The Religious Revolt*   41
    V. *The Commercial Revolution*   43
    VI. *Jews in Germany in the Eighteenth Century*   47

3 THE ENLIGHTENMENT

    I. *Moses Mendelssohn*   50
    II. *Mendelssohn's "Jerusalem"*   59
    III. *Critique of Mendelssohn's Views*   63
    IV. *Cultural and Educational Impact*   69
    V. *Appraisal of Mendelssohn*   73

4 EMANCIPATION AND ITS AFTERMATH

    I. *The French Revolution*   79
    II. *Napoleon Bonaparte*   83
    III. *Emancipation in Germany*   91

PART TWO: EUROPEAN ROOTS

PRELUDE   95

5 TRADITIONAL JUDAISM

    I. *Sources of Traditional Judaism*   98
    II. *Meaning of Orthodoxy*   109
    III. *Ashkenazim and Sephardim*   112

6 HASSIDISM AND NEO-HASSIDISM

    I. *Historical Background*   116
    II. *The Founder of Hassidism*   121
    III. *Doctrines of Hassidism*   125
    IV. *The Habad School*   132
    V. *Opposition to Hassidism*   135
    VI. *Neo-Hassidism*   140

7 THE STRUGGLE FOR REFORM JUDAISM IN GERMANY

    I. *The Early Stage*   156
    II. *The Religious Ferment*   161
    III. *The Later Stage*   167

8 THE HISTORICAL SCHOOL

    I. *Leopold Zunz*   186
    II. *Zacharia Frankel — His Life and Times*   192
    Basic Dynamics of Frankel's Historical School   198
    III. *Solomon Judah Rapoport*   215

9 NEO-ORTHODOXY IN GERMANY

    I. *Orthodoxy and Neo-Orthodoxy*   218
    II. *Samson Raphael Hirsch*   220
    III. *Ideological Approach and Viewpoint*   224
    IV. *Educational Principles*   240
    V. *Agudath Israel and Mizrachi*   244

10 LUZZATTO'S NEO-ORTHODOXY

    I. *Hirsch and Luzzatto*   249
    II. *Luzzatto's Life and Thought*   250
    III. *Jewish Nationalism*   263

PART THREE: AMERICAN SHOOTS

PRELUDE   271

11   ON TO AMERICA!

    I. *Conditions in Central Europe*   274
    II. *Emigration*   280

12   REFORM IN AMERICA

    I. *Struggle for Reform*   285
    II. *Structure and Platform*   296
    III. *Changes in American Reform*   302

13   CONSERVATIVE JUDAISM

    I. *In the Nineteenth Century*   317
    II. *In the Twentieth Century*   324
    III. *Schechter's Doctrines*   331
    IV. *Conservative Ideology*   338
    V. *The Feminist Problem*   344

14   RECONSTRUCTIONISM

    I. *History and Approach*   347
    II. *Judaism as a Civilization*   350
    III. *Doctrinal Interpretation*   359
    IV. *Critique and Evaluation*   364

15   ORTHODOXY IN AMERICA

    I. *Before 1882*   367
    II. *After 1882*   375
    III. *The New Immigration*   392
    IV. *Postscript: What of the Future?*   400

NOTES   403

ABBREVIATIONS   433

SUGGESTED READINGS AND REFERENCES   435

INDEX   451

Foreword

JUDAISM may be truly described as a unity in diversity. It does not demand uniformity in thought or belief, but rather a commitment to common fundamental principles. Generally speaking, these include the doctrine of ethical monotheism, the recognition of the Torah as the source of Judaism and identification with the moral and Messianic ideals taught by the prophets and sages of Israel. The tolerant attitude of Judaism has been epitomized in the Talmudic dictum to the effect that the opposing views of the contending schools of Hillel and Shammai are both the "words of the living God." These diverse opinions are often engaged in a continuous dialogue and a contest for a place within the mainstream of Judaism. The role that a given interpretation is to occupy in Judaism is eventually determined by a tacit concensus of the Jewish people in line with its historical traditions and tendencies. Thus it is that Judaism grows out of the ferment in thought arising from the historical experience of its people. Moreover, it is not the *ideological differences* or debates within Judaism that trouble it as much as *ideological indifference*. Apathy towards its vital issues may bring about the danger of stagnation in Judaism.

This volume may be regarded as a record of the dialogue in Judaism started about two centuries ago and still continuing today. The dialogue was engendered by the revolution in Jewish life wrought by the challenge resulting from the emergence of Judaism from the intellectual confines of the ghetto to the freedom and tolerance of the nineteenth century. The Emancipation marked a crucial turning point in Jewish history which called for a considerable adjustment on the part of the Jew.

The several religious ideological formulations were attempts in this direction. The problem has not been solved as yet. It is to the credit of Judaism that it can indulge the several interpretations and ideologies, and embrace them in an overarching unity.

This work sketches the evolution of the different religious alignments in present-day Judaism against the backdrop of general and Jewish history, and analyzes the social and intellectual forces and dynamics that shaped them. It should be of current interest in view of the discussions and debates now going on in the several faiths and denominations on the question of the revision of their basic doctrines and principles. The book is well researched and lucidly written. It is a scholarly achievement which should have a particular appeal to the student of Judaism as well as the broader area of religion. For the general reader it will serve as an orientation into Judaism, its nature, concept and principle. In sum, the volume is a valuable contribution to the literature in its field.

ABRAHAM I. KATSH
President

Dropsie University
Philadelphia, Pa.

Preface

THIS BOOK focuses on the origin, evolution, and growth of the ideologies of the contemporary religious alignments in principally the Orthodox, Reform, and Conservative tendencies in religious Judaism, and their variants. Since these movements were not born or evolved in a vacuum but have arisen and developed in conditions and events in the Jewish experience in Europe, they are treated in their general and Jewish historical contexts. They could hardly be separated from their historical settings, if for no other reason than the fact that Judaism is so closely interlinked with the history of the Jewish people. The two aspects of the volume are closely correlated, the historical serving as the frame-work for a discussion of the ideological phase. This work, however, embraces in scope more than a mere ideological study with an historical orientation. It enters upon broad related areas which touch on the foundations of Judaism, its character, principles, attitudes, and ancillary themes. Accordingly, the volume affords the reader an opportunity to gain a good insight into the essential and underlying doctrines and values of Judaism. A glance at the list of Contents will reflect the wide range of subject matter covered in this work, which may therefore be regarded as a text in Judaism, examined from the vantage point of its major religious groupings.

This volume is arranged in three parts, each of which is introduced by a prelude which delineates its purpose and purview. The first division, entitled *Backgrounds,* deals with the situation of the Jews in medieval times, the suffering and persecution they underwent which reached a climax in the establishment of the ghetto. It also reviews the factors leading to the Haskalah (the Jewish Enlightenment movement) and ultimately to the attainment of Emancipation, the civic enfranchisement of the Jew. It would seem then, as the eminent Jewish historian Leopold Zunz pointed out, that for the European Jew, the Middle Ages persisted until the French Revolution.

11

The second part of the work, called *European Roots,* begins with a discussion of the nature of traditional Judaism, the only Jewish religious pattern at the beginning of the Emancipation. The Jewish religious unity prevailing at the time was disrupted by the attempt of the Reformers to accommodate Judaism to the new age. The portrayal of the resulting conflict between the Reformers and the traditionalists is perhaps the most natural way of bringing the issues between the two camps into sharp perspective. Other attempts to adapt Judaism to the changed conditions gave rise to additional alignments in religious Judaism—the Neo-Orthodox as the opposite extreme to Reform, and the Historical School in the center. While this struggle was being waged in the nineteenth century in Germany and Central Europe, another religious contest engulfed the Jewry of Eastern Europe—the clash between two Orthodox groups, the Hassidim and their opponents, the so-called *Mithnagdim.* Out of the Hassidic thought of Eastern Europe emerged in the twentieth century the Neo-Hassidic philosophy of the late Martin Buber. Both Hassidism and Neo-Hassidism are presented in this volume, the former as a variant of Orthodoxy and the latter as a synthesis of Hassidism and Western religious ideas. Though Neo-Hassidism, unlike Hassidism, does not represent a religious party in Judaism, it is of considerable interest because of its influence on current Western progressive religious thought.

The final division of this volume, called *American Shoots,* shifts the scene to the New World and traces the development of the respective religious movements on American soil. In addition to Orthodoxy, Reform, and Conservatism, a special chapter is devoted to Reconstructionism, the radical wing of Conservatism. The principles, organizational structure, major institutions, activities, present status, and future prospects of the religious contingents are analyzed in this concluding section of the book.

An impressive array of Jewish thinkers who have exerted a direct or indirect influence on the theories and tenets of the several branches of religious Judaism is presented and discussed in this volume. Among them are the Besht, Mendelssohn, Krochmal, Geiger, Zunz, Frankel, Rapoport, Hirsch, S. D. Luzzatto, I. M. Wise, Leeser, and Schechter in earlier periods; Buber, Kaplan,

Soloveitchik, and others in more recent times. The apposite views of the giants in medieval Jewish thought, Maimonides, Halevi, and Albo, are expounded or at least noted in various connections. The impact, negative or affirmative, of a number of European philosophers on the ideologists of the major religious groupings, is also examined. These include Spinoza, Kant, Hegel, Lessing, Rousseau, Condillac, and several others.

The immediate motivation for preparing this volume was the deeply felt need for a suitable text in the course in Religious Trends in Contemporary Judaism taught at New York University's Washington Square College and the course in Trends in the American Jewish Community offered at the School of Education—the latter on both the graduate and under-graduate levels. We and no doubt colleagues at other colleges offering courses in various phases of Judaism suffer from a dearth of suitable texts in the field and are, therefore, forced to resort to makeshift instruction materials. It is, however, my hope that this book will help to alleviate the situation. It will, I am confident, also meet the needs of adult groups in this area of study.

Though the volume may be employed in a foundational course, more informed students and readers will find much that is new for them in this work. I might observe in this regard that several chapters have been published in scholarly periodicals, including the *Journal of Jewish Sociology, Tradition Magazine,* and the *Herzl Yearbook,* and also in Hebrew in *Bitzaron, Perakim,* and others. Both the Jew and non-Jew, I believe, will find this text a source of edification; the former as a means of expanding his knowledge of his Jewish heritage and the latter to achieve a better understanding of the religion of his Jewish neighbor.

I have tried not to be partisan and to preserve an attitude of objectivity in the treatment of the subject matter, though admittedly this is not always possible. In the main, I have provided the facts from which the reader may draw his own conclusions. I trust that the work will stimulate readers to explore further the vast spiritual treasure that is Judaism. The appended bibliography of general works and chapter references should aid in this pursuit.

The reader will indulge me if I embark on an intimately personal note. In extending recognition to those who have helped me in the

14

various tasks involved in the preparation and publication of this volume I must acknowledge, first and foremost, with deep and abiding affection and reverence, the help of my late dearly beloved and devoted wife, without whom this volume would not have been written. She was a noble and consecrated soul whose inspiration, encouragement, and patience stimulated and enabled me to devote the time necessary for this work. In her passing, I have suffered a tragic and irreparable loss, and my pain and grief are even greater that she did not see the fruition of my efforts. I had originally intended to dedicate it to her as a token of my love and fond esteem, but now it will serve as a memorial and tribute to her loyalty, understanding, and zeal for Judaism and its ideals.

I wish also to express my deep appreciation to my warm friend and colleague, Professor Abraham I. Katsh, *yibodel l'chayim,* a leader and teacher in the true sense of the word, who has aided me in ways too numerous to mention. Professor Katsh is the distinguished founder and occupant of the Chair of Hebrew Culture at New York University and the initiator and director of its Institute of Hebrew Studies. It is he who has given much impetus to the movement for the teaching of modern Hebrew and the Jewish civilization in American colleges and universities.

I should like to thank Mrs. Hilda Karash for her conscientious efforts in typing this manuscript and also Mrs. Shirley Fields for her assistance in this regard.

I wish to express my warm gratitude to those who read various portions of my manuscript and offered many helpful suggestions. These include both colleagues and students, among them: Rabbi S. Michael Gelber, Rabbi Albert Hollander and Rabbi Grainom Lazewnik.

To Miss Nancy Forsberg, who has read the entire manuscript, I am especially indebted for many constructive comments. I am similarly obligated to Dr. Philip Paneth and Mr. Philip Deluty for their aid.

DAVID RUDAVSKY

New York University

Preface to the Third Edition

THE DEMAND for this work in colleges and universities as well as by adult study groups warranted its republication after the second edition was exhausted. This presented a natural opportunity for updating the volume and incorporating in it the changes and developments in ideology and practice that took place in the several Jewish religious alignments since the second edition appeared in 1972. These features represent significant improvements in the book.

The author sincerely hopes that this volume will afford students an understanding and appreciation of the principles, programs, and practices of the several religious groups in American Judaism. What is of even greater importance, however, is the attainment of a knowledge and grasp of the essential doctrines, values, and tenets of Judaism.

March 1979   DAVID RUDAVSKY

Part One

Backgrounds

Prelude

THE ROOTS of the several religious trends in contemporary Judaism are lodged in the Haskalah (Jewish Enlightenment movement) of the eighteenth century, which was an aspect of the general Enlightenment in Western Europe. The Enlightenment presaged the Emancipation of the Jew from his physical segregation in the ghetto and his position as an alien in his native land. These changes catapulted the Jew from his medieval status into the modern world. Culturally, this meant that the Jew was belatedly experiencing the intellectual exhilaration which the Renaissance had brought to Europe four centuries earlier. Thus, whole centuries of slow transition were telescoped for the Jew into a relatively brief period of transformation. Out of the attempt on the part of the liberal segment of Jewry of this era to adjust their Judaism to the new age emerged the major religious ideologies in present-day Judaism.

The Emancipation of the Jews was the product of a complex gamut of many interrelated factors that could be traced to the broadened cultural horizons of Europeans following the Crusades. The new scientific approach that had been gaining currency in Europe, the humanistic movement, the economic, social, and religious revolutions all combined to bring about a mood of skepticism among the intellectuals. The climate of liberal opinion and religious tolerance which pervaded the salons of London, Paris, and Berlin emanated not from the church or synagogue,

17

but from the progressive circles of Rousseau and the Encyclopedists. The latter questioned the authority and authoritarianism
of the Church as of all human institutions. They weakened the
faith in organized religion, but they strengthened the belief in the
innate right of man to life, liberty, and equality.

While such Christian advocates of religious freedom and
toleration as Count Mirabeau and Montesquieu breached the
ghetto walls from without, a group led by the Jewish philosopher
Moses Mendelssohn battered them from within. They endeavored also to prepare their fellow Jews in the ghetto for the era
of Emancipation. Emancipation finally came, but only in the wake
of a violent political eruption. It took the same upheaval that
brought down the walls of the Bastille in Paris to crush the ghetto
barriers. Thus in September 1791, France became the first country in Europe to grant the Jews full citizenship and equality. A
new precedent was thereby established which other European
countries emulated in the course of the nineteenth century.

It would not do, however, to begin our story at this point. The
enfranchisement of the Jew is a climax rather than a starting
point. To grasp the meaning and significance of the revolution it
wrought in Jewish life, we must examine the conditions under
which the Jews lived in their earlier ghetto state, both as individuals
and as a community. But the ghetto is only an episode, though a
climactic one, in medieval Jewish history, in a cluster of other
persecutions and suppressions. A brief sketch of the latter phase
of the Jewish experience in Europe is essential to a proper understanding and grasp of the meaning of the Emancipation.

The introductory part of our study deals with the tragic situation
of the Jew in the Middle Ages. It is intended for orientation purposes and is therefore entitled *Backgrounds*.

1

In God's Name

I. TERROR A LIBEL

Jewish Martyrdom

T CENTURY brought a marked change in the condition of European Jewry. During the earlier millenium of the Christian era, intolerance and violence against the Jews was sporadic and intermittent. Since attacks against them were not as well organized as they were in the later centuries, they were more bearable. Even in the later period, when Jewish suffering was more intense, it was generally diffused in time and place, so that when it was severe in one area, it was relaxed in another. Had it been otherwise, the lot of the Jew might have been more difficult than it was.[1]

The underlying cause of the medieval terror and violence against the Jews was their persistence in clinging to their faith and their refusal to wash away their identity in the baptismal font. It was not, however, their strong religious convictions alone that gave them the courage to resist the pressures of the Church. It was also the fact that the Jews cherished their freedom of conscience and their human right to worship as they deemed proper. Their readiness to undergo oppression and martyrdom for their

19

religion must be seen in this context, as part of the struggle for human liberty. The love of freedom and the spirit of rebellion, it will be recalled, have been instilled in the Jewish people since the days of Pharaoh.

The Crusades

The Crusades brought tragedy and death to the Jews of Europe. During the First Crusade (1096), an undisciplined army of several hundred thousand swept through the Jewish communities on the Rhine and the Danube. "Why be concerned with the Saracen infidels, when the Jewish disbelievers and Christ-killers are so close at hand?" many of the Crusaders asked. Their false piety was often combined with the desire to plunder Jewish wealth. In their great apprehension and terror of the wild mobs, thousands of Jewish men, women, and children took their own or each other's lives rather than fall into the Crusaders' hands. Of course, many more were brutally slain. The temper of the Crusaders may be seen from the fact that when they reached Jerusalem, they assembled all the Jews of the city in a synagogue and then burned it.

These outrages were generally not perpetrated by the clergy; on the contrary, some of them attempted to protect the Jews. In the Second Crusade (1145), St. Bernard of Clairvaux and Emperor Conrad III intervened with only limited success to avert the massacres of the Jews. The subsequent Crusades also proved calamitous for the Jews.

Blood Libel

The medieval Jew lived in constant fear of riot and massacre. It was not difficult to incite the superstitious masses to mob violence against him on one pretext or another, nor to induce the authorities to take "legalized" action against Jewish communities. The charges lodged against the Jews were as fantastic as they were false and outrageous, yet they brought the Jews catastrophe and destruction. At times, no particular accusation was necessary—the mere arrival of the Easter season and its association with the Crucifixion was reason enough to spark an assault on the Jewish quarter.

A favorite provocation was the blood libel. The first recorded incident of this nature occurred in England on Easter 1144, when the corpse of a child, William of Norwich, was found. On the strength of the testimony of an apostate Jew, Theobald of Cambridge, the Jews were charged with killing the lad as an annual Passover sacrifice. Because there was no evidence that the boy had been murdered, no Jew was tried on the charge, but the rumor nevertheless found wings and spread throughout England and Europe.[2] It took on various forms, generally that the Jews required Christian blood for their Passover matzoth (unleavened bread) or other seemingly occult rituals. Entire Jewish communities, as that of Blois, France, in 1171, were burned on that charge. A century later, this slander produced incidents almost every year in Germany. It is of interest to note that the Christians in early times were victims of a similar vilification.

The gullible common people and their leaders ignored the fact that Jews, unlike Christians, were forbidden to consume blood in any form, and that there is no trace of such a practice in rabbinic literature. Moreover, there was no legal evidence to sustain these falsehoods; forced confessions obtained through torture were sufficient. The denunciations and denials of these inventions by the Pope or prominent churchmen were of little avail. The myths had become so deep-seated among the ignorant masses that they persisted to modern times, and as late as 1913, the Mendel Beilis trial in Czarist Russia was staged on this charge.[3]

Desecration of the Host

Another weird libel was the desecration of the Host (*Hostia,* or sacrifice) concocted in 1298 at Roettingen in Franconia. The Jews were alleged to have stolen a consecrated wafer which, according to the doctrine of transubstantiation adopted by the Lateran Council (1215), turns into the body of Jesus. They were accused of torturing or piercing the wafer in mockery of Jesus, causing him pain and agony.

This accusation, of course, is utterly ludicrous and illogical, for it assumes that the Jews themselves recognize the truth of the doctrine of transubstantiation. But the leader of the anti-Jewish attacks that followed these calumnies, a German nobleman named Rindfleisch, was concerned mainly with the slaughter and plunder of the Jews, rather than with intellectual consistency. In the ensuing violence, forty congregations in Austria and Franconia were annihilated.

Black Death

But the peak of cruelty and hostility against the Jews was reached during the Black Death (1348-1351), evidently a form of the bubonic plague, probably carried from India to Europe. In this disaster, from a third to a half of the European population perished. This was attributed to the poisoning of the wells by the Jews, notwithstanding the fact that they also drank the water, or that in France or England, whence the Jews had been banished, the scourge also raged. According to the Nuremberg *Memorbuch* (Memorial Book) three hundred and fifty Jewish communities, including sixty large ones in Spain, Switzerland, and particularly Germany, were wiped out in *Judenbrände* (the burning of Jews). The extermination of Jews meant even more than the pious elimination of Christ-killers. It proved eminently profitable materially, because it also brought about the liquidation of hated creditors. Though it tended to reduce the revenue of the rulers, it helped to divert the attention of the lower classes from their poverty and misery.

The Imperial Serfs

Royalty at the time exploited the status of the Jew to its own advantage. The rulers considered themselves the masters of the Jews, basing their claim on the fiction that they were the heirs of Titus, the conqueror of Israel in the year 70. They regarded the Jews as *Servi Camerae* (serfs of the imperial chamber)—bondsmen who were bound to their lord as a serf to the soil he tilled. The king, in fact, considered them his property which he could treat as he wished; he could barter his Jews, give them away as a gift, sell them, lease them to a baron or bishop for a fee, or pawn them for a loan. Conrad IV in 1242 mortgaged his Jews, permitting creditors to mulct them for the principal and interest he owed. At times, a king would declare himself as the heir of a wealthy Jew, as did Henry II of England (1154-1189) with Aaron of Lincoln, the richest Jew of his day. Rudolph II of Austria (1576-1612) emulated this example four centuries later in the case of Mordecai Meisels of Prague, also the most affluent Jew of his time.

The king accorded his Jews protection from the hostile hoards, but he exacted an exorbitant fee for this service. Thus the medieval Jew became an important source of revenue to the sovereign, resorting to moneylending and usury to raise the heavy sum needed to pay into the king's coffers. He thereby became a sponge which the crown squeezed dry for its own purposes. In 1390, King Wenceslaus IV (1361-1419) cancelled all debts to Jewish creditors in various parts of Germany. He assigned the debts to provinces and cities on condition that they pay him a quarter of the amount.

The medieval Jew was an alien without any political or other human rights. His right of residence could be revoked as readily as it was granted. The simplest way to appropriate the Jews' money was to expel them, at times on a wholesale basis, and then confiscate their property. In 1306, Philip the Fair of France drove out the Jews of his realm, but the need for them was soon felt and they were invited back a decade later. They were banished from France in intermittent years, culminating in the expulsion of 1394. They were exiled from England in 1290 and from Spain in 1492.

Economic Conditions

Though in ancient Palestine Jews were farmers, they were barred from this calling in medieval European countries by custom and law. In the feudal system, which lasted in Europe from the tenth to the fourteenth centuries, the Jew had no place. Feudal society was a religiously dominated system based on a series of Christian oaths of fealty, which the Jew could not take. It also required military service from which the Jew was excluded as an enemy of Christendom.

However, the Jew was needed as the middleman in the feudal economy—as a tradesman, craftsman, physician, or moneylender. He was therefore encouraged to settle in the towns, where, incidentally, he could enjoy the proximity and fellowship of his coreligionists. But the Crusades brought an end to the feudal system. The erstwhile serfs now became burghers and artisans. They were organized into craft guilds, which served for the protection of economic interests as well as religious fraternities. The guilds grew in power after the twelfth century, and they naturally excluded the Jew both as an unbeliever and as an alien to Christian society. The Jew was permitted to retain a place only in tailoring.

There was, however, another niche in the medieval economy open to the Jew—moneylending, a field prohibited to Christians (*Luke* 6:35). Though Jews had been active in this calling earlier, they began to play an increasingly prominent role in the twelfth century. Moneylending was essential to trade, but it bore the stigma of being un-Christian, and the Jew was forced into it because he was denied entry into other vocations. But it became so profitable a venture that by the thirteenth and fourteenth centuries the Lombards and other Christian elements displaced the Jews, particularly in the large-scale operations. True, by an edict of the Third Lateran Council (1179), Christians were barred from this pursuit under pain of being refused Christian burial, but means were found of circumventing the ban. The fee for a loan was called usage instead of usury, or the principal was raised to include the interest, or other subterfuges were used. After being superseded by their Christian competitors, the Jews, in the main, engaged in moneylending on a petty scale only.

II. The Medieval Jewish Community

The Kahal

FROM EARLY TIMES, Jewish settlements in the Diaspora had formed community organizations, known as the *Kahal*[4] or *Kehillah* (assembly). The *Kahal* maintained its own religious and communal institutions: the synagogue, the public bath, the cemetery, the slaughterhouse, the community bakery, and especially the philanthropic services. It also supervised the schools and provided for the education of the children of the indigent. The *Kahal* regulated the social and religious life of the community and generally looked after its welfare. It even fixed weights and measures, wages, prices of food and other commodities. It exercised its police power by means of the *Herem* (ban). This system of Jewish self-government was in operation throughout the medieval period, and functioned also in the ghetto.

The *Kahal* served as a remarkable instrumentality of government and control. Its laws were rigorously obeyed, often in a greater degree than those of the state. One example of the way it operated was its rent-control system. Because apartments in the crowded tenements of the ghetto were at a premium, the Talmudic principle of *Hazakkah* (tenure) was used to ensure the tenant a continuous right of possession. As long as a ghetto tenant paid his rent, his Christian landlord could not dispossess him or raise his rent without his consent, for if the occupant were to move out on this account, no other Jew would replace him, under pain of excommunication. The Jew could bequeath, sell, or assign this valuable right, which was known as the *Jus Cazaka* (*Hazakkah*), to his heirs or successors. This practice had been incorporated in a *Takkanah*[5] (ordinance) attributed to the revered Rabbenu Gershom of Mayence (960-1040), affectionately called the Luminary of the Exile.

Judicial Authority

A primary function of the *Kahal* was to establish and conduct its own courts in which judgment was rendered on the basis of Talmudic law. It enacted its own police ordinances, punished offenders, and in many instances operated its own prisons or at least had special cells in the common jail. The penalties imposed by the Jewish courts included flogging, fines, and imprisonment; perhaps the severest forms of discipline, rarely used, were several degrees of excommunication. Capital punishment was inflicted very infrequently, and that only in Spain upon a convicted *Malshin* (informer), whose crimes endangered the entire community. The death sentences had to be sanctioned by the civil authorities, who also performed the execution.

Taxation

The fact that the medieval Jews were vassals of the king excluded them from the jurisdiction of the local authorities and their courts. This tended to set them apart from the majority of the population. The rulers, moreover, found it convenient to assess and collect the taxes from the Jewish community in a lump sum, leaving it to the Jewish officials to raise the money. These fiscal

powers and responsibilities were an important foundation of the
Kahal's corporate autonomy and existence. It was no easy task
to collect the extortionate revenue demanded of the Jews, the sums
assessed representing a grossly disproportionate share of the taxes
paid by the population as a whole. At times, they were so excessive
as to be expropriatory, reducing the ghetto to bankruptcy.[6] This
was true particularly of a number of self-governing "Jewish cities"
in Poland after the massacres of 1648.

State within a State

As a result of the legal autonomy of the Jewish community and
its jurisdiction over its own affairs, it became an *imperium in im-
perio* (a state within a state). Its members had no relationship to
the civil authorities except through the mediacy of the *Kahal*.
Sometimes, as in the case of the Council of the Four Lands, which
ruled Polish Jewry for almost two centuries (1580-1764), the local
Jewish communities were united into a confederation. The officials
of the *Kahal*, as in Lwow (Lemberg), regarded their own self-
governing community as a distinct and independent entity, and
upon assuming office swore to preserve "our Jewish commonwealth." The *Kahal* operated under a system of *Takkanoth* which
it adopted with the approval of its chief officer, the rabbi. The
Kahal's administrative council, generally composed of seven members known by the Talmudic term *Tovei ha-Ir* (best of the town)
(*Meg.* 27a), was elected by secret ballot. The council was generally patterned on the model set up in the Talmud. The officers
included the *Parnas* (supporter or leader), the *Gabbai* (treasurer),
and other functionaries. The rabbinate and the posts of the two
Dayanim (magistrates) were honorary offices until the thirteenth
century, when salaries were attached to them.

It is to be noted that considerable power was vested in the
scholars. The individual too had a means of asserting his rights.
He could protest against an objectionable act on the part of the
Kahal by an attempt to enlist public opinion in his favor. He could
do so by delaying the public worship in the synagogue or the reading of the Torah until he was promised redress or at least a hearing.
The medieval *Kahal* was a democratic institution forged by a
persecuted minority living in the midst of a hostile majority.

III.　THE GHETTO

Self-segregation

IT WAS NATURAL for the Jews in the lands of their dispersion to congregate voluntarily in separate neighborhoods, much as they and other ethnic groups do today, for social and religious reasons. They felt more at home and at ease among their own people, and also more secure from assault and insult. In those areas, the Jews established their own religious, philanthropic, and social institutions. These districts were predominantly, but by no means exclusively Jewish, for there were Christians living among the Jews and Jews residing outside the Jewish quarter. Jews occupied a special section in Venice and Salerno as a matter of choice toward the end of the eleventh century.

Compulsory Ghetto

In 1179, the Third Lateran Council prohibited Jews and Christians from living together in the same locality, but this regulation seems not to have been commonly enforced. Several decades later, in 1215, the Fourth Lateran Council adopted two stronger measures which were ratified by subsequent Church Councils through the better part of the century. Both edicts were intended for a single purpose—the humiliation and isolation of the Jew, as a moral leper, in accordance with the doctrine of *servitus Judeorum* (servitude of the Jews) adopted by the Church in the fourth and fifth centuries. One decree ordered all Jews to wear a distinguishing yellow badge, thereby branding them as inferior creatures; another required them to live in separate confined quarters in the towns, as a means of ejecting and excluding them from European society.

These edicts prepared the way for the compulsory ghetto. Here Jews were hemmed in by law in a segregated part of town, as a means of preventing their intermingling with Christians, which it was feared might lead to a weakening of the religious fervor of the latter. The first compulsory ghetto in Sicily was created in 1312 in Palermo by Frederick II. In Germany, a ghetto was established in Cologne as early as around 1150. The famous Frankfort ghetto

was started in 1460. In France, one was set up in the fourteenth
century. Ghettos gradually spread to every large city in Central
Europe. In 1496, a ghetto was opened in Kazimierz (near Cracow) and soon also in several other cities in Poland. By the sixteenth century, no Jew could reside outside the ghetto in most of
Europe, and no Christians within it.[7]

The origin of the term "ghetto" is obscure. It is generally believed to have been derived from the word *gietto* (cannon foundry),
because the first legally established and rigidly enforced Jewish
quarter in Italy, set up in Venice in 1516, was situated in the
district known as *Ghetto Nuovo*[8] (New Foundry). It has been
suggested that the name may have originated from the Italian word
borghetto (little quarter). In Germany, it was known as *Judengasse* or *Judenstrasse;* in Bohemia, as in the case of the Prague
ghetto, it was called *Judenstadt;* in France, *Juiverie;* in Portugal,
Carriere and *Judiaria,* and in Islamic countries, the *Mellah.* In
Hebrew, it was referred to as *Messilah* (road) or *Migrash* (court).

The Area

The ghettos established after the fifteenth century followed a
general pattern. They were usually located in unwholesome, low,
and squalid sections. In Rome, for example, the ghetto opened in
1556 was built on the disease-breeding Tiber which overflowed its
banks annually, flooding the lower stories of houses and compelling
the occupants to seek shelter in the upper apartments. In Mayence,
the Jews were cooped up in an unsanitary district known as the
"Swine's Dungheap." Frequently, the ghetto, as in Frankfort and
Paris, consisted of a dismal, narrow alley, flanked on each side by
tall buildings, which shut out air and sunlight. Elsewhere, as in
Rome and Venice, the ghettos comprised larger territories. Within
this crowded area, there was no space for gardens or trees, shrubs
or flowers; nor could its residents leave it for recreation or enter-
tainment elsewhere.

The obligatory medieval ghetto was surrounded by a high wall
with a heavy gate at one or both ends. There was nothing unusual
about this wall, since medieval cities were generally surrounded
by walls. The gates were often guarded by a Christian warden
paid by the Jews. Actually, the ghetto served as much for the

Jew's protection as for his degradation; but it also offered his foes an easy target for attack. The gates of the enclosed Jewish quarter, as of medieval towns generally, were locked from sunset to sunrise, and in some cases also on Sundays and Christian holidays. Upper windows which overlooked the streets outside the ghetto walls were boarded up, so as to prevent Jews from contaminating the churches and the religious processions outside their street with their curious and idle glances.

Restrictions

The area of the ghetto was usually fixed. In order to accommodate the growing population within its borders, the ghetto was expanded vertically, by adding floors to existing buildings. Since many of the foundations of these houses were too flimsy to support the higher structures, the tenements would occasionally collapse over their occupants when subjected to the undue strain of a gathering or celebration. Devastation by fire was an ever-lurking danger in the Jews' district; in 1533, a fire consumed the ghetto in Kazimierz, Poland; in 1571, and 1616, conflagrations destroyed the ghetto in Lwow (Lemberg). In Prague in 1689, a ghetto-wide conflagration took many lives and destroyed a considerable amount of property. In 1711, the Frankfort ghetto and in 1719, that of Nikolsburg were entirely demolished by flames.

The overcongestion in the ghetto was severe. In the ghetto of Frankfort, for example, 4,000 people lived in 190 houses, along a gloomy street only 12 feet wide, with its buildings converging at the top. In the poorer streets of the Roman ghetto, several families occupied a single room. Many ghettos were constantly engaged in a struggle with municipal authorities for the extension of their boundaries. Frequently, homes were used as workshops by day and living quarters by night. Under such conditions, epidemics were common and infant mortality reached frightful proportions. To avoid overexpansion in population, the civil authorities in Germany set a quota on marriages which, generally, were not allowed to exceed the number of deaths. In the German *Judengassen,* only the oldest child was allowed to wed; in Frankfort, marriage was prohibited before the age of twenty-five, and only a dozen marriages per year were permitted in a population of five hundred families. These restrictions, known as the *Familienten-Gesetz,* were particularly obnoxious and irksome to the Jews, with their traditionally high regard for family life.

The hideous yellow badge and the peaked hat that the Jews wore as a means of distinguishing them from Christians, placed them in a category with prostitutes who were distinguished in some localities by a similar mark. This made the Jews an easy mark for the taunts and torments of hoodlums and street urchins. Before the fifteenth century, which witnessed the spread of the formal ghetto, it was sometimes possible for a Jew to purchase his release from these cruel and repulsive regulations; but after the sixteenth century, the oppressive laws were persistently and rigidly enforced. The strict policy was motivated by the belief, current during the Catholic Counter-Reformation, that the Jews had inspired the Protestant Reformation.

Ghetto Life

The ghetto Jew, rejected and oppressed by the Christian world, naturally gravitated toward his fellow Jews, with whom he shared his suffering and humiliation, and in whose midst he could relax and enjoy a sense of sympathy and kinship. As a result, the Jews developed a feeling of mutual responsibility and concern which deepened their Jewish consciousness and loyalty and became an important factor in their group survival. Moreover, though deprived of citizenship and political rights, though oppressed religiously, socially, and economically, the ghetto Jew did not lose his soul. His high standard of ethics gave him a compensating sense of moral superiority over his persecutors. His home, despite its poverty and misery, was his sanctuary. After a trying day of huckstering through the town where he was the butt of the cruel taunts of the populace, he returned to the warmth, comfort, and affection of his family hearth. The Sabbath, too, offered him a welcome respite from the toil and drudgery of his everyday existence. On that day the ghetto Jew cast aside his daily cares and burdens and was transformed into a free man. He donned his festive clothes in honor of the Queen Sabbath; it was for her sake that he stinted the whole week, so that he might eat better on the sacred day. On that day, too, he was endowed with an "additional soul" which enabled him to absorb a full measure of spiritual joy and inspiration to sustain him during the long, hard week ahead.[9]

The Synagogue and School

The synagogue was another place of solace for the ghetto Jew. This center of religious life was usually housed in an unostentatious building, which had to be below the height of the churches in the town, so as not to arouse the resentment or envy of Christian neighbors. The synagogue served not only as the *Bet Tefilah* (house of worship) but also as the *Bet ha-Midrash* (house of study)—an academy for Jewish study which, in Judaism, is regarded as part of worship.[10] Here Jews, returning from an arduous day of toil, shed their badge of shame and forgot their misery in the dialectics and legends of the Talmud or Midrash.

Aside from the synagogue which served as an adult educational center in the ghetto, a number of elementary schools were conducted privately by teachers under various degrees of community supervision. *Yeshivoth* (advanced schools of Talmudic study) were maintained by the community. Until the Renaissance, in the fourteenth or fifteenth century, the Jews were the intellectual leaven in Europe; however, with the spread of ghetto life after the fifteenth century, the schooling of the Jews in Europe, except in Italy, was narrowed down to only religious knowledge, while learning in Europe generally was liberalized and broadened.

Economic Life

Economically, too, the Jews in the ghetto were very much restricted. Displaced from banking and their earlier mercantile pursuits by the Christians, they were reduced to peddling second-hand goods and to pawnbroking, both despised and degraded callings. To keep them from competing with Christians, Jews were forbidden to open shops even in their own quarter. The only handicraft they could engage in was tailoring. They were not permitted to engage in large-scale commercial enterprise, or in the liberal professions, although a small number managed, despite difficulties involved, to become physicians. In Italy, in particular, medicine was often combined with the rabbinate. Curiously enough, Jewish physicians were not infrequently called to the bedsides of wealthy Christians in emergencies, notwithstanding church edicts interdicting it. As a result of their economic disabilities, a large proportion of the medieval ghetto Jews were forced to depend on charity. Many more existed on a minimum subsistence level. The few who escaped the abject poverty of the majority contributed substantially to the maintenance of ghetto institutions and helped considerably in meeting the burdensome taxes, fines, and penalties imposed on the community.

Effects of the Ghetto

Several centuries of seclusion in the ghetto left a marked effect on the Jewish personality. In his dingy surroundings, the Jew was divorced from contact with the soil or nature. Deprived of sunshine, fresh air, and proper diet, he deteriorated physically, became stunted in growth and stooped in posture. Mentally, too, the Jew was confined and limited. Penned in behind the ghetto walls, he was bypassed by the liberal intellectual currents outside. He fell out of touch with the art, science, and geographical explorations that were broadening men's horizons in Europe. The ghetto also had its impact on the Jew emotionally. The precarious existence he led, his sense of insecurity and constant fear, the hostile environment which threatened his destruction, made of him a cringing, timid, distrusting, and, in short, a neurotic individual. The economic strictures in the ghetto compelled him to live by his wits and to resort to sharp practices, in violation of his ethical code.

In the restricted cultural atmosphere of the ghetto, the Jew was denied the opportunity for the stimulus and cross-fertilization of ideas that would normally have come from contact with the world at large. A keen mind could find little room for creative expression in so stagnant a milieu. Since the ghetto Jew concentrated only on his own books and learning, a cultural inbreeding resulted. His study of Talmud degenerated into *pilpulism,* a form of casuistry and abstract argumentation in which subtle hairsplitting distinctions were drawn, with little concern for their practical application. Linguistically, too, the introduction of Hebrew elements combined with a sprinkling of foreign terms into the vernacular used in the ghetto gave rise to a peculiar local dialect, which became known as Judeo-German or Yiddish in Germany, and Ladino in the Spanish-speaking countries; both dialects were written in Hebrew characters. Local characteristic pronunciations and usages also developed. Other *jargons* produced in Italy and elsewhere became additional barriers to normal communication with the outside world.

The segregation of Jews behind the ghetto walls gave Christians little opportunity to know the Jew and appreciate his inner life. Instead, their opinions and attitudes toward the Jews were moulded by rumors and stereotypes current in Christian circles which exacerbated the prevailing prejudices and hostility against the Jew. Even a Voltaire and Goethe entertained the prevailing image of the Jew as a vile and mean creature. On his part, the Jew naturally reacted in kind, with a feeling of bitterness and revulsion toward Christian society.

It was not until the French Revolution, with its slogan of equality for all men including the Jews, that the walls of the ghetto were breached. By 1848, most of the obligatory European ghettos were abolished.[11] The last one, that of Rome, was finally ended by King Victor Emmanuel II in 1875, and its walls were demolished a decade later. It was not, however, easy to undo the sinister effects of the cramped physical and cultural life the Jews had endured for centuries in the ghetto.

2

The Road to Emancipation

I. INTRODUCTORY

The Impetus

THE IMPROVEMENT in the condition of the medieval Jew and his emergence from the isolation of the ghetto was a gradual process spanning centuries. The period of transition was one of major change in European life and thought. These changes can be traced back in greater or lesser part to the impetus of the Crusades. The Crusades, it will be remembered, involved hundreds of thousands of Christians who were engaged in a holy war extending over two centuries, for the purpose of wresting the Holy Land from the Moslems. Their movement, essentially religious in nature, paradoxically produced an opposite result—a greater secularism and a greater stress on mundane values in European life.

A New Outlook

The Crusades brought several worlds together. They brought the inhabitants of Western Europe closer to each other and to their fellow Christians of the Byzantine Empire. They brought the Christians into more intimate contact with the Moslems of the Near East. The Europeans discovered the magnificent and

34

glamorous Moslem Byzantine civilizations. They marvelled at the splendor of Constantinople, which they could only contrast with their own backward villages and towns. They were dazzled by the Moslem achievements in art, medicine, philosophy, and science. They envied the elegance, refinement, and luxury of the East. When they returned home they took along not only new products from the Orient, but also new ideas which made them discontented with things in their native lands. Their broadened horizons prepared the ground for the revolution in thought which characterized the Renaissance and a chain of other currents in medieval Europe. The Renaissance led to the Humanist movement, to the revolt against authoritarianism in science and religion, and to the commercial revolution. These developments contributed to the creation of a greater tolerance and a more enlightened attitude towards the Jews, which eventually led to an amelioration of their lot and their liberation from the ghetto .

II. The Intellectual Revolt

Philosophy and Theology

THEOLOGY DOMINATED all branches of knowledge in medieval Christian Europe. Even philosophy was only the handmaiden of religion. The attempt to explain the Christian faith by reason took the form of Scholasticism, which employed Aristotelian logic. But philosophy was used only to confirm the paramount principles of faith. By 1273 the eminent theologian Thomas Aquinas (1226-1274), who had been influenced in his approach by the Jewish sage Maimonides (1135-1204), completed his *Summa Theologica,* written with the aim of reconciling Christianity with Aristotelian philosophy.

However, to cast doubt on the validity of the Christian faith was to risk heresy. Peter Abelard (1079-1142), the founder of the University of Paris, was denounced by Christian leaders as a heretic for doing just this. In his *Sic et Non (Yes and No)* he compiled a series of contradictory Christian doctrines promulgated by the Church fathers, on the principle that truth can be ascertained through doubt and questioning. He left it to the individual to determine the correct belief. It took great courage to seek truth in that manner in medieval Europe, when the authority of the Church was supreme.

Science

The interest of medieval scholars in theology and philosophy shifted only slightly to science in the eleventh century, when the Arabic scientific knowledge penetrated Europe. The Arabs had preserved Greek philosophy and science which had been all but forgotten in Europe during the Dark Ages. Jews played an important role[1] in the process of transmission of the medical, philosophical, mathematical, and scientific systems of the East to the West. This science, however, like the theology of the age, was authoritarian in nature. Knowledge of medicine came from Hippocrates and Galen; other fields of knowledge were also based on the Greek authorities. The Church frowned on an attempt to probe the secrets of nature, for God had not veiled them from man for the latter to seek to penetrate them.

The Empirical Approach

To break away from this doctrinaire view was a bold step. The medieval scholars who ventured to do so through direct observation of nature and experimentation were intrepid pioneers. Foremost among them was a Franciscan, Roger Bacon (1214-1294), an English scholastic philosopher who objected to the medieval reliance on authority as the source of human knowledge.

Roger Bacon foretold the construction of horseless carriages, oarless, sail-less boats, and flying machines. His ideas resulted in a series of discoveries and inventions by a succession of prominent scientists including Copernicus (1473-1543), the founder of modern astronomy. After long years of study, he concluded that the earth rotates on its axis, and that together with other planets in the solar system, it revolves about the sun. There was also Galileo (1564-1642) whose telescope confirmed Copernicus' theories. Kepler (1571-1630) formulated the mathematical laws which control the movements of the planets. Newton proved by mathematical calculation that the revolution of the planets around the sun and of the moon about the earth was due to the same force of gravity which makes objects fall to the ground.

The same spirit of doubt that prompted men to challenge the old Aristotelian notions of science led them eventually also to question human and social institutions that had been considered sacrosanct. They were now ready to employ the method of reason to seek new light and evolve new principles which might contribute to the improvement of human relationships. The English philosopher John Locke (1632-1704) summarized this new approach in his *Essay Concerning Human Understanding*, in which he declared that knowledge comes empirically through our senses and that we have no innate ideas or knowledge outside experience or the senses. Locke also wrote his *Letters on Toleration*, in which he advocated the toleration of all religious belief as well as atheism. In his emphasis on reason as the arbiter in human affairs, he was a forerunner of the European Enlightenment movement.

III. RENAISSANCE AND HEBREW LEARNING

The Humanities

THE RENAISSANCE, a term meaning rebirth, denotes the new rational mood and temper associated with the intellectual and cultural awakening in Italy in the fourteenth century which in the following two centuries spread throughout Europe, bringing in its train major changes in human life and history. In Italy, the Renaissance marked a renewal of the interest in classical literature, art, painting, sculpture, and architecture. The literary resuscitation was sparked by the work of Francesco Petrarch (1304-1374), an Italian priest, a composer of Latin verse and prose, and a scholar who devoted himself to the study of the neglected Latin classics. His close friend, Giovanni Boccaccio (1313-1375), a poet and novelist, whose short stories represented a model of Italian prose writing, shared with Petrarch the distinction of having been a pioneer in the Renaissance literary movement. The revival of interest in Latin was supplemented a century later by a regenerated interest in Greek, stimulated by Greek scholars who fled from Turkey to Italy after the fall of Constantinople in 1453. Before long, the study of ancient Latin and Greek writings became common.

Soon the humanities (from the Latin *humanitas* meaning secular culture), as this class of literature was called, supplemented and even supplanted the study of theology and speculative philosophy, popular in the Middle Ages when men, despairing of this world, shifted their concern to the hereafter. The humanists, as the advocates of the return to classicism were called, were secularists in outlook, who believed in the perfectability of man and in making this earth a happier abode. For the cultivation of humaneness, the humanities offered a better soil and climate than theology. The former, founded on mind and reason, fostered a bond of sympathy and understanding among people.

While humanists like the Dutch-born Erasmus (1469-1536) concentrated principally, though not exclusively, on the literary treasures of ancient Greece and Rome, others like Johan Van Reuchlin (1455-1522) devoted themselves to the cultural riches of ancient Palestine. To Reuchlin, Hebrew was the sacred tongue "in which God confers directly with men and men with angels . . . face to face as one friend with another." Reuchlin wrote a Hebrew grammar, *The Rudimenta Hebraica,* and other works on Hebrew and on the Cabbala. John Gutenberg's invention of movable type around the 1450's led to the establishment of Hebrew presses a quarter of a century later. This gave further impulse to the spread of Hebrew learning among both Jews and Christians. Soon chairs of Hebrew were founded in a number of universities, notably Bologna in 1488 and Rome in 1514.

A Battle of Books

Interest in Hebrew learning among Christians in Germany was intensified as a result of a curious incident. John Pfefferkorn of Cologne, a Jewish butcher convicted of theft, had converted to Christianity, and, as frequently happened in these instances, the convert's zeal for the new religion prompted him to attack his former faith. Pfefferkorn charged that the Talmud was hostile to Christian doctrine. In 1509, with the aid of the Dominicans in his native city he succeeded in eliciting an edict from Emperor Maximilian, empowering him to confiscate and burn all Hebrew books except the Bible, which meant principally the Talmud. The Jews of Frankfort, supported by friendly Christians, protested vigorously against the proposed destruction of their religious writings. They won the ear of the Emperor who appointed a commission with Johan Reuchlin as a member to look into the charges. Reuchlin had shared the opinion of Christian leaders of his day to the effect that the sufferings of the Jews were a result of their rejection of Christianity. Yet he was opposed to persecution as a means of inducing proselytization, maintaining that only persuasion should be used. In 1511, he rendered a report favorable to the Jews. Reuchlin had not read the Talmud, but he was informed as to its contents and insisted that although it contained superstitious ideas, it also abounded in lofty teachings. There were, Reuchlin conceded, some Jewish works which attacked Christianity and merited destruction, but the post-Biblical Jewish writings, he asserted, did not assume any stand on Christianity. The Talmud, too, Reuchlin proposed, should be employed to clarify the meaning of obscure passages in the Hebrew Bible. In fact, he contended that the rabbinic literature, specifically the Cabbala, contained irrefutable proof of the divinity of Jesus and could also be used to confirm other Christian theological doctrines. Reuchlin demanded protection for the Jews on the ground that they were "fellow citizens of the Holy Roman Empire and imperial burghers," a phrase that reflected a friendliness to Jews that was extremely rare among churchmen of that time.

In the decade that followed, a violent feud broke out on this issue between the obscurantist Dominicans, led by the inquisitor Jacob von Hochstraten, and the more liberal elements, headed by Reuchlin. Martin Luther (1483-1546) defended Reuchlin. This dispute among the clerics, in which the Jews remained largely on the sidelines, contributed much to the widening rift in Christianity that produced the Reformation. The collateral results of the controversy were, accordingly, of far greater moment than the immediate triumph scored against Pfefferkorn. The conflict had drawn attention to the possibility of exploiting post-Biblical Jewish texts in an affirmative manner, rather than as sources of evidence of Jewish hostility toward Christianity. The Talmud, it was recognized, could shed light on the Jewish ideas prevailing in the early Christian period, which had influenced the development of Christianity. Hebrew works might therefore be used as a means of ascertaining the correct text and true meaning of the Hebrew Scriptures which Christians accepted .as an integral part of their Bible. Thus the Pfefferkorn controversy, ironically enough, helped to create a new interest in rabbinic literature among Christian scholars.

Christian Hebraists

The interest in Hebrew learning[2] generated among the proponents of the Reformation carried over to the leaders of the Counter-Reformation. The latter were now constrained to employ the same objective approach in the study of the Hebrew Bible and later Hebrew works which had been initiated by the Protestants in their battle against the Church. This development contributed to the rise of a strong movement for the study of Hebrew by scholars from both Christian camps. The brilliant galaxy of Christian Hebraists in the sixteenth and seventeenth century included such men as Johannes Buxtorfs, father (1564-1629) and son (1599-1644), both professors of Hebrew at Basel; John Seldin (1584-1664), a jurist and student of antiquities; Brian Walton (1600-1661), Bishop of Chester, the editor of the important polyglot Bible, the *London Polyglot;* Edmond Cortell (1600-1685), the eminent orientalist who contributed to the *London Polyglot;* John Lightfoot (1602-1675), the great Christian authority on rabbinics; and Thomas Hyde (1636-1703), a renowned Oxford scholar, who in 1694 published a work containing three Hebrew compositions on chess.

A German professor of oriental languages, Johann Wagenseil (1633-1705), published a collection of Jewish anti-Christian writings from Hebrew sources as a means of exposing Jewish "blasphemies"; however, in one of his works he extolled the Yiddish moralistic literature of his day as a model for the Christian world. Wagenseil, moreover, opposed the persecutions and forced baptism of Jews, and defended them against charges of ritual murder and similar libels. His contemporary, Johann Andreas Eisenmenger (1654-1704), also a German orientalist, followed a different course. In his sensational work, *Entdecktes Judenthum* (*Judaism Uncovered*), he viciously and willfully distorted and misinterpreted rabbinic quotations to prove sinister accusations against the Jews including ritual murder and the poisoning of wells. His work became a sourcebook for anti-Semites in the succeeding decades and centuries. By and large, however, the acquaintance of Christian scholars with original Jewish sources led to a better appreciation of Judaism and a greater sympathy for the Jews.

IV. THE RELIGIOUS REVOLT

The Reformation

HEBREW WAS THE medium by which at least a portion of Christianity returned to the Bible. The Bible thus became the symbol of the Reformation and the revolt against the Roman Church. The Reformation was actually not a new movement; individuals and groups had protested before against the secularization of Christianity by the Church and the abuse of power and privilege by the Pope and clergy. It was, however, Martin Luther (1483-1546) who took the decisive step which marked the beginning of Protestantism. Luther, an obscure professor of theology, rose to prominence when, on October 31, 1517, he posted on the door of the church in Wittenberg his ninety-five theses denouncing the Church's practice of selling indulgences and charging that this destroyed the true spirt of penance. On December 10, 1520, Luther publicly burned a papal bull that threatened him with excommunication, thereby dramatizing his severance of all ties with the Roman Church and the papacy.

Protestantism, in its early stages, did not modify the prevailing Christian attitude of intolerance towards the Jews. Luther was at first well disposed toward the Jews, explaining that they could not have been expected to accept Roman Catholicism because it had drifted away from the Bible and had become a "mere popery." However, he could not see why the Jews did not embrace Christianity in its new and improved form, which was linked to a return to the Bible and repudiation of the sinful Roman Church.

Luther never forgave the Jews for their obstinacy and recalcitrance in rejecting Christianity. In his later writings, he advocated the persecution and expulsion of the "hardened blasphemers" and the burning of their synagogues. The Protestant treatment of the Jews until the French Revolution was influenced by this attitude.

Notwithstanding Luther's opposition to the Jews, the seed of religious liberty had been planted in the concept of nonconformity and individual freedom represented in the Protestant defection. The spirit of rationalism which permeated the Renaissance was evident in Protestantism's challenge of the divine authority on which the Roman Church relied. By asserting their own natural right to differ, the Protestants at least implicitly conceded such a right to others. This meant at least tacitly, a greater religious forbearance for Jews and Judaism.

The Counter-Reformation

The Catholic Counter-Reformation was the answer of the papacy to Luther's revolt. The Roman Church attempted to purge itself of corruption and abuses. The Council of Trent (1545-1563) took steps to refine and purify the Church's practices; it abolished indulgences, forbade luxurious living by clerics, and proceeded to demand strict adherence to the Church's precepts and discipline. The Council, however, reaffirmed the principle of the papacy and the exclusive right of the Church as against the individual to interpret the Bible, thereby affirming its policy of doctrinal uniformity and conformity. The Church blamed the defection of the Protestant heresy on the Jews; its charges, however, were justified only to the extent that the Protestant secession was identified with a return to the Hebrew Bible. To prevent the Jews from further infecting and misleading Christians, the Roman Church repeated its demand for their isolation. Accordingly, we observe two opposing tendencies in the sixteenth century. On the one hand, we see the germination of the spirit of freedom which heralded the coming of the modern age; and on the other, we witness an attempt to suppress Jews and Judaism—a tendency which marked a reversion to medievalism.

The Spirit of Tolerance

The first country to yield to the new spirit of tolerance was Protestant Holland, which had fought a bloody and costly war to throw off the Spanish yoke. The people of that country had known religious oppression at the hands of their Spanish rulers, and, after gaining their freedom in 1580, were prepared to share its blessings with others. *Marranos* (secret Jews) fleeing the terrors of the Spanish Inquisition found refuge in the Netherlands and established a Jewish community in Amsterdam in 1596. This group included men who had been leading figures in politics, business, the professions, and even in the Church in their native lands.

V. THE COMMERCIAL REVOLUTION

Economic Expansion

THE CRUSADES had stimulated trade by creating a market in Europe for raw materials from the Orient, including cane sugar, spices, and precious stones—commodities that Europe lacked. The East also produced high-quality manufactured goods; leathers, textiles, and woolens. In addition to expanding trade opportunities, the Crusades roused an interest among Europeans in exploring and learning more about the world around them, thereby giving impulse to the voyages of discovery and exploration, which in turn increased geographical knowledge.

Only five years after Columbus discovered the American continent, Vasco da Gama found a new route to India by sailing around Africa and the Cape of Good Hope. These expeditions opened up new territories for colonization and enlarged the scope of European commerce, which now spread both eastward and westward. This momentous change in commercial orientation had a decisive effect on the economic, political, and social life of Europe. The trade rivalries that ensued as a result of the increased markets brought Europe great prosperity; but they also caused numerous wars for commercial supremacy.

At first, only the wealthier classes could afford the new wares transported to Europe from the East and West, but with the increase in trade, these goods were gradually brought within reach of the masses whose mode of living, though crude by present-day standards, was luxurious in comparison with what it had been before. To pay for the enlarged quantity of imports, Europe required for export a far greater volume of manufactured goods than previously. As a result, the production for foreign markets often exceeded that needed for local consumption.

To meet the growing demand for the overseas markets, it was necessary to overhaul the prevailing guild system, according to which a master workman in a given trade purchased his raw materials, and sold his finished product directly to the consumer. This simple arrangement was now replaced by the more complicated domestic system in which an entrepreneur furnished the raw materials and sold the completed product. The work was performed by workers and their families in their own homes, using their own tools, for wages received from the entrepreneur. This method of industrial organization continued in Europe until it was supplanted by the factory system in the latter part of the eighteenth century.

Money and Capital

As the domestic system spread rapidly over Europe, the entrepreneur required cash for the purchase of raw materials, the payment of workmen, and other expenses. Money thus became a vital need in the new economy. This was met by the discovery in the thirteenth century of metal resources in Central Europe, and later by the yields of overseas Mexican and Peruvian mines. Thus money was now used as capital—a term which may be defined simply as unconsumed wealth employed for the creation of more wealth. In such an economy, people who accumulated cash could either invest it themselves or lend the use of it to others for a fee. In this way, banking and credit developed both for business operations and for other purposes. Edward III of England (1312-1377) financed the Hundred Years' War by borrowing from Italian bankers.

The role of money in the European economy gave rise to the doctrine of mercantilism, according to which a nation's power depended on its wealth in terms of money, which it sought to attract through a favorable balance of trade or other means. The aims of the government thus coincided with those of business. By the seventeenth and eighteenth centuries, mercantile objectives and problems had become the paramount concern of the rulers and political leaders of Europe, subordinating religious issues. This brought with it an increased degree of religious toleration in Europe.

Capitalism and the Jews

In the new money economy, Jews played a significant role. Those who had amassed fortunes in moneylending or other operations could now employ them in far-flung business and banking activity. In these fields the Jews had an advantage in that they could employ their coreligionists in other cities and countries as trusted agents, with whom they could communicate in a common language—Hebrew. The creation of credit agencies and corporate organizations in business has been ascribed to the Jews, who, it has been said, were able to devise these instrumentalities as a result of their training in the Talmud and its dialectics.[3]

The experience Jews acquired in various phases of commerce and banking led to their appointments as fiscal advisors to the kings, purveyors to the army, and other important and influential posts. In Germany in the seventeenth century, prominent Jewish financiers were appointed *Hofjuden* (court Jews) by the rulers of states and principalities. *Hofjuden* were granted special status and concessions, such as exemption from the special taxes imposed on Jews, residence privileges, and similar favors. Prominent among the *Hofjuden* were Jacob Bassevi of Prague (1580-1634), Samson Wertheimer of Vienna (1658-1724), and Samuel Oppenheimer[1] (1635-1703). These highly placed Jews often intervened with the rulers on behalf of their people.

Commercial Role

Gradually but surely, the importance of the Jew in commerce laid the foundation for the amelioration of his situation. In 1549, the expulsion of the Jews of Antwerp by the Spaniards was averted by the plea of the local merchants that such a measure would bring ruin to their city. Similar episodes took place in Venice, and

later in Bordeaux and Hamburg. In 1623, King Christian IV of
Denmark took the step of inviting the Jews of Portugal to settle
in the newly founded commercial center of Glückstadt, where they
were guaranteed complete religious freedom. He hoped that the
Portuguese Jewish refugees would build up the trade of his country
in the manner of their coreligionists who had found a haven in
Holland from the Spanish Inquisition.

When Menasseh ben Israel (1604-1657) pleaded with Cromwell in 1655 to readmit the Jews to England, from where they had
been expelled in 1290, he stressed the commercial advantage that
was bound to accrue to that country if it were to reopen its doors
to the Jews.[5] Though Cromwell favored Jewish resettlement in
England, both for the economic benefits they might bring and on
humane grounds, he could not permit their immediate formal
re-entry because of the opposition of the merchants and clergy.
He did, however, allow the Marranos who lived in London under
the cloak of Catholicism to remain and trade there; he also un-
officially permitted other Jews to join them and reside in England
unmolested. Several decades later, in 1688, legal recognition was
accorded to the Jews in England.

Settlements of Marranos existed not only in England before
the formal readmission of the Jews, but also in several southern
French seaports, notably Bordeaux and Bayonne, where they
practiced Jewish and Catholic rites side by side until 1730, when
they were officially granted the right to live openly as Jews. By
that time the Jews had become an integral part of the commercial
economy and were held in high esteem, and the governments they
served felt that they should accord them greater toleration. Similar
communities existed in Leghorn, Italy, the West Indies, and other
overseas colonies. In these places, gifted and high-ranking Marranos paved the way for practicing Jews to settle in their midst and
share their privileges.

Jewish Financiers

Capitalism produced an anomalous situation in Jewish life before
the nineteenth century. Moneylending, a degraded calling in medieval times, eventually assumed the dignified character of banking.
Thus, the early restrictions which forced the Jew into moneylending

ultimately proved to be an economic boon. It is paradoxical, too, that a financial establishment that attained the fame and prestige of the Rothschild[6] international banking institution should have been nurtured in the wretched soil of the ghetto. Yet the banking concern founded by Amschel Rothschild made Frankfort one of the great financial centers of Europe. Among the outstanding Jewish banking firms in Europe in the seventeenth century was that of the De Pintos in Amsterdam. Their kinsmen were also prominent bankers in other parts of the world, notably in Brazil and Dutch Guiana at the beginning of the eighteenth century. The wealth of these Jewish financiers and magnates trickled down to their coreligionists, and the social and political influence they acquired helped to strengthen their peoples' prospects of emancipation.

VI. JEWS IN GERMANY IN THE EIGHTEENTH CENTURY

The Schutzjuden

THE SCHUTZJUDEN (protected Jews) in Germany were a vestige of the pattern of protection accorded the Jews as imperial serfs by the ruler in consideration of a special payment. Before the Crusades, the protection was granted Jews on an individual basis, but afterwards it was conferred on the Jewish community collectively. In the seventeenth century, many German princes reverted to the older arrangement and accepted *Schutzgeld* (protection money) from individuals whom they sold special licenses to reside and trade in their territories.

In Prussia during the reign of Frederick the Great (1740-1786), there were "ordinary" and "extraordinary" *Schutzjuden*. The former were permitted to transfer their rights of residence outside the ghetto to their children; the latter could not. Frederick, known as the "enthroned philosopher" and "enlightened despot," supposedly a tolerant monarch "who believed that a man should go to hell his own way," was nonetheless bigoted in his attitude towards the Jews. In 1750, the Prussian king issued an edict restricting the hereditary right of *Schutzjuden* to reside outside the ghetto only to the oldest son, instead of to three sons as had been the practice formerly. The younger disinherited children of the privileged Jews were also deprived by Frederick's order of the right to marry and raise a family. He also imposed new occupational disabilities and onerous taxes on the Jews in his domain.

Frederick's passionate desire to industrialize his country later impelled him to relax his severity. He offered the right of domicile outside the ghetto to the second son of a *Schutzjude* on condition that he open a new factory. The new enterprises required capital, for which the King also turned to the Jews. In consequence, the Jewish population of Berlin, which had been limited to one hundred fifty-two families by the Ordinance of 1750, increased within three decades to one thousand families, in a total citywide population of one hundred forty thousand. In his zeal to attract Jewish money, Frederick accorded equal rights to Jewish bankers, placing them on a par with non-Jews. A number of Jews attained considerable wealth as a result of these measures.

Secular Influences

In the ghetto, the Jews commonly spoke Judeo-German (*i.e.* Yiddish) but the upper class and the more cultured elements who came into contact with non-Jews spoke German. These Jews, together with the Christian intellectuals, were exposed to French cultural influences, emanating from the large French colony in Berlin, which included prominent industrial magnates and financiers. Through them, the Berlin Jewish intelligentsia became acquainted with the liberal currents and progressive thought originating in France and spreading through Central and Western Europe. For utilitarian and social as well as intellectual reasons, the younger generation among the upper-class Jews studied the French language and literature. The criticism of existing institutions by leaders of French thought like Voltaire (1694-1778) and Rousseau (1712-1778) stirred and influenced them. Through them these ideas found their way also into the ghetto.

Secular Education

Worldly learning was relatively scarce among German Jews until the end of the eighteenth century, but it was by no means unknown. As early as the beginning of the seventeenth century, a few Jewish students had been admitted to the medical faculties of several German universities; toward the end of that century, Jews were entering other faculties as well. These students were commonly prepared for their university studies by private tutors. In the eighteenth century, a basic secular education was essential in some of the principalities in Germany. In Hesse Cassel, for example, a law was passed in 1739 requiring that all commercial records and affairs be kept in German. One of the schools of the Portuguese Jewish community in Hamburg at that time taught French. The by-laws of the Jewish orphanage in that city permitted the wards of the institution to study French and German after the age of thirteen, if they showed aptitude in these languages. Several Hebrew texts had been published in the secular field. In 1721 an algebra book written by Asher Worms, a Frankfort physician, appeared. In 1755 a volume on astronomy was prepared by Raphael Levy, a pupil of Leibnitz (1646-1716). Later, Judah Mindlin compiled a Hebrew-German dictionary, with the high-sounding title of *Milim Leloha* (*Words of God*). These works evidence the interest of Jews in general education in the eighteenth century.

The rabbis commonly opposed the dissemination of worldly learning among the Jewish youth, fearing that it would distract them from Jewish study; but some, particularly those who possessed secular knowledge themselves, permitted it. From the eighteenth century on, Jews had another motive for acquiring such knowledge; they hoped thereby to gain the learning that would qualify them for Emancipation. They earnestly believed that their integration into German culture would bridge the gulf between them and their Christian countrymen. In the effort to accomplish this, Moses Mendelssohn played a leading role.

3

The Enlightenment

I. MOSES MENDELSSOHN (1729-1786)

Biographical Sketch

To MENACHEM MENDEL, a poor Torah scribe in Dessau, Germany, was born in 1729 a son, Moses, later known as Mendelssohn.[1] Moses, who had distinguished himself in his early years by his brilliance, received the traditional Jewish training in Talmud and other rabbinic texts. Under the guidance of the scholarly rabbi of the town, David Frankel, the lad of thirteen devoted himself assiduously to a study of Maimonides' philosophical work, the *Guide to the Perplexed.* A frail youth, Moses emerged from this experience greatly enriched mentally, but physically hunchbacked, and in his later years, he often referred to his crooked back as a legacy from Maimonides.

In 1743 Rabbi Frankel left Dessau to assume the post of Chief Rabbi of Berlin. Several months later, Moses, then fourteen, tramped seventy long and weary miles to the Prussian capital to study at the academy of his beloved teacher. During his first years in Berlin, Mendelssohn lived a life of struggle and privation in the attic of a merchant for whom he copied correspondence in lieu of paying rent. But in the big city his educational interests expanded.

He was introduced to a broad range of secular learning by several individuals who were drawn to him by his avid thirst for knowledge. He soon mastered the German language, read its literature extensively, gained an excellent knowledge of mathematics, philosophy, and Latin, and also took up French and English. He did not receive systematic instruction in these subjects, but he managed to learn them with the aid and guidance of sympathetic friends and acquaintances.

After five or six years in Berlin, Mendelssohn accepted a position as tutor in the family of a wealthy *Schutzjude,* the industrialist Isaac Bernhard. He served as Bernhard's bookkeeper, then as his representative, finally, after Bernhard's death, becoming a partner in the firm. Once Mendelssohn had achieved a measure of financial security, he was able to devote his leisure to study and writing. His works on philosophy and aesthetics won him prominence in literary and philosophical circles. His elegant, lucid literary style earned him considerable popularity.

Mendelssohn scored an outstanding achievement in the field of philosophy in 1763 when the Prussian Academy of Science awarded him the first prize in a contest in which the renowned philosopher Immanuel Kant was also a participant. The theme of the contest was "Are Metaphysics Mathematically Demonstrable?" In his winning essay Mendelssohn attempted to prove that the test of reason could be applied to religion as well as to other branches of human knowledge. In recognition of the great distinction Mendelssohn had attained, a friend at the court of Frederick II attempted unsuccessfully to induce the King to award Mendelssohn the full status of a *Schutzjude.* Until that time, despite his wide reputation, Mendelssohn had been permitted to reside in Berlin only because he was employed by a *Schutzjude.* But he had been granted this special privilege only for himself, not as an absolute right which members of his family could inherit. Only later, after he had become a partner in his employer's firm, did he secure the permanent right of domicile for himself and his family.

In 1767, Mendelssohn published his *Phaedon,* a book on the immortality of the soul in which he followed Plato's classical dialogue, the *Phaedo.* In this work he insisted that there must be at least one unique substance in the human personality which is indestructible and survives death. In support of this view, he offered the Cartesian argument that the good and just God would not have planted the idea of a soul in the human mind had there not been one. Mendelssohn attempted to base his conclusion not on religious authority, but on what he referred to as reason and logic. The volume created a sensation in the intellectual world and was published in numerous editions and translated into practically every European tongue. It earned for Mendelssohn the title of the "German Plato" and the "Jewish Socrates." As a result, he was proposed for membership in the Berlin Academy of Science, but the King eliminated his name from the roster of candidates, because he thought it would be an insult to a royal candidate for membership, Queen Catherine of Russia, to have her name on the same slate with a Jew. Mendelssohn's reply to this insult, addressed to several members of the Academy, was said to have been: "It is better that you elect me and the King reject me, than that the King elect me and and you reject me."

Mendelssohn and Kant

Immanuel Kant (1724-1804), an eminent contemporary and friend of Mendelssohn, was the founder of the German idealist school of philosophy. Kant was at first a rationalist who believed that religion could be subjected to the test of pure reason. In later life, however, he revised his thinking and in his *Critique of Pure Reason,* maintained that reason could not be the sole arbiter of religious truths, because the human mind is unable to penetrate beyond the ken of human experience which is limited by the dimension of time, space, and finitude. With our senses we can grasp only phenomena, but not noumena, the *Dinge an sich* (things-in-themselves), as he put it. Ultimate reality, Kant concluded, is therefore beyond our scope.

For this reason, the truths of religion, the existence of God, freedom of the will, and immortality—lie outside of the realm of human knowledge and understanding and cannot be proven. But by the same token, they cannot be disproven. We can, however, make contact with reality through moral experience, by means of the ethical sense, which is associated with the spiritual or transcendental, as distinguished from the phenomenal, self. The existence of a moral inclination in man[2] implies the existence of a moral master and authority in the universe which in turn gives grounds for a belief in God.

Ethical obligation, however, has no meaning without the choice that is assumed in free will. Moreover, it presupposes immortality, for immortality affords an opportunity beyond temporal life for the realization of the moral law, through the reward of the virtuous and the punishment of the wicked. Often this does not occur in this life and must consequently be postponed to the hereafter. It appears, then, that though Pure Reason cannot prove these primary principles of religious faith, it admits they are possible; Practical Reason, however, requires them as a matter of inner conviction, since morality is so closely linked up with them. Kant believed that the conscience of man was the source of an inner, or natural, revelation of the precepts of morality. He thus upheld the autonomy of the moral law, maintaining that it emanates from the rational will alone.

Mendelssohn differed from Kant in that in addition to natural or inner revelation, that is, the conscience, he accepted also the divine revelation of Jewish law. He subscribed to a belief in the theonomy of the Torah and the principles of Judaism as well as their heteronomy, that is, their origin from an external source, not the rational will.[3] Accordingly, we note a dichotomous approach on Mendelssohn's part to this problem.

In his view on religious dogma, Mendelssohn agreed with Kant. Kant opposed the dogmas of Christianity, while extolling its moral principles above those of Judaism. Mendelssohn upheld ritual as an integral part of Jewish law which could not be abrogated. To Kant, however, "anything man does to please God, except through ethical conduct, is religious madness and a putrid cult." Kant, moreover, portrayed Judaism as enthroning a stern God who demanded blind adherence on the part of His followers to His ordained rules and rituals, under the threat of retribution. Mendelssohn could not convince Kant of the intrinsic truth, humanity, justice, and love that form the core of Jewish ethics. Kant appears to have overlooked the lofty doctrines and universalist teachings of the prophets of Israel, which certainly conform to his own exalted moral ideals.

The Lavater Affair

On a visit to Berlin in 1763, Johan Casper Lavater, a Swiss clergyman, discussed intimate religious questions with Mendelssohn, the two men agreeing that the conversation was to be of a private nature. Lavater was highly impressed by Mendelssohn, who indicated that he admired Jesus as a great ethical personage, but not more than that. It then occurred to Lavater to try to maneuver Mendelssohn into a compromising position in which he could be compelled to embrace Christianity. Mendelssohn's refusal to join the church, Lavater calculated, would imply publicly that he considered Judaism as superior to Christianity—an implication that would entail considerable embarrassment for him, if not actual danger. In 1769, Lavater published a German translation of Charles Bonnet's French book on Christian dogma which he called *An Examination of the Evidences of Christianity.* Lavater believed that this work contained conclusive proof of the truth of Christianity. He dedicated the translation to Mendelssohn, and addressed an open letter to the Jewish philosopher in which he challenged him to refute the proofs of Christianity adduced in his volume or submit to baptism.

Mendelssohn was thoroughly shocked by the demand. He had not expected that he would be regarded by a liberal in this condescending manner, as the follower of a superstitious and inferior faith. To him, religion was a personal affair, a question of conscience which he did not feel should be aired publicly. Nevertheless, he had to be cautious in his defense and say nothing that would irritate the censor, his fellow Jews, or the Christians. It was an extremely delicate situation.

He replied by means of a brochure, written in a restrained and moderate tone, acknowledging Lavater's sincerity, though rebuking him for quoting a private conversation. As a rationalist, he declared that he had investigated Judaism from the standpoint of reason and philosophy. Had he arrived at the conclusion that Judaism did not conform with the criteria of philosophy, he would have conceded such a finding publicly. "What could bind me to a religion which is ostensibly more demanding than others, and more despised, if I were not convinced of its fundamental truth?" he challenged. "What would have kept me from accepting Christianity if I were merely a deist, indifferent to both religions alike? Fear of my coreligionists? They lack the power to inspire anyone with fear. Stubbornness or inertia or a mere persistence in the path of tradition? But I have devoted my life to investigating questions regarding tradition and convention and I have never subscribed to anything on the basis of precedent alone. It is only an inner conviction as to the truth of my faith that has kept me in the religion of my fathers and I declare before the God of Truth Who created and sustained Lavater and me that I shall remain loyal to it as long as my soul will not change its nature!"

Mendelssohn then proceeded to discuss the tolerant attitude of Judaism. According to its principles, a non-Jew who observes the *Seven Laws of Noah*[1] is reckoned among the "Pious of the Nations" and has a portion in the world to come. Judaism has no missionaries because it does not expect anyone who is not a Jew to observe the laws of the Torah. "I have good friends among the Christians, good people," Mendelssohn fervently asserted, "and it has never occurred to me to deplore their not being Jews and even less to induce them to adopt Judaism." He conceded that there were foibles even in his own faith, referring to them as "accretions to the core principles of Judaism that obscure its glamour." "But," he added, "who is in a position to assert that his religion is free of human foibles? On my part, I am proud that my religion is not based on doctrines that conflict with logic. Moreover, it has the advantage that it does not pursue proselytes . . . nor does it send missionaries to India or Greenland. If a Confucius or a Solon were to live in my generation I would love and revere him for the great man that he was, without venturing to urge him to accept my faith."

Lavater was moved by Mendelssohn's statement and apologized profusely and publicly for offending "the noblest of men." However, the controversy was continued by others. Mendelssohn was denounced by both sides: by the rabbis for criticising his own religion, and by Christians for yielding to his prejudices and remaining in the Jewish fold. The latter charged that it was fear for his economic interests that impelled him to cling to Judaism. These polemics had a deteriorating effect on Mendelssohn's health, but they also roused him to a more active identification with his people.

Gotthold Lessing (1729-1781)

Mendelssohn's loyal adherence to the faith of his fathers made quite a different impression on his friend Gotthold Ephraim Lessing, who was one of the foremost Christian champions of Jewish rights in the period of the Enlightenment. In 1749, Lessing had written a play entitled *The Jews,* in which he ventured to portray the Jew as uniquely endowed spiritually and culturally. This play aroused widespread debate among the members of the intelligentsia, since it was perhaps the first attempt on the part of a prominent Christian to describe the Jews in so favorable a light. Soon after *The Jews* appeared, Mendelssohn and Lessing met in the home of a mutual friend, and a warm friendship developed between them which was to continue throughout their lives.

Lessing was so impressed by the saintly character of his Jewish friend that he used him as the model for the hero of his famous drama *Nathan the Wise.* This play incorporates a fable from the *Decameron,* which tells of a father who loves each of his three sons equally. In order not to favor any one of them, he has perfect replicas made of a magic ring in his possession, which supposedly has the power of making people love its owner, and bequeaths a ring to each son. After the father's death, each of the sons claims that he is entitled to the genuine ring. Finally, the matter is brought to court. The judge, grasping the deceased father's intention, addresses the disappointed heirs in these words: "There is no need to decide the case now. When one of you in time becomes better loved than his brothers we shall know that he has the original ring."

The moral of the fable is clear. It is far more important that the brothers behave as if they had the genuine ring than that they actually possess it. Proper action or conduct is of far greater moment than abstract truth. The brothers, of course, represent the three major religions: Christianity, Judaism, and Islam. No one can actually determine which is the true faith. What is of greater importance is that the followers of these religions should abide by the morals and ethics taught by their respective creeds, rather than quarrel over the metaphysical question of which theology is the correct one. Each religion has its merits; only through righteous and uplifting conduct can a believer prove the truth of his faith.

The same idea is illustrated in the play again, when the Friar, in admiration of Nathan's truly noble deeds, exclaims, "Nathan, Nathan, you are a Christian! There never was a better Christian!" To which Nathan replies, "We agree. For that which makes me in your eyes a Christian, makes you in my eyes, a Jew!" It should be noted that it took a great deal of courage on Lessing's part to make such a pronouncement and to place Christianity and Judaism on an equal footing, for at that time, in particular, Catholics and Protestants shared a common hostility towards the Jews. Lessing's views were held by only a few, even among the enlightened of his time.

Dohm's Appeal

Another prominent friend of Mendelssohn's, the Prussian Counsellor of State, Christian Wilhelm von Dohm, also pleaded for the rights of the Jews. In an important pamphlet which he published in 1781, entitled *On the Civic Improvement of the Conditions of the Jews,* Dohm described the wretched situation of German Jews and the numerous disabilities they suffered and argued for the amelioration of their plight. He pointed to the fact that Jews were denied the right of domicile in many German states. In others they were permitted to remain temporarily, often only overnight and then only upon the payment of a tax. Where Jews were permitted to reside, their numbers were severely restricted and their taxes were onerous. Dohm also pointed to the effect of the occupational ban on the Jews. Farming was forbidden to them. No craft or trade guild would admit them. Only a few exceptionally gifted Jews who enjoyed the special favor of a prince could enter one of a few professions. Commerce, the only field left to these unfortunates, weighted them down with heavy imposts, leaving as their only outlet petty trade or peddling—a straw grasped by those who had no other alternative.[5]

Dohm alluded to the doctrines of Adam Smith (1723-1790), the celebrated Scottish economist and professor of philosophy, who, in his *Wealth of Nations* (1776), stressed the application of what he termed "natural law" in the field of economics. To produce wealth, Smith wrote, it is important to mobilize the productive capacity of as many people as possible; the greater the number of

productive workers of all types in a country, the greater its prosperity. Dohm referred to the young American republic as a case
in point. America was successful, declared Dohm, because it united
all its people politically, accorded them civil liberties without ethnic
or religious distinction, and encouraged them to contribute their
utmost in any economic field they chose. It was, thus, a matter of
self-interest for a state to emancipate its Jews, he concluded.

Dohm's Proposals

While Dohm was very sympathetic to the plight of the Jews, the
suggestions he made for altering their situation politically were
rather moderate. He urged that the Jews be granted a number of
civic rights, but not full citizenship. He thought it would be best
for the Jews to retain the communal self-government which they
had had in the ghetto, as well as the right to conduct their own
judicial affairs and to punish offenders for religious transgressions
by use of the ban. He also felt that Jews should not hold public
office in the German state, in order not to arouse the ill will of
Christian aspirants for these posts.

Mendelssohn took sharp issue with these proposals. He saw a
grave inconsistency in granting the Jews civic rights and yet keeping
them segregated from the main body politic. Moreover, he disclaimed the authority of a community to penalize or excommunicate anyone for religious infractions, on the ground that such
action interfered with one's right to freedom of conscience. In his
introduction to a German translation of the *Vindiciae Judeorum*,
Menasseh ben Israel's appeal to Cromwell to readmit the Jews
into England, Mendelssohn voiced his objections to Dohm's halfway measures for the enfranchisement of the Jew.

Mendelssohn's views offended both the Jewish and non-Jewish
camps. The rabbis took him to task for opposing their power to
ban or excommunicate. Shortly thereafter, an anonymous pamphlet entitled *The Search for Light and Right* appeared which charged
that Mendelssohn was undermining the foundations of Mosaic law
with his views, for the Mosaic code sanctioned the punishment of
violators. In questioning the propriety of such punishment, the
pamphleteer declared, Mendelssohn had placed himself close to
Christianity, which was based not on laws the breach of which

entail penalties, but on ethical doctrines which are not bound up with a retributive system. In reply to the anonymous author, Mendelssohn wrote a small volume, *Jerusalem,* which became his Jewish *magnum opus.* It was published in 1783, three years before his death.

II. MENDELSSOHN'S "JERUSALEM"

Church and State

THE THEME of Mendelssohn's *Jerusalem* is suggested by its descriptive title, *Concerning Religious Authority and Judaism.* The work consists of two parts, the first dealing with the respective jurisdictions of church and state. Both institutions, Mendelssohn said, are devoted to the promotion of human welfare, though each has its own distinctive sphere of activity. The state deals primarily with secular affairs, those pertaining to the relations of man and his neighbor, an area in which it may employ force in order to secure its legitimate ends. The church, on the other hand, is concerned chiefly with the domain of the spirit and the conscience, and with relations between man and his Maker. In this aspect of life, there is no room for interference, or for the exercise of sanctions, by either church *or* state. Though the state should have no control over the spiritual realm of thought and belief, it should curb disbelief in God, Providence, and immortality, because these beliefs are essential to the maintenance and preservation of the moral order.[6] The church should do no more than use persuasion—without coercion or pressure—in regard to other religious beliefs or doctrines.

The state, moreover, should be entirely divorced from the church; in no way should the rights of a citizen be influenced by his creed or his manner of worship. In religious matters, one must follow the dictates of his own mind and conscience. While a government, or any other group in society, may expel a person from its midst, the church ought not to exercise the analagous right of the ban or excommunication, because to do so would defeat the very purpose for which it was created. The church's function is to guide, teach, and inspire good conduct. Excluding a constituent by the exercise of ecclesiastical authority is akin to the refusal of medicaments by an apothecary to a seriously ill patient. The person the church bars may often be the very one who requires its ministrations and good offices the most. Besides, the church is prone to use its power to cast out members as a penalty for sincere dissent, and this, of course, is morally untenable.

In Mendelssohn's opinion, the voluntary character of the church did not permit it to engage in mundane pursuits, such as owning property or paying salaries. Recognizing, however, that the church as a human institution could not operate effectively without salaried functionaries, he suggested that the government provide the necessary remuneration—apparently not realizing that such an arrangement would break down the wall of separation between church and state which he had advocated. He was at least equally inconsistent in his notion that the state should suppress disbelief in God, Providence and immortality, for that was an outright violation of his principles regarding an individual's right to his own religious beliefs. Despite these contradictions, Mendelssohn was still considerably in advance of his time in his general attitude towards the role of church and state in a free society.

Judaism and Reason

In the second part of *Jerusalem,* Mendelssohn explains his concept of Judaism. He had been exposed to the influence of the general Enlightenment movement which set up reason as the arbiter of human thought and activity. Mendelssohn maintained, as Leibnitz before him, that the fundamental principles of Judaism, the belief in the existence and unity of God, Providence and immortality, is confirmed by "reason, by nature and events," and is, therefore, common to all religions. These ideas are so self-evident as to receive universal assent. They are, therefore, not the product of any particular supernatural revelation. As proof of this assertion, he noted that both the great sage, Joseph Albo (1380-1444) and the deists were almost in complete agreement on these salient doctrines. Thus Mendelssohn made reason the sole guide to religious truth, while Saadya (892-942) and the later medieval philosophers of Judaism made the intellect only a means of confirming and supporting revelation as the principal mode of attaining divine knowledge.

Judaism, Mendelssohn concludes, possesses no dogmas which transcend reason and which its adherents must accept unconditionally as a matter of faith. In the area of theology and religion, Judaism permits freedom of thought, interpretation and opinion. Accordingly, Judaism does not demand uniformity in creed, but rather uniformity in deed. Its laws and statutes are intended to impress the divine will upon the human mind and motivate the individual to pursue a course of conduct that will lead to salvation.

To prove his contention, Mendelssohn points out that among all the precepts and injunctions in the Torah, there is not one that says, "thou shalt believe" or "thou shalt not believe!" All declare thou shalt do or refrain from doing. Sanctions and penalties are prescribed not for disbelief, but for failure to abide by religious laws. Consequently, the Hebrew Scriptures cannot be termed a revealed religion but rather *revealed legislation*—a body of regulations and rules supernaturally given to the Jewish people through Moses. Even the first of the Ten Commandments (*Ex.* 20: 1) does not require belief in God; it merely identifies the historical Deity Who delivered the Jews out of Egypt and upon Whose authority the other commandments are given. In sum, the spirit of Judaism is freedom in doctrine and conformity in action.[7]

To Mendelssohn, the ceremonials and rituals of the Torah are "a kind of writ, living, quickening the mind and heart, full of meaning and having the closest affinity with religious knowledge." Since these laws are of divine origin, we, who are only human, cannot change them. They form an indissoluble bond uniting all who are born Jews, and help to create a salutary religious tone in the community. The precepts of the Torah are designed primarily for its recipients, the Jewish people, by reason of their covenant with God, and are binding only upon them without any implication that theirs is the only true faith. Only the ethical truths not bearing on faith and based on reason, conduct, and the experience of mankind that apply to all men, are essential for salvation, Mendelssohn believes. But the laws of any one religious group cannot be so construed, for it would be unjust on the part of God to restrict salvation to only one people. Non-Jews, too, may merit salvation if they observe the fundamental ethical laws referred to in Judaism as the seven Noahide commands.[8]

Creedal Conformity

Ancient Israel, Mendelssohn observed, was a theocracy, in which the church was identified with the state. The blasphemer violated the law of the state; the desecrator of the Sabbath transgressed basic civic law. When the state disappeared, the penalties against these offenses lost their force, and have not been revived. Yet the laws themselves cannot be abrogated, since they are God-given and only God can annul them. They are obligatory for anyone born a Jew; even Jesus obeyed them. The early Christians, moreover, did not have the right to release themselves or other born Jews from the "yoke of the commandments," by which even Jewish converts to Christianity are bound. It is interesting to note that Mendelssohn stressed the ethnic rather than the creedal element in Judaism, evidently recognizing that Judaism is an ethnic religion.[9]

Biblical and Talmudic Judaism did not formulate any creed. It is true, Mendelssohn conceded, that Maimonides (1135-1204) drew up the celebrated Thirteen Articles of Faith which were incorporated in the liturgical hymn *Yigdal*. Though his Thirteen Articles eventually received general acceptance, there were a number of scholars who criticized them. No one, however, ventured to brand the opponents of Maimonides' creed as heretics. We adhere rather to the maxim of our rabbis: the inferences of the one school of sages and the opposing school are "both the words of the living God"[10] (*Eruvin* 13b).

Mendelssohn objected to what he calls the "fusion of faiths," which corresponds with the Christian concept of "one shepherd and one flock" (*John* 10: 16) and represents Christianity's goal of uniting all mankind under its wing. The merger of religions involves compromises which have no place in the realm of the spirit, where complete freedom of thought and opinion should prevail. It were far better if the different religious groups were to learn to coexist and to respect each other. If the price of civil emancipation for the Jews is to be religious absorption, then it were better, Mendelssohn declared, that Jews forego their enfranchisement. Even if only a handful of people refuse to surrender their religion, they should make common cause and assert themselves accordingly.

III. Critique of Mendelssohn's Views

Dogma in Judaism

MENDELSSOHN, like Maimonides, attempted to reconcile Judaism with philosophy. While the latter tried to harmonize Judaism with Aristotle, the former endeavored to show that it was in agreement with Kant and other rationalists of his age. As noted previously, Mendelssohn was influenced by the deistic movement which advocated natural as distinguished from supernatural religion. The deists, though differing widely on the meaning of the concept of "natural religion," were all united in their opposition to divine revelation. In view of this, it is of interest to observe that though the Berlin Jewish philosopher objected to the notion that Judaism was based on a system of *revealed dogma,* he advanced the idea that it represented a system of *revealed legislation.* The idea of revelation, however, whether involving legislation or any other fixed belief, smacks of dogma, which lies outside the precinct of rational or natural religion. A *dogma,* by definition, *is a theological formulation pronounced by a central ecclesiastical authority, which must be accepted without recourse to reason or logic, as a condition for membership in a religious communion.*[11] The existence of such a belief in Judaism would refute Mendelssohn's contention that Judaism permits complete freedom in religious thought.

It has been suggested that the monotheistic principle expressed in the Scriptural verse which is the keynote of Jewish doctrine and liturgy: "Hear O Israel, the Lord our God, the Lord is One" (*Deut.* 6:4) is essentially a dogma, since all Jews are required to subscribe to it as a matter of faith. It can be argued, however, that the monotheistic concept is recognized in natural or rational religion; moreover, it can be explained in ethical terms. The least that can be said on this question, without reservation, is that in Judaism faith alone without works is of no account. Jewish theology is accordingly a system of morality. In this regard, as has been previously observed, Judaism differs fundamentally from New Testament Christianity which declares: "Believe on the Lord, Jesus Christ, and thou shalt be saved and thy house" (*Acts* 16:31). This thought is also expressed in other verses: "He that believeth and is baptized shall be saved, but he that believeth not, shall be damned" (*Mark* 16:16); "Blessed are they that have not seen and yet believe" (*John* 20:29); "Therefore . . . man is justified by faith without the deeds of the Law" (*Rom.* 3:28).[12]

This doctrine suggests the existence of a dichotomy in Christianity between faith and works. This cleavage is reflected in Jesus' utterance: "Render unto Caesar what is Caesar's and unto God what is God's (*Matt.* 22:21). It indicates a schism between theology and life—belief and conduct. Such a view may have extremely sinister implications, for it may give warrant to the hope of the most depraved villain to wash away his sins in the stream of faith,[13] notwithstanding the wrong and misery that he may have been guilty of. In Judaism, of course, such an idea is untenable, for true penitence requires not faith but actual redress of wrongs committed (*M. Yoma* 8:9).

This is not to say that because the New Testament regards the true faith in Jesus as the sole condition for salvation, that it overlooks the role of proper conduct. The New Testament also extols good works (*Matt.* 5:16, *Gal.* 6:10) though the latter is not a condition for salvation. Paul, who expounds this doctrine of faith, appears to assume that a complete commitment to faith will generate the attitude that will lead man to obey the higher law and the superior morality, instead of the Law of Moses (*Acts* 13:39). In this view, Paul widened the gap between Judaism and the new religion he expounded. Several of the apostles, however, took a less extreme attitude towards the relation of faith to works than Paul. One even insisted that "faith without works is dead." (*James* 2:17, 20).

Precept and Belief

That Judaism is not a faith in the conventional sense of a system of beliefs may be judged from the absence in the Scriptures of an indigenous word for that concept. The Hebrew *emunah,* translated as faith, is not an equivalent; it refers to faith only in the sense of reliance[14] or trust, rather than as a theological credo. The term *Dat,* used to connote religion in medieval times,[15] actually means law, decree, or custom. This fact would appear to confirm Mendelssohn's conclusion that Judaism lacks a fixed creed.[16]

Strictly speaking, from the Halachic and legalistic viewpoint, the primary test of Jewishness is the ethnic one—that of birth, not belief (*Kid.* 68b). One who is the offspring of a Jewish mother is regarded as Jewish. Anyone else must undergo the rite of *Giyur* (conversion) and is then accepted and treated on a par with the born Jew. The quality of one's Jewishness is determined by the degree of his adherence to the laws, ethics, doctrines, and precepts of Judaism. The more closely one clings to them, the more intense is his Jewishness. On the other hand, though one may violate a number of them, he still retains his Jewishness, on the principle that an Israelite "though he sins, is yet an Israelite" (*San.* 44a).

Biblical and Rabbinic Precepts

The nature of Judaism can best be determined by an examination of its sources, beginning with the Hebrew Bible. The prominence of statutes, ordinances, and commands, both ritual and ethical, in the Pentateuch and the conspicuous absence of dogma in the Mosaic writings confirm the conclusion that Judaism is highly pragmatic. The prophets, too, stress moral conduct, not religious belief in the theoretic sense. Typical of the prophetic teachings is Micah's exhortation, "What does the Lord require of thee, but to do justice, love mercy and walk humbly with thy God" (*Micah* 6:8). The psalmist speaks in a similar vein: "Who will go up to the mountain of the Lord? He that hath clean hands and a pure heart" (*Ps.* 24:3, 4). The practical nature of Judaism, requiring proper conduct, is reflected in all the books of the Hebrew Bible.

The Talmud, naturally, follows the same pattern as the Hebrew Scriptures on which it is based. It refers to 613 precepts: 365 negative and 248 positive (*Makkot* 23b), all of which constitute a code of conduct, but not a creed. In Talmudic times, the rabbis saw no special need for regulating the thought of their people or demanding uniformity in belief by means of a series of dogmas. Moreover, there existed no such precedent among the surrounding peoples which the Jews might have been inclined to follow. On the contrary, the Talmud gives expression to skeptical comments such as "There is no Messiah for Israel" (*San.* 99a).[16a] True, there are statements in the Talmud that might be interpreted as dogmatic, such as the passage in the Mishna (*San.* 10:1) . . . "The following have no portion in the world to come[17]: he who maintains that resurrection is not derived from the Torah[18], that the Torah was not divinely revealed, and the Epicurean." These, however, can hardly be considered dogmas, for the penalty prescribed for disbelief in them is neither excommunication nor punishment by a human agency. Violators will merely be deprived of "a portion in the world to come."

The Creed of Maimonides

Since the first century, attempts have been made to draw up a formal compilation of rudimentary principles of Judaism. The stimulus for such a formulation emanated from the outside—from the external challenge of Hellenism or the Christian and Moslem creeds. After the Council of Nicea (325), Church councils adopted various sets of doctrine, which were incorporated in the church liturgy. Islam, though resembling Judaism in its emphasis on precept and duty, also stresses the importance of correct belief, but to a lesser extent than Christianity. Rabbis, at different stages of Judaism, believed that the masses influenced by the religious patterns of both Christians and Moslems needed a clear outline of the basic principles of Judaism. By that time, however, there was no longer a central ecclesiastical body among the Jews, like the Sanhedrin of old, empowered to determine the fixed principles of faith, and the task, therefore, fell to individuals. Among those who ventured such a formulation were Philo (d.ca. 50), Saadya Gaon (892-942), Judah Halevi (1085-1140), Bachya ibn Pakuda (ca. 1050) and others. These endeavors, it should be noted, were deviations from the normal tendencies in Judaism, and there was persistent opposition to the proposed tenets of creed which were essentially matters of individual opinion.

The thirteen creedal principles promulgated by Maimonides at the age of thirty-three in his *Commentary on the Mishna* were, as noted by Mendelssohn, the most popular compilation, and, accordingly, found a place in the prayer book; yet these articles were designated for private, not public, recital. The introduction of a creed into Judaism implied that anyone who did not accept it excluded himself from the Jewish fold. Maimonides thus created an orthodoxy, or a standard of correct faith, and by the same token, a heresy—both of which ideas are alien to Judaism. This was hardly to be expected of an Aristotelian and a rationalist, but it appears that to Maimonides, as to Saadya and other Jewish philosophers, both approaches, the rationalistic and the authoritarian, were equally valid means of attaining religious knowledge and truth. His Thirteen Articles of Faith include the beliefs[18a] that

1. *God, the Creator, exists.*
2. *He is a perfect unity.*
3. *He is incorporeal.*
4. *He is eternal.*
5. *He alone may be worshipped.*
6. *He revealed Himself to the prophets.*
7. *The prophesy of Moses is true and Moses is the supreme prophet.*
8. *The Torah was given by God at Sinai.*
9. *God's Torah is immutable.*
10. *God knows every deed and thought of man.*
11. *God rewards those who observe His commandments. and punishes those who do not.*
12. *The Messiah will come.*
13. *The dead will be resurrected.*

Purpose of Creeds

Why had Maimonides selected these particular beliefs and not others? It is quite likely, as Schechter suggested, that Maimonides incorporated those principles that, in his opinion required emphasis to refute certain doctrines of Christianity or Islam. The Jewish sages may have followed the practice of Church councils and included in their creeds the cardinal ideas they believed to be endangered at a particular period, in order to focus attention upon them. The declaration of God's unity, for example, may have been necessary to combat the Christian doctrine of the

Trinity, while the assertion of the supremacy of Moses may have been directed against the belief in Mohammed or Jesus.

Hasdai Crescas (1340-1410) in *Or Adonai (Light of the Lord)* criticized the Thirteen Articles of Faith because they did not distinguish between the essential and subordinate principles. A disciple of Crescas, Joseph Albo (1380-1440) in his *Sefer Ha-Ikkarim (Book of Fundamentals)* went even further and proposed several classes and ranks of dogmas. There are first, he urged, the *Ikkarim (fundamental doctrines)*, which in his opinion consisted of three main ideas: the existence of God,[19] revelation, and retribution. These three concepts are the pillars of divine religion. They are not peculiarly Jewish, as are the eight *Shorashim* (roots), which represent corollaries of the *Ikkarim*. From the *Shorashim* emerge six *Anafim* (branch doctrines). While the *Ikkarim* and the *Shorashim* are binding on every Jew to the extent that a disbeliever in any of them is a heretic, one who denies any of the *Anafim* is merely a sinner. Some scholars like Isaac Luria (1534-1572) and Isaac Abravanel (1437-1508) saw no justification for singling out any particular doctrine in Judaism above others. The opposition and lack of unanimity in the acceptance of these principles lend support to Mendelssohn's conclusion that Judaism is a religion without dogma.[20]

Albo, like Maimonides, Schechter believed, may have had a practical purpose in ranking the various Articles of Faith, for in so doing he relegated the idea of the Messiah, so vital a tenet in Christianity, to an unimportant role in Judaism. In this manner, he may have intended to combat the claims of the Christians, advanced especially at the religious disputation at Tortosa, Spain (1413-1414), to the effect that Christianity represented the realization of the Messianic aspiration, which the Christians maintained was a cardinal belief in Judaism. Albo had played a prominent part in this disputation which resulted in a wave of apostasy that swept through the intellectual circles of his day, in Spain. In opposition also to the claim of Christianity that it was the true Judaism and its fulfillment, Albo insisted that the laws of Judaism could be changed only by a public revelation like the Biblical one. However the rabbis have ample authority to interpret and accommodate these laws to changing conditions, Albo maintained.[21] To stress his view that deed is of far greater moment in Judaism than dogma, Albo declared that the performance of a single command with proper intent, irrespective of all dogma, will qualify one for life eternal.

IV. Cultural and Educational Impact

Pioneer of Enlightenment

THE INTELLECTUAL HORIZONS of ghetto Jewry were limited by the Talmud. The Yiddish dialect they spoke isolated them from their neighbors. In order to break down the barrier and introduce the masses of German Jews to the broader vistas of worldly culture, Mendelssohn recognized that it would be necessary for them to learn the language of the land. He undertook to teach his fellow Jews German, through the medium of the Hebrew Scriptures, the text most popular and best known among them. He thus made the Hebrew Bible a linguistic channel to general culture for his people. He was confident that if the German Jews were to master German, their fellow citizens would have greater respect for them and would be more inclined to consider them worthy of political and civil emancipation.

Accordingly, Mendelssohn proceeded to translate the Hebrew Bible into excellent German. In 1780, the *Book of Genesis* came off the press; it was followed in the next three years by the other volumes of the Pentateuch. By 1783 the task was completed. The translation, printed in Hebrew letters and known as *Netivoth Shalom, (Paths of Peace)* was intended as a pathway to the Bible as well as to the German language. It was a traditional and conservative rendering, done in the light of the knowledge of the day. In addition to the translation, Mendelssohn also included a Hebrew *Biur* (commentary), prepared with the aid of several collaborators under his guidance.

Mendelssohn also rendered the Hebrew Psalms into verse and wrote a commentary on the *Book of Ecclesiastes;* his German translation of the Song of Songs with its Hebrew commentary appeared in 1788, two years after his death. The German version of the Biblical books evoked a good deal of adverse criticism from the rabbis, whom Mendelssohn branded as "pugnacious proclaimers of peace" whose "opposition, hatred and persecution are aroused by the slightest innovation, no matter how beneficial." Despite the antagonism of the theologians, Mendelssohn's Biblical works were widely accepted, eagerly read both overtly and covertly in Germany and abroad. They had their desired effect; they helped to form a bridge to German culture for many Jews. In a period of several decades, Jews learned German, discarded the distinctive Yiddish dialect, and became absorbed in secular culture, literature, philosophy, and science—all of which they had largely abandoned during their long confinement in the ghetto. Mendelssohn's translation of the Bible thus produced an intellectual revolution in Jewish life.

Revival of Hebrew

At the age of twenty-one, while employed as a family tutor, Mendelssohn, together with a friend, started a Hebrew weekly known as *Koheleth Mussar (Moral Preacher)*. Its purpose was to arouse the interest of young Jewish intellectuals immersed in Talmudic study in the world about them, in nature, aesthetics, ethics, and contemporary thought. The materials published were in the spirit of the deistic and optimistic philosophy of Leibnitz and Christian Wolf, which they correlated with the outlook of the Talmud in epigrams such as "All that God does is for the best" (*Ber.* 60b) or "One must bless God for the evil as for the good" (*Ber.* 33b). The editors, too, expressed their interest in the revival of the Hebrew language. Only a few numbers of the publication appeared, but it was a fortuitous beginning. It is significant that the first literary efforts of the great philosopher of the Jewish Enlightenment were couched in the Hebrew tongue.

Mendelssohn's *Biur,* which appeared three decades after the *Koheleth Mussar,* helped to point up the syntax, beauty, style, imagery, and high literary quality of the Hebrew Bible and the Hebrew language. It encouraged two of Mendelssohn's disciples, Isaac Euchel and Mendel Breslau to establish, in 1783, the *Hevrat Dorshei L'shon Eber,* (Society for the Study of the Hebrew Language). A year later, this organization issued the *Ha-Meassef*

(*Gleaner*) as their official publication. The new periodical elicited considerable enthusiasm in various circles, particularly in Berlin. *Ha-Meassef* became the first successful Hebrew magazine. It was intended as a monthly, but it was published at irregular intervals in Konigsberg, Berlin, and other places. It contained essays on Hebrew literature, poetry, and religious *responsa,* as well as general historical and scientific articles. The journal aimed to introduce its readers to European culture. This function, however, conflicted with the magazine's purpose of striving to effect a revival of Hebrew, for those who became absorbed in general culture frequently abandoned their interest in Hebrew. *Ha-Meassef* did not achieve any outstanding literary excellence, but it attracted readers outside of Germany, particularly Poland, who became apostles of the *Haskalah* (Enlightenment) in their own countries.

Educational Ideas

Naphtali Herz Wessely (1725-1805), a Hebrew poet and a staunch disciple of Mendelssohn, who was associated with him in the preparation of his *Biur,* helped to spread Mendelssohn's educational ideas. He was a sharp critic of the prevailing traditional Jewish educational program and sought to change it. As an observant Jew, he was deeply interested in religious education, yet he insisted that the aim of the traditional Jewish school—to prepare its pupils for the study of Talmud—was not a practical one, for few could gain an adequate measure of proficiency in this field. The majority should therefore, he urged, learn a trade. In addition, they should be given a good grounding in their secular studies and trained to participate in the life about them. The secular instruction should include elementary science, mathematics, history, geography, and the German language. To make these subjects more palatable to the ultra-pious, he related them to the religious subject matter. A knowledge of the vernacular, he explained, was not only important for its own sake but also as an aid to achieving a better understanding and appreciation of the structure of the Hebrew language. Geography, he said, would help the student in locating the places, rivers, and countries mentioned in the Bible and would thus vitalize that study; mathematics would facilitate the comprehension of measurements and calculations in the Bible and Talmud. Despite this rationale, Wessely's progressive views engendered a good deal of opposition from the rabbis and the masses, particularly in Galicia. His views, however, moulded the educational outlooks of the proponents of the Enlightenment and laid the foundation for the system of combined Jewish and secular schooling, later propounded by Samson Raphael Hirsch.[22]

Wessely was favorably impressed by the liberal measures outlined in the Edict of Toleration, which was issued in 1781 by Emperor Joseph II of Austria, who had been influenced by the progressive ideas expressed by Mendelssohn's friend, Christian von Dohm. This law provided for the removal of some of the Jewish occupational and residential disabilities then in force. One of its most lasting provisions required Jews to adopt surnames.[23] The Jews still remained in the status of a tolerated community, but the highly objectionable poll tax was abolished, as well as other restrictions, including those relating to worship and distinctive dress. The Jews were encouraged to engage in commerce, open factories, and learn trades, though they could not become master craftsmen. They were free to send their children to the common schools or establish schools of their own, which were to include secular studies in their programs. The universities, too, were opened to them. Many Jews, including Mendelssohn, found reason to question the Emperor's sincerity in adopting these measures, suspecting that his true purpose was to dilute Jewish learning and disrupt Jewish religious life. In any case, nothing came of the program, for the Emperor died before the new law could be implemented effectively.

An attempt to put Wessely's educational theories into practice was made in Berlin in 1778, when David Friedlander, another of Mendelssohn's followers, established the *Juedische Freischule* (Jewish Free School). The *Freischule* introduced a novel curriculum, combining Jewish and general academic studies with a program of vocational training. In addition to the traditional Hebrew texts, the Jewish program included a new area of instruction, the teaching of the principles of Judaism in German. German, moreover, replaced Yiddish as the official language of instruction in the new school. The liberal wing in the school's governing board demanded the intensification of the secular content at the expense of the religious, but Mendelssohn pleaded for patience, caution, and care in instituting changes. They also advocated the adoption of a radical measure—the admission of non-Jewish children, in order to bring the Jewish pupils into contact with others not of their faith, but Mendelssohn urged that the school evolve a suitable course of study before taking this step. The *Freischule's* progressive approach became a model for others.

V. APPRAISAL OF MENDELSSOHN

De-Ghettoization

WE CAN BEST EVALUATE Mendelssohn's work in terms of his objectives. His goals in the Jewish Enlightenment movement were, in a sense, polar in nature and, therefore, quite paradoxical; he sought to break down the ghetto barriers and transform the Jew into a European, who, at the same time, would retain his Jewishness. Accordingly, the Jew was to be integrated into Western culture and trained to live in two milieux, the worldly and the Jewish, thereby assuming dual cultural responsibility. The first of Mendelssohn's objectives was achieved in a short span of time, in a degree perhaps beyond his fondest expectations. Within a few decades after his death, Jews found themselves very much at home in German culture. In his second purpose, however, he failed, for he did not succeed in inculcating in German Jewry, particularly among the intellectuals, a desire and an inclination to preserve their Jewish heritage.

While Mendelssohn directed his efforts principally to the Enlightenment within the ghetto walls, the progressive thinkers of the day were gradually whittling down religious prejudices. The rulers were also beginning to see the evil and injustice of the ghetto. For the first time in a thousand years, the head of a European state, Joseph II of Austria, recognized that the medieval restrictions were harmful both to the Jews and to the state. Though the provisions of his Edict of Toleration were nullified by the unfriendly policies of his successors,[24] his example was followed by other sovereigns. In 1784, Louis XVI of France and, several years later, Frederick William II of Prussia, abolished the "impost of the cloven foot," a poll tax applicable to Jews[25] and cattle when crossing the border of a province. Further reforms were inaugurated in France and in other countries in the wake of the French Revolution. These could be traced in various degrees to the efforts of Mendelssohn, Dohm, and others among his disciples.

Rationalism and Defection

Mendelssohn made his impact on Jewish life primarily as a fighter for the secular enlightenment of his people, rather than for their enfranchisement. He believed that if the Jews would demonstrate their worth and virtue, the Christian world would be bound to grant them civic equality. Actually the acculturation of the Jew brought other problems in its train, and for those he offered neither a solution nor guidance. In his own rationale for Judaism, there were numerous contradictions; it was largely a rationalization of his own piety and observance, prompted mainly by sentiment and loyalty rather than logic. In his own personality, Mendelssohn represented a blending of Judaism with modern culture; he managed to live effectively both as a Jew and a European without becoming overwhelmed by the problems that frequently assailed the modern Jew. Culturally prominent and economically independent, he could do very much as he pleased. He was able to adhere to strict religious observance with little or no risk to his career, prestige, or comfort. This, of course, was not true of the mass of his less fortunate coreligionists—in his and in later times— who lacked not only his remarkable intellectual gifts, but also his strength of character and conviction.

Many of the enlightened German Jews who were determined to attain emancipation for themselves and their children resolved to do so in what they believed to be the simplest way. In order to rid themselves of the legal disabilities imposed on Jews, they needed merely to renounce their Judaism and join the church. These Jews, like most Germans of the day, believed that total conformity to the religion and culture of the majority was essential for complete loyalty to the Fatherland. They considered the prize of emancipation well worth the price of apostasy.

The upper stratum in German Jewry, seized with high social ambitions, commonly succumbed to this viewpoint. In this group were the so-called "salon Jewesses" of Berlin, whose custom it was to invite German and French celebrities to their drawing rooms for good food, good company, and stimulating discussion of political and cultural questions. Prominent among them was the beautiful, charming, and witty Henriette Herz (1764-1847), wife of the physician and philosopher Marcus Herz (1747-1803), who had written several works in both fields.[26] Henriette Herz, who was considerably younger than her husband, entertained noted statesmen such as Count Mirabeau, the theologian Schleiermacher (1768-1834), and the poet and scholar Friedrich von Schlegel (1772-1829). Soon after her mother's death in 1817, she converted to Protestantism. She followed the example of her close friend, Rahel Levin (1771-1833), another gracious hostess who had introduced Goethe and Ranke to the literary world. It seems that Rahel's close association with her glamorous Christian friends made her overconscious of her Jewishness; she developed a feeling of inferiority which led her to embrace the Lutheran faith in 1814, on the day she married Varnhagen von Ense, a Prussian diplomat many years her junior. It should, however, be observed that though Rahel changed her religion, she never lost interest in the Jews and their welfare.

Dorothea (1763-1839), a daughter of Moses Mendelssohn, deserted her Jewish husband, the banker Simon Veit, to elope with and marry her lover, the celebrated leader of the German Romantic movement, Friedrich von Schlegel. Each had written a novel on free love, but after marriage, they evidently changed their views and joined the Catholic Church. Her two sons, who were also baptized, ultimately became painters of religious pictures in Rome. Three more of Mendelssohn's six children converted to Christianity, and as a result, in less than a century after the Jewish philosopher's death, all his direct descendants were baptized.[27] They were only typical of their confused age.

A number of converts, like the great German poet Heinrich Heine (1797-1856), later regretted their actions. In 1826, only a year after he was baptized, he wrote: "I am hated alike by Jews and Christians. I am sincerely sorry that I submitted to baptism, since I do not see how I have improved my lot since. On the contrary, I have suffered many disappointments." Himself an apostate, he scorned, "the former daughters of Israel, whose crosses suspended on their necks are longer than their noses." Subsequently, in a repentant mood, he composed his *Hebrew Melodies,* recalling his childhood memories of the impressive religious observances in his parents' home. He also wrote other works on Jewish themes. Though he had once exclaimed, "Judaism is not a religion, Judaism is a misfortune!", in his later years he extolled the beauty and the great ideals of his ancestral faith. "Since the Exodus," he declared, "freedom has spoken with a Hebrew accent." At the end of his life, Heine, confined to his "mattress crypt," recognized the tragic dilemma of his life, for he was neither Christian nor Jew and, therefore:

> *None will chant a mass;*
> *No Kaddish*[28] *will be read*
> *Nothing sung, nothing said*
> *At my dying bed.*

Thousands of Jews in Germany who, like Heine, were unable to bear the burden of Jewishness or cope with it streamed to the church. In doing so, they not only depleted the ranks of Judaism, but also deprived it of some of its most talented sons and daughters.

Many of the privileged Jews living outside the ghetto in Mendelssohn's age were obsessed with the spirit of the new humanism, but they were too impatient to wait for the ultimate Emancipation which they hoped would usher in a new era of freedom and good will for them and for all mankind. Having cast off much of their Judaism, a little more did not matter. Why suffer all the discrimination and humiliation they had to undergo if merely entering the church solved these problems and removed all obstacles? This idea was most common among the aristocratic Jewish families in Germany, the young women in particular, for they had been more exposed to secular culture and the non-Jewish environment than their brothers, who were generally restricted to a fundamentally traditional religious Jewish training. Those who defected from Judaism could, moreover, justify their action on the ground that all religions have common underlying truths, and that essentially there is little difference between the moral dictates of one and the other.[29] This explains in a measure, though only in a measure, the rush to the baptismal font of many of Mendelssohn's followers.

Reactions to Mendelssohn

Because of inconsistencies and lack of clarity in his thinking, it was possible for opposing ideological groups in Judaism to consider Mendelssohn their progenitor and ideologist. Traditionalists claimed him as their own because he was a pious and observant Jew who had declared that the laws of Judaism were fixed and permanent. The champions of Reform regarded him as a forerunner and even an initiator of their movement, in consequence of his rationalism. Since Mendelssohn insisted on the "covenant relationship," which obligates only born Jews to abide by all the laws of Judaism, he was regarded as supporting the idea of Jewish peoplehood implicit in the view of Judaism as an ethnic religion— a doctrine that brings him close to the Historical School,[30] which laid the foundation for the Conservative Movement in American Judaism.

Yet some adherents of these same alignments attacked Mendelssohn as an opponent of their principles. Among the extreme traditionalists, there were those who denounced him for his rationalism, which had led him to equivocate about the accounts of miracles in the Bible. He had declared that they had "probably happened," but they had no specific bearing on the nature of Judaism, which is basically a legalistic religion. What the Orthodox disliked even more was Mendelssohn's stress on secular culture and education which they believed was detrimental to traditional Judaism. Some Reformers, on the other hand, criticized Mendelssohn for his Orthodoxy. Nationalists like Peretz Smolenskin (1842-1885) condemned him on the ground that he underplayed Jewish nationalism by stressing the religious aspect of Judaism. These varying reactions may, indeed, reflect the confusion of his age as much as the confusion of his thought.

Mendelssohn had, it should be noted, an important practical influence on Jewish scholarship. His *Jerusalem* and *Biur* prepared the ground for the Science of Judaism movement initiated by Eduard

Gans (1798-1839) in Germany, fostered in Italy by Samuel David Luzzatto (1800-1865) and in Galicia by Nachman Krochmal (1785-1840). These, and others whose names will appear in later chapters, advocated a new, historical, and objective approach to the investigation of Judaism, which served as a vitalizing force in Jewish intellectual life.

4

Emancipation and Its Aftermath

I. THE FRENCH REVOLUTION

The Jews in France

MENDELSSOHN'S movement for Jewish Enlightenment was intended as a step towards political emancipation, which became a reality only a few years after his death in 1786. It first came, however, not to the Jews of Germany but to those of France, with the destruction of special privilege and the liberation of the masses brought about by the French Revolution. Although the Jews had been formally expelled from France in 1394, it is estimated that at the time of the Revolution there were about forty thousand Jews in that country. Since the 15th century, Marranos fleeing from Spain and Portugal had been constantly trickling into the southern French cities of Bordeaux, Marseilles, and Bayonne. Though under constant threat of expulsion, they had managed to remain, largely because of their commercial importance. This consideration, too, led to their being granted the right of domicile in 1723, after which many publicly returned to Judaism. There were also Jews in Avignon, in southern France, who had never been expelled since that territory was ruled by the Pope.

When Louis XIV annexed most of Alsace, as a result of the

Treaty of Westphalia (1648), and his successor, Louis XV (1715-1774) acquired Lorraine, the local Jewish population consisting of Ashkenazim (Jews of German origin) was permitted to remain. An estimated thirty thousand Jews lived in Alsace-Lorraine during the period of the French Revolution. There were also some hundreds of Jews in Paris from the other Jewish settlements in France. The wealthier ones, who generally came from southern France, were tolerated by the Paris police, while the poorer ones were constantly harassed and ejected from the city.

Before the French Revolution, the peasants in Alsace-Lorraine lived under what amounted to feudal conditions. Though legally they were free and, in fact, many owned their own farms, they were virtually enslaved by heavy taxes imposed by the king and the lords. The Jews in Alsace served as middlemen between the landlords and tenants; they were petty tradesmen, tavern keepers, and farmers of revenue, since they were barred from other vocations. A few were employed as purveyors to the army; a large number were moneylenders who, as was then customary, often charged usurious rates because of the great risk involved in their loans. The Jew, it should be observed, was himself crushed by his tax burdens. He had to pay a large variety of license fees for trading, to the king, the dukes, and the village officials. Though in the main the Jews fared better than the masses, they were far from being rich; in fact, in official reports they were described as poverty stricken and ragged. They were intensely despised by the populace as creditors, usurers, and tax collectors.

At times, the hostility against the Jews resulted in mob assaults; at others, it was expressed in oppressive acts by the courts and other government agencies. In 1781, Cerf Berr (1730-1793), the leader of Alsatian Jewry, appealed to Mendelssohn, requesting him to draft a petition to Louis XVI begging for the redress of the wrongs against the Jews and asking for equal rights. Mendelssohn prevailed upon his friend Christian Wilhelm von Dohm, who was well versed in Jewish history and the Jewish problems of his day, to prepare the petition. It was then that Dohm wrote his famous brochure, *On the Civic Improvement of the Conditions of the Jews*.[1] Dohm's radical proposals created a great stir in liberal and enlightened circles in both France and Germany.

Emancipation Achieved

The ten thousand Sephardic Jews in the southern seaport towns, in Avignon, and in Paris were men of the world, who had attained a considerably higher level of secular culture than the thirty thousand Yiddish-speaking Jews of Alsace-Lorraine. In 1787, two years before the French Revolution, delegations of Ashkenazim from Alsace and Sephardim from the southern cities met together to discuss measures for ameliorating their lot, in anticipation of the political and social changes that were in the offing in France. The only result of this effort, however, was to accentuate the differences between the two branches of Jewry.[2] The Sephardim claimed to be pure-blooded descendants of the tribe of Judah, and hence entitled to special consideration. They considered the Ashkenazim to be the offshoot of the presumably inferior breed of the Ten Tribes of Israel. When the National Assembly delayed enfranchising the Jews, the Sephardim, who were relatively few in number, appealed separately to the National Assembly for citizenship. This was granted to them in 1790, while the granting of similar rights to the Ashkenazic majority was postponed.

Count Mirabeau (1749-1791), a prominent leader of the National Assembly, had been impressed by Dohm's pleas to enfranchise the Jews. Together with the Abbé Gregoire and other liberal leaders, he passionately pleaded with the National Assembly to extend equal civic rights to the Ashkenazic Jews of Alsace and other parts of France. After considerable discussion, the Assembly passed a resolution to this effect on September 28, 1791. It was the only logical step that it could take in deference to the principles adopted in its Declaration of the Rights of Man.

In bestowing equal civic rights upon the Jews, the French Assembly implicitly recognized them as free, independent persons, associated with the state directly, rather than as formerly through the mediacy of a corporate group which was not an integral part of the body politic. Each Jew was now a Frenchman in his own right. The new status of the Jew was expressed in Count Clermont Tonnerre's declaration to the National Assembly: "To the Jew as an individual—everything: to the Jews as a nation—nothing."

Actually, the resolution granting French Jews complete citizenship did not place them fully on a par with the rest of the population. Either as a sop to the people of Alsace who were bound to resent the gift of civic equality to the Jews, or as an independent relief measure, the National Assembly, immediately after it emancipated the Jews, also approved a provision to reduce the debts owed by the Alsatian farmers to Jewish creditors, in accordance with a definite scale that it undertook to set up. Moreover, some of the Jewish disabilities continued, among them the discriminatory Jewish oath, which remained in force until 1840. Nonetheless, for the first time in perhaps fifteen hundred years, there was a place in the world in which the Jew was a full citizen.

Jewish Reaction

The warm gratitude of the Jews of France for having been given their civil liberties was expressed by Berr Isaac Berr of Nancy, who, in 1789, had represented the Jews of Alsace in their petition for Emancipation to the National Assembly, in the following language:

> . . . the rights of which we were robbed 1800 years ago have been restored . . . By the grace of God and the act of the French people we have become today not only human beings, not only citizens, but also Frenchmen . . . On the 27th of September, we were the only ones in this great kingdom who were seemingly destined to be eternally confined in the chains of bondage, but on the following day, on that great day which we shall always celebrate, Thou hast put it in the hearts of the legislators of France . . . the prince among nations, to restore to us our rights and help us in renewing our lives . . .

A genuine spirit of patriotism was kindled among the French Jews. One Jew, Samuel Levy, a self-styled exilarch, wrote in a Paris journal:

> France, which has been first to remove from us the shame of Judea, is our Land of Israel; its hills, our Zion; its rivers, our Jordan. Let us drink its living waters, the waters of freedom . . . The people that were enslaved more than any other shall pray for the people that shattered its fetters of bondage . . . for France, the haven of the oppressed.

French Jews expressed their loyalty not only in words but in active participation in the defense of the young republic in her war against Prussia and Austria (1792-1793). Some of the more ardent Jewish patriots, carried away by their zeal and enthusiasm, contributed their most precious synagogue ornaments and appurtenances to the French war effort. In their exuberance and anxiety to please, a few Jews joined the "Cult of Reason," launched in December, 1793. They renounced "their superstitions," as they put it, endorsed the ten-day-a-week revolutionary calendar which interfered with the observance of both Saturday and Sunday as days of rest, and closed the synagogues. Jewish schoolmasters in Paris were required to take their pupils to worship in the Temple of Reason, the former Cathedral of Notre Dame. The extremists discouraged the practice of the rite of circumcision. They also objected to the baking of *matzoth* for the Passover. These excesses forced Judaism underground; but fortunately the religious suppressions subsided in 1794.

II. NAPOLEON BONAPARTE (1769-1821)

Spread of Emancipation

THE ENFRANCHISEMENT of French Jewry marked a turning point in the lives and fortunes of Jews in Western, Central, and Southern Europe. As he swept across Europe, Napoleon introduced the egalitarian principles of Revolutionary France into the various countries he occupied or annexed. The Jews, together with the entire population, benefited from this policy. In Holland, where Napoleon created the Batavian puppet republic in 1795, the French envoy intervened in 1796 to secure complete civic equality for the Jews.[3] In Italy, the restrictions against the Jews were lifted; in 1797, the gates of the Venice ghetto were torn down and burned; in 1798, the gates of the ghetto of Rome were opened. That of Livorno and other cities followed. When the doughty French emperor invaded Spain and Portugal in 1808, he placed his brother Joseph (1768-1844) on the Spanish throne. One of the latter's first acts was to put an end to the Inquisition. It was reinstated in 1814 when the French armies were driven out of the country, only to be abolished completely two decades later.[4]

In 1806, Napoleon crushed Prussia at Jena and seized Berlin. In the next few years, he compelled one German state after another to emancipate its Jewish inhabitants. But after his defeat at Waterloo (1815), the whole German and Italian Emancipation collapsed. Only in France and Holland did Jews continue to be citizens; elsewhere they reverted to their previous status.

Napoleon and French Jewry

In the period following the establishment of the Directorate in 1795, a number of changes took place in the condition of the Jews in France itself. The Jewish population of France proper increased to about sixty-five thousand, and that of Paris reached several thousand. German Jews settled in Alsace-Lorraine, attracted by the new freedom in France and by the fact that they found in their Yiddish-speaking coreligionists people of their own kind. The hostility against them, however, particularly in Alsace, was still intense. The Jews on their part took steps to adjust to French cultural life. They sent their children to secular schools in accordance with the advice of their leader Berr Isaac Berr (1744-1828) of Nancy who urged them to relinquish their Yiddish speech in favor of French. In the general schools, Berr pointed out, the Jewish children would be educated in the French spirit, thereby forging a common cultural bond with the French nation of which they were now legally a part.

But a storm was brewing for the Alsatian Jews. The farmers in that province had bought up the farms and other properties surrendered by the Church and the landed gentry when the feudal structure collapsed in France. The Jews had advanced these peasants large sums on mortgages. But, on coming to power, Napoleon had retired the worthless *assignats* issued by the government when it confiscated the estates of the Church. As a result, the Alsatians were hard put to pay in the new sound currency, and, in consequence, many mortgages were foreclosed. In 1806, an Alsatian official sent a private report to Napoleon, then at the zenith of his career, complaining about the Jewish moneylenders and insinuating also that they were evading conscription. It was not only made to appear that the Jews were not living up to the duties of citizenship, but also that they were in fact mulcting the general population. The impetuous Emperor, who had only a slight acquaintance with Jews, instead of investigating the charges, took precipitous action and declared a moratorium of a year on the payment of all debts by the Alsatian farmers to their Jewish creditors, thus bringing financial ruin upon many Alsatian-Jewish families.

The Assembly of Notables

It was then that Napoleon, with his love of the dramatic and spectacular, fell upon a novel idea. Several years earlier, he had gained control of the Catholic and Protestant Churches; he would now do the same with the Jews. Since the Jews had no central body representing them, he determined to create one, and to this end he formed the Assembly of Notables. This body was to consist of no less than one hundred members of the Jewish faith residing on French soil, to be selected by the *prefects* of the French political subdivisions, from among the rabbis and leaders of the Jewish communities. The Assembly of Notables was intended to serve several important purposes. First, it would become Napoleon's instrument for assuring him of the loyalty of his Jewish subjects. Secondly, he hoped to exploit them through the medium of this Assembly, for the advancement of his policies and the interest and needs of the state.

Napoleon characteristically resorted to a good deal of fanfare in convening the Assembly. Since the pretext for its establishment was the charge of usurious practices committed by the Jews, he presumably called the Notables together for the purpose of "revitalizing in the Jews that civic morality lost during their long centuries of a degrading existence." There was more of a sting and stigma than sympathy in this pronouncement. The Assembly was portrayed as the harbinger of a great historic event, signifying the revival of the ancient Jewish parliament which had been defunct since the destruction of the Jewish state in the year 70. Napoleon thus disguised his insult to the Jews in a mask of glamour; but those who understood his real propagandistic purpose were shocked and dismayed.

It was an impressive assembly of one hundred and ten prominent Jews that met at the *Hôtel de Ville* (City Hall) in Paris for their first session on July 29, 1806. The spectacular gathering included businessmen, bankers, and twenty-five rabbis, all hand-picked by the *prefects* of the various *departments* (provinces) of France. The opening on a Sabbath, was evidently designed as a test to determine whether or not the delegates would subordinate their religious scruples to the orders of the state. Fear of reprisals by the Emperor against their people prompted even those who had vainly demanded a postponement to participate in the first session. Abraham Furtado of Bordeaux, a son of Marrano parents from Portugal, was elected president of the Assembly. Like most Jews of Marrano stock, Furtado was a modernist, who was more interested in the ethics of Judaism than in Talmudic law. At the second session, held the same day, a series of twelve questions[5] drawn up by Napoleon were read to the assembled Notables, which they were told they could answer as they deemed proper. The arrogant and offensive tone of the opening address of Napoleon's commissioner Mole, however, left the delegates little doubt as to what was expected of them; they were also led to understand that failure to comply with the Emperor's wishes might seriously endanger their cherished citizenship rights.

Despite the fact that the Assembly consisted of several factions, it had no difficulty in reaching an agreement on most of the questions posed to it. The president, Furtado, headed the liberal segment. At the other extreme were a number of rabbis of the old school, whom the impact of the Enlightenment had not as yet reached. The center consisted of a more moderate element, led by David Sinzheim of Strassbourg, a patriarchal rabbi steeped in Jewish learning. The final replies to Napoleon's questions in some instances represented a compromise among the several alignments. In general, the Assembly agreed that in case of conflict between rabbinic and French law, they were to be guided by the rabbinic principle that the "law of the state is to prevail" (*Git.* 10b).

The answers to the questions put to the Notables included a declaration that polygamy could no longer be practiced by Jews, since it had been prohibited by Rabbi Gershom's edict in the eleventh century. In the event of marriage and divorce, they agreed, Jews were to obtain prior approval from the state authorities—

thereby making marriage basically a civil, rather than a religious, matter. Under the former practice, it should be observed, marriage and domestic relations had been governed by Jewish law. This decision of the Notables thus challenged and reduced the authority of the rabbis. Judaism, the delegates also affirmed, gave an honored place to agriculture and the handicrafts. In deference to military requirements, Jewish soldiers were exempted from religious duties while in the service of their country. Usury was discredited as being contrary to Jewish law, whether practiced in dealings with Jews or Christians.

Ethnic Judaism

The Notables justly resented the questions as to whether Jews regarded France as their Fatherland and were accordingly obligated to defend it, for they knew that their coreligionists were fighting and dying for it. Nevertheless, the question when read evoked a spontaneous cry from the lips of the delegates: *"Jusqu'a la mort!"* (Unto death!). The Assembly thus proclaimed the patriotism of the Jews to France. They also acknowledged that their relation to other Frenchmen was that of brothers. They further declared that French Jews had nothing in common with their fellow Jews in other countries, except their religious beliefs and practices. The French Jew was thus merely a Frenchman of the Mosaic persuasion and, accordingly, a stranger to the Jews of other lands. Judaism was consequently reduced to a mere religious sect.

This answer was no doubt what Napoleon wanted, but it was less than true, for it overlooked the ethnic factor in Judaism, which is evident in its structure, tradition, and literature. Judaism admits all into its fold who are willing to assume its obligations; yet by and large its membership consists of born Jews. Judaism had been founded, nurtured, developed, and preserved primarily by the descendants of the Jewish group. This is not true of Christianity or Islam, which have been proselytizing religions in a much greater degree than Judaism and accordingly embraced a wide range of ethnic strains. Conversion to Judaism was rare, for it was virtually an invitation to martyrdom ever since Constantine's time (ca. 339).

The literary sources of Judaism attest to its particularistic nature.

The Hebrew Bible is not only the prime source of the principles of Judaism, but it is also the history of the Jews. The Hebrew prophets promulgated universal doctrines of justice, peace and brotherhood for all mankind; yet they had a particular concern for the Jewish people, whom they constantly admonished to walk in godly paths. The major Jewish religious festivals are also of a dual character. In their agricultural significance, they may be said to be universal in scope, yet they are each bound up with the history of the Jewish nationality.[6]

The ethnic element in Judaism has been expressed in another distinguishing manner. Its particularistic character is reflected in the fact that it contains components which may be summed up in the word "culture." Factors such as language and land associated with the Jewish people are endowed with a religious significance, though among other groups they might be considered secular. Thus Hebrew, the ancient language of the Jews, is the language of the Bible and the synagogue and is therefore sacred. So is Zion, the Holy Land, out of which has come forth Torah. It follows then, that Judaism is a unique concept, encompassing a religion, a sense of peoplehood, a culture, history, and language. To deprive it of any of these basic ingredients is to distort it.

The common ethnic, cultural, and religious bonds have created a strong sense of kinship among Jews the world over and a mutual concern for each other's welfare.[7] However, the French Assembly of Jewish Notables did not have the courage to explain this to Napoleon. They might have indicated to him that these natural sympathies and ties among Jews in no way conflict with their primary, exclusive, and single political allegiance to the countries of which they are citizens. They might have also pointed out that the Jews in those lands constitute an ethnic as well as a religious community—a sociological entity, but not a political group.[8]

It is hardly fair to blame the Assembly of Notables for choosing the path of expediency in answering the vital questions put to them. They were faced with a new situation—one with which Jewry had not been confronted in its long experience in the Diaspora. For the first time in Europe, Jews were enjoying complete enfranchisement and were now citizens of a sovereign nation. They feared that if they referred to their ethnic sympathies, their loyalty to France might be questioned, and their hard won civic rights might well be jeopardized. They therefore described Judaism and the relationship of Jews in the familiar non-Jewish vocabulary as a mere religious communion or a creed. In doing so they set the stage for the ideology of classical Reform Judaism,[9] which, unlike present-day Reform, repudiated the ethnic link binding dispersed Jewry. The new formulation of Judaism also led the classical Reformers to disclaim any interest in the particularistic implications of the traditional Messianic hope for a return to Zion. It became a crucial issue between the Reformers and their opponents.

Intermarriage

Another question to which the Assembly of Notables gave an evasive reply concerned the marriage of Jews with Christians. This issue aroused considerable discussion because an approval of intermarriage was contrary to Jewish law and would open the door to assimilation. Napoleon had suggested that every third marriage of Jews should be mixed. The Jewish Assembly, unable to sanction such a proposal, submitted an elusive reply to the basic question. The Bible, they said, prohibited only the marriages of Israelites with polytheistic Canaanites (*Deut.* 7:3; *Ex.* 34:15ff.); but since Christians were monotheists, the marriage of a Jew with a member of that faith was valid. No rabbi could solemnize it, however, since the traditional ritual could not be performed. However, the Jewish party contracting such a union was not subject to the *Herem* (religious ban); he was still regarded as a Jew. Although the latter statement is essentially correct, marriage out of the faith is actually considered a fundamental breach in Judaism, and it is emphatically opposed unless the non-Jewish party adopts Judaism.[10]

The Grand Sanhedrin

Within a few weeks after the Assembly had completed its work, Napoleon, in another grandiose and sensational gesture, convened the Grand Sanhedrin which, like its forerunner of Temple days, numbered seventy-one members. It was organized along traditional lines; its presiding officials were known by the ancient titles of

Nasi (president), *Ab Bet Din* (father, or head of the court, i.e., vice-president) and *Chacham* (sage, *i.e.,* associate vice-president). They sat, as did the Sanhedrin of old, in a half circle around the *Nasi* (*M. San.* 4:3). In the preamble to its resolutions, the French Sanhedrin declared itself to be a legally constituted group, empowered to pass ordinances designed to promote the welfare of Israel and inculcate obedience to the laws of the state. The Talmud, they said, permitted each generation to adopt regulations it deemed necessary for its times.

Many Jews were stirred by the thought that the glorious old institution of the Sanhedrin was to be revived. In its initial session in February 1807, Rabbi David Sinzheim of Strassbourg, who, together with other members of this body, had served in the Assembly of Notables, was elected president of the Sanhedrin. Though a conservative, he cooperated fully with Furtado, an ardent liberal. In reality, the Grand Sanhedrin had little to do except ratify the actions of the Notables, thereby giving religious sanctions to their decisions. In fact, Napoleon hoped or expected that Jews in other countries might consider the Sanhedrin's decisions binding; but this hope was soon dispelled. However, the Reform element in German Jewry, faced with the problem of harmonizing their religious doctrines and practices with their emancipated status, voluntarily accepted the pattern worked out by the Grand Sanhedrin, despite the fact that several of the decisions were the result of compromise and, in fact, coercion. The Grand Sanhedrin thus exerted a distinct influence outside of France.

The Infamous Decrees

The fond hopes of the Jews of France that the Assembly of Notables would inaugurate a new and happier era for them failed. The economic strictures imposed on them by Napoleon on March 17, 1808, which became known in Jewish history as the "Infamous Decrees," struck them like a bolt from the blue. These laws limited the residence of Jews and prohibited them from engaging in trade, moneylending, and other specified occupations for a period of ten years, without the prior and special permission of the *prefects* of the *departments* in France. In point of fact, these regulations were suspended in most of the French *departments* after only two or three years, but by that time thousands of Jewish families had suffered financial collapse. Perhaps even more than the economic effect, the Jews of France felt keenly the degradation implied by the discriminatory legislation; they viewed it as an encroachment on their status of equality and a demotion to second-rate citizenship.

The true motives of the Emperor to restrict Jewish rights soon came to light in another measure, issued in March 1808. It was known as the *Organic Regulation on the Mosaic Religion,* and it declared Judaism to be an officially recognized religion in France. A Central Consistory, or governing body, comprised of rabbis and laymen, was set up in Paris. Branch consistories were established in every *department* or group of *departments* having communities of at least two thousand Jews. The salaries of the rabbis were fixed by the government, but unlike the ecclesiastical functionaries among Catholics and Protestants, the rabbis were not paid by the state.[11] Ostensibly, the consistories were to regulate religious life, but actually they were established as a means of carrying out imperial policy. Their prime purpose appeared to be to facilitate conscription. While Christians could provide substitutes for the army, Jews were not permitted to do so. The consistories were much more concerned with the patriotism of the Jews in France than with their Jewishness. French Jewry, left without strong affirmative guidance and direction, followed a path that led not only to political and cultural, but also religious integration and assimilation. The Jewish government-sponsored consistorial organization in France continued until 1905 when state and church were at last completely separated in that country. A voluntary consistorial system has taken its place.[12]

III. EMANCIPATION IN GERMANY

The Polemics

A GOOD DEAL of public discussion was stirred up by Dohm's brochure describing the plight of the Jews. A decade later, the slogans of the French Revolution roused all Europe. Although the Declaration of the Rights of Man was acclaimed by liberals throughout the continent, the reaction in Germany was far from favorable.

Numerous pamphleteers entered the verbal arena in Germany to oppose Jewish Emancipation on various grounds. These polemicists generally had few objections to the upper crust of *Schutzjuden;* but they could not see how the masses of cringing, uncouth, starving vagabond peddlers who spoke a strange Judaeo-German dialect could ever find a way into German society. The religion Jews observed, their critics claimed, was encumbered with superstitions, curious customs, and fanaticism. Jewish laws calling for early burial of the dead, they insisted, were illogical and dangerous. The excessive number of observances in the Jewish calendar would, they contended, make it impossible for devout Jews to compete vocationally with the gentiles. The opponents of Jewish enfranchisement also found fault with the doctrine of the Chosen People and the authority of the rabbis. Of course, Jews had their champions too, but even they could not condone the Jewish dietary laws or the Jewish prohibition of intermarriage. Moreover, the ardent German nationalists could not see how a Jew who believed in the Messianic restoration could be a loyal German.

Some of the disputants supported the doctrine of the Christian state and maintained that Jews had no right to expect political rights in a Christian country. Some of the leading Germans were as prejudiced as the masses against the Jews. Goethe (1749-1832), born in Frankfort, knew the *Judengasse* in that city and spoke of it as a "prison," the confinement, filth, and crowding of which "depressed his youth", yet he showed little understanding or sympathy for the oppressed Jews. The philosopher Fichte (1762-1814) once declared that the only way to "protect ourselves against the Jews is to conquer their promised land and send them there."

It was quite rare for a writer on the issue of Jewish Emancipation to acknowledge the historical fact that the poverty, insecurity, and low estate of the Jews was a result of the centuries of segregation in the ghetto for which not they, but the Christian rulers were responsible. The Jews in Germany may have had their faults, but these could hardly be sufficient reason for barring them from their human rights. The many favorable qualities of the Jews were rarely mentioned; their enterprise, perseverance, sobriety, chastity, piety, exemplary family life, their concern for their mutual welfare, their charity and good cheer despite their hard lot. It was only seldom noted that these positive traits are a boon to the community and the state. Few voices criticised the opponents of Jewish Emancipation as did Frederick II's finance minister d'Asniers who in 1765 declared in a memorandum to the Emperor that it is to be wondered that "men should reproach the Jews for being useless when these same men prevent them from being useful."

Enfranchisement

The Germans did not willingly grant the Jews equal rights; what they did along these lines was primarily the result of external pressure: the insistence of Napoleon that the countries he occupied accept the French doctrine of freedom and equality for all. This was the case in March 1808 when Jerome Bonaparte, a brother of the Emperor, who occupied the throne of the newly created kingdom of Westphalia, issued an edict completely emancipating the Jews. In the Rhineland in 1811 and as other provinces of Germany came under French rule, the Jews were granted full civil liberties. In several regions in Germany, particularly the cities of the Hanseatic League, limitations were imposed on their citizenship. In Prussia, where Napoleon's influence was less felt, the Jews received their civic rights in 1812 and then only with the proviso that they were not to hold public office.

It now looked as if a new dawn had begun for the Jews of Germany. They could now enjoy almost equal rights as their neighbors, dress like them, send their children to state schools, and vote. They were no longer aliens or interlopers, but citizens; the special taxes required of them in their erstwhile servile condition were generally abolished. The basic prejudice and hostility against them, however, continued with the result that soon after Napoleon's defeat in 1815, one government after another withdrew the rights they had grudgingly given to the Jews in their domains.

Part Two

European Roots

Prelude

IN THE GHETTO, Jews carried on a secluded existence; they had no desire to be like their neighbors from whom they differed in religion, ethnic origin, history, and culture, as well as in outward appearance and dress. The Jews in pre-Emancipation days were regarded by others and looked upon themselves as members of a separate entity—a nation in exile, entirely distinct from and alien to the host nation among whom they lived. Balaam's doubtful blessing, "the people shall dwell solitary and shall not reckon itself among the nations" (*Num.* 23:9), seems to have been applied to the ghetto status of the medieval Jews. Few secular influences pervaded the ghetto, and there was little to disturb its inbred notions and ideas. In consequence, until the Enlightenment and the Emancipation, there was one monolithic brand of Judaism in Europe—the traditional type.

But the Emancipation changed all this. In the ghetto the Jew's physical environment was confined to a single street, and his cultural milieu was restricted to the single area of religious study. In the secular world outside the ghetto, however, religion was no longer paramount. Judaism, like religion generally, was exposed to the test of reason. Those for whom Judaism was of little moment frequently cast it off, together with their ghetto garb. Groups of the loyal, concerned with Jewish survival, sought to adjust their views and customs to the spirit and standards of the new age. This entailed a revision of traditional religious doctrines, practices, and observances.

95

In order to appreciate and appraise the deviation of the various ideological contingents from traditional Judaism, we must first inquire into the foundations and principles of this basic traditional pattern of Jewish observance as a norm. An analysis of traditional Jewish practice will also shed light on the essential nature of Judaism. Two descriptive terms used in connection with Orthodoxy —*Sephardim* (Spanish Jews) and *Ashkenazim* (German Jews)— refer to variants in Orthodoxy which merit explanation. These designations have a geographic connotation and also indicate a difference in ancestry, and to an extent, also in ritual. The initial chapter (5) of this second part of our study will deal with these subjects.

Aside from these divisions in Orthodoxy, there are several ideological shadings. The most prominent group are the Hassidim, who are followers of a tendency in Orthodoxy that originated in the conditions of Jewish life in Poland, a half century before the Emancipation. It was thus remote from the stirrings of the Enlightenment and the Emancipation that shook the Jewries of Germany and Western Europe. Before long, Hassidism had developed a distinctive school of thought—the *Habad*. Two centuries later, Martin Buber formulated the doctrine of Neo-Hassidim in an attempt to fuse Western thought and Hassidism.

The principal tendencies in German Jewry that have diverged from Orthodoxy in the early decades of the nineteenth century— Reform Judaism, the Historical School, and Neo-Orthodoxy—differed on a variety of issues. These included the fundamental problems of Hebrew in the service, the interpretation of the Messianic ideal, and the degree of traditional practice to be retained in Jewish life. There were also other points of controversy; among them, mixed seating in the synagogue, the use of the organ, mixed choirs, the role of women, and the sermon in the vernacular. While the Reformers assumed a radical approach to these problems, the Historical School took a more moderate position. The Neo-Orthodox segment (Chapter 9), however, clung to tradition, compromising with the new environment only to the extent of combining worldly culture with traditional Judaism. Two other versions of Orthodoxy are discussed in relation to German Neo-Orthodoxy, the antinationalist *Agudath Israel* and the pronational

Mizrachi. In Italy, Samuel David Luzzatto evolved a modified form of Neo-Orthodoxy, which is outlined in a separate chapter (10). These alignments,[1] Orthodoxy and its groupings, Reform, the Historical School, and Neo-Orthodoxy, represent the European "roots" or prototypes out of which grew their American "shoots" or counterparts.

5

Traditional Judaism

I. Sources of Traditional Judaism

The Divine Torah

TRADITIONAL JUDAISM, commonly referred to as Orthodoxy, is rooted in the doctrine of divine, supernatural revelation of the Torah at Sinai. It is this belief that the Torah is the revealed word of God, not of Moses or of any other human being, that gives divine sanction to its doctrines and ordinances. To quote from a prominent Orthodox rabbi:

> . . . The one theoretical, metaphysical basis of Jewish life is the faith in revelation, the divine origin of the Torah . . . Beyond this principle Judaism has no dogmas. From time to time, problems have arisen, the formulation of which, or the solutions to which, seemed to touch the foundations of the faith, and during certain of these periods the attitudes of Judaism toward these ideals was considered as of dogmatic importance. But their importance shrank as new problems came to the fore . . .
>
> Besides this dogma . . . of revelation, there is almost no theoretic basis to Judaism. And even this is not a dogma in the usual sense of the word, because its theoretical accept-

98

ance, not reinforced by a life in accordance with the Torah, has no saving power in Judaism.[1]

Orthodoxy requires of the Jew complete compliance with the body of tenets and laws given by God to Moses His prophet at Sinai, and outlined or interpreted in the authoritative sources of Judaism. The vast legal literature of Judaism represents an accumulation of observances and rules designed to guide the Jew in every aspect of his daily life, in business, family, and social relationships. Judaism makes little distinction between the secular and sacred, for every phase of human activity may be hallowed and endowed with spirituality. The physical act of eating is sanctified by a benediction; the table becomes a consecrated altar of God when an ordinary meal is accompanied by a discussion of Torah or of matters spiritual or religious. Thus, Judaism is closely identified and integrated with life by means of its laws and precepts.

Written and Oral Torah

In its restricted use of the term, Torah refers to the Pentateuch, *i.e.* the Five Books of Moses. In a broader sense, the whole body of Jewish law and learning may be encompassed in this term. The Torah, particularly in its narrower connotation, is fixed and fundamental. While the laws of man must be adapted to the conditions of a given age, those of the Eternal need not be. In fact, according to Orthodoxy, the laws of man are subject to those prescribed by God.

The Hebrew Scriptures, especially the Pentateuch, constitutes the *Torah Shebichtav* (*Ex.* 34: 27), (the written Torah) the divine and hence, the supreme law of Judaism which may be interpreted or expounded but not altered, because "God changeth not and He changeth not His law." Actually, the Jewish law has undergone a long process of development. Alongside the written law is the *Torah Shebal Peh* (the oral law) which has served to elucidate and clarify the fundamental written law. For centuries the oral law was unrecorded. It was memorized and transmitted by word of mouth from generation to generation. It had not been reduced to writing in order not to accord it the prestige and dignity of the written law. Traditional Judaism also regards the oral law as having originated at Sinai and, accordingly, includes it in the broad

concept of Torah.[2] The belief in the common divine source of
both the written and oral law is expressed in the Talmudic dictum
to the effect that "The Holy One, Blessed be He, showed Moses
the inferences of the Torah and the inferences of the Scribes[3] and
what the Scribes were destined to innovate in the future." (*Meg.*
19b). This statement is, of course, intended to exemplify the intimate connection between the oral and written law.

The written, as well as the oral, Torah embraces all categories
of law—ethical, civil, criminal, and ritual. The moral and ritual
precepts of the Torah are interrelated. A substantial portion of
the Book of Leviticus, the third volume of the Pentateuch, is devoted to ordinances concerning priestly and ritual practices; yet
the same book contains many ethical principles and moral doctrines. The ceremonials and rituals are important to the Orthodox
Jew because they help him lead a godly life; they are symbols
intended to alert the Jew to his religious obligations. Thus the
Mezuzah (the metal or wooden case containing the *Shema*)[4] is to
be affixed to the doorpost of the Jewish home as a reminder to all
who enter or leave of their sacred duty to God and man.

Rabbinic Interpretation

Curiously enough, the sanction for interpreting the written law
has been derived from the very Biblical verse limiting it; *viz.,* the
injunction prohibiting its augmentation or diminution, "Ye shall
not add unto the words which I command you"[5] (*Deut.* 4:2).
Another verse in the Book of Deuteronomy, "Thou shalt come
unto the priests, the Levites, and unto the judge that shall be in
those days" (*Deut.* 17:9) has been said by the sages to refer to
the need for contemporary interpretation of the law, for "could it
enter your mind that a person would go to a judge who was not in
his days?" (*R. H.* 25b). This reference points up the authority
of the rabbi to expound the Torah for his generation. But the
rabbis have, in fact, not confined themselves entirely to explaining
the law; though they would not concede it, they have enacted what
amounts to new legislation in order to fill in gaps in the law or
adjust it to the thinking, needs, or conditions of different ages.
A case in point is the provision "at the mouth of two witnesses or
at the mouth of three witnesses shall a matter be established"

(*Deut.* 19:15). From the fact that two witnesses and three witnesses are mentioned, Rabbi Akiva (d. ca. 135) inferred that the verse was intended to indicate that the liability of the third witness for testifying falsely is as great as that of the other two. Moreover, the third witness is stopped from claiming that he is innocent of the crime of testifying falsely because actually the evidence of two witnesses is sufficient for the conviction of the culprit, and the third witness's testimony should, therefore, be deemed superfluous and of no account (*M. Mak.* 1:7). Another even more striking instance of an innovation that amounts to legislation is the *prosbul* (Gr. "before the court") enacted by Hillel (d. 10), suspending the operation of the *Shemitah* (law of release) which provides that on the seventh year all debts are to be released or remitted (*Deut.* 15:1-3). This law of release was suited to the earlier agricultural economy of Israel when little credit was required. Not so, however, in the later commercial economy when lack of credit facilities could paralyze or ruin business operations. To avoid a financial calamity in Israel, Hillel created a legal device by which to circumvent the law of release. According to the Biblical provision, he said, an individual could not collect a debt but the court could do so, if it was a witness to the transaction (*M. Shviit* 10:3).

The Mishna

In time, it became necessary to record the oral law, since it had undergone a vast expansion in the course of the centuries. With the multiplicity of sages and opinions, it became increasingly difficult for scholars to memorize the legal discussions or to identify a given decision. Judah the Prince (d. 217 C.E.) undertook the gigantic task of compiling and editing the Halacha, as the oral law is called. The term *Halacha* is derived from the root *Halach* (go or walk), for the Halacha delineates the path for the Jew to follow.[6] Judah the Prince's collection of the Halacha, known as the *Mishna* from the verb *Shanah* (repeat or study) was completed in the third century (ca. 200). Its vast scope may be seen from the titles of its six *sedarim* (orders) or divisions, and the descriptions of the general areas which they treat:

1. *Zeraim* (Seeds) deals with agricultural laws. This division includes the tractate *Berakot* (Benedictions), since the

agricultural yield is closely associated in the religious mind with gratitude and prayer to God.

2. *Moed* (Festivals) discusses the law of the Sabbath, the holy days and holidays, festivals and fasts, and the principles underlying the Jewish calendar.

3. *Nashim* (Women) treats of the Jewish family law and also the regulations concerning vows. The domestic relations laws are of special interest, because they are official for the Jewish community in the State of Israel.

4. *Nezikin* (Injuries) includes the law of torts (civil injuries) as well as the criminal law. This division also includes the tractate *Pirke Aboth* (Ethics of the Fathers) which incorporates the sayings, maxims, and principles of conduct of teachers of Judaism, from the period of the Great Synod (fifth century B.C.E.) to the time of the completion of the Mishna (third century C.E.).

5. *Kodashim* (Sacred Things) outlines the sacrificial cult and the laws pertaining to ritually clean and unclean animals and the rules for slaughtering them.

6. *Tohorot* (Purifications) presents the rules of ritual purity and impurity.

The Mishna contains both the substantive, that is the content phase of the law and the adjective, or procedural aspect, dealing with evidence, pleadings, the organization of the courts, and related matters. Composed in Palestine, it was written in a lucid and compact Hebrew style. This work, representing the aggregation of customs, laws, and interpretations accumulated over the centuries, provided a foundation for further legal discussion and activity on the part of the rabbis.[7]

The Gemara

In the century preceding and following the completion of the Mishna (ca. 200), the Jews in Palestine were crushed by Roman rule and oppression. The collapse in 135 of Bar Kochba's insurrection—a desperate bid for freedom—sent many scholars from Palestine to Babylonia. The refugees helped raise the level of Jewish learning in the latter country. In both the Palestinian and Babylonian academies, the Mishna of Rabbi Judah became the basis for further study and analysis. The debates and discussion in the academies based on the Mishna were included in the Gemara, which amplified and clarified the Mishna. The term *Gemara* is derived either from the Aramaic root meaning "learn" or from the Hebrew root meaning "complete."

Around the year 350 C.E., the so-called Jerusalem Gemara, containing the accumulated legal arguments and debates of the Palestinian schools, was completed. Conditions in Palestine were not such as to encourage intensive intellectual activity and it is, therefore, not surprising that the Babylonian Gemara, completed about a century and a half later, is superior to it. The Babylonian Gemara includes thirty-six of the sixty-six tractates or volumes of the Mishna, three less than its Palestinian (Jerusalem) counterpart, but it is considerably more elaborate and more extensive than the latter. The two compendia demonstrate the differences in the life and conditions in their respective countries; the Babylonian reveals the thriving Jewish life in that country in the early centuries of the present era, while the Jerusalem Gemara attests to the progressive deterioration of the Jewish community in Palestine during the same period. The Mishna and the Gemara together form the Talmud, a term derived from the Hebrew verb *lamed* (study or learn).

The Talmudic text frequently digresses from its discussion of an Halachic (legal) question and wanders off to matters that have no direct bearing on it. The unrelated material, known as *Aggada* (narratives or anecdotes) from the root *naged,* (to tell), consists of nonlegal material, including parables, fables, maxims, aphorisms, homilies, legends, folklore, and even some superstitions of the times. It also takes note of the scientific knowledge of the day in the fields of astronomy, physiology, and medicine, as well as mathematics, philosophy, and other branches of learning. While the Halacha reflects the labors of the rabbis as jurists, the *Aggada* attests to their function as teachers and preachers in the synagogues. Thus the Talmud is a *corpus juris*, a body of Jewish ritual, civil, and criminal law, as well as a compendium of Hebrew lore. It is an encyclopedic work of vast dimensions, representing Jewish intellectual activity extending over many centuries. Its two component texts, the Mishna and the Gemara, are in themselves codes or compilations of Jewish law in various stages of development.

The Midrash

The rabbinic expositions in the oral law were derived from the Bible by the method of *Midrash* (seek, infer) which aimed to find reason or support for a rabbinic interpretation or enactment in a Biblical verse or text. The *Midrash* method was used in one of two ways; if it cited Biblical confirmation for a *law*, it was referred to as a *Midrash Halacha;* if for an *Aggada,* it was known as a *Midrash Aggada.* The oral law was thus linked up with the written. This procedure may be illustrated by an example from a Mishnaic tractate (Sanhedrin 3:7) enjoining the three judges in a civil case from revealing their secret deliberations. The verses "Thou shalt not go about as a talebearer among thy people" (*Lev.* 19:16) and "He that goeth as a talebearer revealeth secrets" (*Prov.* 11:13) are used as the Biblical textual authorities for this regulation.

In the *Midrash Aggada,* an ethical idea or a thought that will impress, appeal, comfort, or interest the congregation is read into or extracted from the text. As an instance:

> And I will make thy seed as the dust of the earth (*Gen.* 13:16). Just as the dust is scattered from one end of the earth to the other, so will thy children be found from one end of the earth to the other; . . . and as the dust of the earth is trodden upon, so will thy children be down-trodden under the heel of other peoples, as it is written, "And I will put it into the hand of them that afflict thee" (*Is.* 51:23). (*Gen. R.* 41:9).

Or take the following admonition to the witnesses in a trial involving a capital crime:

> Know ye . . . that civil cases have a different consequence than capital cases. In civil cases a witness can make restitution and thereby secure atonement. In capital cases, however, he is liable for the blood of the wrongfully condemned person and the blood of his (prospective) children to the end of the generations. So we find in the instance of Cain who slew his brother, where it was said "The bloods of thy brother cry unto me" (*Gen.* 4:10). Not the "blood of thy brother" but the "bloods of thy brother" is said—that is, his blood and the blood of his progeny . . . Therefore, man was created

alone to teach thee that he who destroys a single soul, Scripture holds as guilty as though he destroyed an entire world; and he who saves a single soul, Scripture regards him as though he had saved an entire world. (*San.* 4:5)

Though generally the *Aggadic* material in the Talmud is interspersed with the Halachic, there are also special compilations of Midrashim.

The Responsa

No code is final. This is true in any system of law. The body of American law has grown considerably over the years. Judges are constantly called upon to adapt the law to new conditions. This is a major function of the judiciary; it is essential because it is not possible to anticipate in one period the problems that may occur in another. The rabbis were faced with a similar situation.

After the Talmud was completed, Jewish communities throughout the Diaspora adopted the practice of sending messengers with legal problems to the Geonim (excellencies), the chiefs of the two principal academies of Sura and Pompeditha in Babylonia. The Geonim were tacitly regarded as the spiritual heads of Jewry. The *Shealoth* (questions) they were asked involved matters on which the Halacha was inconclusive or unclear, or for which no legal precedent existed. The *Teshuvot* (*responsa*), the formal answers of the Geonim, were eventually collected and circulated, thereby forging a new link in the chain of legal development.

By the middle of the eleventh century, however, the Jewish centers in Europe had grown, while the Jewish community in Babylonia had declined. The authority of the Geonim waned and ultimately ceased, bringing to an end all central legal authority in Jewish life. Thereafter, individual rabbis succeeded to the position of prestige formerly occupied by the Geonim. Rabbi Gershom ben Judah of Mayence (ca. 940-1028), Rabbi Isaac of Troyes (1040-1105) popularly known by the initials of his name as Rashi, his grandson, Rabbenu Tam (1100-1171), and Maimonides (1135-1204) are among the great medieval luminaries who left behind them records of their *responsa*.

The system of *responsa* has continued to the present day, and by now represents about thirteen centuries of rabbinic achievement. The *responsa* constitute more than mere Halachic literature, for they also portray the social, religious, political, economic, and cultural conditions of the Jews in many countries at different times. Thus, they serve as valuable source material in medieval Jewish history, a period for which our historical information is quite meager and obscure. The *responsa* refer to various phases of community life and customs; they tell of Jewish suffering at the hands of their neighbors and attest to the indomitable faith and courage of the Jews during these gloomy centuries.[8]

Many questions in our own day have perplexed the Orthodox rabbis and provoked spirited controversy among them. The industrial age, for example, has brought to the fore questions pertaining to the use of machinery for ritual purposes. The problem of machine-baked matzoth stirred up a great deal of debate in the latter part of the nineteenth century, and the objections of the rabbis have had little effect in curbing their use. The substitution of electric lights for ritual candles on the Sabbath also engendered considerable discussion. Some Orthodox rabbis were not inclined to permit the employment of these modern appliances, while others thought they were proper.

The Code of Maimonides

The Talmud often presented the opinions and views of various sages on a given question without indicating the settled law. In order to find an Halachic decision, one would often have to search through a maze of discussion and debate. The student of the Halacha in post-Talmudic times was also faced with another problem: successive generations of rabbis had written *responsa* that were incorporated in works or treatises that were not generally available. For this reason, Halachic codes or compilations were attempted in which the settled laws together with the later decisions were arranged systematically under a variety of headings, thereby making them easily accessible.

One such legal digest, prepared by the great Spanish Jewish sage Maimonides[9] (1135-1204), was called the *Mishneh Torah*, (*Repetition of the Torah*)—a name borrowed from an idiom in the Bible (*Deut.* 17:18), which suggests the comprehensive character of the volume. Maimonides devoted ten years to the preparation of this work, which he completed in 1180. It was better known as the *Yad Hachazakah* (Mighty Hand)—a phrase derived from the last verse of the Pentateuch (*Deut.* 34:12). The latter title had a special significance because the two letters of the word *Yad* add up to fourteen,[10] the number of divisions in the code. Maimonides had previously outlined the plan of his book in the *Sefer Hamitzvot* (*Book of Precepts*) in which he tabulated the 365 negative and 248 affirmative precepts forming the traditional 613 precepts said to be contained in the Torah (*Mak.* 23b). A rationalist, who was greatly influenced by Aristotle, Maimonides omitted from his code all superstitious references in the Talmud. He did, however, incorporate sacrificial and criminal laws, despite the fact that these laws had not been in operation since the destruction of the Sanctuary and the Jewish state. He may well have done so in the belief, prevalent at the time, that the Messiah would soon appear and restore the ancient kingdom of Israel, and with it the sacrificial cult in the Temple.[11]

It is of interest to observe Maimonides' view of the Messianic age, which he regarded as a natural development. He considered the belief in the Messiah to be an essential element in Judaism, but he did not consider the Messiah a supernatural being who would perform miracles; the Messiah would merely bring about a religious revival. The paramount difference between normal and Messianic times was that in the latter age:

> Israel will be delivered from its subjection to foreign rulers. The Messianic era, moreover, will be a period when there will be neither famine nor war, neither jealousy nor strife . . . The one preoccupation of the whole world will be to know the Lord . . . as it is written: "For the earth shall be full of the knowledge of the Lord as the waters cover the sea." (*Is.* 11:9).[12]

The Shulchan Aruch

The *Yad* elicited both praise and censure. It was assailed by some on the ground that it presumed to be a substitute for the Talmud, since its author declared that anyone who consulted this work need not refer to any other. Maimonides, moreover, omitted the Talmudic authorities for his statements, which strengthened the prevailing impression that he intended to have his code supplant rather than supplement the Talmud. Over a century later, Jacob ben Asher (ca. 1280-1340), a Jewish scholar who lived in Spain, drew up a similar code, modelled largely after that of Maimonides, but omitting laws associated with the Temple. It was known as the *Arbaah Turim* (*Four Rows*). This phrase alludes to the arrangement of the code in four volumes. The work, however, refrained from giving settled decisions; it merely quoted Maimonides and other sages.

In the next two centuries, considerable additional legal material accumulated; so much so that a new code was considered essential. Joseph Caro (1488-1575) had prepared a commentary much richer in Talmudic sources and the citations of later authorities on the *Arbaah Turim* which he called *Bet Yosef*, after his own name. The *Shulchan Aruch* (*Prepared Table*) was Caro's own briefer adaptation of the *Bet Yosef* commentary. It was designed as a practical guide for everyday use, and it became the most popular of all codifications of Jewish law. Caro, an exile from Spain who had left his native land in the tragic expulsion of 1492 and had settled in Safed, Palestine, was bold enough to issue decisions on moot or disputed questions of law, which he usually decided in accordance with the Spanish authorities. He failed, however, to take into account the attitudes of the French or German scholars, and the customs in vogue in the Ashkenazic communities generally, including the large Jewish community in Poland.

To remedy this defect, the rabbi of Cracow, Moses Isserles (1520-1572), who had criticized Caro's code because its scope was limited, inserted the Ashkenazic customs and laws in glosses and notes which he referred to as the *Mappa* (Table Cover) for the *Shulchan Aruch*. Thus the *Shulchan Aruch* assumed a universal character; it has since served as the major guide in religious practice for Jewry, until the rise of Reform Judaism with its changes in traditional law and observance. Unlike Maimonides' *Yad,* the *Shulchan Aruch* presented supporting citations. Several condensations or abridgements of this work have since been published, the best known of which is that of Shlomo Ganzfried (1804-1886), a Hungarian rabbi, who collected the laws most frequently used. The *Shulchan Aruch* was accepted by Orthodox Jewry generally as a reliable compendium of Talmudic law, thereby providing it with a definiteness, unity, and uniformity that is lacking in the other branches of Judaism.

II. Meaning of Orthodoxy

Orthodoxy, a Misnomer

WITH THE BEGINNING of the Reform movement early in the nineteenth century, it became necessary to find a distinctive name for the main body of Judaism which advocated the *status quo* in Jewish tradition and observance and which resisted the attempts of the Reformers to institute changes and of the nonreligious elements to formulate a secular theory of Judaism. The Reformers originally employed the name *Orthodox* in a derogatory sense to designate the traditionalists and pietists, yet it stuck and in fact was adopted by the latter group. It appears to have been used for the first time in a Berlin journal in 1795.[13] Actually, this term is a misnomer, a label borrowed from Christianity, which cannot properly be applied to Judaism.

The term *Orthodoxy* is derived from the Greek and connotes a correct belief or opinion. Christianity may be said to be a faith, since creed and dogma play an important role in its basic doctrines. Judaism, however, is essentially a praxis, because it stresses *Mitzvot* (precepts) requiring practice rather than dogmas requiring belief. The emphasis that Judaism places on duties and conduct rather than creed prompted a leader of traditional Judaism in America to declare that "Orthodoxy in Judaism has never been concerned about shadings in belief. It has found room for every type of Jew from the most rationalistic to the most mystical."[14]

Dogma and Doctrine

For the sake of clarification, it may be in place to summarize briefly what has been said previously in this regard. It was Moses Mendelssohn, himself a product of the Age of Reason, who contended in his *Jerusalem* that Judaism has no dogma. This does not mean that it has no doctrines, for a doctrine may be a rational concept, while a dogma need not be so. In attempting to define the essential Jewish creed and create standards of correct belief in Judaism, Maimonides met with the challenge of eminent rabbis. There is no parallel in Judaism or in Jewish Orthodoxy to a Catholic dogma as that of the Assumption of Mary,[15] which declares that "when the course of her life on earth was finished, she was taken up body and soul into heaven." When this belief, defined by Pope Pius XII *ex cathedra,* was adopted by the Church on November 1, 1950, no one who denied it could thereafter be considered a good Catholic, or receive the sacraments. A dogma of this nature is of course, worlds apart from the rationalistic Talmudic dictum (*Succot* 5a) to the effect that "Moses and Elijah did not ascend to heaven for it is written 'The heavens are the heavens of the Lord and the earth hath He given to the children of men.' " (*Ps.* 115:16) We have also noted that the idea of salvation in Judaism is not restricted to members of a faith as in Christianity.[16] Maimonides and other Jewish thinkers have held that the daughter religions of Judaism, Christianity and Islam, have advanced the ethical development of mankind and therefore contributed to its salvation.[17] Because of this liberal attitude towards belief, heresy trials were extremely rare among Jews.[18] In view of the absence of a fixed dogmatic creed in Judaism, many traditional Jews prefer to describe themselves as *Torah-True* rather than as Orthodox Jews. Despite the fact that the term *Orthodox* is not a correct usage, we shall continue to employ it in this text as a matter of convenience.

Fundamental Doctrines

Judaism, as we noted, possesses basic doctrines. The Jewish view of monotheism, which is essentially ethical, implies a belief in human morality. The Jewish doctrines of ethics, moreover, are rational and logical, and do not belong to the category of dogma. A Jew may have his own ideas about the metáphysical aspects of the divine unity. The ethical implications of this unity are of far greater significance. The notion of one God as the Father of all mankind occupies a much more vital role in Judaism than the theoretic meaning of the concept. Similar ethical meanings are ascribed to other monotheistic concepts. Thought and idea in Judaism are thus merged with deed and action.

A third-century Palestinian sage condensed the fundamental teachings of Judaism in the following pronouncement:

> . . . The Torah consists of 613 commandments and prohibitions: 365 negative commandments corresponding to the number of the days in the year, and 248 positive commandments corresponding to the number of organs in the human body. Then came David and reduced them to eleven (as in *Psalm* XV). Then came Isaiah and reduced them to six (as in *Is.* 33:15). Micah came and reduced them to three (as in *Micah* 6:8). Isaiah came again and reduced them to two (as in *Is.* 56:1). Then came Amos and reduced them to one, "Seek me and live" (*Amos* 5:4). Then came Habakkuk and reduced them to one, as it is said, "The righteous shall live by his faith" (*Mak.* 23b) . . .

Emphasis in Judaism

There were sages who not only objected to Maimonides' creed, but also took issue with him on some of his rationalistic opinions. Maimonides and his school maintained that God is incorporeal because incorporeality is essential to His unity. However, others followed the view of Abraham ben David of Posquieres (d. 1198), a leading rabbi and scholar of his age, who pointed to the fact that the Bible itself with its anthropomorphisms leads one to envisage God as corporeal. In any event, they felt that the unsophisticated who failed to grasp a philosophical concept about God's incorporeality can yet be pious, for Judaism is concerned with pragmatic actions and not with logical or theological abstractions. It is perhaps this inclination in Judaism that directed its course in the field of law and ethics in which its genius flowered. This too may account for the disposition of the Jew to avoid delving into the occult or the mystical. The Mishna expresses this tendency in the dictum: "Whoever speculates upon four things . . . is as though he had not come into the world; what is above, what is beneath; what before; what after," (*M.Hagiga* 2:1). The Gemara quoting Ben Sira (*Ecclesiasticus*) repeats this injunction and says, "Seek not things that are too difficult for thee, and search not out things that are hidden from thee. The things that have been permitted thee, think upon; thou hast no business with the things that are secret." The suggestion is clear. The Jew is to concentrate on this world and this life and not on what is beyond it (*Hagiga* 13a).

Precept and Practice

Because the sacred law of Scripture is fixed and cannot be changed, Orthodoxy is often rigorous and uncompromising, refusing to make concessions to modernism. As a result, even Biblical regulations have been overlooked by relatively observant Jews. Among the most commonly violated are the laws against shaving (*Lev.* 19:27), the wearing of a garment of mixed wool and linen (*Deut.* 22:11), the laws of ritual purity, and Sabbath rest. The Biblical concept that lighting a fire is labor, appears to many Jews to be entirely inconsistent with our mechanical age. Moreover, in this era of equality, such practices as the religious disenfranchisement of women and the priority accorded in traditional Judaism to the *Cohanim* (males of priestly descent) are considered anachronistic.

The Orthodox rabbinate, of course, finds itself powerless to institute modifications even of rabbinic regulations, not to speak of Biblical laws. Instead, they sometimes add to the severity of the restrictions by imposing others, in accordance with the admonition in the Mishna: "Thou shalt set up a hedge around the Torah" (*Abot.* 1:1). The hedges are intended to protect a more important precept. The effect of this tendency on the part of the rabbis has been to proliferate restrictions.[19] Only a small, isolated, and often intolerant minority of the ultrapious abide by the body of cumbersome ordinances in the *Shulchan Aruch,* and between them and the majority of less observant Jews, a barrier has been set up which threatens to disrupt Jewish unity. In the State of Israel for example, this situation has led to open clashes between the extreme fundamentalists and the general population. Since the Orthodox rabbinate feels powerless to remedy the situation to any extent, a proposal was made in recent years calling for the creation of a synod to re-examine the regulations and attempt to revise them. This suggestion, however, gave rise to the question as to how such a synod should be constituted and who should be authorized to sit on it.[20] Interest in the plan has since declined, largely because it has engendered difficult Halachic procedural problems. The matter has, therefore, been left in the grip of inaction.

III. Ashkenazim and Sephardim

Distinctions

THE ORIGIN of the Hebrew terms *Sepharad,* referring to Spain, and *Ashkenaz,* to Germany, is obscure.[21] The Sephardim are the Jews who lived in the Iberian peninsula and were expelled from Spain in 1492 and from Portugal in 1497. These exiles were dispersed throughout the Mediterranean world, in northern Africa, southern France, Italy, Turkey, Palestine, the Balkans, and other regions. The Ashkenazim originated in Germany[22] and neighboring countries and migrated to eastern Europe in the centuries following the Crusades.

Spanish Jewry, which had been under Moslem rule since the eighth century, drew its tradition from the Jewish spiritual center that had existed in Babylonia. The Ashkenazim, on the other hand, followed the practices of the Italian Jewish communities, which received their spiritual guidance from Palestine, by reason of their proximity to that country. It was natural that the Jewish communities in each of these two orbits of influence should develop common traits, customs, rituals, and speech. While the Ashkenazim have given rise to Yiddish, a form of Middle High German, Spanish Jewry has produced its own dialect, Ladino. Both vernaculars are written in Hebrew characters. Ladino, however, is a purer form of Castilian than Yiddish is of German, and the Hebrew element in Yiddish is far greater than in Ladino. Both Yiddish and Ladino have been progressively declining.

The oriental Jews, like those of Spain, lived in a Moslem environment and were also attached to the Babylonian religious center, which continued as a hub of Jewish religious life until the eleventh century. These factors brought the oriental and Sephardic Jews closer together. They shared the same ritual, customs, and Hebrew linguistic characteristics. The synagogue cantillation of the two groups was essentially oriental. Their common Sephardic pronunciation,[23] morever, differed from that of the Ashkenazim. As a result, the oriental Jews were generally regarded as Sephardic, and the designation of Sephardim was loosely applied to them. Before long, all Jews who were not Ashkenazim were generally classed as Sephardim.

Christian and Moslem Stimulus

In 711, the Moslems conquered Spain and brought deliverance to the Jews from the oppression of its erstwhile Christian Visigothic rulers. Under a succession of liberal Moslem *khalifs,* the Spanish Jewish community thrived, growing in numbers, prosperity, and prestige. Stimulated by the highly enlightened milieu in which they lived, the Spanish Jews ushered in their golden age (ca. 900-1200), during which they produced a rich and varied secular and religious culture. They joined in the cultural interests of their Arab countrymen which embraced mathematics, medicine, astronomy, literature, science, and philosophy. Some also pursued Jewish learning and scholarship—Hebrew grammar, literature, and Biblical exegesis. A number wrote Hebrew poetry, both deeply religious and intensely secular, of a high order of excellence. Many also served their country as statesmen, financiers, patrons of learning and the arts, and as leaders in other fields.

The life of the Sephardic Jews during this period contrasted sharply with that of the Ashkenazic Jews in Northern and Central Europe. The latter were ravaged by the Crusades and suffered under the heel of other oppressions. They lacked the incentive and the relaxed atmosphere that is needed for the kind of creative effort in which their Sephardic brethren engaged. Perpetually harrassed with the immediate problems of survival, they had no time or inclination for mundane culture. In consequence, they confined themselves within the narrow sphere of Talmudism and Jewish law, which they required for guidance in the details of everyday life.

But soon after the Christians reconquered most of Spain, the condition of Sephardic Jewry deteriorated. The bigoted Spanish clergy, spurred by religious zeal coupled with cupidity, instigated the populace against the Spanish Jewish "infidels," whose prosperity and position the masses envied. In recurrent waves of violence culminating in the mob outbreaks of 1391, Jews were forced into baptism, with death as their only alternative. Many of the converts, however, could not be loyal to a faith they assumed through coercion rather than conviction. Some who were driven by remorse became Marranos or secret Jews, who braved the terrors of the Inquisition to engage in Jewish rites and practices. The Church's campaign of persecution against Spanish Jewry ceased only with the expulsion of all unbaptized Jews from Spain in 1492. This final measure was adopted in order to insulate the new Christians from the corrupting influences of their Jewish relations and neighbors. Only a small minority of the Spanish Jews chose baptism to avoid banishment. Thus Spanish Jewry, like the Ashkenazic, demonstrated great courage in the face of trial. The glorious chapter the Sephardim contributed to Jewish history strengthened their *grandezza*—(sense of dignity and nobility), which made them proud of their Sephardic heritage.

Present Status

By the seventeenth century, the Marranos who had fled from Spain and Portugal to liberal Holland established the major center of western Sephardic Judaism in that country. It continued as such until the Second World War, when a large portion of Dutch Jewry was massacred by the Nazis. In the State of Israel, the Sephardim have established their own religious community, which follows Sephardic ritual customs. The same is true of the Sephardic congregations in the Diaspora, which still preserve their peculiar religious traditions and procedures, though they are compelled at times to replenish their dwindling ranks with Ashkenazim. In Israel, the Sephardim and Ashkenazim each have their own chief rabbi.

6

Hassidism and Neo-Hassidism

I. HISTORICAL BACKGROUNDS

The Disaster of 1648

HASSIDISM (pietism) represents a prominent and interesting movement in Orthodoxy. To understand its origin and growth, we must consider the conditions of Jewish life which gave rise to this movement. Prior to the middle of the seventeenth century, the Jews in Poland lived in unwalled isolation in self-contained autonomous communities. They formed a much-needed middle class between the Polish nobility and the peasantry, serving as tradesmen and merchants, agents of the Polish landlords, lessees of their mills and properties and tax collectors. The Jews thus came into direct contact with the impoverished Russian farmers, who lived under feudal conditions in territories occupied by Poland. It was therefore natural for the Russians to make the Jews the target of their hatred as much as, or even more than, the absentee Polish principals.

In 1648, the situation reached a bloody climax. Led by the shrewd and ruthless hetman Bogdan Chmielnicki, rebel Cossack bands swept through the Ukraine, committing the most barbaric atrocities, massacring and maiming thousands of Jews and Poles, and completely annihilating hundreds of Jewish communities. The weak and disunited central government of Poland could not offer effective resistance. Only about half of the Jews of Poland survived the holocaust, which left death, poverty, and ruin in its trail.

The Aftermath

But even after the two-year terror was quelled, the Jews got no respite. In 1654, the Russians invaded Poland from the south and the Swedes from the north, attacking those regions that had escaped Chmielnicki's fury. Because the Swedes had treated the Jews humanely, the Poles charged them with collaborating with the enemy. As soon as the Polish militia had driven out the invaders, they followed the ferocious example of the Cossacks and the Russians and attacked and massacred the Jews. When these riots subsided and the surviving Jewish communities, with some aid from the Polish kings, began their task of rehabilitation, the fanatical Polish clergy harassed them anew with a series of blood libels and other inflammatory charges. These outrages against the Jews were not stopped even after the Pope investigated the blood accusation and issued a declaration in 1763 clearing the Jews of this baseless and vicious slander. A few years later, in 1768, the Jews of the Ukraine were again the victims of a rebellion by the Russian peasants—this time by the Haidemack rebel bands, led by the Cossacks. The wave of violence that resulted culminated in a barbaric slaughter of Jews and Poles at Uman. The riots were soon suppressed, but not before more thousands of Jews had lost their lives and many others were left homeless and penniless. The pall of gloom and dejection cast over Polish Jewry thickened.

Aside from these misfortunes, Polish Jewry after 1648 had to cope with a critical fiscal problem. In addition to the usual heavy tax burden, the *Kahal* (Jewish community organization) was compelled to maintain large numbers of orphans and destitute, rebuild their institutions, and help to rehabilitate the victims of the disasters. The Jewish community treasuries were further drained by exactions of ransoms by marauding bands and by extortions on the part of the Christian clergy. To meet their mounting obligations, the communities had to borrow vast sums at high rates of interest. Consequently, the poll taxes imposed on the depleted Jewish constituencies of the well-nigh bankrupt Jewish communities reached staggering proportions. The resulting hardships served to increase the sense of hopelessness and despair of Polish Jewry.

The terrible events had a deteriorating effect on Jewish intellectual activity in Poland. After the catastrophe of 1648, Lithuania, having suffered less than southern Poland, became the center of Jewish learning in Eastern Europe. The Jews of southern Poland, detached from this cultural hub, sank into ignorance. Their interest shifted from the arid legalism of the Talmud, to the vibrant, warm, inward religion of the Cabbala,[1] a branch of Jewish mysticism. Through their study of Jewish mystic literature, they learned the techniques of alphabetical manipulation. The Messianic calculations in the *Zohar* (radiance), the basic text of the Cabbala, led them to the belief that deliverance and redemption of the Jews from their suffering was at hand.

Shabbetai Zevi

Polish Jewry in particular was longing for the appearance of the Messiah. Had they not already suffered the *Hevlei Moshiach,* the pangs that were to herald his coming? This deep need had been answered by a succession of Messianic pretenders who inspired their followers with the hope that their oppression would soon cease. None of the pretenders, however, created such widespread anticipation and popular confidence as Shabbetai Zevi, an ascetic Cabbalist who charmed people with his personal magnetism. He was born in 1626 in the port city of Smyrna, Turkey, on the Ninth Day of Ab, the fast day commemorating the anniversary of the destruction of both the first and second temples. According to an ancient Jewish tradition, the Messiah was destined to be born on that fateful day in the Jewish calendar. Perhaps it was the account of the cruel tragedy that had befallen Polish Jewry that stimulated Shabbetai's imagination and roused within him the hope and faith that he was the long-awaited deliverer. But whether he was impelled by his religious fervor, or whether he was the downright imposter he turned out to be, he attracted a large host of devoted followers, among them many Polish Jews. The fever gripped both the naive and the highly learned and cultured Jews, though the rabbis in the main rejected Shabbetai's claims.

The mystic year of destiny was 1666. Thousands disposed of

their property and left their occupations to follow "the holy and sainted Shabbetai, annointed of the God of Israel." Shabbetai, encouraged by the faith of his adherents, journeyed to Constantinople, where he was to take over the Sultan's crown. Upon landing there, however, he was promptly arrested. In prison his disciples supported him in regal style. Later, however, he was denounced to the Turkish court by Nehemia Cohen, a rival Polish Messianic aspirant. Hailed before the Turkish ruler, Shabbetai was given the alternative of converting to Islam or suffering a martyr's death.

He chose the former, and a number of his close associates emulated his example. While most of his adherents were disillusioned, a remnant, particularly in Poland, persisted in their faith, even long after Shabbetai's death in 1676, rationalizing Shabbetai's defection in various ways.

Intellectual Climate

The wide gap between the educated and uneducated Jewish elements in Poland gave rise to class distinctions and differences, which were aggravated by another factor. The wealthier Jews and the intellectuals, who formed the ruling oligarchy in the self-governing *Kahal,* did not distribute the tax burdens fairly, but favored their richer friends at the expense of the poor. Unfortunately, not all rabbis protested against this injustice. In fact, some were even parties to the evil, thereby losing their prestige among the common folk.

The rabbis, especially those in southern Poland, sadly neglected their untutored brethren. Instead of imbuing the Jewish masses with lofty ideals and inspiring them with faith, these spiritual leaders devoted their energies to vying with each other in abstract Talmudic debate and casuistry. The populace was thus left in a spiritual vacuum. The resulting void was filled by superstitious beliefs and practices derived from a debased version of the so-called "practical" Lurianic Cabbala. This was disseminated by professional preachers who attempted to impress upon their audiences the vital importance of self-mortification as a means of purifying their souls. Their sermons were embellished with gruesome tales of prowling ghosts and demons, who were said to be ever on the alert to ensnare people into sin, so that in the afterlife they might be cast into Gehenna and tormented by queer, ugly demons. Graphic accounts of the afflictions in hell were drawn from the popular *mussar* (moralist) literature of the day, of the type of Hirsch Kaidonover's *Kav Hayashar* (*The Just Measure*), published in Hebrew in 1705 and translated into Yiddish several years later. Works of this nature were intended to stress to their readers the importance of pious living. They were commonly read on the Sabbath, though they could hardly have added to the joy and delight of the sacred day. Thus, while the daily existence of the Polish Jew was made miserable by the terrors of rioting bands, the dread of the Polish landowners, and the fear of the Catholic clergy, his credulity added to his anxiety and feeling of insecurity in this world, the horrors of the next.

Obscurantist religion breeds superstition and magic. To ward off the *Shedim* (malicious spirits) that they believed inhabited their world, the plain people sought the help of a *Baal Shem,* (Master of the Name). Such a man was thought to possess the occult art of manipulating the letters of the Name of the Ineffable and of His ministering angels, as a means of exorcising demons, driving out ghosts, and avoiding other evils. The juggled letters were combined into new names inscribed in *Kameot* (amulets or charms) or used in incantations. The *Baal Shem* was regarded as especially skillful in curing mental disorders by expelling *Dibbukim* (clinging spirits) said to invade the body of their victim. He was often successful, for these ailments yield to faith healing. Thus, the *Baal Shem* was a combination miracle worker and doctor who sometimes employed talismen, and sometimes dispensed medicines and herbs, which he learned to use with varying degrees of effectiveness.

Such was the gloomy spiritual climate in which the Polish Jewish masses, particularly those in the south, lived during the latter half of the seventeenth and in the eighteenth century. The upper class looked down upon them because of their supersitition, ignorance and credulity; the common people, consequently, developed a sense of social and religious inferiority. The exploited and impoverished folk needed an assurance that, though rejected by their more intellectual fellow Jews, they could yet have a portion in the House of Israel and would also be acceptable to their God. Moreover, since their piety was not based on learning, they required an approach to religion that would bolster their morale and self-esteem. This they found in Hassidism.

The Frankists

Before proceeding to a discussion of Hassidism, we must pause to examine a pseudo-Messianic group which arose contemporaneously with the Hassidic movement. The hard core of Jews in Poland who had maintained their faith in Shabbetai Zevi even after his death formed an underground cult. This cult became perfect game for the machinations of an imposter, Jacob Frank (1726-1791), who posed as a sort of avatar or incarnation of the soul of Shabbetai Zevi. His followers, like those of Zevi, rejected the Talmud, substituting for it the *Zohar*.

A charlatan and swindler, Frank perverted the Cabbala to his own purpose and expounded a doctrine akin to that of the Christian trinity. He initiated his followers into a mystic worship which called for the full exploitation of the physical passions in sex orgies and other debaucheries, as a means of inducing a state of exaltation and self-purification. The rabbis, of course, denounced the sect. The Frankists, seeking vengeance, incited the Polish clergy against them. Finally, the Frankists adopted Christianity, following the example of their Shabbetian predecessors who had converted to Islam. The further disillusionment which this experience brought to Polish Jewry led them to regard any deviation from rabbinism as bearing the seeds of a false Messianism, and helps to explain why they later regarded Hassidism as another heresy to be stamped out.

II. THE FOUNDER OF HASSIDISM

Israel Baal Shem Tov (1700-1760)

ISRAEL BEN ELIEZER, the founder of Hassidism, is often called the *Baal Shem Tov*, (the Good Master of the Name)[2] usually abbreviated as *Besht*. He was born to his aged parents around 1700 in Okopy, a small town in the Ukraine. He left no written record of his life or teachings; what we know of him has been gleaned from legends and tales encrusting his fame. Israel was orphaned at a tender age and became a ward of the community. He was sent to *Heder*[3] but, being a sensitive lad, he could not adjust to this confining environment and frequently went off to roam and meditate in the nearby woods. In deference to his temperament, his guardians thought it best to terminate his schooling and apprenticed him as an assistant to the local teacher, a position which required him to escort the children to and from the school and synagogue. On the way ,he would lead them in singing liturgical hymns and melodies to arouse their religious fervor. His geniality and sincerity soon earned him an appointment as aid to the *Shamash* (sexton) of the synagogue, where he is said to have conducted himself in a curious manner, sleeping by day when the worshippers were there and studying Cabbala at night, after they had departed.

At the traditional age of eighteen, he married; when his wife died a short time later, he moved to Brody, a city in Galicia. Here he quickly acquired a reputation for honesty and practical wisdom. He married the sister of the rabbi of Brody. While she appreciated his piety and saintliness, her brother, embarrassed by his sister's match with a man of little learning, induced the couple to settle elsewhere. They left Brody and established their home in a distant village in the Carpathian mountains, far from any Jewish settlement. There Israel eked out a bare subsistence by digging lime, which his wife sold in town while he remained in the forest, absorbed in prayer and contemplation. In his new surroundings, he learned the use of herbs for medicinal purposes and, before long, became known for his effective cures. He tried several occupations, but he excelled as a *Baal Shem*. He went about the countryside practicing his profession among his rural neighbors, both Christians and Jews, expounding his ethical principles and doctrines, and serving as a healer of both spirit and body. Israel is said to "have revealed himself," as the mystics put it, at the age of thirty-six, at the instance of a divine spirit. This may perhaps be another way of saying that by that time he was recognized as a qualified *Baal Shem* and a religious figure worthy of respect and emulation.

The Besht's Teachings

A man of the people, sincere and upright, the Besht captured the hearts of the common folk with his kindliness and moral teachings. He substituted for the intellectual interests of the educated classes in Judaism, a simple emotional approach that had a particular appeal for the ordinary folk among whom he lived.

One who trusts implicitly in God is closer to Him than the learned sage, he taught, for "God desireth the heart" (*San.* 106b). He loved the lowly people and addressed them in their own way, not by direct didactic discourse, but by means of stories, fables, and aphorisms which they could grasp and appreciate. In time, the Besht's tales, sayings, and parables became an oral tradition which his disciples faithfully transmitted as *Torah* (moral doctrine) to circles of followers. The Besht's teachings, however, have their roots in the classical sources of Judaism including the Hebrew Bible, the Talmud, the Midrash, and the Cabbala.

One favorite tale in Hassidic lore is retold in Ansky's *The Dybbuk,* a popular Hassidic mystic drama. The Besht once decided to impress upon a formerly poor Hassid, grown wealthy but miserly, the lesson of charity and generosity. The Besht summoned the rich man to his room, where he led him to a window looking out on the street and asked, "What do you see through this glass?" "People", he replied. The Besht then showed the opulent one a mirror and repeated the question. "Now I see only myself," was the answer. The Besht then observed: "The window pane is glass and the mirror is glass; but the glass of the mirror is covered with a little silver. Just a little silver and a man becomes blind to others and sees only himself!"

In 1780, two decades after his death, fragments of the Besht's doctrines were published by one of his outstanding disciples, Jacob Joseph Hakohen of Polonea (d. 1782) in a volume of sermons entitled *Toldot* (*History of*) *Jacob Joseph*. This work can hardly be considered a biography of the *Baal Shem* for it contains a crude maze of legends and miracle tales about the saintly man. This material was collected by a son-in-law of the Besht's amanuensis, Alexander Shochet, in a work called *Shivche Habesht* (*Praises of the Besht*), published in 1815, more than half a century after the *Baal Shem's* death. The Besht left no writings of his own.[4] His principles and teachings form the ideological mould into which the doctrines of Hassidism were cast.

Parallels and Differences

Writers on Hassidism, it may be of interest to note, found a number of interesting parallels between the initiator of Hassidism and that of Christianity. Both the Besht and Jesus were of humble origin, both were heroes of the common folk, whom they taught by means of fables and anecdotes. The two religious leaders began their movements as healers and ended as religious reformers who gathered about them a group of disciples to whom they imparted their beliefs. Each of these teachers drew his doctrines from Jewish sources, each emphasizing those phases of Judaism that appealed to him most. Many believe that if Jesus' preaching had not been infused with extraneous elements by Paul, Christianity, like Hassidism, might have remained within the fold of Judaism. This was made impossible, of course, by the fact that Jesus was accepted as the Messiah by his followers.

The Besht's conception of the *Tzaddik*[5] leaves little room for Messianic pretensions on the latter's part. The *Tzaddik,* by dint of his saintliness and his heredity, contributes to the improvement of his own generation as well as to ultimate redemption. He is a link between God and man; he soars high into the realm of the spirit where he communes with God and descends to the world below where he is a guide in the affairs of men. But he is neither a god incarnate nor a Messiah. Not even the Besht himself ventured to assume such roles. The pluralistic nature of the institution of the *Tzaddik* was a strong safeguard against any Messianic claim.

There are other similarities between these two great religious figures. Neither of them left any biographical or doctrinal writings; whatever we know of their thought was recorded by others. The accounts of their lives, which strangely enough, in both instances, were published after their deaths, have been enveloped in a shroud of myth and legend.

There are, of course, differences as well between these two great ethical personalities. Unlike the case of Jesus, neither the birth nor the death of the Besht is associated with miracles. Moreover, in an age ripe with pseudoprophets and would-be Messiahs, the founder of Hassidism did not, like the initiator of Christianity, become a Messianic cynosure. Though he was a contemporary of Jacob Frank, the Besht was never tempted to emulate Frank's Messianic pretensions, nor to establish a new sect. Moreover, unlike the false Messiahs, the Besht at no time absolved his followers from complete observance of the fundamental principles and practices of Judaism; in fact, he demanded complete conformity to its tenets and laws. It is perhaps this insistence that kept Hassidism as a movement or a current within Judaism, while Christianity drifted away.

III. DOCTRINES OF HASSIDISM

God in Hassidism

AS A RELIGIOUS PHILOSOPHY, Hassidism focuses on the concept of God. Hassidism may be said to underscore the love of God, which, of course, is the principal doctrine in Judaism. God is everywhere, the Besht declared, "the whole earth is full of His glory" (*Is.* 6:3). The *Shechinah* (indwelling presence of God) pervades all beings and all matter; creatures and all things possess divine sparks. There is no wall, no barrier between man and the Almighty. Man, if he but looks, will perceive the great love of God in His perpetual work of renewal in the universe. All too often he fails to observe God's love in nature and among His creatures. He is like the deaf mute, who, peering through a window into a room where a great celebration and festivity is in progress, sees musicians going through motions that he cannot understand and playing music that he cannot hear. The people hopping and whirling about ecstatically appear to him to be doing so without rhyme or reason, but were he only to hear the tune he might dance along with them.

All beings listening to the music in nature and sensing the rhythm of the cosmos express their love of God and sing His praises. Even the lowliest worm extolls the Lord with all its power and love. Man should, therefore, always recall and be guided by the verse, "I shall set the Lord before me always" (*Ps.* 16:8). The love of the Creator, like that of mother for child, should be a love for its own sake, without selfish ends. "What need have I of the world to come, if I love God!" once exclaimed the Besht. The way to the Divine is through passionate prayer; by this means one can achieve unity with the *Shechinah* and fulfillment in Divine love. It is quite remarkable that in a world which the ascetic mystics of the day filled with demons and sinister spirits, the Besht with his unmitigated optimism saw God in His love and goodness.

The Besht insisted that "there is no place free of the *Shechinah* (*Nu. R.* 12:4). Epigrams like these quoted by the Besht and his disciples led to the conclusion that the Hassidim were pantheists who equated nature with God. However, nature in Hassidism is regarded as only one of many garbs in which the Ineffable One manifests Himself. God is immanent in the universe, but He is also transcendent, that is, beyond or outside creation. "God is the Place of the universe but the universe is not His Place," the Midrash says (*Gen. R.* 68:9). The Besht expressed his belief in the Creator Who formed the world by His word. Similarly, Rabbi Elimelech of Lizensk, a disciple of the Besht, once said, "all nature is in God and subject to Him." Such a view is not pantheistic but *panentheistic*. The latter term represents the idea that all things are within the essence of God, yet He is more than the totality of all things.

Good and Evil

Without God, nothing can exist, the Besht taught, for it is said, "Thou preservest them all" (*Nehemiah* 9:6). The *Shechinah* permeates all existence, organic and inorganic, good and evil, beautiful and ugly. It is thus present in man even when he is sinful, for without the power of God, man has neither the strength nor the vitality to perform an act, whether it be wicked or virtuous. It follows then that there is a divine purpose and divine force in good and evil. Both are, therefore, not antithetical or mutually exclusive. For in every sin there is concealed a bit of good.[6] In iniquity, the sparks of holiness are to be found in the potentiality for repentance. The hope for improvement lodged in sin is its positive ingredient.

Evil is not an absolute or independent state of existence; it is only a lower rung in the ladder of the good, just as darkness is a relative stage of light; more light implying less darkness and less light connoting greater darkness. This is the meaning, the Besht suggested, of the verse, "And it was evening and it was morning, one day" (*Gen.* 1:5). A complete day involves a unity, a continuity of light and darkness as a single, not a dual, phenomenon.

This concept is, of course, opposed to the common dualistic view according to which evil is aligned against God and the good. The Besht, therefore, explained the verse, "Depart from evil and do good" (*Ps.* 34:15) as an injunction to wrest the good out of the bad. He illustrated his view allegorically. The letters of the word *Tzarah* (trouble) also form the word *Zohar* (light or radiance).[7] Thus it would seem that in every affliction there is a ray of light, a silver lining to every cloud.

Prayer

Prayer in Hassidism is said to form a channel through which the divine light flows upon men. Prayer is a two-way process: it purifies and lifts the soul to the *Shechinah,* and also brings God's blessings down to earth. To ascend to heaven, however, prayer must have wings; it must be a deep, inward, ecstatic and emotional expression. Though the worshipper may not know the meaning of the words, the prayer, if uttered from the depths of the soul, with *Dvekut* (clinging) and *Hitlahavut* (enthusiasm) will reach the Throne of Glory. In such sincere and intense worship, gesticulation is not unseemly, since it is a natural means of appeal or expression, even though it may appear bizarre to an onlooker. Furthermore, the observance of the prescribed hours for prayer is not important; a child may approach his father at any time, not at specific hours of the day. If a proper mood is essential for true worship, one must wait for it to be generated.

Prayer, moreover, may be most meaningful when not confined to a set ritual. This idea is illustrated by the story of the Hassid who arose one dawn to prepare for his morning devotions. He looked out of his window and saw the sun, a patch of gold on the horizon, shining down upon the earth and its creatures. The Hassid soon became so absorbed in thoughts of the benign Lord and His universe that he lost track of the passing hours, until the time for the *Shachrit* (morning service) had elapsed. In the afternoon, he continued to meditate upon the great works of the Lord and the wonders of nature. He was so engrossed in these reflections that before he was aware of it, the time for the *Mincha* (afternoon service) was over. In the evening, he again looked at the heavens. He was so entranced by the galaxy of bright stars shining above, the myriads of planets in infinite space, and the great cosmos in which our earth is barely a speck, that he failed to notice that the midnight hour had struck, and it was too late for the *Maariv* (evening liturgy). Thus it was that the Hassid was too busy communing with God and contemplating His works to pray in a formal manner.

The *Tzaddik* Rabbi Levi Isaac of Berdichev (1740-1810) was famed for his piety and love of his people. He is said to have once held up the solemn *Rosh Hashanah* (New Year) services at the sacred moment of the blowing of the *Shofar,* (ram's horn). Asked for his reason for doing so, Rabbi Levi Isaac explained that he had observed an illiterate worshipper in the rear of the synagogue who had appealed to God in this wise: "I can recite only the letters of the Hebrew alphabet, which I shall repeat over and over again. I entreat Thee O Lord, weave Thou beautiful and appropriate prayers out of the letters of the holy alphabet—prayers that befit Thy grace and glory!" "And now," Rabbi Levi Isaac said, "we are waiting for this truly devout man to conclude his prayers."

There is also the story[x] of the *Tzaddik* of Niemerov who instead of attending synagogue during the solemn Ten Days of Penitence between *Rosh Hashanah* and *Yom Kippur* disappeared from view. Some of his followers insisted that he had gone up to heaven to intercede for his people on these awesome days, but a Lithuanian skeptic trailed him and discovered him in a strange pose. Each morning the *Tzaddik,* disguised as a peasant, went off to the forest, where he chopped firewood for a poor sick old woman living alone in a shack on the outskirts of the town. While kindling the wood in her stove, he quietly chanted the penitential hymns of the sacred season. This act, the Lithuanian recognized, represented a higher level of worship than the conventional synagogue service. When he was again told that the *Tzaddik* ascended to heaven during the Days of Penitence his fervent comment was, "If not higher!"

Doctrine of Joy

The verse "Serve the Lord with gladness, come before Him singing" (*Ps.* 100:2) was adopted as a principle by the Besht. The consciousness of the nearness of the *Shechinah* should inspire man with faith and cheer. A joyous mood should accompany worship, as well as all aspects of religion. Accordingly, the Besht advocated that asceticism, generally discouraged in Judaism, but espoused by the Lurianic school of "practical" Cabbala, be shunned, for it generates a sense of gloom and sadness, which interferes with genuine worship. Inordinate fasting or other form of physical deprivation is, therefore, undesirable. It might weaken the body, so that the soul it harbors may lack the strength to engage in effective worship. This admonition he based on the verse "From thine own flesh thou shalt not hide" (*Is.* 58:7). Even sin should not cause undue distress, for profuse grief evidences distrust in God's power and in His readiness to forgive. The most welcome tears are those of joy and gladness.

To induce a happy state of mind, the Besht encouraged singing and dancing as an accompaniment to worship and religious festivity. He even permitted indulgence in drink, for this purpose. This license unfortunately was carried to excess by some of his followers and earned them the strong censure of their critics.

The Tzaddik

Through Hassidism, the Besht, as we have seen, introduced a new kind of religious functionary into Judaism in the person of the *Tzaddik,* the righteous man, known to his followers by the affectionate term *rebbe.* This designation was intended to distinguish him from the rabbi, also known as *rav* (master), whose primary qualification for his spiritual leadership was his mastery of learning. The *Tzaddik* was not required to be a scholar, though many of them were. Rather the *Tzaddik* was supposed to be endowed with a purer soul and a greater measure of divine sparks than other people. This gift was regarded as a boon from God, which could be acquired principally through the merit of birth, ancestry, and good works—a notion in line with the general tendency in the Besht's doctrines to subordinate scholarship.

According to the Cabbala, a man's actions exert a vital influence in the cosmos; it is, therefore, all the more important to arouse in him greater piety. To this end, the Besht urged every Hassid to attach himself to a *Tzaddik* who would aid and inspire him to lead a good life. The Besht used the favorite Hassidic symbol of Jacob's ladder to illustrate the function of the *Tzaddik*. The *Tzaddik,* he said, stands on the upper rung of the ladder; but he also needs a group of disciples on the lower rungs to make his climb meaningful. He depends on them in very much the same manner as the soul depends on the body. The *Tzaddik,* moreover, has another function; together with his Hassidim, he must strive to raise his generation to a higher spiritual plane. Thus he brings to earth a little of heaven.

Despite the important place that the *Tzaddik* occupied in the religious life of the Hassid, the latter was not to rely on him unduly. The Besht interpreted the rabbinic dictum: "If I am not for myself, who will be for me," (*Abot.* 1:14) as implying that the Hassid must look after his own religious growth. Just as the worshipper in the congregation does not expect the cantor to pray for him, but must do so himself, the Hassid should not shift his own responsibilities to the *Tzaddik*.

The Tzaddik's Motives

According to Hassidic doctrine, the *Tzaddik* must possess the highest ethical qualities, but he must also experience sin in order to understand his followers better. To judge them truly, he must place himself in their position (*Abot.* 2:5). The *Tzaddik* thus appears to sin though he actually does not do so; he is considered too pure to commit the transgressions of ordinary humans. In Cabbalistic language, he is described as rising to the upper spheres: but he may sometimes lack the spiritual strength to sustain himself there. The *Tzaddik* might, therefore, permit himself to drop for a while to a lower level, but he does so only to regain his strength for a still higher ascent. On occasion, too, the *Tzaddik* may find it necessary, according to the Besht, to descend and invade the world of sin, in order to extract and salvage from it the imprisoned holy sparks.

This naive notion provided a license for an unscrupulous Hassidic leader to commit wrongs with complete immunity, on the pretext that whatever he did was for a pure and worthy purpose. The Besht evidently believed that his successors would all follow his moral ways; in the main, they did, but there were also exceptions. Thus it was that *Tzaddikism* harbored the germs of corruption within its own doctrines.

The Tzaddik's Court

The chief disciple of the Besht was Dov Baer of Meseritz, an unusually gifted preacher, who was revered as the ideal *Maggid* (preacher). Dov Baer gathered about him a group of devotees whom he trained and sent forth to propagate his master's doctrines. After Dov Baer's death in 1772, the surviving disciples of the Besht distributed the Hassidic hegemony among themselves. Because scholarship was not an essential qualification for the *Tzaddik's* functions, the sons and close relatives of the earlier, self-appointed *Tzaddikim* inherited this role. The justification for this arrangement was the *Zechut Avot* (the merit of birth and ancestry) which they had acquired by reason of their descent. This system of hereditary *Tzaddikism* may be construed as another phase of the Hassidic rebellion against constituted rabbinic authority.

The early disciples of the Besht lived simply and attempted to imbue their followers with the piety and virtues expounded by the Besht. But among later generations, there were *Tzaddikim* who exploited their positions for their own self-aggrandizement. The custom of giving the *rebbe* a *pidyon* (redemption money) for his blessings spread widely. Some *Tzaddikim* accumulated considerable wealth from this source and were able to set up mansions or "courts," where they lived and received their Hassidim in luxury and pomp. This kind of extravagant living was hardly in keeping with the spirit of humility that Hassidic doctrine demanded; it was, however, justified by its practitioners on the ground that the *Tzaddik* must himself experience riches if he is to pray fervently and efficaciously for these blessings for his followers. In the main, however, the *Tzaddikim* were not guilty of intemperate indulgence, but conducted their establishments in relative simplicity and modesty, serving their flocks as intimate guides and mentors.

There was a good deal of intense spirituality in Hassidic life. A Hassid made a pilgrimage to his *rebbe* at least annually, if he

could, to spend the High Holy Days under the *Tzaddik's* roof.
Here, the Hassidim formed a unique fellowship, united by a common religious purpose and leader. They ate, drank, sang, and
prayed together as one family, sharing each other's joys and sor-
rows and strengthening and fortifying each other's faith. The same
atmosphere was carried over into the *Klaus* or *Shtiebel* (small
house), the prayer room in their home towns which served as a
religious and social center for the Hassidim of any one *rebbe*. Here
they sang the *Nigunim*, (the wordless melodies) sung by their *rebbe*
and danced his dances, which lifted them into a state of spiritual
ecstasy. These common experiences, festivities, and celebrations
welded the Hassidim together into a closely knit religious fraternity.

IV. The Habad School

Shneur Zalman of Ladi

In Lithuania, the stronghold of rabbinism and intellectualism,
Dov Baer made a convert of a brilliant young rabbi, Shneur Zalman
of Ladi (1746-1812),[9] who became the founder of a new school of
Hassidism. The new alignment known as *Habad* derived its name
from the initials of the Hebrew terms *Hokma* (wisdom), *Binah*
(understanding), and *Daat* (knowledge), used in the Cabbala to
designate the three highest of the ten *Sephiroth* (emanations) flowing from God. This choice of a name indicates the unique intellectual principles of *Habad,* which represents a synthesis of the
rationalism of rabbinism and the mysticism of Hassidism.

Doctrines of Habad

Only a few of Shneur Zalman's numerous writings were ever
published, among them his *Likutei Amarim* (*A Collection of Sayings*), more popularly known by the first word of the text as the
Tanya (taught).[10] This work constitutes a brief and concise pre-
sentation of *Habad* Hassidism and its distinguishing rationalistic
principles. It is unique in early Hassidic literature in its logical
organization and analysis, for the classics of Hassidism generally
consist of sermonic fragments or unrelated aphorisms. The volume

is composed of five parts, of which the first is "The Book of *Benonim"* (intermediates). This book propounds lofty ethical goals for the ordinary Jew, who occupies an intermediate rank in piety between the *Tzaddik* and the *rasha* (the wicked one).

The psychological formulation found in the *Tanya* is reminiscent of that outlined by Plato and Aristotle, and by the medieval Jewish thinkers who borrowed from them. Man has two souls: the *nefesh elohit* (divine soul) and *nefesh habehemit* (animal soul). This dichotomy merely implies that man functions along two levels of consciousness. He is a microcosm in whose consciousness is enacted the same struggle between the forces of good and evil that is waged in the cosmos, the two opposing forces continually striving for control over the individual. His good inclinations will lead the Jew towards God; his evil tendencies will draw him away to the *Sitra Achra,* the other side of God as the Cabbala terms it—*i.e.* the ungodly one. The intermediate path which combines both is the *Kelipat Nogah* (shell with a ray of light). This term is used as the Cabbalistic symbol for evil mixed with good, which is a characteristic of the "average man." In this system, the higher soul embodies the three intellectual attributes of wisdom, understanding, and knowledge. It is also endowed with seven emotional powers that are inferior to the intellectual. The lower or animal soul, the seat of the passions, includes the vices—conceit, anger, and the like. The intellectual and emotional phases of a human personality are influenced by motivations and drives which function below the level of consciousness—an idea akin to our modern psychological theory. The facets of our personalities are expressed through the media of thought, speech, and action, the "outer garments" that clothe the naked soul.

Only the *benoni,* the normal or average Jew, is engaged in the conflict between spiritual life and earthly pleasures. The *rasha,* the wicked one, succumbs to the latter; the *Tzaddik* transcends the appetitive desires of his animal soul and is left only with the intellectual and emotional functions of his divine soul. The "average" Jew therefore, should direct his speech, thought, and actions to God and subordinate earthly pleasures in order to achieve a higher spiritual plane. However, he cannot in actuality aspire to the highest sphere, that of the *Tzaddik,* for the capacity to overcome the tendency to earthly desires is a special gift of God that only a few attain.

The "average" Jew must concentrate on Torah and the performance of the *Mitzvot,* because one who is engaged in religious study thinks God's thoughts and identifies himself with his Maker, and thereby enters into a mystic union with Him. Observances of the *Mitzvot* are also important, but a *Mitzvah* requires external expression through the instrumentality of thought, speech, and action. The "average" Jew must resist the use of these media for evil ends. Prayer, utilizing the function of speech or thought, is of great value, but preoccupation with religious learning is the highest good, since it will motivate a Jew to more exalted living. In *Habad* thought, secular knowledge also has its place, either as a means of livelihood or as an aid to religious learning.

The priority given by *Habad* to the mind over the heart, to study over prayer, represents a radical shift in the ideological fulcrum of Hassidism, for the Besht extolled the heart and subordinated the intellect. Shneur Zalman's brand of Hassidism is better adapted to the scholar than that of the Besht. Yet *Habad* has not overlooked the untutored Jew; in regard to him, it accepts the Besht's allegory of the burning bush that was not consumed (*Ex.* 3:2). The humble Jew who can only pray is like the inextinguishable flame surrounding the lowly desert shrub, out of which spoke the voice of God. The *Shechinah* finds its place among the devout and sincere common folk.

The author of the *Tanya* seemed to share the phenomenalist views of Hume, Berkeley, and Kant, who maintained that man cannot grasp inner reality because his reason is limited by his finite faculties. Both the *Tanya* and the Besht agreed that the power of understanding the true essence of ultimate reality is solely within the realm of God, Who is the only true existence, the sustaining force of all matter and life. The Deity alone is Eternity; all else is ephemeral and transitory. What may appear to be suffering to us may not actually be so; it looks so to us merely because we cannot understand God's full plan of the universe, nor do we realize that His concern is with the cosmos as a whole and not only with man. This idea is also found in Spinoza, though it is hardly likely that Shneur Zalman had read Spinoza.

Habad and Hassidism

Perhaps we can see a shade of asceticism in the *Habad* outlook on the *Tzaddik,* the epitome of the highest religious and ethical values. While in the Besht's concept, the *Tzaddik* was permitted riches and earthly pleasures so as to enable him to intervene with the Almighty more effectively to secure these gifts for his Hassidim, the *Tzaddik* in *Habad* was to attain the capacity to transcend them. Yet Shneur Zalman, like the Besht, discouraged undue fasting in repentance from sin. Remorse might be better manifested by a contrite heart and by good, particularly charitable, deeds. These are within the province of the soul rather than the body, and should, therefore, not be affected. The true Hassid, according to *Habad,* can best know God by the fulfillment of his material wants in accordance with the Biblical injunction, "In all thy ways shalt thou know Him" (*Prov.* 3:6). One can attain joy through genuine reliance on the Lord in all matters. To engender such a mood, artificial means such as drink, gesticulation, or strange mannerism in prayer are improper. The *Tzaddik* in Hassidism is presumed to be endowed with mystical powers, while in *Habad* he is essentially a teacher and spiritual leader. In worldly affairs, his followers should pray to God, rather than turn to him—a mere human. The leaders of *Habad,* therefore, avoided the title of *Tzaddik* and preferred the traditional designation of rabbi, which is a mark of learning and scholarship, rather than of mystic power. *Habad* was eclectic in the doctrines of Hassidism it espoused, leaning rather to the rabbinic outlook. It represented a sober and moderate minority in Hassidism, yet it was not acceptable to the *Mithnagdim,* the opponents of Hassidism, who attacked it as they did the other branches of the movement.

V. Opposition to Hassidism

The Mithnagdim

IT WAS ONLY to be expected that the rabbis and intellectuals in Poland would react adversely to the Hassidic movement. The role of the *Tzaddik* in Hassidism was one of the chief causes of their opposition. They saw in the *Tzaddik* not only a threat to their own authority, but to Judaism as a whole. Still haunted by the spectre of Frankism, they denounced the cult of the *Tzaddik* because they feared that it might lead to a Messianic movement. They also maintained that the *Tzaddik* as an intermediary or intercessor in prayer or worship was alien to Judaism; that rabbis should serve only as religious teachers who interpret the law; that they should not lay claim to divine power to perform miracles or bestow blessings.

The rabbis, too, regarded other phases of Hassidic doctrine as contrary to the principles of Judaism. The Hassidic concept of God bordered on pantheism, which negated the principle of the transcendent Deity. Their attitude towards sin and evil, as non-existent rather than as reality, the view that evil possesses sparks of divinity, as we have said, refuted the traditional dualistic doctrine of right and wrong. In subordinating the study of Torah to ecstatic prayer and mystical piety, the Hassidim, the rabbis insisted, were violating one of the basic tenets of Judaism in which Torah study was a supreme objective. The rabbis also charged the cultists with devoting so much time and effort to inducing the proper frame of mind for worship as to neglect worship itself. They accused them of overlooking the substance and content of the prayers in their efforts to generate a high pitch of exaltation, fervent emotion, and ecstasy. They condemned the drinking bouts among the Hassidim. They also criticized the unseemly contortions and gesticulations to which the Hassidim often resorted in prayer. The songs and dances which the Hassidim employed to arouse a state of *Hitlahavut* (enthusiasm) appeared to the rabbis to be highly inappropriate in a synagogue. The fact that Hassidim established their own synagogues heightened the suspicion of the rabbinic leaders. The moderate changes that the cultists introduced into the liturgy when they adopted the *Ari*[11] version which stressed the Messianic motif, as well as the slight modification that they instituted in the method of ritual slaughter, provoked the rabbis still more. Yet strangely enough it was the dissenting Hassidic minority that dubbed their antagonists, who formed the majority of Jews, *Mithnagdim* (adversaries),—a name which has clung to them ever since.[11a]

Elijah of Vilna (1720-1797)

The *Mithnagdim* were headed by a revered intellectual and saintly leader, Elijah ben Solomon, generally referred to as the *Gaon of Vilna,* a title of distinction conferred upon him in deference to his phenomenal learning. The Gaon was not a professional rabbi; he lived on a modest pension granted him by the community from an endowment for the support of scholarship. From his early childhood, the Gaon was recognized as a prodigy; he mastered not only the Babylonian but also the Jerusalem Talmud, which was rarely studied. In addition to Talmudic scholarship, he had also acquired a thorough knowledge of the Cabbala and, though it was unusual in those days, secular knowledge as well, including foreign languages, astronomy, anatomy, and mathematics. He regarded these subjects as essential aids in the study of Talmud.

The Gaon had written some seventy works, including a Hebrew treatise on astronomy, algebra, and trigonometry. An intellectual modernist, he applied the critical approach to Talmudic investigation, seeking first to ascertain the true text, in order to determine its correct meaning, for in the course of centuries, many errors had corrupted the text. For this purpose, he examined and compared various manuscript editions of the Talmud. He opposed the use of the *pilpul* (casuistic method) in Talmudic study on the ground that it served merely as an exercise in abstract logic rather than as a help in determining the law.

The conflict between the Hassidim and *Mithnagdim* began in earnest in 1772, when the rabbinical court of the Vilna *Kahal,* with the approval of the Gaon, issued a ban against the Hassidim and sent a letter of denunciation to the Jewish communities of Poland and East Galicia, urging local rabbis to take similar measures. In retaliation, the Hassidic leaders headed by Dov Baer excoriated the "false learning" of the rabbis, saying they made of the study of Torah "a spade with which to dig," using it to obtain social prestige and financial gain, rather than pursuing it for its own sake. Dov Baer reproved the rabbis for their aloofness from the masses and censured them for their conceit and their preoccupation with the useless hair-splitting of the *pilpul.* In 1781, the rabbis published a second ban, prohibiting loyal Jews from having any social or commercial dealings with the cultists, forbidding marriage with them, and even the burial of their dead. Thus the campaign against "the dishonored followers of the Besht," the "destroyers of Israel," was intensified. Shneur Zalman and one of his colleagues, Mendel of Vitebsk, sought an interview with the Gaon, in the hope of mollifying him, but the latter avoided seeing them. When Shneur Zalman's *Tanya* appeared in 1796, the Gaon denounced its seemingly pantheistic doctrines as blasphemous and declined to accept its author's challenge to a debate, branding him as a heretic. Despite this provocation, however, Shneur Zalman refused to permit his followers to speak ill of the revered Gaon.

In 1797, the Gaon passed away. When a band of Hassidim was found to be celebrating his death in clandestine revelry, the leaders of the Vilna Jewish community were enraged beyond restraint and, at the grave of the Gaon, swore vengeance. At a secret conclave, they decided to seek the intervention of the state in their quarrel. They went to the Russian authorities, whose government had only recently assumed suzerainty over Lithuania, and accused Shneur Zalman of subversive activities and the collection of funds for mysterious purposes. The Hassidic leader was arrested and taken in chains to a fortress in St. Petersberg, where he was imprisoned for several months,[12] being kept under surveillance even after his release.

A year later, the Hassidim repaid the *Mithnagdim* by having several of their leaders arrested by the civil authorities. The rift in the Vilna community grew. In 1800, the *Mithnagdim* denounced the Hassidim as a disloyal group who feared only God, not man— implying that they were defiant towards the Russian government. Shneur Zalman was re-arrested and brought to the capital where, after an additional period of imprisonment, he was again exonerated. A few years later, in 1804, a special government ordinance gave the Hassidim the right to carry on their activities unmolested. Thereafter, the bitterness of the clash between the two factions wore off.

Mutual Toleration

In time, the conflict between the Hassidim and *Mithnagdim* diminished in intensity, though it had left its scars on both groups. On the one hand, Hassidism had been curbed in its radicalism by the opposition of the Gaon; on the other, the Gaon had checked the *pilpulistic* excesses of the *Mithnagdim* in Talmudic study. The intellectualistic *Habad* movement also helped to anchor Hassidism in Talmudism and Halacha. A more rationalistic Hassidism was the outcome—a brand that preserved the warmth, enthusiasm, and broad human sympathies inherent in the movement, without the gross superstition and sharp hostility to scholarship of its early days. The educated *Mithnaged* shed some of his contempt for the ignorant Hassid, and the latter recognized that erudition was worthy of respect. The partition of Poland (1772, 1793, 1795) separated the two warring camps by a national boundary. The Hassidic provinces were ceded to Austria, while the territories of the *Mithnagdim* were taken over by Russia. Within two generations after its founding, Hassidism became institutionalized, and its original creativity and force were greatly dissipated. By the middle of the nineteenth century, almost half of East European Jewry had joined its ranks, but spiritually Hassidism was on the downgrade. The abuses resulting from the *Tzaddik* cult were a major cause of the decline.

In Russia, both the Hassidim and *Mithnagdim* were caught between two common foes, one from without and the other from within. The politically influential Greek Orthodox clergy enlisted the aid of the Russian government in its campaign against the Jews, and a wave of persecution, which became particularly pronounced shortly after 1825, resulted. In addition, the Haskalah (Enlightenment) made encroachments from within the Jewish ranks upon the youth of both groups. As a result, the two opposing parties found themselves, in the latter half of the nineteenth century, between the hammer and the anvil; they were now too preoccupied with their joint problems to continue their internecine strife. While Galician Jewry enjoyed much better treatment at the hands of the Austrian government, it also had to cope with the inroads made by the Haskalah. An attempt at a synthesis of Haskalah and Hassidism had to wait, however, for Martin Buber.

VI. NEO-HASSIDISM

Martin Buber (1878-1965)

THE SIMPLE AND deep piety of the Hassidim found a spokesman and exponent in the eminent Jewish philosopher and scholar, Martin Buber, who became the interpreter of their rich religious life to the Western world. Hassidism's search for God through and within the emotions, Buber believed, gave an additional dimension to Judaism, one that might well serve as an antidote to the exaggerated rationalism that had pervaded Judaism and Western thought since the beginning of the nineteenth century. To Buber, Hassidism was the highest achievement of Diaspora Judaism.

Buber was brought up in the Galician city of Lemberg (now Lwow) in Poland, by his grandfather, a distinguished Midrashic scholar who employed the scientific method in his researches. Young Buber received a traditional Jewish education, but his grandmother also introduced him to secular literature and learning. At the age of seventeen, he entered the University of Vienna. He received his doctor's degree in 1904 on the basis of a dissertation on German mysticism. While still a student, Buber joined the infant Zionist movement, and in 1901, he assumed the editorship of the Zionist journal *Die Welt* (*The World*). His Zionism, however, like that advocated by the Hebrew philosopher, Asher Ginzberg, known by his pen name, *Ahad Ha-am* (1856-1927), attached more importance to the creation of a Jewish spiritual and cultural center in Palestine than to the establishment of a political Jewish state.

As a child, Buber had come into contact with the Hassidim in his grandfather's circle, and he was impressed by their spirituality. He saw Hassidic life as a constant inward renewal—one continuous worship of God. This experience induced him to return to Poland in 1904 to study Hassidism at close range. At first he was stirred principally by its aesthetic aspect, by the wordless melodies of the Hassidim, their rapturous dances, and their folklore. But before long, he became saturated with Hassidic principles, ideals, and doctrines. This led him to compile collections of Hassidic tales and other works on Hassidism which gained for the movement the respectability that it had lacked in the West; in fact, it had been little known in its true essence outside of Eastern Europe.

In addition to his numerous works on Hassidism, Buber, in the ensuing decades, edited several Jewish periodicals and contributed to philosophical and theological journals. With the distinguished Jewish thinker Franz Rosenzweig (1886-1929), he produced a monumental German translation of a number of books of the Hebrew Scriptures which was highly successful in retaining the spirit and cadence of the original Hebrew. After Rosenzweig's death, Buber carried on the work alone.

From 1923 until the rise of Hitler, Buber served as Professor of Jewish Ethics and Religion at the University of Frankfort, the first post of its kind in Germany. During the period of Nazi terror, his leadership was a guiding light and moral force in the spiritual battle of German Jewry against Naziism. When the Jews were expelled from the general schools, he helped to found new ones to accommodate them. Together with Leo Baeck, he launched a network of adult Jewish schools which upheld the morale of the German Jews and enhanced their feeling of self-respect after they had been cast out of German cultural, social, and economic life. He continued in this role until he was silenced by the Nazis in 1938. Then, at the age of sixty, he emigrated to Palestine, where he was appointed Professor of Social Philosophy at the Hebrew University. There he joined Judah Magnes in the small dissident *Ihud* (unity movement) which before 1948 favored a binational state in Palestine and has since persistently advocated a program of Arab-Jewish amity.

In 1951, Buber retired from his academic duties; he later traveled to America and other countries, where he lectured at universities and theological seminaries. Though defended by some, he was violently criticized by others for accepting the Peace Prize of the German Book Trade in Frankfort in 1953 and, a year later, the Hanseatic Goethe Prize in Hamburg. To him, these awards betokened the solidarity among all peoples in their struggle for a unified, common humanity. Buber continued to write until his death in June 1965.

The True Zion

The germs of Buber's doctrines are lodged in a variety of phi-
losophical currents and schools, in the general mood of German
Idealism and Romanticism, and in the mystical strains that entered
German thought after that country's defeat in the First World
War. Buber was also influenced by Kierkegaard's existentialism,
Bergson's intuitionism, Dostoevsky's psychological outlook, and
Freud's psychoanalysis. But Hassidism, both in its mystic and in
its existential approach, exerted a dominating influence upon him.
To him, the Hassidic movement represented an attempt on the part
of Diaspora Judaism to found a true and just society based on
religious principles.

Buber regarded the conventicles of Hassidim, clustering about
their *rebbes* and united by a poignant sense of brotherhood, as
model spiritual communities. He felt, however, that the chief
reason for the failure of Hassidism to achieve a greater role in
Judaism was its lack of a soil and territory of its own in which
it could develop freely and naturally. Thus, Buber linked his
religious ideas with the Zionist aim of establishing a Jewish homeland. Every people, he believed, has its own subconscious soul.
The Jewish spirit will express itself most creatively only when it
is united with its native land. That there is a close affinity between
man's soul and the soil may be seen in the Hebraic concept of
Adamah (earth), which is related to the noun, *Adam* (man). The
Jewish soul has manifested itself in the past in prophetism, in Es-
senism, in early Christianity;[13] in contemporary times, it is reflected in Hassidism and *Halutziut,* the efforts of the *Halutzim*
(pioneers) in rebuilding the Jewish homeland.

No revival in Judaism is possible, Buber believed, without the
Hassidic zeal. The *Halutzim* have captured the Hassidic fervor
in their songs and dances. They have, moreover, also assumed
Hassidism's lofty objectives in their endeavor to erect a social
structure designed for true cooperative living. They attempted to
achieve this in the various types of *Kibbutzim* (collectives) with
which they have been experimenting. These settlements are minia-
tures of the just society which harbors within it the *Shechinah.*
Buber was not concerned with Jewish nationalism for its own sake,
but rather with the creation of the true Zion, which represents

"the holy marriage of a holy people with its holy land." In this way, he believed, the pious Hassid shares with the secular *Halutz* the religious aspiration of establishing the kingdom of God on earth. This is what God expects of Israel, and this is Israel's Messianic goal and mission in the world.

Life as Dialogue

The central feature of Buber's semimystical, semirationalistic thought was his dialogical principle, based on the idea that "real life is meeting." This approach is to be found in the encounter of man with man or of man with God. This is the true aim of human existence. In Buber's view, the reality underlying the world is the vital dynamic relationship of a person to others, which stems from the social nature of man. The *I* withdrawn into its own ivory tower is of no consequence. One can grasp the meaning of *I* only when he reaches out to others. People display one of two attitudes, which Buber poetically described by the primary words *I-Thou* or *I-It*. The two relationships may interchange in different situations.

The *I-Thou* concept designates the complete, direct, reciprocal relationship into which one person enters with another with his whole being. It is a voluntary, active, subject-to-subject affinity— a form of human fellowship in which both persons are on an equal plane, and bear a mutual responsibility to give freely and fully to each other in accordance with their unique proclivities or endowments. The individual in such a give and take is influenced by two opposing attitudes, embodied in the notion that "for my sake was the world created" (*San.* 4:5), commingled with the sentiment that one "is only dust and ashes" (*Gen.* 18:27). One is to be self-assertive in this pattern of human intercourse, yet he must also retain a deep sense of humility.

The obligation to preserve one's own personality in this relationship is illustrated in the Hassidic folk tale of Rabbi Zusya who, towards the end of his days, fretted about the accounting he would be called upon to give in the afterlife. Recognizing his plight, his friends inquired of him, "Is it that you have not been a Moses throughout your lifetime that troubles you?" "No," the aged Zusya answered, "my concern is that I was not Zusya." In other words, the sage regretted that he had failed to live up to his own unique potentialities and that he had not been his true self.

The *I-Thou* bond has been exemplified in the ideal reciprocity that should exist between teacher and student where both learn from each other or, as Buber also suggested, in the psychiatric relationship. One's personality is fulfilled in this type of experience which makes him truly human. True ethical responsibility is founded on the attitude of love and friendship prevailing between the parties in such a communion rather than on external factors such as law or convention. The *I-Thou* dialogue may be spoken or silent, for thoughts, too, may meet. The association depends largely on the attitude and intention of each of the parties to "establish a living mutual relation between them."[14]

The primary words *I-It*, in contrast to *I-Thou*, connote the indirect relation of subject to object, of person to thing; it takes place within a man and not between him and another. If this kind of communion is between people, it involves de-personalization. It suggests the detached attitude of the busy doctor or overloaded social worker towards a person who comes to him for professional assistance, whom he regards as a "case" rather than as a fellow human being. It implies the kind of objective knowledge one seeks in science, in which the purpose is primarily to exploit, control, or manipulate for his own ends. The tragedy in life is that we permit the *I-It* rather than the *I-Thou* relationship to dominate our relations with people.

The Eternal Thou

Among humans, the *I-Thou* relationship alternates of necessity with the *I-It*, since men do at times stand in an objective *I-It* relation to each other. There is, however, one permanent, eternal, and infinite Thou—the force in the universe that is referred to as God. It is the absolute, limitless Thou that permeates all the world, the Thou that can never be It—the Thou that may be addressed but not expressed. The Biblical idiom "I am that I am" (*Ex.* 3:14), referring to Jehovah, should be rendered in the sense of "I am and remain present" and everlastingly so.

God is there in every situation. He is imageless and may appear in a different form at different times, but He is there, both in His encounters with man and in nature. If only man is ready to respond to Him with his whole being, God is not remote. He can be nearer to me than my *I*. It is for us to perceive Him and listen to Him and answer Him. This is not said in a mystical or supernatural sense, but in the Hassidic which presumes that the *Shechinah* of God is everywhere. He is in everything; He speaks to us in the ordinary, everyday events and episodes in life as well as in human history. In theology, the Deity may be transcendental and mysterious, but in this personalized relationship, "God standeth in the congregation of the godly" (*Ps.* 82:1) in intimate contact with man. In mysticism, man seeks to be submerged in the Deity, but in Buber's Neo-Hassidic or neo-mystical viewpoint man and the Deity are in need of each other and stand together in a common alliance on behalf of mankind and the world.

The idea that God enters into every aspect of life is another way of affirming the Hassidic doctrine that there is no true separation between the sacred and the secular—or even the profane. Only *Kavanah,*[15] one's inner intention, is essential to hallow an act—not ritual. To reach God, moreover, one is not to withdraw from the world as does the ascetic contemplating God in isolation. One should encounter God on earth, His laboratory of salvation. It is in the here and now that the Supreme Being joins man in a mutual endeavor to lift humanity to a higher state of sanctity. In this view, Buber differed radically from Soren Kierkegaard (1813-1855), the Danish existentialist philosopher and theologian, who believed that God speaks only to the single one who retires from the affairs of life. But Buber, the Neo-Hassid, maintained that "one cannot . . . have to do essentially with God if one does not have to do essentially with men."[16]

Love of God

The duality in the *I-Thou* relationship is bridged into a harmony through the bond of love between the two individuals bearing this affinity. The concept of love referred to here is used in the sense employed in the Hebrew Bible in the ethical exhortation to "love thy neighbor as thyself" (*Lev.* 19:18). This implies a sense of obligation to respect another's personality and dignity, rather than the emotional sentiment of love. The latter, of course, cannot be ordained. In Judaism, the love of man is raised to the level of the love of God.

The same is true of Hassidism. Buber used many examples from the sayings of the *Tzaddikim* to illustrate this doctrine. A *Tzaddik* once reminded a Hassid that the traditional *Siddur* (prayer book) prescribes the recitation of the ethical precept to love one's neighbor as oneself before prayer. Another *Tzaddik* pointed out that the injunction in the Bible to love one's neighbor ends with the phrase, "I am the Lord," to indicate that God is present in a relationship in which human love prevails. There is also the saying of a Hassidic *rebbe* to the effect that whoever says that he loves God without loving man is telling a falsehood.[17] The Seer of Lublin had declared that he who loves other Israelites acquires divine sparks which increase as he loves more of them. When he loves all of Israel, he attains the true love of the Almighty. The love of God is thus not complete without the love of man. To love the Deity alone is to love a solitary, lonely God, the God of one's soul, not the God of the universe. The *Baal Shem Tov* once explained the Golden Rule in this manner; as you love yourself with all your shortcomings, you must love your neighbor with all of his. [18]

Redemption from Evil

Buber was profoundly influenced by the Hassidic conception of man's purpose on earth, as formulated in terms of Cabbalistic symbolism. Man is to be allied with the Divine in releasing the sacred sparks of the *Shechinah* that are confined in all life and matter. Man is charged with the task of raising a segment of his environment to a higher rung of sanctity or perfection, and in so doing, he himself is lifted to a higher stage of spirituality. This implies that everything waits for sanctification. Moreover, there is nothing absolutely unholy or evil in itself, for what we regard as sin or evil is only the tension and turbulence caused by the onrushing sparks of divinity struggling for liberation. The divine sparks imprisoned in the *Kelipah* (shell), the symbol of iniquity and sinfulness can be released and restored to God through *Teshuvah* (turning or repentance). Everything and every thought of man can help to this end; everything and everyone can be redeemed. "Thus man lifts up heaven," said a *Tzaddik*.

The idea of *Teshuvah* in Judaism is a direct refutation of Paul's doctrine of original sin and forgiveness by means of divine grace and vicarious atonement through the death of Jesus. Judaism has always opposed a belief that sin is congenital, for that negates the idea of free will and free ethical choice (*Deut.* 30:15; *Abot.* 3:15). The Talmud maintains that one may follow the road he selects (*Mak.* 10b). One may be held in the grip of his own sin, not anyone else's (*Pr.* 5:22). Buber explained his view of sin, *Teshuvah*, and forgiveness in the following passage:[19]

> . . . According to Jewish doctrine sin is the disturbing by man of the fundamental relationship between God and man, so that as a result man is no longer identical with the creature of God. Forgiveness is the restoration of the fundamental relationship by God after man through turning to Him is set again in the condition of this creatureliness. Turning, provided the individual exerts his whole soul to accomplish it, is not prevented by anything, not even the sin of the first man. . . . Man always begins again and again as God's creature, although henceforth under the burden of a humanity cast out from Paradise into the world and history. . . . That he sins belongs to his condition, that he turns back belongs to his holding his own in it. He sins as Adam sinned and not because Adam sinned. . . . . Because the way of humanity ever begins again, no matter how far it has gone astray, the man who prays speaks the truth when, on waking every morning he says to God: "The soul which Thou has given me is pure." True, everyone sins, but everyone may turn back. "The gates are not closed" (*Midrash Tehilim on Ps.* 65) or, as Jesus expressed it, "Knock and it shall be opened to you." God withholds nothing from him who turns back "unto God." . . .

Judaism, Buber further pointed out, does not see the holy and unholy, the good and the evil as a sharp dualism. The energy and impulse that generate the latter may, if properly directed, bring forth the former. Buber found support for his opinion in Jewish sources. Human passion, he maintained, leads to sin only when it is not directed in a godly path. The *Yetzer Hara* (evil inclination) is merely "the elemental force which is the sole origin of the great human works, the holy included."[20] According to tradition, the phrase "that it was very good" (*Gen.* 1:31) is regarded as referring to the evil inclination. The injunction "and thou shalt love the Lord thy God with all thine heart and all thy soul" (*Deut.* 6:5) is explained by the rabbis as referring to the two inclinations, the evil and the good. It is man, not God, that has made evil the so-called evil inclination.

There is yet great corruption in the world; moreover, there has been no full redemption at any time or anywhere. For this reason, the Jew cannot accept the Christian idea that the Messiah has come. Then, too, there is no limit to holiness. The Biblical Korah was satisfied with the level of his people's sanctity and was, therefore, "extirpated" from his people (*Nu.* 16:33). All peoples must strive for divinity and cooperate in a joint effort to redeem the world and establish the Kingdom of Heaven, the symbol of the fulfillment of God's justice on earth. Though in actuality the attainment of this goal is hardly more than a Utopian vision "for the end of days" (*Is.* 2:2), man must remain committed to it and strive to attain it.

God and the Torah

Man, according to Buber, was created for the purpose of communicating with God. God entered the world because of man. The great contribution of the Hebrew religion is not the idea of monotheism but rather that "the real God is the God Who can be spoken to because He is the One Who speaks to man,"[21] but Jews are not the only people that carry on a dialogue with God— they have merely concentrated on it most. The vast religious literature they produced evidenced the extent to which they carried on the dialogue. The role of the Jews in it, moreover, is one of activism. This implies not only that the Jew feels free to engage in it; his is the task to initiate it, though he cannot complete it. This activism is characteristic of Judaism, in which deeds, not faith, are the decisive factor.

Buber regards the Hebrew Scriptures as the record of the dialogue between God and Israel in the course of history. In the

Bible, God is always the *I* Who reveals Himself not in His essence but in His relation to man. Man is the *Thou* whom God addresses, as is evidenced by the fact that the pronoun *thou* is the key word in the Decalogue. The Torah is neither literally infallible truth nor mere folk literature; it is both human and divine. It is actually one work, in the sense that one common central theme—the confrontation of a people with its God—unites all its diverse elements and components. The miracles in the Bible simply reflect the wonder of the Israelites at fateful episodes intervening in their history.

The Torah, as Buber saw it, is not to be observed as a distinctive, binding body of law, unless one believes it to be divinely ordained in the fundamentalist sense. The term Torah means instruction and refers essentially to God's instruction, direction, or information. It is erroneous to render it as "law" as does the Greek original of the New Testament. The Hebrew noun *Moreh* connotes teacher (*Job* 36:22; *Is.* 30:20) and Torah is the ever fresh, vital, living word or teaching of God in His constant dialogue with man.[22]

This view of Torah, Buber conceded, involves a risk, but it is the risk of all who search for God. It is simpler, of course, to find shelter behind the law, but this is not the way of those who seek after truth.

Buber failed to recognize that Judaism is essentially a system of precepts, both ethical and ritual, embodied in law. He explained that the observance of Torah as law signifies a belief in a one-time revelation in the past rather than in the God of the dialogue Who speaks His Word dynamically to each of us out of the present. Buber rejected the objectification and freezing of Torah. Yet he criticized Paul for his view that since the difficulty of full observance of the law leads to frustration, the law may be abrogated[23] and replaced with a dogmatic faith. Buber differed from Paul on the grounds for casting aside the Torah as law, but the effect of the two views is very much the same.

God of Paul and of Judaism

Paul, reared in a Hellenistically dominated milieu, envisaged a dualism of faith and law, grace and works. This gave rise to a dichotomy in which the principle of God's judgment is separated from the idea of His redemption; the first having presumably been visited upon the people before the crucifixion and resurrection, while the second followed it. This view contradicts the doctrine of God's love expounded by Jeremiah (*Jer.* 31:3) and other prophets. Paul, accordingly, created two dominions and two gods in the world, an "unrestricted rule of wrath" and "a sphere of reconciliation." Buber, the Jew, of course could not countenance such a dualism, for to him "God is One and His Name is One" (*Zech.* 14:9).

Jewish religiosity is based on the Biblical idea of *Emunah*[24] (faith)which alludes to man's faithfulness and trust in his relationship with God, Buber explains. The concept of *Emunah* also means, he points out, that one who maintains a dialogue with the Divine Being can rely on a recurrent and renewed revelation for his guidance in the human enterprise, and does not need to abide by the vestiges of an ancient Scriptural code. Dependence on a rigid law is further objectionable to Buber, since it relieves one of the responsibility for making a moral choice, which admittedly involves a "holy insecurity" or uncertainty. Such conformity, Buber stresses, implies an acceptance of the Greek doctrine of *pistis* or belief in the immutability and permanent validity of the law rather than the Hebrew idea of *Emunah*.

This kind of outlook, too, Buber warns is bound to interrupt the immediate and direct bond of communion of man with God. He quotes Rabbi Mendel of Kotsk, a prominent Hassidic teacher who has appositely said one must not make an idol of even a precept. The truly pious Jew, Buber declared, will rely on the spirit of Jewish tradition to point the way to new Jewish legislation and doctrine, which a creative Jewry will evolve in its natural environment, on its own soil, in consonance with the needs of the times. Buber's position on this question offended the Orthodox segment of Jewry, who challenged it as antinomian, destructive of Jewish law, and a rebellion against the divine Torah.

Jesus and Judaism

Buber was also criticized severely for his pro-Christian leanings. He saw Jesus as an outstanding figure in Jewish history, though he differed from the Christian viewpoint in a number of vital respects. Buber declared:[25]

> I firmly believe that the Jewish community, in the course of its renaissance, will recognize Jesus; and not merely as a great figure in its religious history, but also in the organic context of a Messianic development extending over millenia, whose final goal is the Redemption of Israel and of the world. But I believe equally firmly that we will never recognize Jesus as the Messiah Come, for this would contradict the deepest meaning of our Messianic Passion . . . In our view, redemption occurs forever, and none has yet occurred. Standing, bound and shackled, in the pillory of mankind, we demonstrate with the bloody body of our people, the unredeemedness of the world. For us there is no cause of Jesus; only the cause of God exists for us.

Though an admirer of the great ethical personality of Jesus, Buber could not accept him as the Messiah. The Messiah is portrayed as a "hidden quiver" (*Is.* 49:2) which is, Buber thinks, what Jesus should have remained. It appeared to Buber, however, that shortly before the crucifixion, Jesus developed a "Messianic consciousness" which he imparted to his disciples. Had he remained a "hidden quiver," he might have been included among the Servants of the Lord (*Is.* 53), the Hebrew prophets, Buber suggests. As a Messianic figure, he was challenged by the Jews, Buber observes, and soon became for them the first of a number of false Messiahs. Actually, Buber indicates, Jesus had much in common with the prophets; like them, he subordinated ritual and ceremony to ethical precepts. Unlike Paul, however, Buber notes, Jesus upheld the law, declaring that "not one jot or tittle shall in any wise pass from the Law, till all be fulfilled" (*Matt.* 5:18).

Just as the Deity reveals Himself to man, He sometimes hides from him (*Is.* 45:15), as is evidenced by the tragic plaint of Job and the anguished cry of the Psalmists; yet God hides only to reveal Himself in another manner. But He does not take on any specific form, as depicted in the Christian doctrine of Incarnation. It is true that Paul and John, not Jesus, propounded this idea, which also injected an intermediary between God and man, and made of Jesus the only "door of salvation" (*John* 10:9). These notions in themselves negate fundamental principles in Judaism; they represent, moreover, a shift from the Hebraic concept of *Emunah*, or trust in a direct relationship with the One and Only, to the Greek *pistis,* or the inherent faith in the truth of a proposition.[26]

The God of the Bible is described as imageless (*Deut.* 4:12). This, however, did not deter Buber from expressing his conception of God as the Absolute Person, to represent the encounter with Him as a loving Father. This is the relationship of the Hassid towards the Deity. In characterizing God in this manner, Buber was concerned not with the spiritual God of Judaism, but rather with the attitude envisaged in the eternal *Thou* or the divine *I* of his *I-Thou* dialogue.

> . . . one may understand the personality of God as His act—it is, indeed, even permissible for the believer to believe that God became a person for love of Him, because in our human mode of existence the only reciprocal relation with us that exists is a personal one.[27] . . .

Buber used the anthropomorphic idiom—a symbol of the reality that man could comprehend. Yet even as such, it represents a paradox, for this term represents a limiting concept, while God suggests the idea of the Infinite. In respect to the question of the essence of God or similar theological problems, Buber "stands on the narrow ridge of uncertainty." In fact, these issues have no place in his religious existentialist outlook.

The Ideal Community

The Jewish people, Buber believes, has been chosen as the special instrument of God's redemption: an obligation and a burden, not a privilege. The Jews are particularly qualified to build the true society because they are endowed with a perspective of time and history,[28] rather than space, as may be observed from the fact that Jews excel in music and not the plastic arts. They have given rise to the Messianic conception, which evidences an historical goal of social advancement. In evolving the Utopian society, righteous means must be employed. This is the reason, according to one *Tzaddik,* for the repetition of the word "justice" in the verse, "Justice, Justice shalt thou pursue" (*Deut.* 16:20)—one mention signifies the means; the other, the end. One who uses evil to produce the good is bound to destroy the good in the process. The doctrine of justice must apply to individuals as well as nations. Buber insisted also that the Jewish majority in the Jewish homeland should conduct itself in accordance with the principles of the prophetic ethics. They must live with the Arabs, not only next to them.

The ideal community is to be made up of those who can truly say "thou" to each other; for only such individuals "are capable of truly saying 'we' with one another." The genuine society consists of free men, each retaining his identity and selfhood. Such a group must not become a mass, a totalism that swallows up the individual, leaving him a mere abstraction. The proper balance must be struck between individualism and collectivism. "Individualism in the sense of isolation is bad, because it sees man only in relation to himself" Buber said, "but collectivism does not see man at all."

Buber's social ideal was therefore the small community, in which a man's individuality can be asserted. Israel has been effective in implementing this ideal in the *Kibbutz* (collective village) organization that it has fostered in its homeland. In these settlements the *I-Thou* relation has not degenerated into the *I-It.* Israel may, therefore, yet serve as a model to other peoples in this regard. In fact, it is aiding other states, through its Afro-Asian program, to create a social structure based on economic justice, in which the *I-Thou* values will be fostered. In view of its geographic location on the crossroads between East and West, the Jewish state may be in a position to influence both regions in this manner, and thus further the development of the overall world community.

Buber's Influence

Buber rendered a vital service to Western Jewry in unlocking for it the great spiritual treasures of Hassidism: its lore, its principles, and its aesthetic appeal. His Hassidic writings are impressive, both because of their content and their magnificent style. They did much to bolster the respect of Western Jews for the spiritual life and values of their downtrodden and unprogressive East European brethren. In consequence, the feeling of religious and cultural propinquity between these two sections of Jewry was strengthened.

In Germany, Buber exercised a profound impact on his generation through his books and numerous writings. He influenced many Jewish men of letters including Arnold Zweig, Max Brod, and Franz Rosenzweig, and he contributed to the regeneration of an interest in Judaism among them. His popularity, however, was far greater in Central Europe than elsewhere. Buber's prestige in America has risen in the last decade and a half, owing to the translation of an increasing number of his works into English. However, in view partly of the organization and institutionalization of Jewish life and religious viewpoints in the United States, his outlook on religion as a personal relationship has not taken root. Because he was not observant in the traditional sense and was charged with "flirting" with Christianity, and because he idealized Hassidim and prophetic Judaism and subordinated the Halacha, Orthodox Jews have generally opposed his philosophy. In Israel, where he lived for over a quarter of a century, he was isolated from the main currents of his country's spiritual life, for he was neither a religionist in the conventional sense, nor a secularist. Buber's concept of religious life as a dialogue relation gained him many followers among outstanding Christian Protestant leaders, notably Karl Barth, Nicholas Berdyaev, Emil Brunner, Rheinhold Niebuhr, and Paul Tillich. Paul Tillich (1886-1965) once expressed the hope that Buber's existentialist *I-Thou* philosophy could be a powerful stimulus in reversing the victory of the *It* over the *Thou* and the *I* in present-day civilization. Buber's leading Catholic disciples included Gabriel Marcel, Theodore Steinbuchel, Ernest Michael, and Karl Thieme.

It is significant that among the few papers found in the wreckage of the plane in which the late Dag Hammarskjold, Secretary General of the United Nations, met his death, there was a copy of Buber's *I and Thou,* and a number of scattered pages of Hammarskjold's Swedish translation of that work. The Secretary General had visited Buber and read his works and had been inspired by him. What Buber and Hammarskjold had in common was the aspiration for an ennobled humanity in which the *Shechinah* shall dwell. Through Buber, the doctrines and principles emanating from Hassidic and other Jewish sources have reached out beyond the Jewish group into the Christian world. His impact on religious thought was such that no liberal religious thinker could venture to overlook his approach and his teachings. Buber envisaged God not as a force or power but as a living reality who encounters man in every experience of life, and instructs him in the ways of love and justice towards his fellow.

7

The Struggle for Reform Judaism in Germany

I. The Early Stage

David Friedlander

THE LENGTHS to which an exaggerated rationalism in religion may lead is illustrated by an incident involving Mendelssohn's wealthy disciple, David Friedlander (1765-1834).[1] Friedlander, a deist, had little regard for the customs and rituals of Judaism. Like so many rationalists, he was concerned only with its ethical principles. Towards the end of the century, Friedlander apparently became convinced that the prospects for civil emancipation for German Jewry were dim and distant. Though he had himself deplored the stampede of Jews to the baptismal font, he nevertheless proposed a novel plan whereby he hoped to acquire civil rights for Jews on the basis of a partial conversion.

In 1799, Friedlander wrote to Pastor Teller, Counsellor of the Prussian Ministry of Religion, on behalf of several Jewish householders, offering to join the Lutheran Church on condition that they would not be required to subscribe to certain Christian theological dogmas, such as the Trinity or the divinity of Jesus, which they regarded as contrary to reason. They did not mind, they said, going through the rite of baptism, as "an outward and visible sign of an inward and spiritual grace," but only as a symbol, not as a sacrament. Since they had rejected the rituals of Judaism, the religious gap between them and Christianity was so narrow that they felt they could bridge it easily.

Naturally, the clergyman rejected the proposal for a "dry baptism," as many facetiously termed it.[2] His answer to Friedlander was polite, though stinging. Those Jews who had purged their Judaism of its ceremonial precepts, he indicated, had already come close to the teachings of Christ, who had come down to earth to redeem all mankind. For his own part, he wrote, he would perhaps be ready to accept the prospective Jewish converts into the church without insisting on complete compliance with all the dogmas and beliefs of Christianity. However, he observed, he did not know whether that would be sufficient for the government to grant them political enfranchisement. With this innuendo, Pastor Teller scorned Friedlander's motives for apostasy. He also indicated that with conditions as they were, Friedlander and his group would do best to remain Jews and, as such, influence their coreligionists to emulate their example and cast off the yoke of the Jewish observances.[3]

Rejected by the Lutheran Church, Friedlander set himself to the task of revamping Judaism, so that it would not be a barrier to Emancipation. He urged that the references to Zion be deleted from the liturgy, to avoid their being used as a pretext for impugning the patriotism of the Jew. He also advocated the use of German instead of Hebrew in the synagogue service, as a means of modernizing it. Friedlander was thus a forerunner of the Reform movement.

Israel Jacobson

The father of the Reform movement in Germany was Israel Jacobson (1768-1828), a rich Jewish philanthropist who, in 1801, started a modest boarding school in Seesen, a townlet near the Harz mountains. The school was nonsectarian and liberal for its times. It offered a combined program of religious and vocational training, in which agriculture occupied an important place. The general subjects were taught by Christians, while Jewish teachers expounded the Hebraic content. As an adjunct to the school, Jacobson maintained a small private synagogue in which he believed he could alter the worship with less difficulty than in a regular community synagogue. He called it a "temple" to distinguish it from the traditional synagogue.

Jacobson instituted several reforms in the temple service of a pragmatic nature, and not on the basis of any set theory or policy. He abbreviated the Sabbath ritual at the Seesen Temple and inaugurated hymns and choral singing in German, for the purpose of enriching the worship aesthetically. He also included a regular sermon, delivered in German, as a part of the service. This in itself was an innovation.[4] In 1808, Jacobson erected a synagogue at Seesen at his own expense and installed an organ in the new edifice. The traditional male choir was replaced by a mixed one— another radical digression from the prevailing custom and practice.

A year earlier, in 1807, Napoleon Bonaparte had placed his brother Jerome on the throne of the new kingdom he had carved out for him in Westphalia. Jacobson, who became financial advisor to Jerome, was appointed president of the consistory[5] that was established in Westphalia on the French pattern. The consistory soon opened a school in Cassel, which Jacobson modelled after the one in Seesen. There, in 1810, Jacobson initiated the first confirmation exercises ever to be held in a synagogue. Five boys were confirmed in that first ceremony, which was conducted immediately after the Scriptural reading on a Sabbath. The confirmands had previously been subjected to a public examination on the principles and doctrines of Judaism, which was referred to as a catechism. This term, borrowed from the church, implied that Judaism, like Christianity, was based essentially on a creed. The confirmation ceremony itself was patterned after the Protestant rite of the same name—it had neither precedent nor roots in Judaism. This reform produced a storm of protest in the ranks of Orthodoxy, and Jacobson had to resort to the authority of the state to silence opposition. But his power was shortlived, for in 1813, with the defeat of Napoleon, the Kingdom of Westphalia collapsed, and Jacobson went back to Prussia.

The Berlin Temple

Jacobson then moved to Berlin, where he ventured to open an adult synagogue along the new lines in his home. Soon several other laymen did likewise. Among them was Jacob Beer, father of the composer Meyerbeer. In 1817, however, influential Orthodox elements persuaded the authorities to close the new synagogues under a law enacted in 1750, which prohibited Jews from worshipping outside their regularly established community synagogue. The King is said to have declared that he was opposed to any improvements in the service, because a modernized worship might check the stream of Jews flocking to the church. It seems, however, that what the Prussian government really feared was that religious reforms might open the door for political change.

Before long, however, the private temples in Berlin were permitted to reopen temporarily, while the principal synagogue was being repaired and enlarged to accommodate the expanding community. This, however, gave rise to the question as to whether or not satisfactory provision would be made for the Reform group in the rebuilt community synagogue. The Prussian government settled the problem in its own way; on December 9, 1823, the King issued an order providing that the "religious services of the Jews must be conducted in accordance with the traditional ritual, without any modification in language, ceremonials, prayers or hymns."[6] This ended the Reform service in Berlin for two decades. The Orthodox had ostensibly triumphed—but their victory was a Pyrrhic one. The numerous conversions among Jewish youth in the ensuing period may be charged in some measure to the closing of the temples which had exercised a restraining influence.

The Hamburg Temple

One of the preachers at Beer's closed temple, Edward Kley, left Berlin in 1817 for the more liberal climate of Hamburg, where he accepted a position as director of the newly founded Hebrew *Freischule* (free school) in that city. Kley soon succeeded in recruiting a number of influential Jews to help him in establishing a temple locally. The Hamburg Temple, dedicated in 1818, introduced still more liberal practices than its predecessors had in Berlin. One of the most important innovations of the Hamburg congregation was to recast the prayers for the Jewish national restoration in universal terms, so as to refer to a general redemption for all mankind rather than to the redemption of Israel alone. The traditional petition for the coming of the Messiah to lead the return back to Zion was replaced by a prayer for an era of justice and brotherhood for all humanity. Another modification involved the reading of the weekly Torah portion in the Sephardic rather than the Ashkenazic pronunciation.

By 1822, the Hamburg Temple had established confirmation exercises as part of the regular synagogue service. Originally, Jacobson's school at Cassel had limited the ceremony to boys; but the Berlin private temples had extended this ceremony to girls as well. Before long, the confirmation exercises spread among the Reform temples. They were held by common consent on *Shavuot* (the Feast of Weeks), which is associated with the giving of the Ten Commandments at Sinai. Unlike the *Bar Mitzvah* which was conducted as an individual rite for a boy who attained the age of thirteen, the confirmation exercises were performed as a group ritual for both sexes, climaxing the religious education of the confirmands.

The changes introduced in the Hamburg Temple represented a significant break with tradition. The Orthodox rabbis could not condone what they regarded as flagrant violations of religious custom, nor could they see sufficient justification for revising or omitting prayers that had expressed the hopes and yearnings of their people for seventeen centuries. On their part, the Reformers contended that their action was primarily a matter of intellectual honesty. How could they pray sincerely for the restoration of Zion when they regarded Germany as their Fatherland? It seems, however, that more than consistency was at stake; the Reformers were no doubt actuated by the fear that the Jews' "outmoded" nationalistic prayers would distinguish them more sharply from their non-Jewish neighbors, and prejudice their case in their struggle for Emancipation and equal political rights.

The opposition to the reforms of the Hamburg Temple was led by Isaac Bernays (1792-1849), the erudite rabbi of the Orthodox congregation in that city. Bernays combined profound Jewish with secular learning[7] and took the initiative in expanding the secular instruction in the local Talmud Torah, the Jewish community school. He vehemently opposed the actions of the Reformers who, curiously enough, sought sanction in the Talmud for the changes they advocated. Although they did not as yet venture to omit completely, but only to modify, the prayers for the coming of the Messiah and the Jewish national restoration, Bernays felt obliged to place the Hamburg Reform prayer book under ban, when its second edition appeared.

II. THE RELIGIOUS FERMENT

The Polemic Literature

WHILE THE CONFLICT between the Orthodox and Reform factions was raging in Hamburg, Israel Jacobson, in Berlin, together with several friends, engaged Eliezer Liebermann, a Talmudic scholar, to solicit the sanctions of European rabbis for the changes instituted in the worship in Reform temples. Liebermann, the scion of a rabbinical family, was well-rounded in his Jewish knowledge. In 1818, shortly before the Hamburg Temple was dedicated, he published a small volume entitled *Nogah Hatzedek*[8] (*Light of Righteousness*), consisting of the *responsa* of four rabbis who had approved the changes adopted by the Reform temples. Two of them, Shem Tov of Leghorn and Jacob Hai Recanati, Italian rabbis, were men of small fame, though the latter was head of the Rabbinical Collegium of Verona. They maintained that instrumental music in the service on the Sabbath was entirely proper, since it was used for a sacred purpose. The third, Moses Kunitzer, a pious Hungarian rabbi in Ofen and *dayyan* in Budapest, shocked the traditionalists by defending the use of the organ in worship on the ground that it could attract many to the synagogue who had drifted away from it. He sanctioned the introduction of the Sephardic pronunciation in the service, and also the addition of prayers in the vernacular. The last, Aaron Chorin of Arad, Hungary, a veteran rabbi of liberal tendencies, declared in his *Kinaat Haemet* (*Zeal for Truth*) that the Talmud distinctly permits the recitation of prayers in any language, since worship requires concentration which is possible only in a tongue one understands. In support of his opinion, he quoted the well-known dictum, "The Shema may be read in any language that one understands" (*Ber.* 13a). Chorin appears to have been of weak moral fiber, since he retracted his statement because of the pressure of Orthodox colleagues and congregants; but later, towards the end of his life, when the pressure was relaxed, he reaffirmed his earlier position.

Liebermann's Appeal

To the rabbinic responsa in his *Nogah Hatzedek* Liebermann appended his own plea on behalf of Reform. He pointed to the lack of decorum in the traditional synagogue and proposed that it could be improved by enhancing the aesthetic tone of the services. The Reformers of the day were justified in this criticism. For centuries Jews had been accustomed to assemble in their houses of worship not only for prayer and study, but also for the discussion of community affairs. The informality that prevailed at the latter gatherings was carried over into their worship. The Reformers also found fault with what they described as "oriental" customs and procedures, lacking dignity and reverence.

In his work, Liebermann cited a number of rabbinic rulings in support of his contention that prayers in German were permissible, among them the statement in the *Shulchan Aruch* to the effect that "one may pray in any language he wishes" (*Orah Hayim* 101:4). He based his fervent appeal for the introduction of German hymns and prayers on a curious argument. German, he explained, is a suitable medium for worship, since it is a "pure" tongue possessing a grammar and syntax, and in this regard differs from the degraded Yiddish jargon spoken by East European Jews, who must, therefore, pray in Hebrew.

To bolster his contention, he also resorted to a distortion of the facts of Jewish history, charging that Jews had been oppressed throughout the ages because of their bizarre practices and obscurantism. Their sufferings could have been avoided, Liebermann maintained, if they had not excluded secular learning and culture from their educational programs and had demonstrated greater loyalty to their sovereigns and greater devotion to the countries in which they lived.

These claims were patently untrue for, as is commonly known, the Jews in the Middle Ages had been persecuted for no other reason except their loyalty to their religion. They had been cast out and excluded from European society not because they chose to be isolated, but because of the hostility of the Christian world, engendered by their refusal to surrender their ancestral faith. Moreover, when given the opportunity, the Jews had never failed to serve their sovereigns faithfully. The services rendered by Jews to the governments of Christian and Moslem Spain attest to this fact. Wherever Jews lived in the Diaspora, they heeded the advice of the prophet Jeremiah: "Seek the peace of the city whither I have caused you to be carried away captive, and pray unto the Lord for it, for in the peace thereof ye shall have peace" (*Jer.* 29: 7). What Liebermann did was to turn the victim into a culprit, and in so doing he exposed his own insincerity.[9]

Anti-Reform Responsa

Liebermann's contentions in his *Nogah Hatzedek* evoked angry replies from the Orthodox camp. In 1819, a year after the publication of that volume, the Orthodox rabbinate in Hamburg published its *Eleh Divrei Habrit* (*These Are the Words of the Covenant*),[10] a collection of twenty-two *responsa*, including several from leading rabbis outside Germany. Most of these *responsa* had been assembled by the venerable Rabbi Abraham Eliezer Halevi of Trieste, on behalf of a group of Orthodox rabbis in Germany. These opinions, condemning the Hamburg reforms, were published in the original Hebrew with a German translation, printed in Hebrew letters, appended to the volume. One of the writers, a prominent sage, Rabbi Akiva Eger of Posen (1761-1837), held that the sanction to pray in any language applied to private or incidental prayers, but not to formal public worship. His son-in-law, the celebrated Rabbi Moshe Sofer (Schreiber)[11] of Pressburg (1763-1839), insisted that after the destruction of the Temple the prohibition of the rabbis interdicting music in the service could not be rescinded by a later authority, unless it was "greater in wisdom or number" than the earlier one which had set up these restrictions. For the same reason, he disapproved of even minor departures from tradition, among them, the reading of the Scriptural portion in the synagogue without cantillation. Another prominent rabbi, Mordecai Benet (Banet) of Nikolsburg, Moravia, insisted that a Jew should pray only in Hebrew because the letters of the Hebrew prayers contain occult allusions which could not be transmitted in any other language. These scholars appear to have been much more concerned with prayer as a matter of rote performance than as "a service of the heart."

The anti-Reform *responsa* regrettably missed the historical issues at the crux of the controversy; instead they offered pedantic legal- isms and casuistry, taking scarcely any account of the crucial cul- tural and spiritual problems behind the attitude of the Reformers. Neither the great Rabbi Eger nor any of the champions of the traditionalist view raised important objections to the changes instituted by the Reformers; they rarely mentioned for example, that the use of the vernacular or the organ in the service was likely to give the synagogue the air of a church. The narrow formalism of the Orthodox rabbis is evidenced in Benet's criticism of his adversary for supporting his conclusions with logic rather than with Talmudic citations. The same rabbi mentioned only incidentally the consequence of abandoning tradition: the danger that the Reform group might, if it carried its tendencies far enough, cut itself off from the main body of Israel and become merely a dissenting sect. The opponents of Reform also resorted to virulent and vitriolic invective and name calling instead of ad- vancing rational arguments; in their polemic literature, they de- scribed the liberals as "infidels," "wicked," "rascals," "traitors," "mixed multitude" (*Ex.* 13:38), "neither Jews nor Christians," "destroyers of God's vineyard," and worse. These tactics, of course, generated much heat but little light.

The Reformers, too, were not without blemish in their logic; for example, they supported their views with quotations from the Talmud, a work which they often repudiated. The champions of Reform also refuted the attacks of the Orthodox. In his *Brit Emet,* (*Covenant of Truth*), published under a fictitious name, David Caro, an educator, advocated that a rabbi should acquire ade- quate secular knowledge as a qualification for office; moreover, he should teach human tolerance and endeavor to adjust the reli- gious practices of his congregation to the cultural environment of the day. One of the founders of the Hamburg Temple, Mayer

Israel Breslau, published anonymously a biting satire against the Orthodox, written in a beautiful and terse Hebrew style, which he called the *Herev Nokemet Nkam Brit*,[12] (*The Sword Avenging the Vengeance of the Covenant*).

The clash became more bitter as other pamphleteers entered the fray. In 1819, soon after Liebermann's *Nogah Hatzedek* appeared, Nachman Berliner of Lissa printed a leaflet followed by a voluminous work entitled *Et l'daber* (*Time to Speak*)[13] in which he deprecated the "venom" in Liebermann's writings and warned that the inner religious revolt among the Jews might spread to non-Jews and, in consequence, become a cause of social unrest in the world. Berliner concluded that it was therefore necessary to suppress Liebermann's *Nogah Hatzedek* and ban its author. Rabbi Jacob of Lissa, and others went even further, urging that the Reformers be treated as a subversive element.

Government Intervention

It was this kind of reasoning that impelled the Orthodox to take the deplorable step of instigating the government to outlaw the Reform temples. Naturally, the government was far less concerned with the merits of the dispute and the welfare of the Jewish community than with its own interests. In Hamburg, the government refused to intervene in the conflict, and as a result the Hamburg Temple was not troubled for several decades. In the Duchy of Westphalia, too, the government declined to take sides in the controversy, but in Berlin, as we have seen, the King of Prussia interceded.

The Reform group also sought the government's intercession at times. In 1833, the district rabbi of Saxe Weimar, Dr. Mendel Hess, an ardent Reformer, went to the civil authorities and secured the issuance of a *Judenordnung* which imposed a series of drastic reforms on the Jewish community. It included an order that virtually the entire synagogue service was to be conducted in German, and that the *Kol Nidre*[14] and several other prayers were to be eliminated. The opposition to this regulation was so strong that its enforcement had to be delayed for several years.

The polemical literature produced during this early period in the clash between the two camps in German Judaism dealt with changes in the externals of worship. It was generally published in Hebrew, since it was intended for circulation primarily among rabbis and Hebrew scholars. The dispute thus helped to stimulate Hebrew writing and style. It is ironic that a movement concerned with minimizing Hebrew should have contributed to its revival.

Growth of Reform

During the first half century after Mendelssohn's death (1786) until well into the 1830's, the initiative in the Reform movement was taken by laymen who introduced revisions into the synagogue service on a pragmatic rather than on a philosophic basis.[15] These changes in liturgy and in worship gradually spread from Berlin and Hamburg to other cities. In 1820, a branch of the Hamburg Temple was opened in Leipzig for the purpose of demonstrating the Reform service to the hundreds of Jewish visitors who came to the famous Leipzig Fair, in the hope that they would bring the innovations back to their home communities. From Germany, the movement spread to Denmark where, as early as 1814, confirmation exercises were introduced into the synagogue at the behest of the civil authorities. A program of revision in worship, adopted by the Reform congregation in Vienna in 1826, served as a model for others in Bohemia, Hungary, and elsewhere. Even in far-off America, a brief experiment in Reform was attempted by a group of dissenters of congregation Beth Elohim in Charleston, South Carolina, in 1824.

But while the Reform movement in its early decades was growing in size and influence, it did not seriously undertake to formulate an ideology. The earlier Reformers, who, as we have seen, were mostly laymen, did not possess sufficient Jewish learning to venture to establish a theoretical foundation for their programs. They could not enter into polemics themselves and depended on the few rabbis who shared their viewpoint to do so on their behalf. But around the 1840's, a new type of rabbi came to the fore who took over the initiative from the lay leaders. These rabbis were at home in both Jewish and secular learning; they were consequently more secure in what they were doing than the laymen, and they proceeded to adopt bolder reforms. In their approach to

Jewish doctrine and practice, they often assumed the critical attitude fostered by the new movement for *Juedische Wissenschaft* (the Science of Judaism). Abraham Geiger (1810-1874), a pioneer of the movement and Samuel Hirsch (1815-1889), both rabbis, who were influenced by Hegel, became the ideologists of Reform Judaism.

III. THE LATER STAGE

Hegelian Thought

THE IDEOLOGY of Reform Judaism is grounded in the idealistic philosophy fostered in Germany mainly by Immanuel Kant, Friedrich von Schelling (1775-1854) and George Wilhelm Friedrich Hegel (1770-1831). The key to Hegel's doctrine lies in the term *evolution*. According to Hegel, all existence is an integral part of a single unity or whole—the objective or Absolute Mind—which is itself in a perpetual flux and in a continuous process of unfolding, resulting from an inner drive to achieve self-realization. Thus, the Absolute, or God, is in itself a potentiality. The same is true of man, who is only a small miniature of this principle of Unity or the Absolute Idea in the Universe. Human history, ethics, laws, religion, and social institutions are simply aspects of this process of development. The tendency towards constant evolution may be explained by analogy with the acorn, which has as its major purpose its eventual growth into an oak. The highest manifestation of the Absolute Idea or Spirit is to be found in art, philosophy, and religion.

Hegel pursued his thinking to the point where it took on a deterministic aspect. He suggested that the Idea, *i.e.*, God, at times exploits the passions of men for the accomplishment of its ultimate ends. Thus, it would seem that "world history is world justice." If this is true, then wars have to be accounted as just. In fact, all occurrences in history are merely to be regarded as steps in the unfolding and self-realization of the Absolute Spirit. A prominent idealistic philosopher, Francis H. Bradley (1846-1924) expressed the same principle when he said, "This is the best possible world, and everything in it is a necessary evil," meaning that the state of the world, its good and evil, is merely a passing stage towards further progress. Such a theory clashes, of course, with the ethical doctrines of Kant and the moral tenets of humanity in general. Unlike Kant, Hegel believed that we could know the world only through our mental processes. Accordingly, there is no reality beyond what we can perceive with our senses, and no meaning in the unknowable "things in themselves." We grasp what is true by means of immediate experience, through the insights and concepts we develop. Our reason, therefore, can penetrate all phases of human culture, including religion.

Hegel developed a dialectic which he maintained explained the development of ideas from lower to higher forms. Every *thesis,* that is, every attempt to formulate a concept about the universe is carried to a degree where it becomes untrue. The doctrines of democracy, for example, may be stretched to a point of anarchy. The thesis, will thus give rise to an *antithesis,* or a contradictory hypothesis. Out of the original thesis and antithesis, a new *synthesis* will result which will incorporate the essential truths in both. The latter synthesis is on a higher plane of reality and is accordingly different from each of the component theses. As this process is continued, it is bound to culminate in a final, perfect, or complete synthesis—the one all-embracing truth, the foundation of all reality. The end of the struggle of the Absolute for self-realization is reached in a full comprehension of the universe. This theory of the evolution of ideas influenced the thinking of the leading Reform ideologists and other Jewish thinkers as well. The most prominent among the latter was Nachman Krochmal (1785-1840), a founder of the *Juedische Wissenschaft* movement, who adopted some of Hegel's ideas.

Nachman Krochmal

Nachman Krochmal was born in 1785 in Brody, a flourishing city in northern Galicia. His father, a wealthy merchant, was an adherent of the Haskalah movement. Despite this, Nachman received the traditional Jewish education typical of the devout religious environment in which he lived. His parents paid an annual fine as the alternative to sending Nachman to a secular school. They did so probably in deference to the sentiments of pietist neighbors. As was customary at the time, young Krochmal married at the age of fourteen. He lived at the home of his father-in-law in Zolkiew, and while there, acquired a secular education, with the aid of friends and tutors. He spent a number of years studying German, French, Latin, Syriac, mathematics, and natural science; he managed, too, to delve into philosophy, which he believed to be the foundation of all knowledge. During this period, he also mastered Maimonides' *Guide for the Perplexed.*

After ten years of strenuous application to his studies, Krochmal became seriously ill as a result of overwork and went to Lemberg for medical treatment. He spent many months there in a long convalescence. A number of young people, attracted by his fame and scholarship, formed a circle of disciples about him, and Krochmal, in the peripatetic manner of a Socrates, discussed various aspects of philosophy and culture while promenading with them in the fields. It was for people like these young scholars, troubled by the problem of harmonizing Judaism with contemporary thought, that Krochmal, in the last years of his life, wrote his only book, which he intended to call "Portal to a Purified Faith." This volume was left unfinished at his death; it was edited and published posthumously by his friend Leopold Zunz, under the title of *Guide for the Perplexed of the Time,* for it attempted to do what the great Maimonides had done in his own work. Both shared a common purpose; the reconciliation of reason and religion. Krochmal's work, written in Hebrew, turned out to be the most original Jewish philosophical treatise of the nineteenth century. It was the first attempt after Judah Halevi (1085-1140) to present a philosophy of Jewish history.

In the first part of his *Guide,* Krochmal enumerated the three forces that, in his opinion, threatened all true religion. The first is the religious fanaticism and formalism that lead to superstition and the belief in demons and evil spirits. The second danger is of an opposite nature—materialism and atheism, which may bring about a moral decline. The third is the mechanical adherence to precepts without peering into their inner meaning. The latter approach, which represents a middle path between extreme religiosity and rationalism, is not a solution, for it leads to compromise, not truth. To determine the genuine currents of faith, Krochmal indicated, it would be necessary to dig down to its wellsprings and trace its mainstream through various epochs. Once this is accomplished, Krochmal claimed, it might be possible to separate its essence from the excrescences and adhesions that had attached to it in the course of its existence. For this task, he felt a thoroughly critical historical approach was indispensable.

The Science of Judaism

Before Krochmal's time, scholars had little organized knowledge of post-Biblical Jewish history. They were accustomed to pore over rabbinic texts with the purpose of seeking out or ascertaining the settled Halacha (law) with little concern for its evolution—its historical context or relationships. Krochmal, influenced by Hegel, thought that Judaism could be better understood as being the result of an evolutionary process, and advocated the use of the scientific historical method in Jewish studies. This assumption represented a radical departure from the earlier procedures in the exploration of Judaism, and gave rise to the so-called *Wissenschaft des Judentums,* the movement of the "Science of Judaism."

Krochmal maintained that the two major factions in Judaism in his day, the traditionalist and the liberal, suffered from the lack of an adequate sense of time, *i.e.,* the historic sense. The latter disdained the past and refused to reckon with it and its values, while the former rejected the present and the spirit of the age. Both alignments failed to see Judaism in the proper perspective as the product of the impact of ideas and events. Krochmal was convinced that the only way to discover the true foundations of Judaism was to ferret out from all available sources, non-Jewish as well as Jewish, the primary and related data that had a bearing on a given subject or theme. The cultural contacts of the Jewish people, the doctrines they borrowed from others, as well as those they cast aside, provided original material which could be useful to an investigator. This information could demonstrate not only how the Jewish people had survived past perplexities, but might also point to a pattern for survival in the new rationalistic age. This new method of historical inquiry influenced Krochmal's colleagues and disciples in his own generation as well as the later Jewish scholars down to our own day.

Krochmal's Interpretation of Judaism

In accordance with the divine plan, man is a social creature. This fact lies at the root of society and history. Society is organized into families, tribes, and nations. With Hegel, Krochmal maintained that the Absolute Spirit (using Hegel's term for the concept of God) demonstrated its social purpose and plan in the world, in the evolution and progress of peoples and nations. The Absolute Spirit has expressed itself in different forms in the various nationalities. Among the Greeks it became evident in art and philosophy; among the Romans, in law and government; and so with other nations. Israel's peculiar faculty was the search for the complete spirituality—its God. The different spiritual inclinations added to humanity's common spiritual reservoir. There need, therefore, be no rivalry or conflict among them.

The spiritual essence that represents the concept of the God of Israel differs from the deities or the highest ideals of the other peoples, in that the latter bear only a partial spirituality and include a degree of materialism. The Hebrew God is the embodiment of pure virtue and ethical perfection. The Jewish spirit is thus universal and incorporates the spirits of the other peoples to the extent of their spirituality. Thus, the all-embracing universal Jewish spirit encompasses the spirits of other nations in an harmonious unity.

Krochmal was influenced by the cyclical theory of growth and decline of nations expounded by Giovanni Battista Vico (1668-1744), the Italian philosopher and jurist who attempted to apply the scientific method to the study of history. According to Vico, there is a natural law in history to the effect that a nation, like a biological organism, passes through three major stages in its career: the early or formative period, an era of maturity, and ultimately disintegration and extinction. The permanent aspects of the national spirit of a people survive its physical decline and become a part of the heritage of others and eventually of mankind. The Jewish people, however, Vico intimated, have been able to avert this fate.

According to Krochmal, the Jewish people went through the three cycles in the course of its history. The first extended from Abraham to the end of the First Commonwealth (586 B.C.E.);

the second ranged from the Return (536 B.C·E.) to the defeat of Bar Kochba (132); and the third from Rabbi Judah Hanasi (ca. 200) to the expulsion from Spain (1492). But Israel is an exception to this principle of genesis and death in human history, for from its very inception as a people, it strove to attain the Absolute Spirit, the source of all ideals, which is all spirituality and therefore eternal. The Jewish people is impelled by a will to live, to lead mankind to the attainment of the Absolute. This has been Israel's goal through the ages, and it must survive in order to accomplish it.

Because of this affinity between Israel and its God, the Jewish group must now embark upon a new cycle in its history. The Emancipation, he implied, will usher in the new era of regeneration, rebirth, and florescence. This, it may be inferred, was Krochmal's unexpressed conclusion in his uncompleted *Guide*. His reinterpretation of Jewish history in these terms gave it a philosophy which influenced the religious and nationalistic currents in present-day Judaism.

Impact on Reform Judaism

The Reform movement borrowed a number of fundamental ideas from Krochmal's view of Jewish history, notwithstanding the fact that the philosopher himself was a traditionalist and observant Jew. Krochmal's suggestion that the Jewish people had been designated as "the teacher of the nations" is a cue to the doctrine of the Jewish mission of Reform Judaism. The Reformers arrived at this notion by overlooking Krochmal's particularistic conception of Judaism, with its stress on the role of the Jewish group. They highlighted only the humanistic phase of his doctrine, thereby adapting it to their own purposes.

The prospect of beginning a new epoch in Judaism appealed to the Reform theorists, and one of their foremost ideologists, Abraham Geiger, exploited this idea in his rationale for the movement. In the main, however, Krochmal did not answer the crucial question he posed: how to resolve faith and reason. In his analysis of Judaism, he seemed to say merely that it appeared pointless to exchange the eternal truths of Judaism for the passing fancies of modernism or the ephemeral ideals of another culture, particularly since Judaism has a vital spiritual goal for which to strive.

Abraham Geiger (1810-1874)

Abraham Geiger, an outstanding leader in the Jewish Science movement, was born to an Orthodox family in Frankfort in 1810. A child prodigy, young Abraham is said to have learned to read the Hebrew Bible at three, the Mishna at four, and the Gemara at six. He also received a good secular education and, in 1829, embarked on his studies in classical languages, history, and philosophy at Heidelberg. He resumed them at Bonn, where he met and developed a warm friendship with Samson Raphael Hirsch who later, as founder of Neo-Orthodoxy, became a bitter ideological opponent. In 1832, Geiger was awarded a university prize for a work entitled *What Mohammed Borrowed from Judaism;* he subsequently received his doctorate from the University of Marburg. Already in his first rabbinical post at Wiesbaden, which he occupied from 1832 to 1837, Geiger showed his inclination towards Reform in the changes in worship and decorum he instituted in the synagogue. The opposition of his congregants to choral singing and other minor reforms led him to resign his pulpit. In Wiesbaden, in 1835, he launched a scholarly periodical, the *Zeitschrift für Jüdische Theologie (Journal of Jewish Theology)*, which continued until 1839.

In 1838, Geiger was elected junior rabbi of Breslau. The senior rabbi, Solomon Tiktin, was a leading champion of Orthodoxy, who vigorously attacked his assistant because the latter had introduced a regular sermon, prayers in the vernacular, clerical robes, and other innovations in the service. Germany was then divided into many independent principalities, and Geiger, a native of Frankfort, was a foreigner in Prussia. In order to assume a rabbinical office in the Prussian city of Breslau, he had to be naturalized. Tiktin's supporters invoked the aid of the state authorities, who denied Geiger's application for naturalization. But Geiger successfully countered these objections and was naturalized some fifteen months later, whereupon he assumed his rabbinical duties.

The feud between the two rabbis continued. Two years later, Geiger took the offensive and sought Tiktin's removal by officials of the Jewish community and of the government. The community, supporting Geiger, suspended Tiktin, who proceeded to appeal to the Orthodox rabbinate in various countries to endorse his views. He published a work containing the opinions of numerous rabbis denouncing Reform. The· Breslau congregation, led by Geiger, issued a two-volume collection of statements by rabbis favoring Reform and upholding the right of a rabbi to freedom of thought. Finally, Tiktin's suspension was invalidated by the government,and he was restored to his post. But the conflict did not end then; it persisted even after Tiktin's death in 1843, when Geiger became the senior rabbi and Tiktin's son was designated as his assistant. Some six years later, the congregation was split, one group turning to Reform and the other to Orthodoxy, but they were reunited in 1856. The controversy in Breslau exemplified the prevailing hostility between the traditionalists and the Reformers.

Geiger was a leading figure at the conference of liberal rabbis convened in 1844, and the two subsequent years. He had been one of the foremost exponents of the idea of establishing a modern rabbinical seminary in Germany, and had in fact secured an endowment from one of his congregants for this purpose. However, much to his chagrin and disappointment, Geiger was not chosen to head the institution. A rabbi of a more moderate religious outlook, Zacharia Frankel, an opponent of Geiger, was appointed to that office. Not until 1872, did Geiger secure an academic post. That year, he was appointed director of the *Hochschule für die Wissenschaft des Judentums* (Institute of Higher Jewish Studies), a Reform rabbinical seminary that was then opened in Berlin. His academic career was, however, ended shortly afterwards, with his death in 1874.

Geiger was an outstanding and all-embracing Jewish scholar, a philologist and historian in one. His investigations, published in books and in hundreds of articles, covered practically the entire range of Jewish learning. He devoted a good deal of time to the study of medieval Hebrew literature and wrote a work on Maimonides and Ibn Gabirol. He also translated some of Judah Halevi's poetry into German. In 1862, he founded his Journal, the *Jüdische Zeitschrift für Wissenschaft und Leben* (Jewish Journal of

Life and Letters), which continued until his death in 1874. In his principal work, the *Urschrift und Übersetzungen der Bibel* (The *Original and Translations of the Bible*) published in 1857, Geiger sought to prove that the Biblical texts reflected the changed conceptions of Judaism of the periods in which they were written and similarly so with the Bible translations. In his essay on the Pharisees and Sadducees (1860), he demonstrated that the former party in Judaism, much maligned in the New Testament, was actually the progressive one, since it was opposed to the inflexible and stagnating attitude of the Sadducees towards the Bible. The results of Geiger's researches were vital contributions to Jewish historical knowledge.

Geiger's Analysis of Judaism

Geiger's thinking was influenced by Hegel and Krochmal, as were the views of the Reform theorists generally. He maintained that religion in its principles, ideas, and practices, like all human institutions, undergoes a process of development and change. The Jewish tradition, itself endowed with creative power, helps to shape the Judaism of a given age. The historical process of evolution is an ongoing one; any generation may deviate from the past and embark on a new era. Each age has the same right as every other, if not the duty, to forge a new link in the chain of creativity. The current generation is of greater, not lesser importance than its predecessor, because it must play a cardinal role in the further development of Judaism. If each age makes its contribution to the Jewish heritage, Judaism will grow to a higher level. Thus, while the rabbis of the Talmud venerated the past, declaring that "if the earlier authorities are like the sons of angels, we are like the sons of men" (*Sab.* 112b), Geiger and his school stressed the present.

The Jewish people, Geiger asserted, has a genius for religion. The Bible is the product of revelation, which to Geiger meant a subjective, momentary flash or enlightenment, not the manifestation of a supernatural phenomenon. Revelation is a one-time occurrence, the result of divine inspiration, the experience of an individual, while tradition is a continuous dynamic process in which the entire Jewish group is involved. The original source of Judaism is revelation, but revelation is preserved in the continuous tradition, which must keep it alive. Both together—the product of revelation coupled with tradition—constitute the Judaism of a given generation.

Geiger, like Krochmal, examined Jewish history in close detail and divided it into specific stages of cultural creativity. Geiger saw the first period, that of revelation, as evidencing the deep inner springs and the original sources of creativity out of which Judaism grew. This epoch ended with the completion of the Hebrew Scriptures. The second was the Talmudic period, which evidenced the dynamic, vibrant force inherent in Judaism. This vitality was reflected in the process of rabbinic interpretation, which did not hesitate to take liberties with the practices and laws developed in the previous era. The rabbis had no scruples about criticizing their religious tradition; nor did they regard the values of their own times or of a later age as fixed and eternal. Only in the third period, beginning with the completion of the Talmud (ca. 500) and ending in the middle of the eighteenth century, was Judaism transformed into a stultified, paralyzed system, "a stubborn legalism."

It is the task of the fourth, the current stage, which according to Geiger began with Mendelssohn, to raise tradition to a higher level by means of a critical appraisal of the principles and tenets of Judaism. The essential character of the Jewish tradition must be raised from a narrow system of laws and obligations to an ethical creed of universal scope and application. This, Geiger believed, was the purpose and function of Reform. It must free Jewish life from the shackles of precepts and regulations, which are often incompatible with the spirit of the age. Reform must chart a new course; it must inject the highest ideals of the times into the Jewish tradition, even though it may modify it in the process. As an evolving and changing religion, Judaism has new ideals and aspirations to offer the individual Jew as a substitute for an unsatisfactory system of ordinances and rules; it will thus help him resolve the existing contradiction between his modernist inclinations and the demands of his faith. The concern for the adjustment of Judaism to the individual, it may be noted, reflects a Protestant

tendency; Orthodoxy was generally not troubled by this consideration, since it expected the individual to conform to the regimen
of laws set down for the Jewish group.

For Geiger and the intellectual leaders of Reform, this rationale
justified the changes they were introducing in Judaism. For the
Orthodox Jewry of those days, however, this interpretation represented a revolt against the only kind of Judaism they knew and
the tradition they cherished. They regarded Judaism as a discipline
of life, commanded by God, which every Jew was to follow;
hence it could not be onerous. It was not merely a creed, as the
Reformers maintained, for its laws and tenets gave Judaism its
natural character and dynamism. Judaism, moreover, could not
overlook its ethnic elements; nor could it be forced into a Pro-
crustean bed, to fit every age and fashion. For their loyalty to its
code, Jews through the ages had suffered martyrdom; now the
detractors and destroyers of Judaism were coming from within.
Even if they did not succeed in wrecking Judaism, they might yet
cause a schism in the ranks of Israel. This the traditionalists were
determined to resist with all their power.

Implications of Geiger's Theories

It may be well to examine the specific application of Geiger's
principles. Judaism, as a living, ever-developing faith, Geiger assumed, has no room for what he called fossilized, outworn relics
and customs. Tradition is an important guide in Judaism, since
"the present cannot break with the past." But this does not mean
that every precept or tenet must be retained, no matter how it
clashes with the spirit of modernism. The principles of ethical
monotheism as expounded by the prophets, Geiger considered fixed
and binding. But rituals and ceremonies are merely ways of exem-
plifying religious truths and are not, in themselves, immutable and
permanent. Practices that may serve and inspire one generation
may be objectionable to another; they are not sacrosanct and may
be discarded or altered as the need arises. Even the basic rite of
circumcision, ordained in the Scriptures, may be abrogated. In a
letter to Leopold Zunz in 1845, Geiger described this rite in the
terms used by French radicals during the Reign of Terror, as "a
barbarous, bloody act . . . the sacrificial idea which invested the

act with sanctity in former days has no significance for us." For the dietary laws, Geiger had no use whatever. He referred to the "doglike" obedience of those who adhere to Jewish law not as a matter of strong, inner conviction but merely because it is prescribed in classical Jewish sources.

Though Geiger regarded Judaism as essentially a creed, he held that the Jewish group must continue as a religious community in order to spread its doctrines; but he would not accord the Jews the status of a people. The Jews were entrusted by God with a special mission, to be "a light unto the nations" (*Is.* 42:6), to teach mankind the true meaning of ethical monotheism and foster universal peace and justice. For this purpose, God had dispersed the Jews among the nations. Thus, the scattering of Jewry was a divinely ordained blessing, rather than—as the Jews had regarded it for centuries—a punishment for their sins.[16] It follows then that the Jews must surrender their ethnic or nationalistic characteristics and become entirely like their neighbors in every way, except that they are to retain a different religious confession. This notion impelled Geiger to delete all references to the Messianic hope and the restoration of Zion from the prayer book he published in Breslau in 1854. In place of the Messianic petition, he inserted a prayer for the achievement of the millenium for all mankind.

Geiger, as other sincere pioneers of Reform, may well have been motivated in his stress on the universalistic aspect of Judaism by a deep conviction that the Emancipation was the harbinger of the Messiah, who would usher in a new era of freedom and equality for the Jews and all mankind, when all particularism would vanish from the earth. Judaism as a universal religion, he believed, would be held in higher esteem by the Jewish intellectuals in Germany, who deprecated it because of its nationalistic character. Geiger may also have had a vision of Judaism as a world religion. Not all the Reformers of his day shared this ideal. Some were doubtlessly impelled by opportunism. Reform appealed to them as a means of removing a barrier that prevented their acceptance by their fellow Germans. Reform, too, may have appealed to them as a "religion of convenience" in view of its less onerous regimen of observances than that demanded by traditional Judaism.

The Hebrew language, Geiger believed, should be retained in

the liturgy, for the sake of tradition, but it should not be unduly prominent. This idea evidently prompted him to preserve the Hebraic character of his Breslau prayerbook. In theory, however, he believed that one should pray in his own mother tongue, as his normal medium of expression. What is perhaps surprising is his declaration that the German hymn elicited in him an emotional response that the Hebrew did not. Geiger insisted that history had pronounced its judgment against the Hebrew language, though this judgment had not as yet been carried out in his day. No protest, he declared in Hegelian terms, is justified against the forces of history. These views expressed at the Frankfort Conference (1845), resulted in the dramatic withdrawal of Zacharia Frankel, a moderate, from the meeting. Though very liberal in his views on Reform, Geiger was not as drastic as his colleague, Samuel Holdheim.

Samuel Holdheim (1806-1860)

A native of the province of Posen, which had a large population of Jews of Polish rather than German background, Samuel Holdheim had received a thorough Talmudic training in an East European Yeshivah, and it is quite possible that his religious radicalism was a sharp reaction to his experience there. He later attended the Universities of Prague and Berlin, where he gained a fair grounding in philosophy and other branches of secular knowledge. As rabbi of the community at Frankfort am Oder from 1836 to 1840, he introduced mild reforms in the synagogue service. For the next six years, he served as *Landesrabbiner* or chief rabbi of Mecklenburg-Schwerin, after which, in 1847, he readily accepted the pulpit of the Berlin Reform Congregation, which Geiger had refused chiefly because it was a separatist and private group operating outside the community orbit. He wrote prolifically, but his main work was his *Worship Addresses*, which consisted of several volumes of sermons. One of the reforms he advocated in this work was a change in the function of the rabbi, who, he urged, should no longer be concerned with deciding ritual questions or matters of Jewish law, but should rather act as the minister of the congregation, in a capacity similar to that of the Protestant clergyman.

A disciple of Hegel, Holdheim contended that Reform represented improvement, that history in its unfoldment is constantly advancing, and that the later steps in the ladder of progress must supercede the earlier ones. This, of course, signified a break with the past and with the chain of religious continuity, the hallmark of tradition. Tradition is not concerned with the age or the need for adjustment to new conditions; but Holdheim insisted that Judaism must yield to the temper of the times.

Holdheim's Radicalism

In his work *On the Autonomy of the Rabbis and the Principles of Jewish Matrimonial Law,* published in 1843, Holdheim expounded some of his other theories of Reform. The underlying foundation of his thinking was the denial by the Paris Sanhedrin of the natio-ethnic character of Judaism. Lacking Geiger's broad secular training, Holdheim was unable to use the latter's historical and critical approach and supported his conclusions by means of casuistic reasoning on the basis of Talmudic dicta. His main contention was that the religio-ethical and humanistic elements in Judaism were to be divorced from the nationalistic ones, since the latter had lost their binding force with the destruction of the Jewish state. The autonomous community life which Jews had led throughout the centuries should be replaced with the autonomous right of the rabbis to inaugurate changes in Judaism, in keeping with its religio-ethical nature and the spirit of the times.[17] Now that Jews were no longer citizens of their own but of other states, their customs and observances must be adjusted to the needs of these states.

To provide a Talmudic rationale for his opinions, he cited two Mishnaic principles: "The law of the State is the law" (*Ned.* 28a) and "laws depending on the land (of Israel) are to be observed only in the Land (of Israel) and a precept that does not so depend is observed both in the Land (of Israel) and outside it" (*M. Kid.* 1: 9). Holdheim distorted the meaning of the phrase "laws depending on the land," construing it to mean "country" rather than "soil," though the latter is the clear interpretation given to this phrase in the Talmud and subsequent sources. Thus, he said, all laws which existed under conditions of Jewish sovereignty have no force outside the Jewish state, since the Jews dwell in other countries. Accordingly, he claimed, though the Sabbath is a religious institution, it need not necessarily be celebrated on the seventh day as in Palestine, but, under prevailing conditions, may be shifted to Sunday.[18] By the same token, he argued, the detailed regulations concerning the Sabbath may be discarded; moreover, functionaries in the public service, among them teachers, lawyers, and others are not subject to the Sabbath regulations enjoining work, since they are exempted by the rabbinic law of *Shevuth* (abstinence from work), which permitted those engaged in the Temple service to carry on their labors on the Sabbath. The fact that the parallel was inapplicable did not trouble Holdheim.

The religious regulations pertaining to marriage and divorce should be supplanted by the civil law, Holdheim insisted. In his only Hebrew work, *An Essay on Matrimony*,[19] he also attempted to prove that intermarriage was religiously permissible, since its prohibition was only a national interdict. He also accepted the ruling of the Paris Sanhedrin that because Christians were monotheists, the Biblical injunction (*Deut.* 7:3, *Ex.* 34:15ff.) against intermarriage did not apply to them, and he readily officiated at weddings of this kind. The same principle, he argued, is true of circumcision. In the stormy debate stirred up by the Frankfort Society of Friends of Reform in 1843 on the question of whether or not "the covenant of Abraham," *i.e.* circumcision, was a basic condition for the admission of the male into the Jewish fold, Holdheim published a pamphlet in which he declared that not circumcision but birth determines who is a Jew and that a male child born of a Jewish mother is Jewish, regardless of whether the rite has been performed or not. From the strictly Halachic viewpoint, Holdheim was indeed correct, yet he failed to take into account the sensibilities of the Jews who regarded circumcision as a sacred practice, hallowed by martyrdom since the days of the Hadrianic persecutions (117-138), when Jews had observed it on the pain of death. Though Geiger entertained views similar to those of Holdheim, he did not deem it appropriate as a rabbi to express them publicly, as Holdheim did. In general, it may be said that Geiger had a far greater respect for tradition than Holdheim. The latter did not hesitate to declare from the pulpit that circumcision, like other religious institutions, was optional in Judaism. In view of these opinions, it is not surprising that Holdheim advocated unrestrained abrogation of vital Jewish traditions.

No temple in Germany was as radical in its reforms as Holdheim's congregation in Berlin. He upheld the views of the French Assembly of Jewish Notables[20] that Judaism was a mere creed and Jews were "followers of the Mosaic persuasion." He took liberties with traditional practices on the basis of a dominantly rationalistic approach. Of all the fast days in the Jewish year, he retained only *Yom Kippur,* the Day of Atonement. He abolished the second days of the major festivals, believing that since the calendar was now fixed by accurate chronometric calculation and no longer depended, as in ancient times, on the observation of witnesses of the phases of the moon, it was not necessary to add an additional day to a festival, in order to correct any error that might have occurred in fixing its date.[21] In introducing this change, Holdheim insisted that he was returning to Biblical Judaism, but he ignored the sentiments of the majority of the Jews of his day who felt that an ancient custom assumed the character of a religious law and should not be meddled with.

In deference to modernism and church practice, he instituted mixed pews and a mixed choir in his synagogues, which, of course, was regarded as a violation of religious tenet. The *talis* (prayer shawl) was discarded, as was the headgear worn by male worshipers. The reason for this and other changes, as explained by David Philipson, a leading writer on Reform Judaism, was that:[22] ". . . our Occidental habit is to show respect by the uncovering of the head, as is the Oriental habit to keep the head covered . . . To keep the synagogue Oriental with an entire Hebrew service, worship with covered heads, separation of the sexes, while the Jew in all things outside the synagogue was Occidental, was to institute a divorce between the synagogue and life, which could not but be detrimental to the best interest of Judaism." The Orthodox rabbis, however, challenged the authority of the Reformers to modify religious practices and observances.

Holdheim also discarded the custom of blowing the *Shofar* on *Rosh Hashanah,* the Jewish New Year. Because the priestly benediction traditionally recited on festivals by the *Kohanim* (the worshipers of priestly descent) was regarded by the Reformers as merely an historical link to the sacrificial service in the Temple (*Nu.* 6:24-26) with no significance in modern times, it was also omitted in the Berlin temple. Holdheim transferred the recital of the priestly benediction to the rabbi, the active religious leader of the congregation. These and other changes in the service made Holdheim's temple in Berlin the most extreme Reform congregation in Germany, as well as throughout Europe. It served, however, as a model for Reform in America.

Decline of Reform in Germany

Enthusiasm for Reform in Germany waned quite noticeably towards the middle of the nineteenth century. After the revolutions of 1848, a wave of reaction swept through Europe, similar to that which had followed the defeat of Napoleon and the Congress of Vienna in 1815. The hopes of the Jews for complete emancipation were shattered when the restrictions against them were revived. They recognized that their enfranchisement had little to do with the modernization of their religious doctrines and practices. To gain their complete civic rights, many Jews diverted their energies towards attaining *political* instead of religious reform.

The decline in interest in the Reform movement in Germany may be judged from the fact that no conference of liberal rabbis was convened for almost a quarter of a century from 1846 until 1869. In the latter year, a synod was held at Leipzig, comprising both rabbis and laymen representing the various Reform congregations in the country. Two years later, the synod was reconvened at Augsburg. These gatherings accomplished little because, in the main, each Reform congregation in Germany preferred to follow its own independent course—so much so that not even a common Reform prayer book was adopted until 1929. The Reform conferences appear to have had little positive results, except to exacerbate the opposition of the Orthodox.

There were other reasons for the lack of progress of the German Reform movement. The Reform congregations were private organizations which were not supported by the community. The government in Germany taxed every professing Jew for the maintenance of community institutions, and membership in a Reform congregation entailed an additional financial obligation. Moreover, the

Prussian government also used its authority to prohibit the establishment of congregations that deviated from the traditional pattern. Then, too, after 1848, an increasing number of German Jews, disillusioned by conditions in their native land, emigrated to the United States. Among them were gifted individuals who either as rabbis or lay leaders could have helped to advance Reform Judaism in Germany. These people found a more fertile soil for their ideological principles, efforts, and interests in free America.

Despite the violent and turbulent controversy on Reform in Germany in the earlier decades of the nineteenth century, religious life in that country appears to have been stabilized toward the latter decades of that century. The German Jews were granted complete citizenship rights in 1871, soon after the Franco-German War, but this did not have any effect on their religious tendencies. A substantial portion of German Jewry at the time was not observant in any real sense; a minority followed various shadings of Orthodoxy, while the majority of the religious element was only moderately Reform. In fact, in 1928, when David Philipson, the noted American Reform rabbi, visited typical Reform congregations in Germany, he reported that "judging by the American standards of Reform, the German Reform service was distinctly Conservative, if not Orthodox. A service conducted almost completely in Hebrew, men and women separated, the women being relegated to the gallery, the men worshiping with covered heads—all this seemed unreal at a liberal Jewish convocation."[23] However, what the Reform movement lost in momentum in Germany, it gained in America.

Influence of Reform

It is difficult to appraise the over-all effect of German Reform on Judaism in general. While some claim that it was a halfway station to baptism in the nineteenth century, others are convinced that, by and large, it checked the drift to conversion. The Reform movement has been strongest in the United States, where it can be credited with having exerted a considerable impact on the other alignments in Judaism.

Conservatism has borrowed a number of the innovations instituted by the Reform wing. Orthodoxy, particularly in America, has done likewise, though to a lesser degree. Among these changes are the improved decorum, the use of the vernacular and the regular sermon at services, as well as confirmation exercises in various forms. Mixed pews, the organ, and the elimination of the benediction by the priestly caste are among the modifications adopted by the Conservative congregations. Women have been given an important place in the affairs and activities of the synagogue and the religious schools among both Orthodox and Conservatives. On its part, American Reform has in recent decades restored some of the traditional observances and doctrines it had previously abandoned. It is worth noting that many of the ideas and practices that were violently opposed as being against tradition a century and a half ago, or less, have been introduced in congregations purporting to be traditional. These are simply the vagaries of time.

8

The Historical School

I. Leopold Zunz

The Moderates

PRACTICALLY ALL THE INITIATORS of the Science of Judaism movement were moderates in their religious views. Only a few were as radical as Geiger. The predominant majority was identified in the main with the religious principles then formulated in Europe by Zacharia Frankel and later, in the United States, by Solomon Schechter. While Frankel's ideology was associated with the Historical School, Schechter's became the basis of the Conservative wing in American Judaism.

One of the leading pioneers of the Historical School in Germany was Leopold (*Yom Tov Lippman*) Zunz (1794-1886), who was a founder and dedicated exponent of the Science of Judaism. This eminent Jewish scholar was born in Detmond in the Rhine province, eight years after Mendelssohn's death, to a family in very modest circumstances. Orphaned at an early age, he was sent to the Samson Free School at Wolfenbüttel, an institution for poor Jewish children. The major subject of instruction in this institution was Talmud. On Friday morning Bible was taught, and each week several hours were devoted to the secular disciplines. At Wolfenbüttel, young Zunz already showed his liberal inclinations, when, together with a classmate, Marcus Jost, who later became a noted Jewish historian, he studied Hebrew grammar surreptitiously.

A new director of the school, Samuel Ehrenberg, discovered Zunz's great intellectual gifts and guided him in his educational career. In 1811, the youth was graduated from the local *Gymnasium* (high school), the first Jew to receive a diploma from that institution. Four years later, he entered the University of Berlin, where he studied and acquired the methodology and spirit of the historical approach in the investigation of various phases of human culture. Zunz received his doctorate at the University of Halle in 1818. His doctoral dissertation dealt with a review of rabbinic literature, an area shunned by the earlier proponents of the Haskalah, but one that Zunz regarded as a monumental achievement of the Jewish genius. In his work, Zunz classified the rabbinic writings in accordance with the historical periods in which they were produced. He also pointed up the potentialities of this literature as a rich source of information and data on the various epochs it embraced.

The Kulturverein

After the Congress of Vienna (1815), the state of confusion and perplexity of the enlightened sector among young Jewry in Germany mounted appallingly. Many in that generation had received a good general education. Some were university graduates, equipped and ready to take their places in secular society; but the religious barriers restrained them. The reaction and measures adopted at the Congress restored the earlier disabilities against the Jews. Their resulting frustration knew no bounds; having tasted freedom, they could not return to their former inferior status. Their disillusionment was aggravated by the re-echoing cries of "Hep-Hep",[1] the anti-Jewish rallying cry which emanated from many quarters, including intellectual circles. Mendelssohn had led the German Jews out of the ghetto to a point of no return; yet he had not shown them the way to the Promised Land. They were thus left stranded, not knowing where to turn. In their predicament, considerable numbers found a refuge in the church.

In this period of intellectual uncertainty and confusion, Zunz and several colleagues joined in an attempt to resolve the dilemma confronting their generation. In 1819, he, together with Eduard Gans

(1798-1839), a brilliant jurist and follower of Hegel, Moses Moser (1796-1838), an erudite merchant, and others, formed the Union for Jewish Culture and Science. Later, the poet Heinrich Heine joined the society. The members of the organization were convinced that true emancipation could be achieved only from within. They undertook to make known the basic achievements and significance of Judaism to the enlightened circles of German Jewry, by means of a critical and scientific study of Jewish sources. They hoped thereby to raise the prestige of Judaism in the eyes of the Jews, and thus reduce the surging waves of baptism that threatened to overwhelm German Jewry. A knowledge and appreciation of the Jewish past would, they were confident, also inspire Jewish youths with a sense of dignity and self-worth that would strengthen their Jewish moorings. Among the Christians, too, they believed, a better understanding of Judaism would heighten respect and regard for the Jews and lessen the prevailing anti-Jewish bias. The Union for Jewish Culture and Science planned, accordingly, a wide and ambitious program of research and popular Jewish education.

Their plans entailed more than the dissemination of Jewish culture. They also intended to train young Jews in agriculture, so as to draw them away from mercantile pursuits, thereby minimizing what they thought was a major economic cause of the animosity against the Jew. These grandiose schemes, however, soon came to nought, for the liberal elements in the Jewish community of Berlin were apathetic to their efforts and the pietists objected to the new type of critical investigation of the sacred texts that the well-meaning society fostered. The society was dissolved in 1824, when Gans, its president, was himself baptized in order to secure a professorship at the University of Berlin. Heine, too, followed suit, so as to "gain a passport into Christian society," as he put it. In his case, the passport implied admission to the Prussian bar, though later he did not enter legal practice, despite his brilliant performance in his examinations. Heine was of an erratic nature, as may be seen from a letter he wrote to his friend Moser:"It would distress me much if my own conversion would appear to you in a favorable light. I assure you that if the law permitted the stealing of silver spoons, I would never have been baptized."

But the aims of the defunct Union were realized at least to the extent that Zunz's efforts in Jewish Science yielded an abundant harvest of scholarly work. Marcus Jost (1793-1860), the historian Heinrich Graetz (1817-1891), Abraham Geiger, Zacharia Frankel, and other German Jewish scholars were motivated to undertake a wide number of Jewish historical studies. This method soon spread to other lands; in Italy it was adopted by Samuel David Luzzatto (1800-1865) and in France by Salomon Munk (1803-1867). The Jewish Theological Seminary of Breslau, established in 1854, was dedicated to the critical study of all facets of Jewish learning. In several countries, including the United States, rabbinical seminaries and other academic institutions following this pattern trained their students to pursue their investigations in the new spirit.

Motivating Factors in Jewish Science

Many factors gave impulse to the movement for Jewish Science, which was the product of the fateful encounter between the spirit of Emancipation and tradition in the area of Jewish scholarship. The subjection of the Jewish classical texts to critical inquiry marked a break with the traditional attitude of authoritarianism in which they had been enshrouded. Moreover, though some were concerned with the vital role that the new scientific method could play in advancing Jewish learning, others regarded it merely as a proper means of compiling and bringing to a fitting climax the long process of Jewish cultural activity which they now deemed to be at an end, for they believed that Judaism was bound to succumb to the overpowering forces of secularism and Emancipation. The Jewish past, they thought, could not be further enriched by an extended literary or scholarly creativity, and an appraisal of its contribution was, therefore, in order. Zunz and his colleagues hoped that the new pattern of Jewish scholarship would be organized into an academic discipline, which could be taught in institutions of higher learning on a par with other dead or defunct historic civilizations, like the Greek and Roman. They wrote their works in German in the hope of reaching out beyond the limited confines of rabbinic circles, aspiring to attract as wide an audience of Jews and non-Jews as possible.

It should be noted that Zunz lived at the convergence of the eighteenth and nineteenth centuries, and the confluence of their streams of thought. Hegel's absolute idealism, with its emphasis on the evolutionary interpretation of history, society, culture, politics, and religion, now combined with the spirit of Romanticism which gripped Germany after the defeat of Prussia at Jena in 1806. The latter movement was a reaction to the triumph of the rule of reason epitomized in the French Revolution, as well as a compensation for the humiliation the Germans had suffered at the hands of Napoleon. Romanticism represented an escape from the dull present, its reality and the cold logic of existence, to another age, notably the medieval period, when man was regarded as the vehicle of spiritual forces. The currents of Romanticism permeated all facets of cultural life, learning, and the arts in Germany as in other countries; they also had an impact on Jewish scholarship, guiding it back to the past.

In contrast to the reverence of Renaissance scholars for the ancient civilizations of Greece and Rome, the Romanticists adopted as their model the culture of the Middle Ages, with its devout religious faith, unbridled supernaturalism, and mysticism. While the rationalists looked upon the medieval period condescendingly, *de haut en bas,* the Romanticists glorified it. However, the period probed by the scholars of the movement for Jewish Science usually went back beyond the Middle Ages to post-Biblical times. It extended generally from the Talmudic and Gaonic period through the Spanish expulsion. In Jewish Science, moreover, Romanticism was merged with its opposing rationalist current, the former element providing the motivation and the latter, the objective, critical mode of investigation.

Zunz and Reform

Zunz had been a tutor in the home of Marcus and Henriette Herz in Berlin, where he came in contact with the leaders of Reform and was imbued with their ideas. He had preached at Beer's private Reform temple, which had been closed by the King of Prussia in 1823, presumably on the ground that the worship and sermon in the vernacular violated Jewish tradition. To disprove this claim, Zunz embarked on an important study published in 1832, *Devotional Addresses of the Jews,* in which he demonstrated that preaching in the popular tongue had been an institution in the synagogue since the days of Ezra (444 B.C.E.). He also showed that the liturgy had undergone numerous changes in the course of its development and, accordingly, the innovations adopted by the Reformers were simply another phase in the evolution of Jewish ritual. Thus it was that the attempt to justify Reform served to stimulate the Science of Judaism.[2]

When Zunz was appointed director of the Berlin Teachers' Seminary around 1840, he modified his earlier views on Reform. A number of his friends thought that this change was motivated by expediency, but he appeared too sincere to have been influenced by mundane considerations. He had proved this when he had previously resigned his pulpit in the Prague Reform Synagogue because his religious views differed radically from those of his congregation. His attitude towards Reform may be judged from a sharp letter he sent in 1845 to Geiger, who had criticized his shift to traditionalism:

. . . The reforms in the dietary laws are repugnant to me. Those who delight in waging war against Judaism which cannot defend itself, may do so. The yardstick by which to gauge religion is religion itself, that which has been accepted by the people and hallowed from generation to generation . . . We must reform ourselves not our religion. We may attack only unwholesome practices that have entered our religion from within or without, but an assault on the Talmud generally is the resort of apostates. . . .

In an article on *tephillin* (phylacteries) published in 1843, Zunz spoke of the inspiring and edifying rituals, essential to the survival of Judaism. These precepts, he explained, serve an important purpose as outward reminders of fundamental ethical and religious doctrines. Without them, Judaism is bound to remain an abstract concept. He stressed the same idea in his *responsum* on circumcision, published a year later, in connection with the controversy stirred up by the Frankfort Friends of Reform, who had denounced this rite. This practice, Zunz maintained, is of the very essence of Judaism. Judaism cannot serve merely as a system of moral tenets or a refutation of pagan teachings. Its universal principles, Judaism holds in common with other religions; its particularistic observances are necessary to preserve its distinctive character. Jews, moreover, must not barter any of their sacred ideals or institutions for Emancipation or civic rights, for they are entitled to them as human beings, and they will eventually attain them without surrendering their religious values or principles.

In these and other writings Zunz insisted on the retention of the time-honored rituals and customs of the Jewish people—not because he believed they were divinely ordained, but because they had emerged from the life and experience of the Jewish people. His rationalism did not permit him to subscribe to the fundamentalism of Orthodoxy. Though Zunz favored the modification or elimination of "unwholesome customs and practices," he vigorously opposed the Reformers who were inclined to abrogate Jewish observances out of deference to what they called the "spirit of the times" or merely for convenience, or with the opportunistic objectives of achieving political enfranchisement. Zunz thus followed a compromise course between Orthodoxy and Reform and, in so doing, helped to set the stage for Frankel's Historical School.

II. ZACHARIA FRANKEL — HIS LIFE AND TIMES

Career

ZACHARIA FRANKEL (1801-1875), a leader of the Jewish Science Movement in Germany, is regarded as the founder and theorist of the so-called Historical School in Judaism. Born in Prague to a well-to-do family, he combined a thorough Talmudic training in the local Yeshivah with a good secular education. In 1831, he earned his doctorate in classical languages at the University of Budapest. That same year, he also received his rabbinical ordination and subsequently accepted a call as *Kreisrabbiner* (district rabbi) of Leitmeritz, and as rabbi at Teplitz, the leading congregation in the district. In the latter post, Frankel gave evidence of his liberal ideas by the innovations he introduced in the synagogue worship: a male choir, a sermon in the vernacular, the omission of the *piyutim*[3] in the service, and other mild reforms.

Several years later, in 1836, he assumed the post of *Oberrabbiner* (chief rabbi) of Dresden, which he occupied until 1854, when as the "man of the golden mean," he was elected in preference to Abraham Geiger, the scholarly leader of Reform, to the presidency of the newly founded rabbinical training school, the Jewish Theological Seminary at Breslau. He chose to devote his energies to the school rather than the pulpit, because by temperament he was an academician and teacher, rather than a rabbi and preacher. At the Seminary, which he headed until his death, Frankel prepared rabbis and scholars, who were imbued with his critical ideas and his ideals. Many of them made significant contributions to various phases of Jewish history and literature.

Writings

Frankel wrote prolifically. His special field of interest was the Halacha, which he regarded as the structure and framework of Judaism. In his doctoral dissertation entitled *Preliminary Studies in the Septuagint,* Frankel investigated the status of the Jewish legal tradition in the third century B.C.E. This study foreshadowed his life-long interest in the development of Jewish law. As professor of Talmud at the Breslau Seminary, Frankel recognized the need for a text to be used as an aid in the teaching of Talmud and, accordingly, in 1859, he published a Hebrew work entitled *Darkei Hamishna* (Methods of the Mishna.) It was a history of the Halacha, and it stimulated others to pursue further research in this field. Frankel's suggestion, borrowed from Krochmal,[4] that the oral law was of rabbinic and not Sinaitic origin evoked a storm of protest on the part of Samson Raphael Hirsch and the Orthodox rabbinate.[5] His other major Hebrew work, the *Mavo Hayrushalmi,* was designed as an introduction to the Jerusalem Talmud, which had long been neglected because of the far greater devotion of scholars to the Babylonian Talmud. He also published several tractates of the Jerusalem Talmud, for which he wrote a commentary that he called *Ahavath Zion* (Love of Zion), as a token of his faith in the restoration of Zion, in opposition to the Reformers.

In 1844, in order to stimulate interest in Jewish Science, Frankel launched a journal, the *Zeitschrift für Jüdische-Religiöse Interessen* which lasted only three years. Later, in 1851, after he had placed his Seminary on a firm footing, he established the *Monatschrift für Geschichte und Wissenschaft des Judentums.* Frankel edited the latter publication for eighteen years until 1869, when he turned it over to a devoted colleague, the noted Jewish historian Heinrich Graetz, then Professor of Jewish History and Biblical Exegesis at the Breslau Seminary.[6] A leading Jewish scholar in his times, Frankel made a lasting contribution to Jewish thought and learning.

Reason and Sentiment

Frankel was influenced by the strong Romantic currents which permeated all phases of intellectual life in nineteenth-century Europe. Essentially, Romanticism was a revolt against the rationalism of earlier generations; a reaction against the assumption that all human activities, even politics and morality, are subject to the mechanical and arbitrary laws of nature. Romanticism stressed individualism and introspection, the freedom of man and his ability to transcend the natural level and strive for the Infinite. It regarded man as a complex creature, endowed not only with reason but also with emotion, imagination, and intuition, who should mobilize all his faculties in his search for beauty and truth. In so doing, he was not to be encumbered by formal rules, precedents, and artificial restraints.

The impact of Romanticism is evident in Frankel's insistence that the feelings and sentiments of the Jewish masses towards tradition must not be overlooked. The same tendency is reflected in his exhortations to the Reformers not to apply rationalism unduly to the solution of the religious problems confronting them. He often reminded them that by excluding sentiment from Judaism, they dilute it. Reason is as cold as the north wind, and though it appeals to the intellect, it cannot satisfy the emotions, nor can it console or bring peace of mind or happiness. True Judaism genuinely inspires and brings joy and delight to its followers.

Effects of Jewish Science

Frankel was instrumental in improving the political, religious, and social status of the Jews in Germany. While at Dresden, he helped to restore to the Jews of Saxony their long-deprived right to public worship and the erection of synagogues. Frankel believed that the prime function of the Science of Judaism was to advance

Jewish learning and enhance the prestige of the Jew, rather than to achieve practical ends. Nevertheless, one of Frankel's studies, *The Jewish Oath in Theological and Historical Context,* published in 1840, served a useful purpose; it helped to convince the government of Saxony that there was no valid ground for the *More Judaico,* the special oath[7] required of Jews testifying in court proceedings. Jews had been compelled to take this odious form of avowal because they were presumably absolved each year from binding vows and commitments by the *Kol Nidre*[8] ritual, recited as a preliminary to the *Yom Kippur* eve service. Frankel proved that this degrading procedure should have been abolished in 1838, when the Jews were granted the status of subjects by the King of Saxony, though strangely enough they had to swear their allegiance to the King on that occasion by this humiliating pledge. Saxony soon (1839) replaced it with a much more dignified one. Other states in Germany followed this example, Prussia abolishing the oath only in 1869.

Within the Jewish community, the movement for Jewish Science helped to curb the two extreme fringes—the ultrapietists and the assimilationists. The liberal attitude of free investigation implicit in the concept of Jewish Science resulted in moderating the rigorous traditionalism of the most extreme Orthodox elements. On the other hand, the new esteem which Judaism gained from the efforts of the Jewish Science school helped to strengthen the loyalties of many who saw little reason for Jewish continuity.

The German Historical School

Aristotle spoke of the *Jus Naturae* (the natural law) which he believed to be a product of the rational nature of man—a law which is uniformly unchangeable "as fire which burns here as well as in Persia." This idea was developed in modified form by the great Dutch jurist, Hugo Grotius (1583-1645). Grotius saw natural law as sanctioned by human morality rather than by divine revelation. To him and his disciples, natural law was the ideally just law, fixed, static, unalterable, and eternally valid for all people everywhere—a norm or objective standard against which all enacted law and legal institutions could be measured.

The German Romantic tendency affected the fields of philosophy and law and helped to shape a different doctrine in legal philosophy. Under the influence of the German philosopher Friedrich W. J. von Schelling (1775-1854), the jurist Gustav von Hugo (1768-1844) rejected the theory of natural law as a metaphysical abstraction, and laid the groundwork for the Romantic conception of the Historical School. Friedrich K. von Savigny (1779-1861), his disciple G. F. Puchta (1798-1846), and others developed this idea further. They viewed the law through the prism of history and advanced the notion that the law of a culturally advanced people, like its language, customs, and manners, has originated as far back as prehistoric times in the unique popular character or *Volksgeist* of a nation, as the result of the operation of silent and unconscious forces. Customary law,[9] which is the outcome of custom, practice or popular belief, is only a manifestation of that spirit. Law is thus not the gift of legislators, but rather the result of the organic life of the group. It grows and develops with the people, and declines when the people loses its uniqueness. For this reason, the law cannot be codified or changed. It is, however, different with legal scholars who understand the *Volksgeist* and may, therefore, be said to be authorized by the community to interpret or apply it. The law in this view is an expression of dynamic group life, as well as a branch of knowledge to be cultivated by a body of erudite specialists, charged with the "sacred duty" of keeping alive the historical link between a nation's present and past, as a vital part of the nation's spiritual life. The object of legal history "is to trace every established system of law to its origins and thus discover an organic principle whereby that which still has life may be separated from that which does not, and must, therefore, be relegated to the realm of history."

Without entering into a thoroughgoing critique or evaluation of the theory of the *Historische Rechtschule,* (Historical School of Jurisprudence) it may be said generally that the theory has a number of fundamental flaws. Though a people's peculiar character might affect its legal system, it can hardly be claimed that the sole or even major source of a nation's law is its popular spirit. The complex aspects of law, among other elements, cannot be attributed to its *Volksgeist.* A nation's economic, social, and cultural conditions tend to shape its law. Moreover, Savigny's theory might lead to the conclusion that an ancient tradition, which is presumably embedded in a people's *Volksgeist,* is superior to later legal enactments. Savigny regarded the law, like language, as a phase of a nation's natural development—but the fact is that language is not generally a distinct national product, for many of its elements have other origins. It was no doubt romantic and mystical to extol the *Volksgeist,* and this idea may have been congenial to the nationalistic mood prevailing at the time Savigny propounded his views, the period immediately following Napoleon's downfall—but this does not make the doctrine any more correct or true. Notwithstanding its Romantic fallacies, Frankel, like many intellectuals of his day, was impressed and influenced by the theory, the principles of which he attempted to apply to Jewish religious law and practice, thereby creating the Jewish Historical School as a parallel to Savigny's *Historische Rechtschule.*

Influence on Frankel

The basic concept shared by both Frankel and the German Historical School is the nationalistic factor. Frankel, like Krochmal, pointed to the Jewish people as the source of Jewish law and tradition. Out of this view there later emerged the principle of *Kelal Israel* (the totality of Israel) as the arbiter of change in Jewish practice, advocated by Solomon Schechter, the architect of the Conservative movement in American Judaism, which inherited the tenets of the Historical School. Frankel himself, in line with one of the basic notions of the Historical School, devoted his life to a study of the evolution of rabbinic law and its roots in early times, as a means of discovering his people's *Volksgeist* and the true essence of Judaism. He hoped to evolve from this investigation a criterion by which dead elements in his people's past could be separated from those that retained their vitality; the former to be discarded, while the latter were to be preserved. He determined that Hebrew, the Messianic hope, and other values in Judaism belonged to the category of fixed and eternal components in Judaism. These notions constitute the foundations of his philosophy of Positive Histórical Judaism. Frankel also challenged the rights of individuals to change Jewish practice unless they were the recognized representatives of the Jewish community. These and other views of Frankel indicate his affinity to the German Historical School.

BASIC DYNAMICS OF FRANKEL'S HISTORICAL SCHOOL

Jews and Judaism

IN CONFORMITY with his Romantic viewpoint, Frankel defined Judaism in natio-ethnic terms as the religion of the Jews, implying thereby that Judaism, as the historical achievement of the Jewish genius, is lodged primarily in the Jewish people, rather than in the principles of ethical monotheism that underpin the Jewish faith. Judaism may thus be regarded as the sum total of the doctrines, values, and outlooks on life which the Jews have developed in the course of their history and retained as their spiritual heritage. The Jews were the beneficiaries early in their history of a directly communicated, supernatural, divine revelation at Sinai, recorded in the written Torah. There is, however, another, indirectly transmitted divine communication, continuous and natural in character. This revelation is manifested in the concensus and will of Israel to accept, disseminate, preserve, observe, and expand the primary communication represented in the written Torah. The subsequent revelation is an extension of the earlier one. It is incorporated in the oral law, which is the result of man's reason and experience. Strictly speaking, the written law is too sacrosanct to be tampered with by man or subjected to the normal process of change; but the oral law, which is of human origin, though also divinely inspired, may be accommodated to the needs of the times. The heteronomous written law, embodied in the Holy Scriptures, thus appears to differ from the autonomous oral law, contained in the rabbinic texts, primarily in regard to source and permanence. The former, being of divine origin, transcends the impact of time, while the latter, a human product, does not.

The distinction between the two kinds of law is, however, actually nominal rather than real. The Torah can have meaning only insofar as it is applied to the life of the Jewish people, who have guarded and clung to it steadfastly. Without Israel to interpret it and give it concrete expression, the Torah is an abstraction. It has permeated the consciousness of Israel through a process of elucidation and adaptation to practical situations. At times, this method of development, through interpretation or enactment has added to the stringency of the Scriptural regulations by erecting numerous *Syagim* (fences) around them, while at others it has lightened and relaxed them. An illustration of the latter is the punishment of the culprit whose victim suffers a loss of limb by money damages rather than the infliction of like injury in accordance with the literal construction of the Biblical provisions, (*Ex.* 21:24, *Lev.* 24:20). Thus the two levels of legislation, the divine and the human, have been fused organically into a unified code so closely identified with the Jewish group as to give Judaism an ethnic character. Judaism may thus be said to comprise the triad of basic value-components noted in the dictum in the *Zohar* (*Lev.* 73a) which describes them as "intertwined one with the other; *viz.,* the Holy One, blessed be He, the Torah and Israel."

Schechter's and Ginzberg's Views

Professor Solomon Schechter (1847-1916) explained the relationship of Bible and tradition as seen by the Historical School in the following terms:

> ... It is not the mere revealed Bible that is of importance to the Jews, but the Bible as it repeats itself in history, in other words, as it is interpreted by Tradition[10] ... The Talmud ... lends some countenance to this view by certain controversial passages in which "the words of the scribes"[11] are placed above the words of the Torah. Since, then, the interpretation of Scriptures, or the Secondary Meaning, is mainly a product of changing historical influences, it follows that the center of authority is actually removed from the Bible and placed in some *living body,* which, by reason of its being in touch with the ideal aspirations and the religious needs of the age is best able to determine the nature of the Secondary Meaning. . . .
>
> ... Another consequence of this conception of Tradition, is that it is neither Scripture nor primitive Judaism, but general custom which forms the real rule of practice. Holy Writ, as

well as history, Zunz tells us, teaches that the Law of Moses was never fully and absolutely put in practice. Liberty was always given to the great teachers of every generation to make modifications and innovations in harmony with the spirit of existing institutions . . . The norm as well as the sanction of Judaism is the practice actually in vogue. . . .[12]

Professor Louis Ginzberg (1873-1953), another outstanding scholar and ideologist of the Conservative movement, writing in a similar vein, said of the Historical School:[13]

> . . . For an adherent of this school, the sanctity of the Sabbath reposes not upon the fact that it was proclaimed on Sinai, but on the fact that the Sabbath idea found for thousands of years its expression in Jewish souls. It is the task of the historian to examine into the beginnings and developments of the numerous customs and observances of the Jews; practical Judaism on the other hand is not concerned with origins, but regards the institutions as they have come to be. If we are convinced that Judaism is a religion of deed, expressing itself in observances which are designed to achieve the moral elevation of man and give reality to his religious spirit, we have a principle, in observance of which reforms in Judaism are possible. From this point of view, the elevation of a law is independent of its origin, and thus the line of demarcation between biblical and rabbinical law almost disappears. . . .

These statements demonstrate the attitude of the Historical School towards tradition and change in Judaism and the way in which it differed from both the Reform and the Orthodox positions. The Reformers were concerned primarily with the present in Jewish life, and were ready to repudiate the past in order to bring Judaism into rapport with modern times. The Historical School, like the Orthodox, placed its accent on the past, stressing the role of Torah, Talmud, and later rabbinic works as vital links in the growth of Judaism. The traditionalists, however, regarded the past as decisive and its customs and traditions as fixed and unalterable, while the Historical School viewed it as a fluid, formative period. It considered Judaism to be a dynamic and evolving historical force, a perennial stream, as expressed by the Mishnaic metaphor of a "spring flowing with ever-greater strength," in contrast to the Orthodox who thought of it as a "cemented cistern that does not lose a drop" (*Abot.* 2:11). The Historical School believed that Judaism might be adapted in a measure to modernism, but that progress and change must start and reckon closely with tradition. Frankel applied this principle as a guideline in his approach to the problem of altering Jewish ritual and practice in conformity with the times.

The Hamburg Temple Dispute (1842)

Frankel entered the polemical arena in the dispute on the Reform Hamburg prayer book, a revision of which appeared in 1841. This new edition was actually less dramatic in its departures from the traditional *Siddur* (prayer book) than the earlier one, published in 1818, but it still omitted a number of passages considered vital by the Orthodox. The *Chacham* Bernays, Chief Rabbi of the Hamburg Orthodox congregation, warned that the ban issued some twenty years earlier against the Reform prayer book was still in force, and that those using it did not discharge their religious obligation of worship. Frankel, together with twelve other rabbis, was invited to give his opinion in the controversy, and he did so in a long statement in the *Orient* (1842) chiding both parties to the dispute.

With Bernays' ruling that one who employs the Reform prayer book does not discharge his religious duty, Frankel disagreed. The primary question, he insisted, was not whether or not the prayer book met the legalistic requirements set down by authorities, for the implications of the question transcended the immediate, local issue. Public worship was a matter which affected the Jewish people as a whole, and it should be viewed from this angle. Bernays, on his part, should not have interdicted the prayer book in the manner in which he did. The temple leaders were justified in resisting suppression in matters of conscience, and it was not fair to brand them, as did Bernays, as atheists and destroyers of the faith. The effect of such tactics might well be to curb unduly the spirit of freedom and progress, and produce a type of mechanical and insincere piety. The excessive zeal displayed by Bernays was bound to cause an irreparable rift in the ranks of Judaism. Persuasion, rather than coercion, should be employed in matters of this kind.

But Frankel did not spare the Reformers either. It was true, he declared, that not all customs and practices were God-given, nor all precepts sanctioned by divine authority; yet the extreme ardor for change displayed by the liberals was fraught with the danger that they might be impelled to go beyond the bounds of propriety, particularly since they had no acceptable criterion for selecting or rejecting rituals and practices. The Reformers lacked a sense of history; they failed to understand that in questions of public worship, one had to be concerned with the spirit and tradition of the people, which could not yield to dispassionate reason and logic. To determine whether or not the modification of a portion of the liturgy was proper, one had to probe the attitude of the Jewish people towards it; it was important to bear in mind that human beings and their emotions are not rooted in the present alone, nor in the spirit of modernism only; they are deeply embedded in sentiment and historic experience. It was, therefore, wrong to delete the *Avodah,* the account of the sacrificial service in the Holy Temple on the Day of Atonement incorporated in the traditional liturgy of the solemn day, for these passages arouse sacred memories of the ancient days when the national sanctuary existed in all its glory. The *Avodah* service, too, had become in-grained in the consciousness of the people. "Our centuries-old history supports Bernays," Frankel concluded. No single group or institution had the right to take it upon itself to modify tradition, for to do so would destroy its value as a common bond in Israel. Only the people as a whole, not the officials of one temple or another, might institute changes in custom or ceremonial; only the community of Israel as such might discard or revise a religious usage.

The Messianic Hope

Frankel had also criticized the Reform Hamburg temple for having deleted the prayers for the restoration of Zion from its liturgy. This question had become a stormy issue between the traditionalists and the Reformers. The belief in a personal and nationalistic Messiah and the re-establishment of the idealized

Davidic dynasty was deeply embedded in Jewish hearts and had brightened the long, dark centuries of exile, ghetto, and persecution for the Jews, inspiring them with a will to survive. The Jewish people were, therefore, reluctant to surrender it.

The Reformers, however, fearing that this ideal would be regarded as inconsistent with national patriotism, adopted the doctrine of the Jewish mission, which made the Diaspora the norm of Jewish existence, willed by God. In support of this position, the Reformers adduced the Talmudic doctrine, "The Lord did a kindness to Israel by scattering them among the nations" (*Pes.* 87b),[14] indicating that exile was not a penalty imposed on the Jews for their sins, as Jewish tradition had had it, but rather that the dispersion was providential, enabling the Jews to become a "light among the nations" (*Is.* 42:6) so that they might teach the world the true meaning of ethical monotheism as envisaged by the Hebrew prophets.

Frankel was outspoken in his protest against the omission of the prayers for the rebuilding of Zion by the leaders of the Hamburg Reform temple asserting that:[15]

. . . The idea of an independent Jewish homeland is in itself ennobling and full of vitality. There is nothing wrong in the aspiration to reestablish our nationality in a corner of the globe associated with our most sacred memories, where it could again stride forward freely and gain the respect of the nations, which, sad experience teaches us, is extended only to those who possess worldly power. In this hope, there is no inkling of hate or disparagement of our present Fatherland; nor should it arouse a suspicion that we regard ourselves as aliens in the Fatherland and that we desire to flee from it . . . This merely proves that despite millennia of suffering and oppression, we have not yet despaired and we are still in a position to grasp the idea of independence and regeneration. In any case, this is a far loftier concept than the constant subservient accommodation of our people to external conditions, an attempt which frequently culminates in a vapid, superficial cosmopolitanism. . . .

Jewish Nationalism

Gotthold Solomon, preacher of the Hamburg temple, challenged Frankel to reconcile his view of nationalism with the struggle for complete enfranchisement then being waged by German Jewry. Like the extremist Reformers of today, he raised the spectre of dual loyalty. Frankel defended his position by pointing to the parallel situation of the Greek citizens of Austria, who had participated actively in the movement for the liberation of Greece from Turkish domination without anyone having cast suspicion on their loyalty to the Hapsburgs. "Similarly," Frankel argued, "why should Jews not desire the creation of a Fatherland for their unfortunate brethren suffering in Sardinia, Czarist Russia and elsewhere?" As far as Germany was concerned, he explained, the Jews there had a Fatherland. They were in a far better position politically and economically than those in Eastern Europe and other countries, for in Germany, Jews now enjoyed almost complete egalitarian rights. However, should conditions in Prussia, for example, where Jews had been accorded almost full legal equality by the Edict of 1812, deteriorate or retrogress to what they had been during the oppressive period of post-Napoleonic reaction, the Jews there might also need a land of their own where they could live undisturbed and unmolested. But, as matters now stood, the German Jews differed from their Protestant and Catholic fellow citizens primarily in their religion. For this reason, Frankel intimated, the Jewry of Prussia rejected the plan of King Frederick William IV who, upon ascending the Prussian throne in 1840, was ready to grant them special national rights, but not full equality. Frankel declared:

> . . . Wherever the Jew finds a Fatherland which recognizes him as a legitimate son, he renounces his Jewish nationalism; he must renounce it, if he wishes to regard himself as a true son of the Fatherland; he himself demands of the Fatherland that it grant him this status—and once it is bestowed upon him, his Jewish nationalism ceases of itself, for Jewish nationalism is something imposed from without. . . .

As we can see from the above statement, Frankel's notion of Jewish nationalism was quite confused;[16] or perhaps he felt that he had to be cautious in what he said, in order not to prejudice his coreligionists' case in their struggle for Emancipation. It is possible that for this reason he spoke of Jewish nationalism as something negative, forced on the Jews from without by their oppressors and denigrators who sought to treat them as aliens and intruders, rather than as a positive sentiment fostered by the Jewish group. Moreover, Frankel failed to ascribe to Jewish nationalist aims any affirmative meaning, such as the establishment in the Jewish homeland not only of a refuge for oppressed Jewry but also a cultural center, a "refuge for the Jewish spirit." Such an objective had been suggested as early as 1805 by one of the early proponents of Reform in Hungary, Rabbi Aaron Chorin[17] (1755-1844). It was formulated in a clear and articulate manner toward the end of the century by the East European Jewish thinker, Asher Ginzberg, better known by his pen name, Ahad Ha-Am[18] (1856-1927).

It is evident that Frankel failed to distinguish, as we generally do today, between the concept of nationhood and nationality; the former term designates a political entity, while the latter connotes merely an ethnic or cultural group, like the various language groups in the Swiss Confederation. Before they attained independent statehood, the Irish were a nationality, as the Scotch and Welsh still are today, a part of the British nation. According to this viewpoint, the fact that the Jews of Germany belonged to the German nation in no way contradicted their status of nationality and religious, spiritual, and ethnic affinity with their fellow Jews throughout the world. Only one's political affiliation is exclusive; but neither that nor one's citizenship is in conflict with membership in a variety of family, community, religious, or ethnic groups, all of which tend to exercise a broadening influence upon the individual.

Influence on Zionism

Frankel's idea of Jewish peoplehood was only the core of Zionist ideology, as it was later formulated and crystallized. To Frankel, the idea of the return to Zion was not, as has been suggested, a mere religious belief, to be confined to the prayer book but not to be translated into actuality. Gotthold Solomon[19] and others of Frankel's moderate opponents might have been ready to agree to such a compromise in order to avoid a cleavage in Jewry on this question. Of course, Geiger and the radical Reformers would have objected to such a concession, as not being consistent with what they claimed was a purer and broader ethical concept of Judaism and a higher truth. Frankel also advanced another principle that Zionism, particularly in the West, later adopted. As a compromise between the traditional view of *Kibbutz Galuyot,* (the ingathering of exiles), that is, the resettlement of the Jews of the entire world in Zion, and the Reform negation of the traditional aim of the Messianic redemption in its totality, Frankel advocated that the Jewish homeland should be rebuilt primarily for the homeless and persecuted in Jewry. A similar thought had been advanced at the beginning of the nineteenth century by Aaron Chorin.[20]

The Frankfort Conference

The first conference of Reform rabbis in Germany was convened in 1844 in Brunswick at the instance of Ludwig Philipson, founder and editor of the popular Jewish weekly *Allgemeine Zeitung des Judenthums, (General Journal of Judaism)* for the purpose of strengthening the Reform movement through a substantial measure of coordinated action on doctrine and ritual. The second conference of the liberal rabbis was held the following year (1845) at Frankfort. Frankel was not expected at this gathering because he had criticized the earlier one severely; but he came, in the hope of exercising a moderating influence and curbing the aggressive design of the extremists.

To understand the mood of the Frankfort Conference, it is necessary to note the atmosphere in which it met. At the time, the currents of German nationalism had penetrated the German intellectual as well as the liberal religious circles. A movement had arisen for the creation of a separatist German Catholic church detached from the Church of Rome. Similarly, the so-called rationalistic *Lichtfreudliche Gemeinden*[21] (Communities of Enlightened Friends) among the Protestants repudiated the doctrine of the Trinity and other Christian dogmas and undertook to establish a nationalist Protestant church. The radical *Berlin Temple Verein* (union), organized two months before the Frankfort Conference, issued an *Aufruf* (appeal) to the Conference "to redeem Judaism, our most precious heritage, from all antiquated forms." The thoroughgoing leftist constituency of this new Berlin congregation, and its declared intention to institute drastic changes in the liturgy, led many to believe that it was planned as the Jewish component of the nationalistic German religious movement. The extremist tendencies of the group were manifested in the adoption of a ritual almost completely in the vernacular, the introduction of the practice of worship with uncovered heads, and the shift of the principal service from the Sabbath to Sunday.[22] Despite these innovations, it turned out that the Berlin temple did not actually plan to join the contemplated German nationalist religious tendency. The Reform rabbis at the Frankfort Conference, however, gained courage and confidence from the aggressive attitude displayed by this ultraradical congregation,[23] which sent a delegation to the Conference.

Question of Hebrew

A major issue at the Frankfort meeting concerned the place of Hebrew in the synagogue service, a question that had specific nationalistic overtones. Geiger, the leading spirit of the Conference, argued that Hebrew was not and could not be considered indispensable in Jewish worship, since language is a national element, while Judaism is not a national but a universal religion; moreover, Hebrew is a segregating influence and should, therefore, be eliminated. Others who shared Geiger's views pointed to a precedent for the use of the vernacular in the liturgy in the fact that important prayers like the *Kaddish,* recited by mourners, were composed in Aramaic. The *tehinot,* the devotions of pious Jewish women, were in Yiddish, not in Hebrew. It is a disparagement of the lofty ideals of Judaism, they maintained, to insist that Hebrew must have so high a priority in the synagogue, despite the fact that it is so little understood by the people. The sages, too, they insisted, did not declare Hebrew to be the obligatory language of worship—quite the contrary. The Mishna and Talmud distinctly declare that even the *Shema* may be uttered in any language (*Ber.* 13a); moreover, the *Shulchan Aruch* maintained that "one can pray in any tongue he desires" (*Orach Hayyim Hilchot Tefila* 101:4), and the *Sefer Hassidim* specifically states (588,785) that it is better not to pray at all than to pray in a language one does not understand. Actually, the Reformers claimed, the use of the vernacular in the service is bound to strengthen rather than weaken the pillars of religion. The language does not sanctify the prayers; the converse is true. German, too, if used in the services, might eventually become a hallowed language, the Reformers contended.

Frankel expounded the role of Hebrew in public worship in an entirely different light. Religion is in itself abstract, he said, and Hebrew is the concrete form in which it is expressed; it is an integral and organic ingredient in Judaism, for it is the holy tongue in which the doctrines, concepts, and ideals of Judaism were created and preserved; it also adds the aura of a mystic element to the religious service. Terms like *Adonay* (Lord) could not be adequately translated, because of the subtle meanings and overtones they have acquired in the course of the centuries. If Hebrew is omitted from worship, it is bound to lose its place in religious education as well, and this will have a disastrous effect on Jewish survival. This actually happened in the period of Philo (50 C.E.), when Greek superceded Hebrew, and Philo himself resorted to the Septuagint for his allegorical explanations, a number of which, based on almost ludicrous mistranslations of the original,[24] turned out to be distortions which vitiated the traditional precepts. Greek influence, too, led Philo and his school to approach the Scriptures from the vantage point of philosophical speculation, unlike the sages, who examined philosophy in the light of the Scriptures. Judaism has unique and cherished values, symbols, and institutions, yet a dissenter can attack any or all of them on the specious ground that Judaism as an institution cannot conceivably depend just on this or that tenet. If this is carried far enough, Judaism may eventually be reduced to a mere creed, which, of course, is alien to its very nature. Worship in Hebrew is a sacred bond uniting scattered Jewry. There must be historic continuity as well as unity in Judaism, and "he who objects to the preservation of our hallowed tongue, actually destroys a vital historic element in our religion."

The views of Geiger and his followers on this question were upheld by a vote of fifteen to thirteen of the rabbis present with three abstentions, though they unanimously agreed that, for the time being, it was "advisable" that Hebrew be retained in the service. Frankel strongly objected to the position taken by the majority, and in protest, he and a colleague, L. Schott, dramatically left the meeting and withdrew from the Conference. In a letter which he published subsequently, he explained that he had done so because the decision of the assembly of rabbis was in violation of the principle of "positive historical Judaism" to which he was committed.

The Frankfort Conference also took a definite stand on the issue of the inclusion in the liturgy of the prayers for a personal Messiah, as well as the broader problem of Jewish nationalistic regeneration. The majority supported a resolution to the effect that "the Messianic idea should receive prominent mention in the prayers, but all petitions for our return to the land of our fathers and for the restoration of a Jewish State should be eliminated from the liturgy."[25]

Positive Historical Judaism

Although Frankel insisted that Judaism could be meaningful only if it pursued a "positive historical" approach, he did not explain this rather vague term which became the shibboleth of the Historical School and later of its American offshoot, the Conservative movement. Frankel provided a clue to the meaning of this phrase in his exposition to the Frankfort meeting of the role of Hebrew in public worship. He agreed to the introduction of non-Hebraic prayers into the liturgy, but he demanded that the service should remain predominantly Hebraic, in deference to the demands of "positive historical Judaism."

Accordingly, Frankel implied that in the historical experience of the Jewish people, the Hebrew language has become a positive, that is, a firmly entrenched, value. It was the soil in which Judaism was nurtured in the past and the only one in which it could flourish in the future. Though Hebrew had become associated with Judaism in the course of history (that is, within the process of time), it had ultimately become a permanent feature in Judaism, transcending time. Thus, Hebrew which has served as the external form in which Judaism is articulated, has become as timeless as the essence itself. It is not then, the letter of the law or fixed tradition which determines what is basic in Judaism, as the Orthodox would have it, as much as the unique place a given usage, such as the Hebrew language in worship, has attained in the consciousness of the Jewish people. By the same token, it is not the rationalistic spirit of the age that serves as the yardstick as to what is to be preserved or discarded in Judaism, but the sentiments of the people. This is true not only of Hebrew but of other institutions in Judaism as well.

The outward forms are of particular importance in Judaism, Frankel maintained, because Judaism is a religious code—a complex of affirmative and negative precepts, not a system of theological speculations and beliefs. The praxis in Judaism delineates the path of moral and ethical conduct for the Jews; without it Judaism is inchoate and abstract. Frankel thus supported the Orthodox position which regards ritual and ceremonial observances as inseparable from the doctrines with which they are linked. The Reformers, however, have discarded these practices as externals, as mere shells; they purported to retain only the inner kernel or core of ethical ideas—an approach which they regarded as liberal and progressive.

Adaptation to Modernism

But if one facet of the historical process in Judaism comprises its rooted eternal patterns which withstand the impact of time, another yields to it. In its centuries-old experience, Judaism has come to grips with other cults and cultures; it has rejected those currents of thought that clashed with its tenets and doctrines, but it has accepted others that conformed to its nature. Moreover, in the course of its development, certain of its laws and customs have undergone modification in accordance with the spirit of a given era or epoch. Frankel combatted the reluctance of the Orthodox to acknowledge that there is room for change in Judaism and need for it to adjust to the modernist outlook. His contemporary, Samson Raphael Hirsch, the founder of Neo-Orthodoxy, however, averred that it is not Judaism that has to conform to the spirit of the age, but rather the spirit of the age that must conform to Judaism. To Frankel, however, an attitude which makes precept and ritual rigid, inelastic, and an end in itself spelled a form of paganism and idolatry.

Judaism, Frankel indicated, has never considered all of its laws immutable. Through interpretation and sometimes through the enactment of new regulations, the ancient rabbis modified practice in accordance with the needs or views of a given era. Thus, Hillel found a legal means of circumventing the law of release[26] (*Deut*. 15:1) when the conditions of the age demanded it. The importance of this policy in Judaism is evidenced in the dictum in a classical historical work, which among other subjects, deals with the controversy between the Sadducees and the Pharisees. The Sadducees, it will be recalled, were literalists who insisted on a rigorous construction of the Scriptural law, while the Pharisees were liberals who believed in the pliancy of Biblical precepts. "That day," it is asserted, "was a festival for Israel, when the Pharisees prevailed in their interpretation of the law of 'an eye for an eye' . . . 'a hand for a hand' (*Ex.* 21: 24), rendering this verse in terms of monetary compensation rather than retaliation in kind."[27] The triumph .this celebration marks does not lie in the humanitarian aspect of the rabbinical version, important as that may be, Frankel explained, but rather in the fact that it established the principle that not the letter but the spirit of the law must prevail and that this spirit must raise the law to a level where it can serve as a suitable guide for man, who is himself endowed with the divine spirit.

Permanent and Transitory Values

In sum, Frankel's concept of positive historical Judaism envisages a bi-polarity of values and institutions in Judaism—its hallowed tenets or practices belonging either to a primary or a secondary category. Among the first are the inner, positive, or preservative principles and observances in Judaism which cannot give way to an ephemeral *Zeitgeist* or the test of rationalism or to mere convenience. This group includes the permanent components of Judaism which, though they have evolved as a result of the temporal process, have transcended it. Among these usages and concepts are Hebrew, the Sabbath, the Messianic hope, and certain other ideas and ideals which have been hallowed by the Jewish people for generations.

The secondary category contains the external and transitory doctrines and practices in Judaism, those that may be said to be subject to the fluctuations of time. The Reformers, however, place all the traditions, precepts, and practices of Judaism in this secondary group, claiming that since all elements in Judaism have been generated at a given point in time, they are exposed to its normal effects. The Orthodox also see only a single rank in the practices and concepts in Judaism, but only the primary one, which is fixed and constant and beyond the influence of time. Frankel sought a balance or mean between the two classes of elements in Judaism, the fixed and the fluid ones. This was one of the chief dilemmas confronting him and his school of thought.

Change in Judaism

But how can change be implemented in Judaism, even in the subordinate category? According to Frankel, this may be done on the basis of critical inquiry into Jewish law, lore, and history for the purpose of ascertaining how deeply embedded a given practice or usage has been in the Jewish past; how sanctified it has become in the heart of Jewry, and the extent to which it functions as a strengthening and binding force among the people. Frankel, however, cautioned that: "Jewish science is not a mere autopsy on the corpse of Judaism. By means of it we must inquire into the prncipal foundations of Judaism from ancient times, for the preservation of which we must wage a determined struggle. We may not tamper with these fundamentals. They are memorials that have been acquired at the cost of blood and great sacrifice." From this point of view, the origin or even the nature of a ritual is of far less importance in resolving whether or not it should be retained than the place and significance it has attained in the Jewish tradition.

The aim of contemporary Judaism is to preserve tradition, Frankel went on to say, and yet to forge ahead on the path of progress. To this end we must find the golden path between the two seemingly contradictory goals. We have no right to modify practices that the people cherish, even on the strength of the results of scientific inquiry into the nature of these practices. "Any Jew is at liberty to pursue independent thought or investigation, but only the Jewish community as a whole has the authority to bring about reforms in Judaism. What has been fully accepted by the people and sealed in its history is sacred."

The Voice of the People

This attitude accords with Frankel's view of Judaism as a uniquely nationalistic religion in which the few cannot act for the many. Only those modifications in practice introduced by the people in its entirety may be countenanced, on the principle of *"vox populi, vox dei."* No group of rabbis may exercise such authority, for the rabbis do not constitute a sacerdotal class in Judaism. This democratic principle, Frankel believed, will safeguard Judaism. The body of Jewry will not admit reforms lightly, on impulse; it will shun anything that may lead to its injury or destruction. Actually, of course, in the past, the rabbis did effect changes and innovations in practice, through the process of interpretation or enactment, but in doing so they served as representatives of the community; they had the confidence of the people that they would reflect their views and sentiments. The Reform rabbis, however, Frankel contended, were not inclined to strengthen but rather to weaken the role of the *Mitzvot* and doctrines in Jewish life; as a result, they shocked the religious sensibilities of the majority of Jews. Consequently, the Reform rabbis lacked the confidence of the Jewish public and, therefore, had no right to presume to act for it. Quite the contrary, the Jewish masses regarded them as unrestrained transgressors of the law and its precepts, who must be checked and curbed.

The Talmud, too, maintains the view that the will of the people is a vital factor in Jewish law. A Talmudic principle advises those who would ascertain the law, to "go and see how the people comport themselves" (*Ber.* 45a). It also maintains that "a custom supercedes a law" (*Jer. Yevamot* 12a); moreover, no decree may be imposed on the community unless the majority is able to abide by it. The practice of the people is to prevail, the sages held, even in the case where the use of a prohibited item has spread during a period of stringency among the majority of Israelites (*Avodah Zarah* 36a).

Frankel's opponents at the Frankfort Conference objected to his contention that the people alone and not they, a group of rabbis, had the authority to effect changes in Jewish practice. They claimed greater competence to do so than the rank and file of Jews, for they understood better the trend and the spirit of the times. For the same reason, they did not feel bound to reckon with the sentiments or opinions of the masses. Only demagogues who were not sincere and responsible spiritual leaders with definite and well-considered ideas of Judaism could pursue Frankel's line.

In his references to the people who are to decide on changes in Judaism, Frankel made it clear that he had in mind not the entire Jewish community, a large portion of which may be ignorant of Jewish law or indifferent to it, but rather the teachers, scholars, and those who are concerned with the preservation and advancement of the Jewish tradition and heritage. Frankel's stress on the authority to be exercised by the Jewish people, indicates that he thought of Judaism as a pluralistic rather than a private concern— and in this regard, Judaism differs from Christianity, more especially Protestantism, which emphasizes the role of the individual in religion. The Sinaitic revelation was a collective experience; the Hebrew prayers are formulated in the plural; public worship is preferable to private and requires the participation of a *minyan* (quorum of ten). Numerous other doctrines and practices in Judaism can be adduced in support of the view that Judaism is a group discipline. Geiger and his colleagues, however, believed that individuals with a specific plan and outlook are competent to mould the image of Judaism in accordance with what they deem to be its fundamental principles and outlooks. The Reformers, moreover, appear to have accepted the religious divisions in Jewry as a fact and were, therefore, ready to rely on a segment of the community to institute innovations in Judaism. Not so Frankel, who hoped for a strong and unified Jewry.

Significance of Historical School

Frankel's Historical School did not form a separate movement in Germany as did Reform, yet it gained many supporters in Germany and elsewhere. Frankel did not formulate a set ideology or program, his main contribution having been to restrain Reform and adapt traditional Judaism in a measure to the spirit of modernism. He thus steered, as was previously observed, a middle course between the principles of stability advocated by the Orthodox and that of flexibility and change upheld by the Reformers, but in pursuing this compromise, he became a target for both camps.

III. SOLOMON JUDAH RAPOPORT

Life and Works

IN EXAMINING THE ROLE of Solomon Judah Rapoport[28] (1790-1868), an early adherent of the Historical School and a forerunner of the American Conservative movement, we shift the scene from Germany to Galicia, then a part of Austria. Rapoport, like Zunz, Frankel, and Geiger, employed the Science of Judaism and the historical method to shed light on the development of Judaism. In this approach, Rapoport was influenced by Krochmal, a fellow Galician; in fact, Rapoport antedated Zunz in the use of this pattern of study. Though an observant Jew, Rapoport aroused the ire of both the Hassidim and the Orthodox because he supported the Haskalah among Jews. For this, and for reading the Bible in Moses Mendelssohn's German translation, Rapoport and a friend were banned in 1816 by the local rabbi, Jacob Orenstein. They appealed, however, to the government, which had forbidden the use of the ban, and the rabbi was forced to rescind it.

In his earlier years, Rapoport was the manager of a commercial enterprise which farmed the taxes on kosher meat from the government. Later he served as rabbi of Tarnopol, and for the last twenty-eight years of his life, he occupied a rabbinical post in Prague. Whatever time he could spare from his daily work, he devoted to study, his major area of historical research having been the obscure *Geonic* period.[29] Among his literary works, he published a number of *Toldot*,[30] biographical monographs on the tenth and eleventh century *Geonim,* which shed light on the life and times of these great luminaries. Rapoport, like Krochmal, wrote in Hebrew, his style contributing substantially to the advancement of modern Hebrew literature.

Views on Reform

Rapoport disagreed with the Orthodox, but he was also violently opposed to Reform. In the 1840's he denounced the activities of the Reformers as "the great abominations and the disgraceful deeds that are being perpetrated in German Jewry. Many of the so-called rabbis lead the people astray from the divine path and brazenly proclaim to Israel 'You have no portion in the Talmud or even in the Law of Moses.'[31] Thus the leaders of the people are causing them to err." In 1845, he published a pamphlet entitled *A Public Censure by a Veteran Rabbi,* which consisted of two impassioned pleas to the Frankfort Rabbinical Conference.

The first, addressed to the historian Marcus Jost, a member of the Conference, warned that Reform was provoking a schism in Jewry, which had formerly been firmly united by the bonds of the Torah and the Hebrew tongue. "If there is anything in our customs and laws that needs to be changed, let it be done not by man, but by time," he pleaded. Time has swept away many outworn customs in Judaism and it will do so again, he contended. He warned that the children of the Reformers "may prefer other faiths to a denuded and inferior religion of their own, stripped of soul and spirit. Not because we have observed the Sabbath and the second day of festivals or because we read the Book of Lamentations on the Ninth Day of Ab,[32] have we been persecuted in medieval times, but only because we refused to convert to Christianity or Islam. Shall we desert our convictions now that our situation has improved?" he challenged.

In his second plea, addressed to the Conference as a whole, Rapoport indicated that the leading rabbis throughout the ages who had instituted changes in the marital, divorce, or dietary laws had done so in the knowledge that the entire Jewish people would accept them and that the unity of Jewry would not thereby be threatened. "Who in this generation," Rapoport queried, "regards himself or is recognized by others as sufficiently competent to revise Jewish law?" He cautioned the Reformers who had abolished the second days of the festivals that they were likely to appear as Karaites[33] to those who observed them. As for the elimination of the Messianic hope from the prayer book, Rapoport insisted that nations friendly to the Jews would continue to regard them as loyal citizens though they prayed for the return to Zion, but that their foes would not surrender their hostility towards them, even if they did renounce their nationalistic aspirations. It was true that the Jewish people was sick and required healing, but the cure did not lie in the elimination of customs, traditions, and laws. The remedies Rapoport prescribed were those of the typical proponent of the Enlightenment: the cultivation among the Jews of a love of labor, science, and humanity.

The majority of Jews, Rapoport declared, would not follow the Reformers. They were bound to become a small, isolated sect like the Karaites and Samaritans,[34] "and this sect of transgressors will be left . . . without hope of redemption, without Torah and inspiration, and their lives will be reduced to a dull and drab existence unrelieved by flowers and the delights which stimulate spirit and soul." Reform, thought Rapoport, was too impatient to wait for a normal process of evolution of their religion, saturated with poetry and mystery; theirs was an insistence on a rationalism devoid of any emotion. History and the Jewish people would not condone the actions of the Reformers, who conspired against Judaism only to find favor in the eyes of transgressing youth, or the Gentiles. It would account them seducers to false worship and brand them as "sinners and those who cause others to sin, kindlers of the flame of controversy in Israel, lovers of the material and foes of the spiritual."[35]

Rapoport generally supported Frankel's moderate views on Reform. He was also swayed by the Romantic tendencies of his day. His attitude towards nationalism, tradition, and change, as shown in his writings, was in line with the ideology of Frankel's positive Historical School, who attempted to interpret Judaism in the light of history and continuous tradition.

9

Neo-Orthodoxy in Germany

I. ORTHODOXY AND NEO-ORTHODOXY

Old Orthodoxy

IN THE TURBULENT EARLY YEARS of the nineteenth century, the clash between traditional Judaism and the Haskalah in Germany gave rise, as we have observed previously, to Reform. From this conflict, Orthodoxy did not emerge unscathed and unaltered. It made concessions to modernism and gave rise to an alignment that has been referred to as Neo-Orthodoxy, to differentiate it from old Orthodoxy.

The staunch ultra-Orthodox segment in German Jewry opposed the intrusion of modernism and worldly ideas. Dubbed the *Altgläubigen* (Old Believers) by the Reformers, they continued to live as they had in the ghetto, in a milieu dominated entirely by Talmudic concepts and precepts. They regarded the culture of the outside world as hostile to Judaism and inconsistent with it, and therefore to be rejected and shunned. This fundamentalist view was shared by Jewish pietists in other countries, particularly those of Eastern Europe.[1]

A leading spokesman for this rigorous viewpoint in European Judaism was Moses Sofer[2] (Schreiber) (1763-1839), a great rab-

218

binic authority of Pressburg, who in his *Tzavoat Moshe* (*Testament of Moses*) forbade his children to read works by "Moses of Dessau," that is, Moses Mendelssohn. He exhorted them also not to acquire a general education, attend the theatre, or engage in worldly pursuits generally. "Nor may you contend," the eminent sage declared, "that times have changed, for we have an Ancient Father, Blessed be His Name, Who did not and will not change."

Neo-Orthodoxy

A more moderate reaction to secular culture among the devout in German Jewry was initiated by a younger contemporary of Moses Sofer, the renowned Isaac Bernays[3] (1792-1849). The fact that Bernays was a graduate of the University of Wurzberg prompted the Hamburg Jewish community to elect him as its rabbi in 1821, in the hope that a man of his caliber and modernity would succeed in winning back to Orthodoxy the errant youth that had strayed to the Reform temples. It was left, however, to Samson Raphael Hirsch, his ardent disciple, to formulate the basic rationale of German Jewish Neo-Orthodoxy.[4] Actually, the revised form of Orthodoxy was not a new phenomenon in Jewish life, but merely a reversion to the pattern of Judaism prevailing in Arab and Christian Spain, where Jews participated actively in the common life and general affairs of the community. The supporters of the new trend in traditional Judaism in the nineteenth century did not, of course, capitulate to the Enlightenment as completely as the Reformers; they merely came to terms with it.

Neo-Orthodoxy and Romanticism

Neo-Orthodoxy was born in the Romantic atmosphere that gripped Germany during the period of its rise, in the first half of the nineteenth century. In its very nature and essence, Orthodoxy contained much of the Romantic spirit, so that it is difficult to appraise the extent of the influence upon it of the Romantic movement. Neo-Orthodoxy, like Orthodoxy, underscored faith and tradition. It upheld supernatural revelation as the source and sanction of Jewish law, both Scriptural and oral. It also espoused the belief in the miracles recorded in the Bible, and in general, stressed the validity of the customs and practices of the past. Neo-Orthodoxy was doubtless strengthened by its affinity with the principles of German Romanticism. In its acceptance of the Enlightenment and German secular culture, Neo-Orthodoxy absorbed a phase of the German Romantic tendency. In doing so, it attempted in a degree, to combat the Reformers with the latter's own weapons.

II. SAMSON RAPHAEL HIRSCH

Youth and Training

THE CHIEF EXPONENT of Neo-Orthodoxy in Germany, Samson Raphael Hirsch (1808-1888), was born in Hamburg to a devout family that had moved there from Frankfort-on-Main a century earlier. His father was a merchant and a leader of the Orthodox section in the local Jewish community. As a boy in his father's home, Hirsch had heard a good deal about the radical views and activities of the Reformers, and the strategy to be employed in combatting the Reform *Neuer Israelitische Tempel Verein* (The New Israel Temple Association) founded in Hamburg in 1817 by Eduard Kley.[5]

A bright and gifted lad, imbued with religious zeal, Samson preferred the rabbinate to the business career his parents had planned for him. While attending the local *gymnasium* he pursued his Jewish studies under the guidance of the *Chacham* Bernays, from whom he acquired a good grounding in the Bible as well as an enthusiasm for piety and tradition.[6] Young Hirsch continued his studies at the Yeshivah of Rabbi Jacob Ettlinger at Mannheim, where he acquired an impressive knowledge of Talmud and other rabbinic sources. Soon after his ordination in 1829, he matriculated as a student in philology at the University of Bonn.

At Bonn, Hirsch was brought face to face with the mounting religious liberalism and rationalism that characterized the period. He formed a warm friendship with a Jewish fellow student, none other than Abraham Geiger,[7] who, as we have seen, later became one of the leading theorists of Reform. Together they organized a Jewish students' debating society at the university. The group met on Sabbath afternoons for a discussion of Jewish religious questions. This forum gave Hirsch an opportunity to impress his fellow students with his unusual mental agility, his forensic powers, and his firm religious convictions. Years afterward, Geiger, by then a violent opponent of Hirsch, wrote of him, "I admired him for his superior intellectual qualities and virtuous character, and I loved his kind heart."

Rabbinical Career

In 1830, at the age of twenty-two, Hirsch accepted a call to the post of *Landesrabbiner* (district rabbi) of the Grand Duchy of Oldenburg, where traditional Judaism was at a low ebb. Because of pressure from liberal elements, he was compelled to eliminate the *Kol Nidre* from the *Yom Kippur* service and to inaugurate several other more moderate reforms. He undertook to improve the religious situation through a broad program of education. After eleven years in Oldenburg, he moved to Emden, where he served for five years as chief rabbi of East Friesland.

The large and well-organized Jewish community of Nikolsburg, known for its eminent rabbis, appointed Hirsch as its district rabbi in 1846 and, a year later, named him as *Oberlandesrabbiner* (chief rabbi) of the entire province, which then had an unusually large Jewish population of fifty thousand souls. The community had been torn apart by numerous factions, and everything the rabbi did provoked the displeasure of one group or another; yet despite this, Hirsch succeeded in establishing a Yeshivah which attracted students from far and wide. In his capacity as chief rabbi, he served as a member of the Moravian parliament where, by dint of his eloquence and persuasive power, he did much to win civil equality for the Jews of the province. This achievement prompted Hirsch to appeal to his constituents to intensify their religious observance with these words, "What value will there be to our attainment if we shall be Jews no longer!" He also initiated a move to aid Jewish youth to train for careers in agriculture and the crafts.

It is particularly interesting to note that Hirsch was branded a Reformer in Nikolsburg, because there, as in Oldenburg, he introduced several minor changes in ritual practice. He performed weddings inside the synagogue instead of outside, as was the traditional custom; he delivered his addresses on these occasions, as well as his sermons in the synagogue, in German instead of the prevailing Yiddish. At services he and the cantor also wore clerical attire, a distinct innovation. Hirsch, moreover, eliminated the sing-song chants commonly used in the prayers and in the study of sacred texts.

The Frankfort Community

At this time, a violent tempest was brewing in the community of Frankfort, which had previously been a center of traditional Judaism. For several decades, the local community council, dominated by the Reform wing, had militantly opposed the Orthodox group. Since 1818, when the council had rejected a bequest for the erection of a Talmudical academy on the grounds that such an institution was "opposed to modern culture and the goal of training the Jews for citizenship," it had persistently used its powers to prevent the creation of this school. The council also neglected to keep the traditional synagogues in proper repair; the ritual baths were closed, the religious burial society was disbanded, and the practice of supplying hospitals and prisons with kosher food was discontinued. In protest, eleven Orthodox Jews had petitioned and received permission from the municipal authorities to launch their own *Religionsgesellschaft* (Religious Association) within the framework of the community. The group soon grew to a hundred families, and in 1851, after Hirsch had been in Nikolsburg for five years, the Religious Association of Frankfort offered him its rabbinical post. It is a tribute to Hirsch's courage and character that he was ready to leave his important and impressive rabbinical office in Nikolsburg to accept the call of this small and obscure congregation.

No sooner had Hirsch arrived in Frankfort than he embarked energetically on the task of strengthening and enlarging the Orthodox camp. He proceeded to establish the *Bürger* and *Real Schule,* Jewish elementary and secondary day schools which taught both the Jewish and secular studies. Hirsch's aim was to offset the influence of the *Philanthropin,* an institution in Frankfort which conducted similar schools, but along Reform lines. The *Philanthropin* had gained great prestige in the half century of its existence, and an attempt to compete with it required considerable daring. Both of Hirsch's day schools represented the embodiment of his principle of *Torah im Derech Eretz* (Torah combined with worldly fashion) (*Abot.* 2: 2), by which he meant the harmonization or symbiosis of Jewish religious and secular culture. There were few modern schools at the time in Germany which gave adequate attention to the Jewish curriculum, and Hirsch's schools served as a model in this regard. With the financial aid of the Rothschilds, he stabilized the budget of his schools and also erected an imposing synagogue edifice. In the worship in this synagogue, he inaugurated the changes he had previously introduced in Nikolsburg. He remained in Frankfort for almost four decades, until his death in 1888, leaving behind him a strong, well-functioning Orthodox community.

Secessionist Policy

Hirsch was not satisfied merely with the *Austritt,* the partial withdrawal of his Orthodox Religious Association from the Kehillah, the over-all Jewish community, for this gave his congregation autonomy but not complete independence. The members of Hirsch's Religious Association were still required to meet their assessments to the common community fund in addition to supporting their own synagogue and institutions. Hirsch insisted that the differences between Orthodox and Reform Judaism were greater than those between Catholicism and Protestantism, and it was, therefore, mandatory for the traditionalist party to secede entirely from the Frankfort Kehillah. To achieve this end, he induced a friend in Berlin to persuade Edward Lasker, a liberal Jewish deputy in the Prussian Diet, to sponsor a bill legitimizing the complete severance of the Orthodox from the central community on the ground of freedom of conscience. Such a law was passed on July 28, 1876, and on the following *Simchat Torah* (Festival of the Rejoicing of the Torah), Hirsch dramatically announced his resignation from the local Kehillah. The law thus sanctioned the division of the Jewish community.

The old Frankfort families who had a sentimental attachment to their historic Kehillah objected to a total split. The fact that the latter retained ownership of the cemetery may have been an additional reason for their opposition. The relative newcomers in the

Orthodox wing, who had no deep-seated loyalty to the Kehillah, followed their rabbi's example. Thus there came into existence two Orthodox congregations in Frankfort: one within and the other outside the Kehillah. The majority of the Orthodox rabbis, among them the renowned *Würzburger Rav* Seligman Ber Bamberger, a vigorous champion of traditional Judaism, protested against this separation, which he regarded as setting a precedent for sects in Judaism.[8] Hirsch, however, was adamant, insisting that not he but the majority had virtually withdrawn from true Judaism by their disloyalty to tradition, and he was, therefore, not guilty of violating Hillel's doctrine against separation from the community (*Abot.* 2:5). The separatist movement and its policy, known as *Trennungs Orthodoxie,* caused a furor throughout Germany, but actually only a few communities beside Frankfort (notably *Adath Israel* in Berlin, organized in 1869) followed Hirsch's example. The secession law, however, served as a weapon which the traditionalists could wield on occasion to force concessions from the Kehillah.

III.   IDEOLOGICAL APPROACH AND VIEWPOINT

Writings

AT THE AGE OF TWENTY-EIGHT, while yet in his first rabbinical post at Oldenburg, Hirsch anonymously published a small volume, *The Nineteen Letters of Ben Uziel,* which caused a stir in Jewish circles in Germany. The work, an eloquent plea for Orthodoxy, was written in an impassioned and impeccable German style. It purported to be the correspondence between a young rabbi, Naphtali, and his friend, Benjamin, whose contact with European civilization had caused him to abandon his religiosity. Naphtali, however, attributed this to his friend's lack of knowledge and understanding of the essentials of Judaism, and he therefore undertook to enlighten him on the ethical principles and doctrines of his faith, as well as on the problems brought about by the Emancipation. Under the guise of an exchange of correspondence on this subject, Hirsch outlined his fundamental philosophy of Judaism.

Another volume, entitled *Horeb,* which Hirsch had written earlier but published two years later, was intended as a text to explain the Biblical and rabbinic laws and practices of Israel to "Israel's thinking young men and women." The title of this work was suggested by the name of the sacred mountain in the Bible (*Ex.* 3:1). Only the laws "not bound up with the Land of Israel" were treated in *Horeb,* which may be regarded as the companion volume to the *Nineteen Letters. Horeb* is arranged in accordance with the same six divisions outlined in the *Nineteen Letters,* which are:

1. *Toroth* (Doctrines). The basic religious teachings of Judaism, relating to the belief in God and His Unity, the Love and Fear of Him, human pride, humility, suffering, virtue, and the purpose of man.

2. *Edoth* (Testimonials). The "action symbols" designed by God for the training of Israel. Among these symbols are the Sabbath, the festivals, fasts, rites, and ceremonials.

3. *Mishpatim* (Judgements). The laws promulgated for the advancement of social justice and the protection of the individual's person and property, encompassing also the prohibition of deceit and defamation.

4. *Chukim*[9] (Arbitrary Ordinances). The statutes concerning man, plants, and animals; the dietary regulations, the prohibition of cross-breeding of plants and animals, gashing and disfigurement, the rules of physical modesty, cleanliness, and vows.

5. *Mitzvot* (Commandments). The precepts pertaining to family relations, education and training, penitence, obligations to others and the community, oaths, the "desecration and hallowing" of God's name.

6. *Avodah* (Worship). The function of prayer, religious worship, the language of worship, the sanctity of the priesthood.

To the author of *Horeb,* these laws were God-given, the product of the revelation at Sinai, and therefore immutable. It is not possible to change them, but merely to seek out their inner meaning by means of meticulous study. Religious observance will help to mould a person's character, train him to be just and noble, and aid him in attaining the high, ethical status of the *Yisroel-Mensch* (Israel-Man), the religious and humanistic Jew who attains spiritual fulfillment in a just and holy life. Judaism, Hirsch pointed out, is a religious discipline designed to ensure the cultivation of the traits that comprise the ideal Jew.

Hirsch wrote prolifically.[10] Among his important works, in addition to those mentioned previously, are his commentaries on the Pentateuch, the Psalms, and the prayer book—the last named having been published posthumously. Hirsch also wrote polemical essays and brochures, as well as numerous articles in his monthly *Jeschurun,* which he founded in 1854 and edited for many years.

Method and Approach

To Hirsch, the Torah was as genuine a reality as heaven and earth. Therefore, he posited two revelations, nature and Torah, both of which he regarded as equally indisputable sources of truth and divine wisdom. The phenomena of nature are a matter of experience; so is revelation which is a confirmed historical event, witnessed by two and a half million souls around Mount Horeb.[11] Since Torah is the gift of the Divine Lawgiver at Sinai, it is not a human document. Being independent of human thought or participation, the laws of the Torah, like those of nature, are beyond the impact of time and the processes of history, temporal continuity, or change. With this rationale, Hirsch attempted to counter the Reform notion that Judaism was the product of an on-going evolutionary process throughout history, which is subject to the process of change. The supernaturally revealed character of the Torah would make any attempt to study its doctrines or its precepts in an historical framework meaningless.

According to Hirsch, only one of the two alternatives was possible: either the Torah is divine or it has no meaning whatever —not even a humanistic value. To be understood properly, it must be explained from itself, from the language in which it is written, which reveals its spirit. Hirsch employed a curious system of speculative etymology based on phonetic or sound similarity, which in the main lacks philological support. He referred to *eretz* (earth), for example, as the "swift runner," because the noun resembles the root *rutz*[12] (run). The word *Torah,* Hirsch suggested, is derived from *horoh*. One form of this verb may be rendered as "impregnate," implying that the Torah intends "to implant the seeds of truth and morality."[13] The Hebrew term *shamayim* (sky) is related to *sham* (there), and because of the suffix *yim* (two), Hirsch rendered the word as "double over there," which he said, refers to the upper and the lower portions of space.[14] This method provided Hirsch with a basis for homiletical elucidation which he utilized extensively in *Horeb* and in other writings, though it lacked scientific validity. In its essentials, it is a revival of the metaphorical approach used by Philo-Judaeus of Alexandria in the first century. Philo assumed that since both the Bible and Greek philosophy were true, the teachings of both could be reconciled, and he undertook to do so with the aid of allegory. [15]

Hirsch applied his *Symbolik* (symbolical method) as a means of avoiding literal interpretations of Scriptural law which might clash with the rationalistic outlook of his times. Symbolism, he pointed out, was no less a medium of human communication and thought than language. The Torah frequently alluded to signs (*e.g. Deut.* 6:8) and remembrances (*e.g. Nu.* 5:15). This manner of interpretation, however, was to be used within the context of Judaism in an attempt to discover in the Bible inner meanings and fundamental religious truths. Hirsch employed this device especially in his *Edoth* (testimonials), the division in which he discussed the "symbolic observances." Circumcision is intended, he indicated, as a moral imperative in physical life and a reminder "to keep even the body and its organs pure and holy and to shun all that leads to bestiality." The phylacteries teach us to dedicate ourselves to the service of the Almighty; the *Mezuzah* (the sacred inscription on the doorpost) consecrates the Jewish home as a sanctuary. The various types of sacrifices, too, are given figurative[16] significance and are thus presumed to illustrate religious ideas.

This kind of analysis can easily be pressed too far, as may be seen from his amplification of some of the *Chukim* (arbitrary ordinances). For example, Hirsch explained that the flesh of certain animals is forbidden as food because they are possessed of predatory instincts, while animals which generally eat grass and chew the cud resemble in their passivity unconscious plant life, which may be eaten. This, he asserted, is commonly true of the "clean fowl."[17] Hirsch also attributed a symbolic meaning to the rule against mingling meat and milk in cooking, which he attempted to explain as symbolizing the need for preserving the divine order in nature.[18] *Shatnez* (the prohibition of mingling of wool and flax in garments) and the cross-breeding of plants or animals[19] are proscribed for the same reason (*Gen.* 1:20 ff). In shaving his beard, a man changes the physiognomy God gave him (*Lev.* 19:27); in wearing a woman's garment (*Deut.* 22:5), a male tends to disturb the pattern that the Lord has ordained for his external appearance.[20] The head should be covered, he explained, for reasons of modesty. Only those parts of the body which are essential for work, like the hands and face, should be uncovered.[21]

In the Orthodox view, the religious laws and rituals are vested with an inherent sanctity and must be regarded as ends in themselves.[22] Hirsch criticized Maimonides for explaining some of the Biblical precepts on what might be termed cultural-anthropological grounds; yet though Hirsch did not concede or recognize it, his symbolic method also violated the Orthodox concept. In his approach Hirsch intended to stimulate more widespread observance of the precepts, yet he was actually indulging in apologetics. This course was really contrary to his fundamental assumption that the rituals and laws must be followed primarily because they are divinely prescribed symbolic acts by which godly thoughts enter the human mind.[23]

While Hirsch stressed the idea that the religious practices were the declared will of God, he failed to see that in referring to them as symbols, he invited the suggestion that as such they could easily be dispensed with or replaced by others. Hirsch's symbolic method has, nevertheless, yielded a positive contribution to Jewish thought in terms of the new ideas, meanings, and values that he discovered in Jewish religious tenets.

Mission of Man

In the first of the *Nineteen Letters,* the young skeptic, Benjamin, inquires of the rabbi whether happiness and human perfection are not the ultimate purposes which religion must help mankind attain.

In his answer to this challenge, Naphtali, the rabbi, questions the validity of either goal as a major objective in life, explaining that the pursuit of happiness may at times imply the kind of sensual pleasure or the satisfaction of desires which may lead to antisocial or even criminal conduct. Another possible purpose, the perfection of one's being, is an objective which can be realized only by a select few. The masses of humanity must, in consequence, seek other goals from among those expounded by thinkers and philosophers through the ages. For the Jew, the task is quite simple, for he need merely turn to the Torah for guidance. The very first story in the Bible depicts God in all His majesty as the Creator of the Universe. The study of the natural sciences will reinforce the reverence for God. The rabbi eloquently describes the great and wondrous works of the Lord:[24]

> . . . Seest thou the heaven in its eternally silent, unchanging course, bearer of light and heat, and all the motive forces of our earth, supporter of the earth-world. Seest thou it with its millions of starry worlds, or resplendent with the refulgence of the magnificently radiant sun-ball or the earth, the swift runner, with its eternal circles of originating and passing away, of blooming and withering, of life and death, eternally struggling from ceasing fading, and death, to ever-new existence, bloom and life . . . Seest thou the universal ocean, with all-encompassing arm of flood embracing the earth, or the springs which burst forth from the fissures of the rocks and flow on as rivulets, brooks, and mighty rivers? Dost thou rejoice in the firm surface of the earth upon which thou walkest safe and secure together with thy dear ones; hast thou pleasure in its meadowy expanse or its leafy trees, or in all the living beings which stir so animatedly in the waters and in the air, or dwell with thee on earth? Dost thou see sun, moon, and stars, which from their celestial positions above thee regulate the times of day and month and the seasons of the year, and determine the recurring periods of waking and sleep, of rise and fall, of bloom and decay on earth? . . .

All beings have been created by the One God; each in its place, each in its time. All His creatures are here to serve Him; in obeying His will they fulfill their destiny and contribute their share to the work of the universe. There is a harmony in the universe controlled by a rotating cycle of mutually dependent forces, each assisting in maintaining the others. God thus manifests His great love in the world. "As His love supplies matter and force to work, so also does the finger of His justice point to limitation, goal, and measure."[25] In the interdependency of all elements in nature there is love; in the limitation of their functions there is justice.

> . . . Thus water, having penetrated the earth, is collected in cloud and sea; light, having pierced the earthy crust and brought forth plants, children of light and heat, is concentrated again into sun, moon and stars; the germ, offspring of earth, is taken from the earth and given to the crown of ripened fruit, which henceforth the earth must receive that it give—thus one glorious chain of love, of giving and receiving, unites all creatures; none is by or for itself, but all things exist in continual reciprocal activity; the one for the All, the All for the One. . . .[26]

Man is also part of this great chorus of servants of the Lord. The earth is the Lord's; it must, therefore, be respected as divine and its inhabitants must love their fellow-creatures as children of God. Man has not been placed on the earth merely for the purpose of enjoyment or suffering but rather to work out the ends of righteousness and love. Happiness and perfection are not final goals in themselves; they are only inner and external endowments to be employed in accordance with the will of God. Man's uniqueness lies in the fact that "whereas the voice of God speaks in or through all other creatures, to him it speaks directly that he accept voluntarily its precepts as the propelling force of his life activity." Complete compliance with God's will through an observance of all His commandments, is thus the chief function and destiny of man. The epithet "a God-intoxicated man" that was applied to Spinoza, the pantheist, may well describe Hirsch, who clung to his faith in a transcendental creator with great love and fidelity.

Hirsch and Kant

Hirsch, of course, assumed the rabbinic principle that one must perform the religious commandments because they are the will of

God (*Abot.* 1:3, 2:4, 5:23). God, the fountainhead of all law and morals, has revealed them in the Holy Scriptures for the benefit of man. The law may thus be said to be theonomous, that is, its origin is from God; it may also be regarded as heteronomous, since it emanates from a source outside man. The chief justification for obedience to the Torah is that it is the will of God; its effect on human welfare is of little concern. This idea may be said to conform with that of Immanuel Kant (1724-1804), who had influenced Jewish thinkers, including Hirsch. Kant, who was famed for his theories of knowledge and metaphysics, regarded ethics as the most important philosophical problem. His doctrine of the categorical imperative, which called for the discharge of moral actions regardless of consequences, might well be judged to be congenial to the attitude of the Mosaic law which, as Hirsch pointed out, demands unqualified obedience to its precepts. The positive and negative tenets of the Torah expressed in the form of "Thou shalt do" and "Thou shalt not do," are of such a nature.

Kant's philosophical view as to the source of ethics, however, differed from that of Hirsch, the theologian. Kant believed that human ethics have their origin in the inner conscience of man. The moral law associated with the conscience is autonomous, self-regulating, and self-determining. It alone is the censor which passes on one's ethical judgment and acts. Any other laws, even the theonomous or divine law, are scrutinized by the autonomous conscience before being accepted by the individual. The conscience, of course, is a rationalistic and humanistic concept. Hirsch attempted to reconcile his conception with Kant's view by saying that the conscience is not the exclusive source of virtue, nor is it entirely autonomous, for it is a creation of God and a medium for communicating His moral teaching to man. A divine morality, he argued, is more reliable than that of man, for the laws of the Eternal are beyond time, change, and flux. The laws of the Torah are therefore superior to human laws. Moreover, one who accepts God and His Torah as the highest moral authority identifies his will with that of the Divine. In this manner, Hirsch adapted his view of Judaism to the demands of both humanism and religion. This combination of a suprarationalistic and rationalistic outlook led Hirsch to support the ideals of social and political democracy which inspired the Revolution of 1848.

Despite his rationalistic outlook, Hirsch maintained that the Jew had no right to select those tenets or doctrines of the Torah that he believed to be suitable to his time or to his reason. He must accept the laws of the Torah in their totality; moreover, the ritual and ceremonial practices in Judaism are for him on a par with the ethical. This last notion would, of course, have been rejected by Kant.

Mission of Israel

If man's mission is to serve God, Israel must be exemplary in this regard and devote all its energies to this end. "Everything that you have or will have is given to you only that you may fulfill the task of Israel in your life," Hirsch exhorts the Jew in his *Horeb*.[27] The Jew must help his people attain its mission and destiny:[28]

> . . . Because men had eliminated God from life, nay, even from nature, and found the basis of life in possessions and its aim in enjoyment, deeming life the product of the multitude of human desires, just as they looked upon nature as the product of a multitude of gods, therefore, it became necessary that a people be introduced into the ranks of the nations which through its history and life, should declare God the only creative cause of existence, fulfillment of His will the only aim of life; and which should bear the revelation of His will, rejuve--nated and renewed for its sake. unto all the parts of the world as the motive and incentive of its coherence. This mission required for its carrying out, a nation poor in everything upon which the rest of mankind reared the edifice of its greatness and its power; externally subordinate to the nations armed with proud reliance on self, but fortified with direct reliance on God. . . .

Israel, according to Hirsch, was created for the Jewish religion and not the Jewish religion for Israel.[29] The Jewish people is merely the instrument for the achievement of God's purpose, which is to improve the moral state of man. To achieve this objective, Jews must preserve their isolation and aloofness, preserve their own way of life, and not stoop to the lower moral and ethical levels of other peoples. This segregation, however, is to be of a religious, not of a social nature. Only in the remote future, when mankind, refined and purified by the teachings of the Hebrew prophets, turns to God and acknowledges Him as Ruler, will Israel's mission be accomplished. The period of the Second Commonwealth was a preparation for Israel's mission in the Diaspora; in fact, Christianity aided Israel in its task by "rendering intelligible to the world the objects and purposes of Israel's election."[30] Hirsch's concept of Israel's mission, as of the Diaspora, was similar to that of the Reformers. He believed that the Jewish people has benefited considerably from the lessons learned in exile: that power and force are only transitory, and that their own strength lies mainly in upholding the laws of the Torah. As a result of this experience, they have a rich moral message for humanity. In this respect, the *Galut* has not been a liability, but rather an asset to the Jews.[31]

Israel is a priestly people; it was chosen so only in a spiritual and moral sense, as the people who chose God. That Israel is distinguished primarily as a religious, rather than a political entity may be seen from the fact that it is referred to in the Bible by the term *Am* which connotes a spiritual aggregation, rather than a political one. This is confirmed by the historic fact that the Jews were a people even before they entered the Promised Land, as well as after its destruction. [32]

Judaism and the Zeitgeist

All of Judaism, according to Hirsch, both the oral as well as the written law, is the product of a single revelation. The oral law is an organic part of this revelation, because it is indispensable to a proper understanding of the Biblical text. This idea is in harmony with the rabbinic dictum that even what an authoritative sage is bound to declare in the future is not new, but has already been stated at Sinai (*Jer. Peah.* 2:62).[33]

Because the Torah is divine, we must adhere to it closely. The Torah is timeless, and instead of complaining that Judaism is no longer modern, we should deplore the refusal of our age to conform with Judaism. Judaism, as a divine creation, should shape life, but life cannot shape Judaism. History shows that from the very beginning Judaism and the Jewish people were out of tune with the fashion and demands of the day. Abraham walked alone with

God, in opposition to the popular trends. During long centuries, Judaism was the sole voice of protest against a pagan world;[34] if now there is less of a gap between Judaism and the spirit of the times, it is because the world is responding more and more to the word of God.

Hirsch, like Luzzatto, criticized Maimonides for his attempt to reconcile Judaism with Arab and Greek rationalist thought. The Bible, being the word of God, requires no sanction from without. Mendelssohn, who like Maimonides was an observant Jew, had made a similar blunder, in Hirsch's opinion. In deference to the rationalistic spirit of his generation, he had treated the Bible philologically and aesthetically, but he had failed to teach it in its own context and build it up from within itself. But Judaism is self-sufficient and does not need to be gauged by alien standards.

Secular Culture

Though Hirsch insisted that Judaism need not accommodate to the spirit of the age, he nevertheless challenged the ultra-tradi--tionalists who opposed the Neo-Orthodox attempt to liberate Judaism from its intellectual isolation. He attributed a large measure of the defection of the Jewish youth to Reform or to the Church to the ghetto's exclusion of modern secular culture from Jewish life. He believed in the employment of secular learning as a means of supporting and strengthening religious education. He maintained that the estrangement between Judaism and general culture was not necessarily characteristic of Judaism, but was only the product of the ghetto and the forced segregation of the Jew.

Hirsch criticized the mechanical observance of religious tenets on the part of the superficially pious who, lacking all inspiration, "had seized upon the laws of life and meaning, and reduced them to mummies without any lucidity or spiritual fervor."[35] Judaism as a dynamic, vibrant religious faith should evoke the spirit of joy and dedication in the performance of its precepts. He also deplored the inclination of the Talmudic scholars of his day toward *pilpulism* in their study of rabbinic law. Hirsch's Neo-Orthodoxy was intended to correct those flaws in Orthodoxy and make it more palatable to the modernists.

Emancipation

In the Emancipation Hirsch saw a great opportunity for Israel to develop the ideal Jew who would observe the tenets of his religion in greater freedom, and perform his obligations as a Jew. "In the centuries of persecution and scorn, our mission was imperfectly attainable, but the age of mildness and justice now begun, beckon us to that goal," Hirsch declared.[36] "Emancipation," he warned, " is not the prime objective of the Jew, nor an end of his *Galut*"; he must regard it "only as a new condition of the Jewish people's mission, a new trial, much severer than the trial of oppression."[37] The danger to which the Jew is exposed under the sun of Emancipation is that he may yield to the temptation of pursuing pleasure and gain, and be lured to laxity in following his religious precepts. He may be led to profane the Sabbath for fear that his livelihood will be jeopardized; but in so doing, he will surrender his reliance and trust in the Lord, Who gave his ancestors in the wilderness a double portion of manna for the Sabbath.[38] Hirsch displayed a bold faith in a supernatural Providence.

Adherence to the dietary laws, Hirsch conceded, may erect a wall of separation between Jew and non-Jew and tend to make the Jew unduly conspicuous. But Judaism, he argued, segregates the Jew for the ultimate benefit of mankind, in order to preserve for the latter the great ideals of the Hebrew prophets and sages. This separateness is essential for the Jew to perform his sacred mission. With those Jews who are troubled by the possible effects of these divisive practices on non-Jews, Hirsch fervently pleaded:[39]

> ... Practice righteousness and love as the Holy Law bids you; be just in deed, truthful in words, bear love in your heart for your non-Jewish brethren, as your Law teaches you; feed his hungry, clothe his naked, console his mourners; heal his sick, counsel his inexperienced, assist him with counsel and deed in need and sorrow, unfold the whole noble breadth of your Israeldom, and can you think that he will not respect and love you, or that there will not result as great a degree of social intimacy as your life can concede? ...

Reform Judaism

One as staunch in his Orthodoxy as Samson Raphael Hirsch might well be expected to be bitter and belligerent in his denunciation of Reform; yet in his *Nineteen Letters,* he took a surprisingly tolerant attitude towards that movement. He credited the leaders of Reform with good intentions; he explained that they erred in their comprehension of the truth. The blame was not entirely theirs, for "the entire past bears the responsibility together with them." They erred because they assumed a pattern of life and view of the nature of freedom that is alien to Judaism. Yes, said Hirsch, we need reform; but reform of a different type:[40]

> . . . progress to the Torah height, not however, lowering the Torah to the level of the age, cutting down the towering summit to the sunken grade of our life . . . merely to seek greater ease and comfort in life through the destruction of the eternal code set up for all ages by the God of eternity, is not and never can be reform. . . .

In his foreword to *Horeb,* Hirsch summarized his basic premise: "The divine law must be the seed out of which your intellectual and spiritual life is to grow, not the reverse." When the Jew uses his mental faculties to examine the laws critically, in order to determine which to fulfill and which to nullify, he is sitting in judgment on the Almighty and His perfect Torah. The proponents of Reform, notwithstanding their recognition that the human mind is limited, were nonetheless ready to make their acceptance of the laws of the Torah depend on their own reason. This, to Hirsch, was a logically untenable position.

Science of Judaism

Since Hirsch based his view of Judaism on a one-time divine revelation, he could not subscribe to the historical and evolutionary methods in the study of Judaism advocated by the exponents of the Science of Judaism movement. He could not insist that Jewish law was eternal and immutable if he agreed that Judaism had undergone a process of development. Hirsch extolled the virtue of the traditional Jewish learning and described the Science of Judaism as a "mere idle display of fireworks," which lacked the substance that the old method of the study of Jewish texts contained for the nourishment of Jewish life. The knowledge of the past acquired by the researchers in Jewish history was "dust from the tombs of decomposed corpses blown out over the barren steppes of the present." Hirsch felt that these scholars used their knowledge to cover up and to rationalize their violations of the Jewish law.

In his attitude towards the movement for the Science of Judaism, Hirsch assumed the viewpoint of the ultra-pietists. He thus adopted a policy of *noli me tangere* toward the whole religious tradition, maintaining "that the method of the Science of Judaism pretends that the later authorities (in Judaism) did not understand the earlier, nor the latest, the later . . . and so insinuating that the basis on which living Judaism rests at the present day . . . is nothing but one deception built upon another by guides stricken with blindness and ignorance."[41]

In order to refute the fundamental evolutionary premise of this movement, he attempted in his *Commentary on the Pentateuch* to link Biblical verses with related passages in the Talmud and Midrash, to demonstrate the intimate interconnection between them, and to prove that the rabbinic explanations are implied in Biblical texts.

Prayer

Hirsch's attitude towards prayer was a singular one. Etymologically, he pointed out, the Hebrew word *hitpallel* (prayer) is a reflexive verb derived from the root *pallel* (judgment). The term *hitpallel* suggests a process of self-judgment. Prayer, accordingly, "is not only a request or petition for divine aid" nor even an outpouring of devotion and adoration; it denotes an honest attempt in the presence of God to get a true picture of one's self and to compare what one is with what he ought to be, in order to purify and strengthen one's spiritual powers. Prayer, in this sense, is directed towards the individual; its prime purpose is to arouse a feeling of self-sanctification and self-purification and train the worshiper for submission to God's will.

Since, however, prayers serve as a substitute for the sacrificial service, they constitute a set regimen of worship which brooks no omission or modification. There is a close kinship between sacrifice and prayer; "what the sacrifices achieved by deed-symbol, prayer achieves by word-symbol."[42] In fact, in the fullness of time, when God shall restore the Jewish people to the Holy Land, the sacrificial system and the priesthood will be reinstated as ordained in the Torah. It is a hope voiced in the prophets (*Mal.* 3:4) and the traditional prayer book.

Like the Reformers, Hirsch was not concerned with the revival of Hebrew as a living tongue, but unlike them, he insisted on the use of Hebrew in the prayers, maintaining that they could not be translated properly, nor could their spirit and flavor be transmitted in any other language. He also advocated the retention of the synagogue service because he felt that this would serve as an incentive for Jews to learn the holy tongue, and Hebrew would thus be preserved as a bond among dispersed Jewry. Hirsch conceded, however, that if one knew no Hebrew, he could recite his prayers in a good translation.

Jewish Nationalism and Citizenship

In his attitude toward Jewish nationalism, Hirsch differed radically from the protagonists of what might be termed the Zionism of his day, espoused by Zevi Hirsch Kalischer (1795-1874) and Moses Hess (1812-1872). He adhered literally to the Talmudic dictum not to "force the end" of *Galut*.[43] It is possible, of course, that he was influenced in his thinking by a belief that an effort to rebuild the Jewish state was inconsistent with a German Jew's loyalty to his native land.

> ... We mourn over the sin which brought about the downfall (of the Jewish State), we take to heart the harshness which we have encountered in our years of wandering as the chastisement of a father imposed on us for our improvement, and we mourn the lack of observance of the Torah which that ruin has brought about. Not in order to shine as a nation among nations do we raise our prayers and hope for a reunion with the land, but in order to find a soil for the better fulfillment of our spiritual vocation in that reunion and in the land which was promised and given, and again promised for our observance of the Torah. But this very vocation obliges us, until God shall call us back to the Holy Land, to

live and to work as patriots wherever He has placed us, to collect all physical, material and spiritual forces, and all that is noble in Israel to further the weal of the nations which have given us shelter. It obliges us further to allow our longing for the far-off land to express itself only in mourning, in wishing and hoping; and only through the honest fulfillment of all Jewish duties to await the realization of this hope. But it forbids us to strive for the reunion or the possession of the land by any but spiritual means.[44]. . .

As a rigid pietist, Hirsch could not accept a doctrine which called for the restoration of the Jewish state through human intervention. "Israel may not wrest its independence by its own efforts," he said.[45] Moreover, the crux of *Galut* to Hirsch was not the persecution of the homeless Jew or his people, but the banishment of the *Shechinah* from Zion. The Jewish people are not a nation in the ordinary sense of the term—not a political entity, but one that exists for the Torah, the symbol of spiritual redemption, for which not only Israel, but the entire world yearns.

The Jew in his native land owes his allegiance to the country which has given him protection, in conformity with the admonition of Jeremiah "to seek the peace of the city whither I have caused you to be carried away captive and pray unto the Lord for it; for in the peace thereof shall ye have peace." (*Jer.* 29:7). He must obey its laws in compliance with the Talmudic principle that "the law of the state is the Law" (*Git.* 10b). Hirsch interpreted this view in extreme terms. The state is supreme, and even if it oppresses the Jew, he still owes it complete loyalty. Hirsch spoke to the Jew of his duty towards the state in the following terms:[46]

> . . . This duty is an unconditional duty and not dependent upon whether the State is kindly intentioned towards you or is harsh. Even if they deny your right to be a human being, and to develop a lawful human life upon the soil which bore you, you shall not neglect your duty. Render justice . . . fulfill the duty which God lays upon you: loyalty towards king and country . . .

One wonders if this extreme idea of duty to a wicked government is Jewish in essence. Judaism demands the suppression, not the enhancement, of the forces of evil. It insists on justice. Succumbing or yielding to oppression hardly helps in eliminating injustice. Turning the other cheek or resigned obedience to tyranny was never regarded as right or proper in Judaism.

Hirsch's sentiments towards Germany did not in any way affect his religious sentiment towards Zion. He chided the Reformers for eliminating the fast of *Tishe B'av,* the Ninth day of Ab, commemorating the destruction of the Holy Temple. He and his followers prayed for the restoration of the divine glory to Zion—a religious aspiration without a nationalist motivation.[47] Moreover, the attainment of this goal was entirely God's province, not man's. Hirsch's interest in Hebrew was also purely a religious matter; he had no concern for its revival as a modern spoken tongue. Hirsch's own works were almost entirely in German. In general, he shared the anti-nationalist outlook of the Reformers, though his traditionalist opinion would not permit him to adopt their rationale. His own conformed to the viewpoint of the extreme pietists.

IV. EDUCATIONAL PRINCIPLES

The Complete School

HIRSCH WAS A gifted educational theoretician as well as a practical administrator, who translated his pedagogic ideas into reality in the elementary and secondary schools he established in Frankfort. Hirsch's educational principles were derived from his synthesis of traditional Judaism with the spirit of the Enlightenment. He summarized this view in his epigram *Torah im Derech Eretz.* Both elements were to be combined into a harmonious whole. In terms of subject matter, this meant a combined curriculum of Jewish and general content, a pattern which has been emulated in Jewish day schools in America and abroad.

To refute the notion held by many traditional Jews of the day that general studies were a corrupting influence, Hirsch pointed out that it was only in the ghetto, where the Jew had been separated from the mainstream of European cultural life by the high, somber ghetto walls, that he had excluded secular learning from his educational program and concentrated solely on the religious phase.

Moreover, the cramped physical conditions of the ghetto discouraged the Jew's interest in nature, as a consequence of which he neglected the study of natural science. Since, too, "fetters and burnings at the stake were the spectacle that world history offered to the Jew . . . he was not inclined to read its pages"[48] But this was true only in the ghetto; before that time Jews had been at home in both mundane and Jewish knowledge, and they played a prominent role in both.

The two areas of study, however, are not on a par. Hirsch regarded the religious instruction as primary and the secular as secondary, in contrast to the leaders of the Enlightenment. "The core of all knowledge for every Jew is Torah," he said. He maintained that religious training should be accorded priority because the existence of society depends on its religious foundations. The truths of Judaism should serve for the Jews as the test of all doctrines, views, principles, and attitudes of mundane culture. To preserve the prestige of the religious component in education, it should be taught in the same school as the secular content, and also within the regular school day. If the Jewish program is taught in a supplementary school, outside the usual school hours, it will in all likelihood assume a subordinate role, particularly if the additional schooling will tax the child unduly.

The Jewish youth should be exposed to a worldly education, for Judaism has nothing to fear from contact with any other culture; it looks towards the constant intellectual and moral advancement of mankind and welcomes every phase of human progress. It is, perhaps, the only religion that requires one who enters into the presence of an eminent sage of any faith to recite a benediction praising the Lord "for bestowing His wisdom on flesh and blood." The Jew should, accordingly, not reject or neglect general learning; he should pursue it for its own sake, as well as a means of gaining a better understanding of the intellectual milieu in which he lives. Judaism, however, must not lose its identity in the dominant cultural currents of Europe, though it must not be isolated from them. To provide Jewish children with a one-sided Jewish schooling may eventually lead them to regard Judaism as the "thief of their youth."

The reader of today cannot help but be impressed by the

modernist overtones of Hirsch's rationale for a sound Jewish training, both from the viewpoint of the minority as well as the majority group. Judaism, Hirsch pointed out, is not merely a creed which can be taught by means of a catechism, as the Reformers attempted to do. The teaching of its religious literature, like German or any other, is designed to "open its treasures to the young, and improve their hearts and minds through a life-long communion with the great spirits of their people."

To be understood and appreciated properly this literature must be studied in the original. Only the original words "can convey the flame from mind to mind, from heart to heart; translation destroys the charm." The study of a language and culture contributes to its survival. It also enriches the individual and the civilization in which he lives. As a living example, Hirsch pointed to the German immigrants in America who maintained their spiritual bond with their people by teaching their children the German language and literature. This, Hirsch explained, they did in their own interest as well as for the benefit of their children and their new Fatherland.[49] In culturally pluralistic America, with its diversity of men and peoples, each ethnic group adds its own national spiritual heritage to the great symbiosis of civilizations that make for a more resplendent and greater America.[50]

General education, which should serve as a handmaiden to the Torah, is likely to help open and reinforce Jewish knowledge and give it perspective. The study of the politics and life of other ancient peoples enables the Jew to see the contrast between Jewish law and ethics on the one hand, and Egyptian tyranny and Syrian depravity on the other. The exhortations of the Hebrew prophets become more meaningful to the student if examined within the framework of the political and religious civilizations of ancient Babylonia and Egypt to which they make constant reference.[51] The study of Hebrew, as is true of any foreign tongue, is an aid to developing a mastery of one's native or spoken language. A bicultural training of this kind makes it possible for the student to appreciate Judaism from the standpoint of humanistic culture. As a result, he will emerge better prepared to perform his mission in the world.[52] Jewish and humanistic education are thus complementary; together they will produce the *Yisroel-Mensch,* the ideal Jew, who by the same token will be an ideal human being.

Integrated Education

To accomplish these ends, Hirsch felt the two modes of training should go hand-in-hand and be thoroughly integrated. The teachers in each branch of learning should, therefore, be equipped with both. To bring about an effective blending of the two areas of content, Hirsch proposed that both fields of instruction be taught by the same teacher. The religious spirit, however, should permeate all secular instruction.

> . . . The course of each star and each seed on earth should proclaim to us not only the Creator but also the Legislator Whose will has been realized in inimitable perfection in physical laws in heaven and earth and Who awaits the free realization of the moral law by man in progress aspiring to perfection. It is a single conception in which this view comprises both the Seraphim at the throne of God and the fly in the sunbeam. . . .[53]

The German Jew, as Hirsch envisaged him, was an organic part of German society. One of the important aims of Hirsch's educational program was, accordingly, training for citizenship, which implied, of course, the cultivation of a patriotic sentiment among the students. A radical innovation in traditional Jewish education was his idea of coeducation in all Jewish subjects, except Talmud. In fact, Hirsch introduced such a plan in his elementary school, where it was maintained for many years, setting a precedent in Orthodox schooling.

Hirsch's *Real Schule* (secondary day school) was operated in the same spirit as his lower school. Its combined Jewish and secular curriculum was a pioneering venture, which was emulated by others. Hirsch properly regarded Jewish education as the main artery of Jewish life. He made an original contribution in this area which had a lasting impact on Jewish educational thinking and practice both in Germany and other countries, including Israel and the United States.

V. AGUDATH ISRAEL AND MIZRACHI

Organization of Agudah

IN 1886, about two years before his death, Hirsch founded the *Association for the Interests of Orthodox Judaism,* which consisted of Orthodox Jews in Germany who had detached themselves from their respective Jewish community councils and formed their own independent community organizations, in accordance with the law of secession passed in 1876. In 1907, Jacob Rosenheim proposed a plan for broadening the scope of the Association to include like-minded Jewish groups in other lands. Two years later, the delegates of the Orthodox communities in Lithuania and Poland met with representatives from German Jewish Orthodoxy, in order to iron out ideological differences between the Eastern and Western contingents, which hinged primarily on the role of secular culture in Jewish life. The Eastern Jews, who had been much less influenced by the Enlightenment, regarded general culture as alien and repugnant to Judaism and a threat to its survival; the German Jews, identified with Neo-Orthodoxy, insisted that Judaism and mundane learning were entirely compatible.

This preliminary meeting preluded a conference convened in 1912 at Kattowitz, on the Upper Silesian border, attended by several hundred delegates of traditional Jewry from a number of countries, at which the *Agudath Israel,* (Union of Israel) was launched. The founding of the new organization was accelerated by the defeat at the Tenth World Zionist Congress, held the previous year, of a resolution introduced by the *Mizrachi,* the Orthodox wing of the Zionist organization, providing for equal support for its religiously oriented educational institutions in Palestine, on a par with that accorded the schools of the general Zionists, conducted along nonreligious lines. A number of *Mizrachi* leaders who withdrew from the Zionist movement on this account now joined forces with the anti-Zionist sponsors of the *Agudath Israel.* As a result of the activity of the *Mizrachi* elements in the *Agudah,* as the union was popularly called, the issue of Zionism was kept alive in its discussions.

Agudah Program

During the First World War, the leadership of the *Agudah,* originally in the hands of the Russian rabbis, shifted to the Frankfort group in Germany. Before long, the *Agudah* was firmly established as the international voice of Orthodoxy. It called for close adherence to the Torah and rabbinic law, as expounded by traditionalist rabbis of recognized erudition. Hirsch's antinationalist stance was adopted. The religious nature of Judaism was stressed. "God is the Sovereign of the Jewish people and His law is supreme," the platform of the *Agudah* stated. This implies that Jews are a unique entity; they are unlike any other people in that they are a supernatural group, beyond the ken of history. Because *Galut* represents God's punishment visited on Israel for its sins, *Geulah* (redemption) can come only from God. It was therefore sinful to attempt to hasten it, as the Zionists were doing.

Despite its anti-Zionist position, the *Agudah* encouraged colonization in the Holy Land as a religious duty, in accordance with the Biblical precept of *Yishuv Haaretz* (settlement of the land) (*Deut.* 26:1, 17:14). Spurred by a crucial need for a haven for European Jewry, the *Agudah* intensified its colonization efforts in Palestine after the rise of Hitler in 1933. The *Agudah* continually and unhesitatingly agitated against Zionism and the Zionist effort before the League of Nations and the British mandatory government in Palestine. Because of its violent opposition to women suffrage and other issues, the *Agudah* constituency refused to join the *Knesset Israel* (the Assembly of Israel) which the mandatory government recognized as the official representative body of the Jewish community in Palestine. In its opposition to Zionism, the *Agudah* at times went to the extreme of cooperating with the Arab Nationalist Committee, the avowed enemy of a Jewish Palestine. On this issue, the ultra-Orthodox pursued a line similar to that of the extremist wing of classical American Reform, the American Council for Judaism.[54]

In the years since the creation of the Jewish state, the *Agudah* has persisted in its views. It demands that the State of Israel be governed entirely by religious law as a theocracy, and not as a secular state. It maintains that secular sovereignty of the Jewish state is to be articulated only in its relationship and its dealings with other nations; in its internal affairs, it should be bound by the laws of the Torah. For several years the *Agudah* was represented in the first coalition cabinet, but it had since withdrawn from it, only to return in 1977, with the establishment of the Begin government. Begin is himself an Orthodox Jew.

In its efforts to propagate its ideas, the *Agudah* created a system of schools in pre-war Poland and other countries, the core of which was the network of *Beth Jacob Girls' Schools*.[55] These schools, first established in 1913 in Cracow, Poland, through the zeal of a Jewish seamstress, Sarah Schnierer, were taken over by the *Agudah* in 1929. Schools for girls represented an innovation in Orthodoxy, which had little, if any, tradition of organized Jewish education for girls. In 1929, the year that the *Agudah* took over the girls' schools, it set up an agency, *Horev,* for the purpose of establishing a network of boys' schools. A decade later, these had an enrollment of over fifty thousand boys, while the girls' schools numbered forty thousand. Both school systems in Europe were destroyed during the Nazi catastrophe.

Schools under *Agudah* sponsorship have been reorganized in Europe and have spread to the United States and Israel; in Israel they are detached from the regular government system and comprise the *Hinuch Atzmai* (independent schools). In the latter school network, the sexes are separated, the religious subject matter is given priority over the secular, and the nonreligious content is adapted to the pietist viewpoint of the *Agudah*.[56] There is promise, however, that the intransigence of the *Agudah's* separatist policy in Israel in educational matters will eventually wane, as has been the case in a measure on the political front after the *Agudah's* loss of its power base in Eastern Europe following the Holocaust.

The Mizrachi

The extreme Orthodox elements were content merely to mourn and lament the destruction of the Jewish homeland, and wait and pray for the coming of the Messiah to restore the Jewish people to their land. But Zevi Hirsch Kalischer[57] (1795-1874), a leading traditionalist rabbi in his day, believed differently. Disillusioned by the failure of the Emancipation in Germany and the persecutions of the Jews in eastern Europe, he wrote his *Derishat Zion (Quest for Zion)* in 1862. In this work, he proposed the idea that colonization and a practical program of work were to precede, not follow, the coming of the Messiah. This revolutionary proposal gave impulse to the organization almost half a century later of the religious Zionist movement, the *Mizrachi,* which represented a synthesis of Jewish nationalism and religious traditionalism.

In 1901, only a few years after Herzl summoned the first Zionist Congress in Basel, Rabbi Isaac Jacob Reines (1839-1915) convened a conference of religious Zionists at Vienna at which the *Mizrachi* party was founded. Reines was elected as the first president. The name of the organization is a combination of the initial and final letters of two Hebrew words, *Merkaz Ruhani* (spiritual center) which calls attention to its purpose of making the land of Israel the center of religious Judaism. The name *Mizrachi,* itself meaning "eastern," refers to the organization's objective to rebuild the Jewish homeland. *Mizrachi* has branches throughout the world.[58]

The *Mizrachi,* as an Orthodox alignment, regards Judaism as a religion based on divine revelation of the Torah, which it believes should dominate Jewish life; its objectives are summarized in the slogan "The Land of Israel for the People of Israel according to the Torah of Israel." *Mizrachi* expounds the view that the Jewish people is distinguished from all others by the fact that it is founded on the Torah. Jewish nationalism, according to this principle, should serve primarily as a medium for the advancement of religious Judaism. Unlike its rightist sister organization, *Agudath Israel,* which operates on a separatist program, *Mizrachi* affirms the national unity of the Jewish people and functions within the framework of Zionism. In the state of Israel, *Mizrachi* is represented in the cabinet and participates in the religious bloc, which demands the observance of Jewish religious laws in government and in all agencies and institutions. It conducts a network of schools in Israel which is part of the government system. Before World War II, it maintained many schools in Eastern Europe, but hardly a vestige remained of them after the Nazi holocaust. In the United States, the philosophy of the *Mizrachi* is epitomized in Yeshiva University, which serves as the educational archetype of the movement.

10

Luzzatto's Neo-Orthodoxy

I. HIRSCH AND LUZZATTO

Similarities

NEO-ORTHODOXY IN JUDAISM may be broadly defined as the acceptance of the totality of Jewish law and practice within a framework of modernism. In Italy, its chief exponent was the brilliant and versatile Jewish scholar, Samuel David Luzzatto (1800-1865) who, with the other ideologists of his school of thought, shared an *a priori* belief in the divine character of the Pentateuch. It was their view that the basic doctrines of Judaism fall outside the realm of reason, which, being the product of human perception alone, is not as reliable a guide as divine revelation. On this account, too, it is not possible to question the miracles or supernatural events related in the Mosaic books, for they are beyond nature and experience. In general, the Neo-Orthodox, like the Orthodox, followed the teachings of Judah Halevi (1085-1140), who extolled religion and faith over philosophy and logic.[1] Luzzatto declared that anyone who did not subscribe to the Sinaitic revelation and the Mosaic authorship of the Pentateuch undermined Judaism.

Differences

But there were also points of disparity between Luzzatto's and

249

Hirsch's positions. Italian Orthodoxy, unlike that of Germany and other parts of Europe, did not have to contend with the problem of secular culture, for among Italian Jewry worldly knowledge was taken for granted. Moreover, Luzzatto was closely associated with the *Wissenschaft des Judentums* movement, which had gained a foothold in his native Trieste. Luzzatto employed the critical method in the investigation of some of the externals surrounding the text of the Pentateuch, and he applied it more freely in the analysis of other books of the Bible. Hirsch, as we have seen, denounced the evolutionary approach of the Science of Judaism as doing violence to the basic principles of Judaism.

II. Luzzatto's Life and Thought

Biography

Samuel David Luzzatto was born in Trieste, when that city was still under Austrian domination, to an old Italian Sephardic Jewish family that traced its ancestry to Moses Hayim Luzzatto of Padua (1707-1747) the noted Jewish scholar, poet, and mystic, who on account of his dramas and other works is often considered to have been the founder of modern Hebrew literature. Samuel was also descended from Ephraim Luzzatto (1739-1793), a Hebrew poet and physician, who in 1768 published in London a volume of Hebrew songs and poetry. Hezekiah, Samuel's father, was a deeply religious man, inclined towards mysticism. Though only a wood turner by trade, he possessed considerable Jewish and general learning. A *Luftmensch* by temperament, Hezekiah was continually preoccupied with grandiose plans. He had schemes for constructing a perpetual-motion machine and similar contrivances. As a result of these distractions, he found it difficult to concentrate on earning a livelihood for his family. Because of his poverty, and also in keeping with numerous rabbinic injunctions, Hezekiah taught his son a trade², but the latter from his early youth preferred a scholarly career.

Samuel was a precocious and gifted lad. He received his basic education at the Trieste Talmud Torah, a liberal institution organized along the progressive principles laid down by Mendelssohn's disciple, Naphtali Wessely (1725-1805), which called for a combined program of Jewish and general studies. After completing his formal schooling in Bible, Talmud, general science, and ancient and modern languages at the local school, young Luzzatto continued to acquire further learning through his own efforts, and also with the aid of his father. He earned his livelihood as a tutor. In 1829, Luzzatto left his native city to accept a professorship in the newly established *Collegio Rabbinico* in Padua, the first modern rabbinical seminary in the world—a post he was to occupy for the rest of his days. His academic work gave him both opportunity and motivation for study and writing.

Luzzatto exhumed old manuscripts from archives and libraries, thereby saving them from oblivion. One of his most important works was the publication, with an introduction, annotations, and corrections, of some eighty-six religious poems of Judah Halevi, in the *Divan* (1864). This volume helped to open the portals of medieval Hebrew poetry to the Jewish scholarly world. Some years earlier, he had prepared his *Mavo* (1865), an historical and critical introduction to the *Mahzor* (festival liturgy) according to the "Roman" version. He also composed the first Jewish critical commentaries on a number of Biblical books. He translated the Pentateuch, the *Haftorot*[3] (1860), and the Hebrew daily prayer book into Italian. In addition, he wrote Hebrew grammatical and philological treatises and theological studies in Hebrew and Italian. Aside from these and scores of other works, Luzzatto contributed hundreds of articles and essays to practically every Jewish scholarly periodical of his day, in Hebrew, German, French, and Italian. He did much for the revival of Hebrew *belles-lettres*. This vast literary activity covered a period of five decades.

Chief among his writings is a work entitled *Iggrot Shadal*[4] (*The Epistles of Shadal*), a compilation of some seven hundred letters written by him to a large circle of scholars on a miscellany of subjects. This material, published posthumously (1882-1894) in nine volumes, evidences the extensive erudition and encyclopedic learning of its author. Luzzatto's sons selected some ninety of these letters and assembled them in a collection called *Peninei Shadal* (*Pearls of Shadal*)[5] (1883). They cover a wide range of biographical, literary, exegetical, theological, grammatical, and historical themes, and include also letters, discussions of dreams, Aristotelian and Spinozean philosophy, and other topics. Luzzatto's thought is not organized in any volume or group of volumes, but is scattered throughout his books, essays, and letters.

Romantic Influences

In the case of the Jewish scholars and literati of the nineteenth century including Luzzatto, the Romantic tendency, as was previously noted,[6] was expressed in the return to Jewish tradition, the regeneration of Jewish learning, the Hebrew language, literature, and poetry. It stimulated the study of the evolution of Judaism which lay at the foundation of the Science of Judaism movement. Not only the European, but also the Italian Romantic movement affected Luzzatto, who specifically mentioned in one of his letters the impact upon him of his contemporary, the outstanding Italian Romantic writer Alessandro Manzoni[7] (1785-1873), author of the historical novel *I Promessi Sposi* (*The Betrothed*). Other Italian Romantic writers, among them the dramatist Silvio Pellico (1788-1854), also left their imprints on Luzzatto.

Two centuries before Shadal, Blaise Pascal (1623-1662) espoused the emotional approach to religion, declaring that "the heart has its own thoughts, which reason does not know." Shadal's attitude toward religion was strongly influenced by Rousseau (1712-1778), whom Luzzatto mentioned frequently and who, like Luzzatto, gave expression to both the rationalistic and the Romantic viewpoints. Rousseau had started out as a rationalist, a disciple of Voltaire and the French Enlightenment, but in his later years, he became its most violent opponent. In other words, he at first challenged tradition and later defied the Enlightenment. Luzzatto did not evince both tendencies at successive periods, but did so simultaneously. He disapproved, for example, of the critical investigation of the Pentateuch, on the ground that the sacred text was too carefully guarded to permit errors to creep in. Yet, he unhesitatingly assailed the traditional view that the *Nikkud,* (the phonetic or diacritical signs used in Hebrew)[8] is of Mosaic origin, contending instead, as had Elijah Levita (1469-1549) almost four centuries earlier, that they were devised considerably later, during the Gaonic period, which began after the sixth century. Because of his contradictory tendencies, he was regarded as a *Maskil* (adherent of the Enlightenment) by the ultra-Orthodox and as a fundamentalist by the *Maskilim*.

The Intellect and Emotions

Actually, one could easily attack the notion that because reason is an essential criterion in many aspects of life, it must be the sole test in all. We are equipped with sentiments and emotions that we should at times exploit in preference to logic. Rousseau pointed out that in the area of religion and conduct, we may do better to rely on sentiment and feelings, rather than on syllogisms. In his prize-winning essay on the subject, "Has the Progress of the Arts Corrupted or Advanced Morals," he insisted that culture was not an unmitigated blessing. As an example, he pointed to the revolutions and unrest which the invention of printing had indirectly caused in Europe. He ventured to suggest that reflection was contrary to nature and urged that too rapid an intellectual development had its dangers and that it was, therefore, desirable to train the heart and emotions. Luzzatto similarly declared that man was not only mind, but also possessed feelings. Man's soul and religion were given him to steer his emotions in the direction of the good and the right. If, however, philosophy should venture to guide religion, both would perish.[9]

Another philosopher who exercised as great an influence on Shadal as Rousseau was the sensationalist Etienne de Condillac (1715-1780), to whom Luzzatto referred in his autobiography as his master and teacher. Condillac expounded the idea that the content of the mind's conscious activities is derived solely from sense perception. He illustrated his theory with a figurative statue, endowed only with the sense of smell, which receives the successive stimuli of each of the other senses as they are added. Out of the same process of perception and in the same manner, Condillac taught, the passions and ultimately the moral will are developed. Condillac was a disciple of John Locke (1632-1704), who advanced the theory that all knowledge and experience emanate from the senses and that "there is nothing in the mind that was not first in the senses." The mind is a *tabula rasa* on which sense impressions are recorded.[10] Both Condillac and Locke thus regarded personality as an aggregate of the sensations.

These ideas, however, lead logically to atheism and determinism. To forestall them, Condillac appended a treatise to his main psychological work, the *Traite des Sensations,* in which he repudiated both antireligious conclusions and upheld the doctrine of free will and generally also the substantive reality of the soul as a sort of sixth human sense. Luzzatto not only accepted the religious principles outlined by Condillac, but in line with the latter's sensualism, asserted that what cannot be ascertained through sense perception cannot be investigated.[11] Consequently, abstract questions, such as the existence of the Deity or the soul or immortality, or even the problem of Biblical miracles, fall outside the realm of human inquiry. Nevertheless, Shadal attempted to prove in one of his Italian works[12] on the basis of the rationalistic argument, from order, harmony, and the laws of nature, that there must be a divine guiding force in the universe.

Luzzatto's thought was a strange combination of critical and Romantic ideas. This accounts for his numerous inconsistencies and for his failure to develop a systematic philosophy. On the one hand, he followed a rationalistic course when he rejected mysticism as a current of thought foreign to Judaism. He did so again when he declared that the *Zohar* could not have been the creation of Simeon Bar Yochai, the second-century sage, since it discusses the Hebrew diacritical marks and accents which, as previously observed, were the product of a considerably later age.[13] Despite these rationalistic opinions, he nevertheless believed that the dead appearing in dreams confirm the existence of another world.[14] We discern another logical incongruity in his stance on the Book of Isaiah. Though Shadal did not insist on the absolute incorruptibility of the Hebrew prophetic books, he found sufficient reason to uphold the unity of the Book of Isaiah, including the latter portion following Chapter 40, which Krochmal and practically all Biblical scholars since the nineteenth century have agreed was composed by one or more later prophets. In fact, he broke with his friend Solomon Judah Rapoport, a noted Hebrew savant, on this question. Luzzatto simply maintained that the same author could employ various styles of writing; moreover, that it would be a slight and an insult to earlier generations to charge that they had not accurately transmitted so important a work as that of Isaiah. This opinion, however, did not deter him from making corrections in its text, as he did in other non-Mosaic books of the Bible.

Shadal adopted the critical viewpoint when he conceded that the Book of Ecclesiastes was of much later date than that assigned to it by tradition. Moreover, notwithstanding the fact that the Book of Ecclesiastes was part of the sacred Scriptures, he opposed its pessimistic outlook. However, he upheld in the main the traditional view that the Psalms were the work of King David, though he admitted that there were some later Psalms. He believed, too, that the Book of Job was of Mosaic authorship (*B.B.* 14b)[15] and not a product of the post-Biblical period, as Biblical scholars generally held. Though he regarded the Torah as being letter-perfect and insisted that it "does not dread the light nor does it fear true criticism," he nevertheless maintained that it should not be exposed to question and scrutiny.

Scriptural Truth

The Jew, Luzzatto urged, must accept on faith the fundamental doctrine of the divine origin of the Torah and its corollary, the existence of one God, as the only binding dogma in Judaism. From this belief is derived the sanction for all religious laws and observances. There may be other principles in the Torah, but they are not considered as primary in Judaism. For this reason, Luzzatto pointed out, as did Mendelssohn before him, Jews could differ among themselves on a host of religious matters without being considered heretics, as illustrated by the examples of Hasdai Crescas (1340-1410) and his disciple Joseph Albo (1380-1440). These medieval scholars took issue with Maimonides for failing to distinguish in his Thirteen Articles of Faith between rudimentary and derivative doctrines. Crescas even questioned the doctrine of free will, while another sage, Gersonides (1288-1344), subscribed to the theory of creation from primordial matter and not creation *ex nihilo.* The piety of these men, however, was not impugned, for Judaism does not lay stress on man's beliefs and opinions, but places its major emphasis on practice. The Torah aims to lead men into paths of righteousness, to improve their ethics through obedience to its laws, rather than to ensure a correct and uniform faith.

Luzzatto was firmly convinced of the truth of the miracles recounted in the Bible, as well as of prophecy, for he declared that all natural laws are of necessity a product of God's will[16], since the natural forces are not self-propelling. Man knows only the laws of cause and effect, time and space, but those are merely a matter of the sensations and experience—while supernatural events are beyond the domain of sense perception. It is not impossible that something may take place outside the limits of experience. Prophecy, too, falls in this category; it contradicts experience and experience cannot, therefore, be invoked to confirm it. Like Saadya (892-942), Judah Halevi, and other Jewish thinkers, Shadal regarded the miracles associated with the Exodus as historical, since they were confirmed by six hundred thousand living witnesses[17] on their way from Egypt.

Despite these beliefs,[18] Luzzatto asserted that the Torah was esteemed by God, not so much because it was the depository of absolute truth, as for its major function—that of fostering better human behavior. The search for pure truth is the domain of philosophy; the purpose of religion is to preach virtue and guide people in the righteous path. The Deity, moreover, cannot always employ perfect truth in His communication with man, for it is beyond human power to grasp it. Society, too, cannot be sustained on the basis of genuine truth; it may well have to resort to the kind of illusion that nature itself occasionally resorts to in performing God's will. Nature, for example, conceals the underlying biological purpose of marriage and wedlock, procreation and the attendant responsibilities and burdens of parenthood, behind the overpowering emotions of romantic and parental love. Similarly, the Bible hides the true reason for sacrifice and worship behind the simple notion that the Lord is concerned with these rituals, when their prime purpose is actually the psychological effect on the worshiper, who is to be impressed by the ritual with a sense of humility and reverence.

Ethics of Judaism

Luzzatto regarded Judaism as a religion of the heart rather than of the mind or intellect;[19] its doctrines, he observed, gave evidence of the spirit of compassion with which man is naturally endowed,[20] and which impels him to do good for its own sake. This sense of pity, he believed, is an outgrowth of the normal human tendency of self-love, projected toward another being. This impulse animates many of the Scriptural and rabbinic precepts, exemplified by the Biblical provision for return at night of the pledged garment (*Ex.* 22:25) or the institution of the Sabbatical year (*Deut.* 15:9) which cancels all debts and relieves the poor man of a paramount financial burden. Characteristic of this trait, too, is the rabbinic law prohibiting an employer from depriving the porters of their wages, because they had accidentally broken the barrel of wine they were carrying (*B.M.* 83a). The charitable attitude towards the widow, orphan, and stranger exemplifies the quality of mercy in the Mosaic and Talmudic laws. It is for this reason that also the pagan peoples in ancient times acknowledged the high morality of Israel, for even the royal sinners in Israel, like Ahab, extended forbearance and kindness (*IK.* 20:31).

The Bible, of course, also includes precepts which may appear to us as brutal. There is, for example, the command, "Thou shalt not suffer any soul to live" (*Deut.* 20:16) from among the Canaanites condemned to annihilation (*Deut.* 7:2). This, Shadal was at pains to refute. He pointed to the catastrophes in nature—earthquakes and other such cataclysms—and drew a parallel between the Biblical injunction and natural disasters, for he saw both nature and the Torah as manifestations of God. In his complete faith and trust in the righteousness of God, he condoned the natural cataclysms, as though they offered a justification or an excuse for man's inhumanity to man. Moreover, Luzzatto was himself so unalterably convinced of God's mercy and justice that he failed to see that to the skeptic these calamities might reflect on God's ability to control the sinister forces of nature.

Another pillar of Judaism, according to Shadal, is the doctrine of divine retribution, a vital principle which he believed to be one of the cornerstones of society. Reward and punishment, Shadal insisted, are meted out in this world and not, as Mendelssohn suggested, in the next. Mendelssohn's idea, Luzzatto feared, would be injurious to morals. It is, he maintained, not correct to assume that the wicked prosper, though it may appear so. In a poem entitled *Equal Portions,* which is suggestive of the idea expressed by Emerson in his *Essay on Compensation,* Luzzatto maintained that God, who sees not only the external acts of a human being, but peers into his heart, assigns each person a like portion of good and evil, joy and sorrow, and none receives "flowers without thorns." Shadal's unshakeable faith in divine mercy is especially moving. It is remarkable that the poet retained so strong a religious faith in view of the many trials and tragedies he suffered in his family life. He spent his life in poverty. His first wife died in 1841, following an eight-year siege of melancholia after the death of a young child. His children were constantly ailing. His eldest son, Ohev Ger (Philoxenus),[21] a highly gifted and promising young scholar, died in 1854, at the age of twenty-five. His only daughter Miriam, who was very talented linguistically, passed away unexpectedly at eighteen. Despite his adversities, Luzzatto remained steadfast in his faith and piety.

Abrahamism and Atticism

Western civilization, Luzzatto declared, is composed of two antithetical forces; Atticism, the culture of ancient Greece or Athens, and Abrahamism, the religious thought of the Jews. Abrahamism originated with Abraham, chosen of God because he rejected polytheism. God also charged Abraham and his descendants with the duty of preserving both Judaism and universal ethics for posterity. The Jews were given special precepts regarding diet, circumcision, laws of purity and sacrifices as a means of setting them apart from other peoples. Only in the distinctive rites essential to Jewish group cohesion and survival does Judaism differentiate between Jew and gentile. As other Jewish thinkers before Luzzatto had stressed, Judaism unlike other faiths promises salvation to the righteous of all people, not exclusively to the Jews. Accordingly, all men are God's children, but the Jews are his chosen people, for they are a "kingdom of priests and a holy nation" (*Ex.* 19:6) and as such must bear a particular regimen of ethical and ritual responsibilities and obligations. Their selection is thus merely an application of the idea of *noblesse oblige*.

According to Luzzatto, mankind is indebted to Israel for morality and the love of the good. Such notions as justice, equity, and kindness were received as divine gifts from Sinai.[22] On the other hand, Greece gave to the world philosophy, science, and art, a love of harmony and splendor. Our predilection for the beautiful and pleasant over the good and beneficial, our preference for delightful rhetoric over genuine truth, for theoretic abstraction over integrity and honesty, and, generally, the pursuit of pleasure, pride, and wealth, Luzzatto attributed to Athens. He saw no virtue in technocracy; he pointed up the moral lag in our culture to which Rousseau and others had made reference. This, too, he charged to Athens and its rationalistic doctrines. "When were there as many great inventions as in this generation? Yet, have these new discoveries eliminated war, murder, robbery, poverty, disease, envy, hate, oppression and untimely death?" he challenged. He reproached man for having improved his machines but not himself.

The Greek elements in our civilization, Luzzatto complained, have produced a meaningless intellectuality, suitable for philosophers, but not for the masses, who require the vitamins of morality.[23] The exaltation of reason is foreign to Judaism, Luzzatto maintained. He criticized Ibn Ezra (1093-1167) and Maimonides for their rationalistic inclinations, which, he believed tended to divert Judaism from its true course into alien channels of thought. He attacked Maimonides for not citing the rabbinic authorities for the decisions he adduced in his Code, and even more for his advocacy of Aristotle's golden mean. The true path of the Lord, taught by Abraham (*Gen.* 18:19)[24] is not the golden mean but the uncompromising way of justice and righteousness, as ordained in the Scriptures. Ibn Ezra's leanings[25] towards Hellenistic rationalism, he charged, lead to speculation and not to concrete action toward the goal of human betterment. The philosophers, after centuries of contemplation, have as yet failed to agree on any one system of thought; they have, however, made pessimists of people. On the other hand, Torah and Judaism demand of the individual that he follow the divine precept in order to attain the lofty heights of the righteous, who, according to the Talmud, are even greater than the heavenly angels (*San.* 93a). To achieve true progress, civilization must strengthen its religious and ethical structure while combating and countering its immoral, atheistic Greek foundations. This attitude prompted Luzzatto to proclaim feelingly, "My God is not the God of Kant, but the God of the *Tanakh!*"[26]

Luzzatto and Spinoza

Luzzatto's views were sharply opposed to those of Baruch (Benedict) Spinoza (1632-1677), who appeared to Luzzatto to be the epitome of the philosopher. A son of Marrano parents, Spinoza received a good Jewish schooling upon which he later drew for some of his philosophical speculations. He was influenced by the rationalistic approach of Maimonides' *Guide for the Perplexed* and by Ibn Ezra's Biblical criticism, by the deterministic doctrines of Crescas, and by other medieval Jewish thinkers. It was, however, the French philosopher René Descartes (1596-1650) who helped to mould Spinoza's thinking most. Spinoza borrowed both his presuppositions and his mathematical method from Descartes. The latter began his philosophical system with the premise *Dubito ut intelligam*—one must doubt in order to know; one must doubt everything except the thinking process itself, or doubt in itself. Thus, a man can be certain only of his own state of consciousness, which represents existence. Hence, Descartes concluded, *"Cogito ergo sum"* ("I think, therefore I am").

God, to Descartes, is the perfect Being, who cannot and will not deceive us for He could not be perfect if He did. God has implanted in us innate ideas, among which are the mathematical truths, the notion of God, and a natural belief in the external world.[27] These are clear and distinct ideas, and hence true. The physical world has the property of extension or space, which may be described in terms of mathematical relationships. The manner in which God is related to mind is, however, different from His relation to spatial or material things. God is the link between the mechanical world of the senses and the rational world of the mind. Thus, the universe is a dualism, composed of matter and mind, spirit and body, the world and God.

At this point, Spinoza the Jew, steeped in monotheistic thought, diverged from his master, Descartes. For Spinoza there was only one infinite substance, God, who is not a separate independent force but *Deus sive natura* (God is nature)—the natural order and God are one. Everything that exists or occurs in the world is an aspect of one of the two attributes of God, thought and extension. The spiritual or mental life of man is as much a part of God as the sand and the water of the sea. God is the most abstract unity conceivable. He is undefinable, for to define or to ascribe any quality to Him is to limit Him. He is not the Creator of the world, for He is the world. Accordingly, too, His infinite thought is not our finite thought, nor His extension our finite extension. God is, then, not a personal God in any sense. He is a logical necessity, and His world is only the necessary outcome of His divine essence, as indispensable to the universe as the three sides or angles of a triangle to triangularity. Thus, Spinoza was a pure monist.

This view of God led the German mystic and Romanticist Novalis to describe Spinoza as "God intoxicated" while others like Shadal branded him an atheist. Spinoza's God is not Luzzatto's Creator of the universe, the ethical God of Judaism or its daughter religions, Christianity and Islam. These religions are predicated on a belief in a living, loving, moral God who is concerned with the conduct and welfare of his creatures. Spinoza's God lacks a moral purpose in the universe. Spinoza, too, was a rigid determinist, in the tradition of the ancient Stoics. He maintained that "all things which happen, happen according to the fixed law of nature." One's selection of a course of action or behavior is, it follows, the product of preconditions, psychological or other natural factors; there is, then, no free choice or free will. Nothing is inherently good or bad in the world; all good and bad are relative to a given situation. The two are, therefore, not opposing concepts. Man must learn to surrender to the natural sequence of events, not to react to them emotionally, but rather to free himself from the shackles of his normal sentiments and live as *sub specie aeternitatis,* (under the aspect of eternity) according to a broader outlook and the values or appearances of the eternal cosmos. The highest goal of man should be the intellectual love of God, which one can achieve through a better knowledge of the world. Such knowledge will endow man with greater power and control over his environment.

Without attempting to analyze the reasoning or assumptions of either Descartes or Spinoza, we shall touch merely upon some of their implications. Spinoza's God is too detached from humanity to have any moral influence upon it. He is not the God of revelation or the God Who inspired the Hebrew prophets to protest against iniquity and injustice and who, when catastrophe struck their people, brought them solace and comfort. Spinoza's doctrine of resignation would make the sacrifices of the Jewish martyrs—in fact the entire struggle that is Jewish history—meaningless. Also, Spinoza's attitude towards good and evil deprives men of the motivation and clarity of choice that religion provides; moreover, it nullifies the message and purpose of the teachers and sages in Judaism and their lofty ideals. Spinoza, by his beliefs, had read himself out of Judaism; by his own admission, he did so even before his formal excommunication in 1656.

Spinoza's fundamental philosophy and metaphysical outlook were thoroughly repugnant to Luzzatto. His extreme rationalism sharply clashed with Luzzatto's Romanticism. It is logically point-less for any one to assume an attitude of piety or worship towards a divinity that represents merely the fixed and immutable order of nature or a mechanical process. Luzzatto, moreover, extolled the human emotions, while Spinoza claimed they merely enslaved man and that one had to liberate himself from them in order to achieve true happiness. A man who does not love or hate, Luzzatto asserted, is not human, but merely a flint or rock. Luzzatto assumed, further, that compassion was the source of Judaism, but Spinoza regarded this emotion as a weak, feminine virtue. Luzzatto cherished the Jewish precepts and rituals, while Spinoza failed to see any intrinsic sanctity in them. The precepts of the Torah, which Luzzatto considered eternal, Spinoza saw only as having been designed for the government and survival of the ancient Jewish state.

These differences in viewpoint led Luzzatto to denounce Spi-nozaism and to carry on a polemic war with its disciples. Luzzatto regarded Spinozaism as the confirmed enemy of Judaism. "Only he whose heart is stone can see merely determinism in the miracles of nature," Luzzatto declared. He further maintained that one who believed as Spinoza did was bound to be an immoral person, for the doctrine that there is no moral law or moral judge in the world could well lead to ethical chaos. Luzzatto's views were thus entirely irreconcilable with those of the seventeenth-century Dutch Jewish philosopher.

III. Jewish Nationalism

Nationalistic Influences

To the extent that Romanticism focused on the history of a people, it gave impulse to the growth of its nationalistic spirit. Romanticism concentrated on the early centuries and the primitive state of the group, when it was relatively free from the shackles of law, custom, and convention of later ages. It held the tribal or ethnic unit in high esteem and sought out its distinctive traits and characteristics.

The nineteenth century was marked by the nationalistic revolt in European countries. It was particularly intense in Italy, which had enjoyed a taste of national unity under Napoleon I, but was again dissected by the action of the Congress of Vienna into a mere geographical abstraction. The example set by the Italian heroes in their battle for unification could not but have impressed Shadal. There was Giuseppe Mazzini (1805-1872), to whom the struggle was a religious crusade. Count Camillo Benso di Cavour (1810-1861), prime minister of Sardinia-Piedmont, had contributed his diplomatic gifts to the success of the Irredentist movement and Giuseppe Garibaldi (1807-1882), his considerable military prowess. These influences, and the nationalistic atmosphere in which Luzzatto lived, no doubt affected his outlook on the question of Jewish nationalism. Though Luzzatto often shifted in his thought between the Romantic and the rationalistic approach, he was entirely consistent and unflagging in his Jewish nationalistic zeal.[28]

Jewish Particularism

Shadal emulated Judah Halevi (1085-1140) in his nationalistic as well as religious outlook. In Judah Halevi who regarded the Jewish people as a select group, the heart among the nations,[29]

Shadal saw a kindred spirit. His love for the nationalistic poet led him to publish Halevi's *Zionides* in 1840, in a special volume which he entitled *Betulat Bat Yehudah* (*Virgin Daughter of Judah*) after the biblical metaphor (*Lam.* 1:15) for Jerusalem, which was considered inviolate.[30] It was Luzzatto's nationalism that prompted him to devote his life to an intensification of the Jewish consciousness through an exploration and interpretation of Judaism's great classical and medieval literature.

Luzzatto referred to his conception of Judaism as Abrahamism, thereby stressing its ethnic element. The special precepts given Israel were a means of guarding the group's distinctiveness, but the universal ethical principles of justice, righteousness, and morality were designed for the protection of society and humanity generally. Thus, Jewish nationalism was not a narrow chauvinism; it served humanity as a whole. In surrendering his particularism and uniqueness, the Jew not only did violence to Judaism, but also deprived mankind of an important ethical force. The moral temperament which has characterized Judaism is, however, a psychic, not a racial trait; it is not transmitted to Jews in their genes, but is an important element in their religious teachings.

Luzzatto's nationalistic ideas were permeated by Romanticism. As an extreme example of this fusion of the two currents of thought, we may cite his poem for the Ninth of Ab, written in short, pithy phrases[31] pleading for the deliverance of his people from suffering, the restoration of the Jewish state, and with it, too, in a nostalgic vein, the revival of the priesthood and the sacrifices. Already Maimonides had tried to explain away[32] the sacrificial cult as a concession to the primitive, pagan, idolatrous impulses; for a rationalist and a follower of the Haskalah, the sacrificial worship would appear to be crude, if not barbaric. Yet, to Luzzatto, this ancient ritual was an integral part of the basic religion of the Jewish people, to be restored with the regeneration of the political state!

Luzzatto saw nationalistic implications in essentially religious institutions. Maimonides, the rationalist, saw as the primary purpose of the single sanctuary[33] prescribed in the Bible (*Deut.* 12:26) the discouragement of the sacrificial system; Shadal,[34] the nationalist, saw the unification of the Hebrew people as the primary objective. Shadal envisaged the same purpose in the provision for Sabbath rest. But Maimonides regarded the sacred day as a means of focusing the attention of the Jew on God, the Creation, and the fact that as free men Jews could keep the Sabbath in accordance with God's precept—something they could not do as slaves in Egypt.[35] Thus, Luzzatto interrelated the major religious and nationalistic values in Judaism and wove them into a single unity.

Emancipation

Shadal's nationalism was evident also in his attitude towards Jewish Emancipation. In pursuing the spirit of modernism, many Jews, Luzzatto said, surrendered their Jewish individuality and distinctiveness, in return for which they expected to be granted civic equality. In fact, these Jews, Luzzatto insisted, were prepared to surrender their national values even for a mere shadow of egalitarianism, let alone complete liberty. Such equality, however, Luzzatto could not regard as true emancipation; it spelled bondage and servility. The principal goal of the Jew, he felt, should be to achieve inner freedom, which is the only kind worth striving for.[36]

Emancipation, Luzzatto stressed, is not a panacea for all the ailments of Judaism. The survival of the Jewish people depends far more on the creation among Jews of an *esprit de corps,* a feeling of brotherhood and kinship. Their major goal should not be the attainment of political parity with their neighbors, but rather the development of a sense of national pride, which should stimulate the study of the Torah and the Hebrew language and should discourage the spread of the spirit of Atticism among them. Nor is Emancipation an unmixed blessing; in France, Belgium, and Holland, where Jews have been completely enfranchised, Jewish creativity has declined, Jewish religious growth has been stunted and the Torah and Hebrew language forgotten. The proffered freedom in these countries was an invitation to fusion[37] and assimilation. In one of his poems,[38] Shadal inveighed against those *Maskilim* (proponents of Enlightenment) who neglected their own heritage, preferring Goethe and Schiller to the Hebrew prophets and sages:

Perish he who shames his mother
and ridicules his father's old age
Who makes of Emancipation a fetish.

May my tongue cleave to my pallet
May my right eye be dimmed
May my right hand wither,
If I forget thee, Oh Zion.

Shadal pleaded for the freeing of Judaism from foreign cultural influences, in the conviction that one of its crucial problems was to preserve its original purity. He had little use for philosophers generally and took up the cudgels particularly against Spinoza, whom he regarded as the embodiment of the antireligious tendencies in philosophy. Accordingly, too, he attacked Maimonides, who sought to blend Judaism with Aristotelian philosophy, as a "stumbling block" and "the source of our troubles."[39] In borrowing from Aristotle, he charged, Maimonides had converted Judaism from a religion of the emotions to one of the intellect. It was not possible to fit Judaism into the Greco-Arab mould of thought, as Maimonides had attempted, and have it retain its true nature. His venture in this direction had led him to curb freedom of thought among Jews by fixing thirteen definite articles of faith[40]. Luzzatto went even further in his attack against Maimonides. He charged the medieval sage with concealing his true antitraditional views. By contrast, he alluded to Rashi as "a humble and wholesome personality."[41]

Shadal carried his Jewish nationalism and opposition to the infusion of foreign currents in Judaism to an extreme when he censured the noted Jewish historian Heinrich Graetz for asserting, as Jewish scholars commonly do today, that the Babylonian Talmud is superior to its Jerusalem counterpart.[42] This viewpoint brought Luzzatto into sharp conflict with the *Maskilim,* among them Nachman Krochmal, who advocated a synthesis of Judaism with European culture.[43]

The debate on the intrusion of alien elements into Judaism brings to the fore the question of cultural cross-fertilization, whether Judaism should remain rigidly monolithic and exclude the cultural ingredients of its environment, or should adapt itself to them. It must be conceded that Judaism could hardly have survived if it had lacked the vitality to adjust to the dominant cultures among which it lived, or if it had failed to absorb those external ideas congenial to it, while rejecting others. For that matter, Shadal himself yielded to the rationalistic and secular currents, though he vigorously stressed the danger that if outside thought were to influence Jewish doctrines and principles unduly, Judaism was bound to be submerged and disappear.

The Science of Judaism

The pursuit of the objectives of the movement for the Science of Judaism brought in its wake apologetic tendencies on the part of many Jewish scholars, who underscored the humanistic rather than the nationalistic and distinctive values in Jewish literature and lore. Shadal objected strenuously to these efforts and urged that the Science of Judaism be made an instrument for Jewish survival. He denounced those who were concerned with the Jewish past in the manner of antiquarians, whose paramount interest in exhuming ancient civilizations, such as those of Egypt, Assyria, and Babylonia, was primarily academic and little more. Luzzatto saw the Jewish past as a link to the Jewish present and future, as a current in an ever-expanding stream of Jewish cultural creativity. Any other type of Jewish learning is bound to die out, he warned. The function of the Science of Judaism, he insisted, is to train scholars imbued with a love and reverence for Judaism, who will dedicate themselves to the task of fostering and extending Jewish knowledge as a phase of an ongoing and burgeoning Jewish life.

Reform Judaism

From his early days, Luzzatto was an implacable opponent of Reform. In 1818, his old teacher, Abraham Eliezer Halevi, visited Italian rabbis in order to solicit their opinions against Reform and counter the efforts of Eliezer Liebermann,[44] a Talmudic scholar who toured the country to gain rabbinical support for the movement. Young Luzzatto on that occasion wrote his *Vision of the Seduced Cities*,[45] a poem denouncing the offenses of the Reformers against tradition, notably their attempt to replace Hebrew by the vernacular in Jewish houses of worship in Berlin, the very city in which Naphtali Wessely and Mendelssohn had done so much to revive it. "Today, Israel abandons its sacred language," the poet predicted, "tomorrow, it will surrender its Torah!" He also protested vigorously against the attempt by the Frankfort Reform Society in 1843 to abolish the rite of circumcision and other time-honored Jewish practices.

Luzzatto ridiculed the "mission" theory of the Reformers as an empty dream and a "vain comfort." It was the Jewish belief in revelation and Torah, Luzzatto averred, not the Reform doctrine of the Jewish mission, that had inspired the Jew to undergo sacrifice and martyrdom. That the mission theory had little practical significance might be judged from the fact that the Bible, which had been disseminated among civilized nations for over eighteen hundred years, had not as yet brought any degree of perfection to humanity. There was less reason to believe that the religious liberals with their inclination toward Atticism would succeed in doing so.

To achieve the Utopian state envisaged in the concept of the Jewish mission, Shadal maintained, the human heart would have to undergo a fundamental reconstruction bordering on the miraculous. Futhermore, the Messianic ideals expounded by the Hebrew prophets, unlike the mission theory of the Reformers, did not call for an absolute universalism; the Hebrew prophets viewed the Messianic era merely as an epoch of just nationalism in the world, in which Israel, a paragon of justice, would live on its own soil and assume the role of judge among the nations (*Is.* 2:2-4). To attain this ideal, Jews should cling to their faith with greater devotion and loyalty and not whittle it down, as the Reformers were doing.

Hebrew

Luzzatto acquired a mastery of Italian, French, and, to a lesser extent, German; he also studied oriental tongues, as well as Greek and Latin, but his favorite medium, with which he identified himself, was Hebrew. To him, it was a national and not only a holy language, and he spoke of the "love of the sacred tongue that burns within me."[46] He referred, moreover, to the Bible both as a religious and a national classic. Jewish literary and cultural enterprises, he urged, must be carried on in their natural medium, the Hebrew language. He refused to have his commentary on Isaiah translated into German, lest that should militate against its publication in Hebrew, declaring that "my chief desire and aim is the resuscitation of Hebrew."[47] Little wonder then that Luzzatto took occasion to chide his colleagues in the Science of Judaism circles in Germany for writing in German rather than in Hebrew. Previously, Luzzatto pointed out, Jewish scholars wrote in Hebrew for an intimate audience of readers and they expressed their thoughts freely. Now that they wrote German, French, and English, they "must reckon with what the gentiles will say," and they adapt their works to the expectations of outsiders and often give them a Christian flavor.[48]

For many years Luzzatto devoted himself to the advancement of the Hebrew language. He composed Hebrew poetry, much of it quite stultified. But, if his Hebrew style is poor by present standards, it should be remembered that his was a pioneering venture. He evidenced considerable skill in his Hebrew grammatical works. He expressed the hope that all his writings would eventually be published in Hebrew[49] and urged the establishment of a special Hebrew publishing house.[50] Religious education, he felt, should be carried on in the original Hebrew and the rabbinic texts taught in the original and not in translation. To him, the Hebrew language was a bridge between the classical and modern cultures of the Jew, and the only means by which Hebrew literature could be revived and a love for Judaism sustained.[51]

The Jewish Homeland

In 1850, Luzzatto wrote to Rabbi Nachman Nathan Coronel of Jerusalem:[52]

> . . . to endeavor to bring back the Jews of the Holy Land to their ancestral occupation, agriculture, and thus support themselves by the toil of their hands as do other peoples, who also take pride in doing so. If they should succeed in such a plan, they will not only rehabilitate themselves, but they will restore the Jewish homeland into a land flowing with milk and honey. Farming, too, could thus become the core of a productive economy, and would stimulate its growth. . . .

Shadal proposed also that instead of financing the migration of Jewish boys from Asia to Europe, to be corrupted by Western civilization, egoism, and atheism, philanthropic effort should be directed towards bringing them to Palestine, where they could engage in rewarding enterprise. The land of Israel, if worked by Jews, could be restored in time to its former state of bloom and blossom, particularly if the effort enjoyed government protection.

Luzzatto was not only concerned with the economic resuscitation of the Jewish homeland, but also with its cultural aspect. Since Judaism stood for justice and righteousness, the Jewish homeland should become a center from which these ideals could flow forth to the entire world. He proposed that competent judicial authorities be trained in the Holy Land to dispense true justice to all who would come before them for judgment from every part of the earth —Jews and non-Jews alike. This idea is suggestive of the broader objective later advocated·by Ahad Ha-Am, of creating in Palestine a Jewish cultural and spiritual center to serve the Diasporal periphery.[53]

In sum, the currents of Jewish nationalism are evident in Luzzatto's pattern of thought. The Jewish people occupied the central position in his philosophy. In his inclinations towards Jewish nationalism, Luzzatto was close to Zacharia Frankel, the founder of the Historical School in Judaism; in fact, he was bolder and clearer in his nationalistic aspirations than Frankel. Both Frankel and Luzzatto, as fellow disciples of Krochmal, participated in the Science of Judaism movement, which Samson Raphael Hirsch, his Neo-Orthodox colleague, strongly opposed, because it represented Judaism as a product of a centuries-long process of historical development, rather than as Hirsch represented it, as a direct product of the Sinaitic revelation. But in his general religious outlook, Luzzatto concurred with his younger contemporary, Samson Raphael Hirsch.

Part Three

American Shoots

Prelude

The third and last part of our study deals with the American offshoots or branches of the several Jewish religious movements which originated in Europe in an attempt to adjust Judaism to the challenges of the Emancipation. The growth of these religious alignments on American soil can be told only as part of the story of the dramatic development of American Jewry from an insignificant group of two-thousand five-hundred at the time of the American Revolution to a community of five-and-a-half million souls today. The Jews of America represent the largest and the most powerful and prosperous aggregation in the four thousand years of history of the Jewish people. The remarkable increase in the Jewish population in the New World since the creation of the American republic is largely a result of several waves of Jewish immigration. This mass exodus followed the anti-Jewish reaction and the bigotry that had returned to Germany and Central Europe after the collapse of Napoleon's military adventures in 1815.

The ideas of Reform first penetrated the slender ranks of American Judaism in 1824, when an attempt was made to institute changes in the religious services of congregation Beth Elohim in Charleston, South Carolina. The steady flow of Jewish immigrants from Central Europe in the 1830's and 1840's which spread throughout the east and constantly pushed westward brought the Reform doctrine to both the newly organized and existing Jewish congregations throughout the country. The same wave of newcomers carried exponents of the more moderate Historical School

271

who introduced their principles into Jewish religious life in America. The massive immigration changed the image of American Jewry radically. It was no longer Sephardic in form but dominantly Ashkenazic; it was no longer uniformly Orthodox, but now embraced more liberal sectors.

Later, the influx of Jews from Eastern Europe began in earnest. It assumed vast tidal proportions after the oppressive May Laws of 1882, with their prelude of pogroms and riots. From a quarter of a million Jews in 1880, the Jewish population in the New World climbed to a million by the turn of the century, and to three-and-a-half millions by 1920. The new arrivals superimposed their East European brand of Orthodoxy, steeped in Jewish learning and warmly disposed toward Jewish nationalism, on the staid and dignified native Orthodoxy. The new arrivals were mainly Yiddish speaking; occupationally, they were dominantly struggling workmen, shopkeepers, and petty traders. They overflowed the crowded slum sections of the cities.

The more acculturated second generation of the East European immigrants who had advanced to middle-class status flocked to new neighborhoods in the cities. Their offspring moved to the suburbs. In these areas, the children and grandchildren of the East European immigrants founded or joined Conservative synagogues, and the wealthier ones among them frequently became members of Reform congregations. Both wings of Judaism were considerably strengthened by this influx. The ideological distinction between them, however, was not quite distinct.

While the earlier Reform congregations could turn to the antinationalist and antitraditionalist Pittsburgh Platform of 1885 for doctrinal guidance and direction, the Conservative movement had only a vague and undefined set of principles to go by. A liberal segment among the latter group formed the Reconstructionist "school of thought" which espoused a philosophy based on a rationalistic and naturalistic approach to Judaism.

History makes and breaks ideological convictions. Events between the two world wars intensified the nationalistic sentiments of Jewry. The need for a Jewish haven grew apace of the mounting anti-Jewish hostility in this period. On the one hand, the *Protocols of the Elders of Zion,* the Ku Klux Klan in America, the economic depression, and the Nazi anti-Jewish campaign produced an unprecedented upsurge of anti-Jewish bigotry and anti-Semitism in America. On the other hand, the Balfour Declaration and the remarkable progress of the *Yishuv* (the Jewish community in Palestine), despite the many difficulties it faced, brought the dream of a Jewish homeland closer to reality. Both positive and negative forces contributed to a rise in Jewish nationalistic feeling among all shades of Jewry. In 1937, the Reform wing gave expression to this growing nationalistic sentiment in its Columbus Platform, which reversed its earlier antinationalist and antitraditionalist position (Chapter 12). The triumphant struggle for the rebirth of the Jewish state which culminated in 1948, and the subsequent goal of aiding in its upbuilding, united American Jewry. The religious divisions, however, persisted.

The Nazi persecutions and holocaust created a new mass departure from Europe to America. This stream of newcomers who arrived before and after the Second World War included a large contingent of Orthodox Jews, along with a substantial segment of Hassidim, all of whom were anxious to continue their mode of living in free America. This influx infused new blood into American Orthodoxy. The Hassidic newcomers reinvigorated the Hassidic enclaves in the large Jewish centers throughout the country. These episodes and their impact on the Jewish religious thought and movements in America will be surveyed in the ensuing final section of this volume.

11

On to America!

I. Conditions in Central Europe

Reaction

THE NAPOLEONIC WARS ended in 1815 with Napoleon's defeat and downfall. In these conflicts Jews fought on both sides and fell on the battlefields of opposing armies, side by side with their countrymen. Nonetheless, the collapse of Napoleon's armies was a signal in Germany for the revocation of the rights that German Jewry had won while Napoleon was in power. As a result, many Jews, particularly among the progressives and liberals, lost hope in Emancipation and sought to improve their lot through emigration to far-off America and other lands. This exodus brought the currents of Reform and more moderate alignments in Judaism and some of their leading spirits to America.

The Congress of Vienna

After the allies took Paris in July 1815, Napoleon was exiled to the distant isle of St. Helena. The Congress of Vienna was convened to restore the "legitimist" regimes of Europe. In the drama enacted at that Congress, the chief actor was the arch-reactionary Metternich, Chancellor of Austria-Hungary, who feared and hated

274

democracy. The cynically named Holy Alliance, consisting of Austria-Hungary, Prussia, and Russia, revived and strengthened the theocratic and monarchial principles which had prevailed before Napoleon's victories. In the new political climate, the reversal of the liberal Jewish policies introduced by Napoleon seemed certain. The Jewish leaders in Germany saw the handwriting on the wall and sent unofficial representatives to the Congress to plead their cause and forestall, as far as possible, the revocation of their liberties. A few highly placed Jews in Vienna, whose elegant salons were frequented by Austrian and Prussian diplomats, attempted to influence their guests in favor of Jewish rights, but it availed them little.

In may 1815, even before the Holy Alliance was concluded, the Jewish question had arisen at the Congress in connection with the broad issue relating to the formation of a German Confederation. A resolution was adopted to the effect that the "Jews were to continue to enjoy the rights accorded them in the various States," but upon the demand of the German free cities, the preposition *in* in the last phrase was replaced with the word *by*—a seemingly innocent and harmless substitution. This change, however, nullified the meaning and intent of the framers of the original resolution, for now any signatory could claim that it was not bound by the rights previously granted to the Jews in its territory, but only by those which it had given to the Jews *voluntarily*. With the exception only of Prussia and Mecklenberg, Jewish Emancipation in the thirty-six German principalities had been bestowed upon the Jews as a result of Napoleonic pressure. These rights were now subject to revision. The liberties of German Jewry were thus suppressed by a preposition.

Restrictions

In the wake of the Congress of Vienna, the government of the numerous German states imposed a variety of disabilities on the Jews in their territories. In many parts of Germany, Jews were herded back into squalid ghetto neighborhoods. In others, they resisted the attempt to return them to ghetto status, but with only limited success. The Jews of Frankfort, for example, who had paid vast sums for the rights they acquired after the Napoleonic conquests, were relegated in 1824 to the status of "Israelitish citizens." This arrangement, reached after ten years of harassment and negotiations, entailed a number of economic limitations and a quota of fifteen marriages per year for a community of three thousand souls. Similar abridgments of Jewish rights were effected in Bavaria. The Jews of Hamburg were deprived of their political privileges; they were also limited in their pursuit of trade, handicraft, and the ownership of real property. In Saxony, they were not admitted to the guilds. They were expelled from Lübeck and Bremen in 1816. The Prussian Emancipation Act of 1812 was interpreted as permitting the adoption of numerous economic prohibitions against the Jews and their exclusion from various occupations. They were also barred from employing Christian servants or using Christian names. The brief egalitarian interval thus ended in grief.

Defamation and Defense

Many members of the conservative Christian clergy in Germany regarded the Jews as the symbol of the despised French Revolution, for only as a result of that uprising had they attained their freedom. This hostility prompted these clerics to blame the Jews for the economic instability of the times, the prevailing unemployment, poverty, and the Napoleonic wars. The spirit of medievalism which accompanied German Romanticism heightened the religious animosity against the Jews, which was now fanned into a burning hate.

Intellectual leaders joined the forces of Teutomaniac hate. Friedrich Ruhs, professor of history at the then newly founded University of Berlin, published an inflammatory pamphlet (1816) in which he insisted that the Jews were responsible for Germany's defeat by Napoleon. He contended that Germany, as a Christian state, should treat the Jews as aliens, as if the principles of Christianity negated any other course. He urged that the Jewish population in the country be restricted, that their participation in economic life be curbed, that a special tax for their protection be imposed upon them, and that they be required to wear a distinctive badge. Only a baptized Jew, Ruhs proposed, should be eligible for citizenship. Thus the position of the Jew was to retrogress to that of the Middle Ages.

A professor of natural science at Heidelberg University, Wilhelm

Fries, a Romantic nationalist, went even further. To him, the "natural" hatred of the Jews, not a display of humanitarianism, represented a healthy nationalistic sentiment. The Jews of Germany, Fries wrote in a pamphlet, published in 1816, had seized half of Frankfort's capital. Unless they were destroyed by means of legal controls limiting their marriages and by the infliction of other disabilities, the Jews would enslave the Germans in a matter of a few decades. The shades of the ancient Pharoah, his fears and countermeasures, were conjured up once again, in a modern guise. The Jew-hater "Count" Hartwig Hundt, a writer of cheap novels, advocated in his *Judenspiegel* (Jewish Mirror) that Jews should be sterilized, their womenfolk consigned to houses of infamy, and their children sold to the Englishmen in the West Indies as slaves for their plantations. The atrocities suggested by these moulders of German thought in the first part of the nineteenth century foreshadowed the program of murder and annihilation inaugurated by the *Herrenvolk* a little more than a century later. Even the great poet Goethe was addicted to this dangerous bigotry and advocated that all the humiliations and oppressions of the ghetto be reimposed on the Jews in Saxe-Weimar.

The Jews, however, had their Christian defenders too. John Ewald, an erudite clergyman of Baden, demanded civil equality and an opportunity for the Jews to develop their capacities for the service of the state. The Prussian minister William Humboldt (1767-1835) had introduced the original resolution at the Congress of Vienna calling for complete emancipation for the Jews. Prince Hardenberg (1750-1822) had supported him in this measure. But on the other hand, some of the Jewish journalists and pamphleteers failed to aid the forthright efforts of these Christian champions of Jewish rights. Instead these Jews indulged in apologetics. They did not come out with a straightforward demand for the enfranchisement of their people on humanitarian grounds. They merely pointed to the refined Reform Jews as evidence of the readiness and ability of Jews to be integrated into German society. Accordingly, they argued, there was hope for the Jews, if they were only permitted to prove themselves.

The campaign of vilification and incitement inevitably led to violence by the masses. On August 2, 1819, the old medieval cry of "*Hep, Hep,*[1] *Jude Verrecke!*" (Jew perish!) was renewed by the students of Würzberg University. From there, it reverberated through other German towns and cities. A wave of terror began in Bavaria, spread to Franconia, then through all Germany. Murder of Jews, looting and burning of their property, was the order of the day in these places. German Jewry was shocked by the on-slaughts; many among them, sadly disillusioned in their hopes for the attainment of egalitarian status, sought avenues of escape. Some entered the church, while others looked for different means of improving their lot.

In multinational and polyglot Austria-Hungary, the center of reaction, the Jewish situation in the post-Napoleonic period was equally bad, if not worse. Except for several hundred privileged Jews in the Hapsburg kingdom, the majority were forced back into narrow and gloomy *Judengassen.* Again they were required to take the *more Judaica,* the special humiliating oath demanded of Jews in law courts. Discriminatory residence and business laws were common. Special licenses were demanded of Jews who desired to engage in business enterprises, and these were granted only on pay-ment of excessive levies. Jews were excluded from the rural districts of Moravia and Bohemia. These restrictive measures weighed heavily upon the Jews and broke their spirits to the point of despair.

Economic Factors

A vital economic factor affecting Europeans generally aggravated the situation. The population of Europe during the nineteenth century climbed from one hundred and seventy-five million in 1800 to about four hundred million in 1900. This rapid rise in population resulted in a land scarcity and a consequent increase of urbanization in Germany and other countries.[2] Cities became overcrowded and the expanding economic opportunities which had followed in the wake of the industrial revolution shrank, forcing many Germans to seek their fortunes in less densely settled regions and territories.

The Jews however, suffered not only from the impact of general conditions; they also had to contend with the disabilities and the special taxes imposed on them. Their plight was thus more difficult. In 1836, a financial depression added to the miseries of the German people. All these developments combined to produce a mass exodus from Germany in which a sizeable number of Jews participated.

Gabriel Riesser

Some Jews hoped to gain political and economic equality through flight, while others were determined to continue the struggle for Emancipation at home, adopting, however, a change in tactics. Instead of fighting their battle as Jews, they joined the revolutionary movements in their native lands in considerable numbers, thereby casting their lot with their liberal countrymen in a common struggle for freedom and democracy. Gabriel Riesser (1806-1863) was a leader in this movement. He was a grandson of the Orthodox chief rabbi of Hamburg, his native city, and he had joined the Reform movement. He had refused to follow the well-trodden path to the baptismal font as a means of securing the professorship in law that he merited, and to which he had long aspired, and had remained a staunch and dedicated Jew.[3]

In answer to the contentions of the theologian Paulus, and other exponents of the doctrine that Germany was a Christian state in which only Christians could be full-fledged citizens, Riesser declared, "We did not emigrate here, we were born here, and either we are Germans or we are stateless." He regarded the Jewish people as a religio-ethnic group, whose ethnicity was the sole vestige of their former political nationhood in Palestine. This characteristic, however, he insisted, in no way contradicted the exclusive political loyalty of German Jewry to their native land. Riesser succeeded in making the repeal of the legal disabilities of German Jewry and their unconditional enfranchisement a plank in the platform of the Young Germany movement, of which he was a founder.

Revolution of 1848

The European revolutionary movement of 1848 began in Paris, when barricades were erected against Louis Philippe I, his oppressive government, and the ruling classes. The spark ignited, and its flame quickly spread to Germany and other European countries. In the Berlin street fighting against the imperial forces, at least twenty Jews were killed. On the basis of a popular election, a *Vorparlament* (Preliminary Constitutional Assembly) was convened at Frankfort to draw up a constitution for a united Germany. In recognition of his dedicated services to the liberal cause, Riesser was elected a vice-president of this body. When Frederick William IV of Prussia scornfully rejected the emperor's crown, some of the radical German leaders ventured to establish republics, but these attempts were ruthlessly suppressed.

The spirit of revolt and the movement for national liberation also reached Austria. In Vienna, the arch-reactionary Metternich was forced to resign and flee, and the helpless Hapsburg monarch had no alternative but to grant his people a constitution and promise other reforms. In the Magyar uprising in Hungary, led by the national hero Louis Kossuth, some twenty thousand Jews, including a special Jewish battalion, fought, but the republic they set up was shortlived. The revolutionary attempts launched in other countries failed as well. Consequently, the concessions made or promised by the various states were withdrawn; yet though the rebellions collapsed, they were successful in relaxing the strong grip of the aristocracy on their governments. But before the gains were consolidated, a period of reaction set in, in consequence of which the liberals lost their faith in the triumph of their cause, at least within their own times. These reverses gave further momentum to the migration of the intellectual elements from Central Europe.

II. EMIGRATION

Jewish Emigration before 1848

THE AGITATION FOR JEWISH MIGRATION was heard both in government councils and among the hostile elements in the population. In the Bavarian Diet, public pronouncements were made to this effect. These demands evoked a response in Jewish circles. Heinrich Heine and Ludwig Börne declared in the early 1820's that America must become a haven from European oppression for all freedom-loving peoples, including the Jews. In 1822, several leaders of the *Verein für Kultur und Wissenschaft der Juden* (Union for

Culture and Science of Judaism) wrote to Mordecai Manuel Noah (1785-1851),[4] the leading American Jew of his day, advocating the migration of European Jews to America.

Bernard Behrend, a Hessian Jew, had proposed in 1832 and again in 1840 to Baron Amschel Rothschild and Gabriel Riesser that a vast area be acquired in North America for a settlement of German and Polish Jews. Neither Rothschild nor Riesser acquiesced in the plan. The latter conceded that the problem of emigration was of utmost importance for the Jews but, because he would not himself leave his native Germany, he did not feel he could press others to do so.

By 1840, the condition of the Jews in Germany had not improved substantially. Hesse did grant the Jews an ample measure of equality in 1833, but this was exceptional. German Jewry, in the main, still remained disenfranchised and impoverished. Consequently, the flow of Jewish emigrants from Germany continued and even gained in momentum. It is of interest to note that a small trickle of Orthodox Jews also journeyed to Palestine to settle on the soil. In Palestine, saturated with Jewish history and Jewish memories, they hoped to live an intense Jewish life and avoid the danger of assimilation that frequently accompanied the Emancipation of Jews in Europe.

In the 1830's Jewish university students in Prague had aroused considerable discussion of a proposal to restore the Jewish state and to resettle Jews there. They took their cue from the burgeoning nationalist movement in Bohemia. The ritual murder charge in Damascus in 1840, which became an international issue, provoked greater interest in the idea. Adolphe Crémieux, the brilliant French Jewish lawyer and orator, was sympathetic. Sir Moses Montefiore, the noted English Jewish philanthropist and leader, endeavored to interest the British government in a plan to colonize several hundred villages in Palestine. They were encouraged by influential Britons, among whom were Colonel Charles Henry Churchill, the British Consul in Jerusalem, Lord Shaftsbury, and Lord Palmerston, the foreign secretary. These were all precursors of the Zionist movement, launched six decades later.[5]

Jewish Emigration after 1848

Leopold Kompert, a noted Bohemian Jewish novelist, was one of those who had lodged his hopes for freedom in the revolution of 1848. Disillusioned by the outcome, he wrote an article entitled *On to America,* in which he urged his coreligionists to flee to America in order to avoid the reaction that he expected in Europe. In response to his call, and to the similar pleas of other Jewish leaders, new emigration societies were formed to facilitate both departure from the European countries and settlement in America. Adolph Brandeis, father of the late United States Supreme Court Justice, Louis Dembitz Brandeis (1856-1941), was in a contingent of immigrants who left Prague in 1849.

In the earlier decades of the nineteenth century, primarily individuals and single people joined the migration; in the later ones, family groups journeyed to the New World. The German Jewish immigrants before 1848 were on a lower intellectual level than those who came afterwards. The latter saw little opportunity in factory work or industry, nor were they trained for other occupations. With little capital, the only business venture they could undertake was peddling. Many went to the Midwest, where there was no language barrier between them and their German countrymen who had settled earlier in that region. They pushed westward toward the coast, finding homes and creating Jewish settlements as far west as San Francisco. To the rural areas, the German Jewish hucksters brought the comforts of civilization on their wagons or their backs. A number also participated in the gold rush of 1849. In time, some fortunate individuals accumulated sufficient wealth to open dry goods, clothing and general stores in midwestern cities, Detroit, St. Louis, Cincinnati, Cleveland, Milwaukee, as well as in urban centers in the South and West. A few of these enterprises eventually grew into department stores.

In the wave of two million immigrants from Central Europe who landed in the United States in the single decade following 1850, there were about one hundred thousand Jews, mostly from Austria, Hungary, Germany, and Bohemia. Of the one hundred fifty thousand Jews in America around 1860, about forty thousand lived in New York, and half that number in Philadelphia, while sizeable Jewish communities were developing in Boston, Newark,

New Orleans, and other cities. The newcomers either joined existing congregations in those places or founded their own. In the outlying areas, the Jewish immigrants established new synagogues as soon as they could gather the requisite *minyan* (quorum) of ten male worshipers. Some of those who came after 1840 organized *Reform Vereine,* associations which propagated the ideas of Reform and in time developed into Reform congregations.

Among the intellectuals who came to America during this period, there were young rabbis with Reform leanings. Ordained rabbis had been a rarity in the United States, the rabbinical functions having been performed by *hazzanim* (cantors) or *shochtim* (ritual slaughterers) employed by the congregations. The Reform rabbis of the caliber of Leo Merzbacher, who came to America in 1841, Max Lilienthal, who arrived in 1845, Isaac Mayer Wise, who landed in 1846, Bernard Felsenthal, in 1854, and David Einhorn, in 1855, were men who combined a rabbinic training with a university education. They exerted considerable influence over their congregations. In the New World, their radical religious views found fertile soil among their fellow immigrants, some of whom had belonged to the Reform wing in Germany. The liberal rabbis were not inhibited in their efforts to introduce reforms in their American synagogues, as these were entirely independent and autonomous bodies, not subject, as they had been in Germany, either to governmental control or to the domination of a legally entrenched community organization. The Reform synagogues could follow as divergent a line as their constituencies desired or approved. The rabbinical leadership of Reform Judaism consequently guided the destinies of their movement far more effectively in the United States than in their native lands.

American Jewry

The Jewry that the German Jewish immigrants found on their arrival in America was small; in 1840 it is believed to have been as little as fifteen thousand in a total population of seventeen million. The newcomers swelled the figure to fifty thousand out of an over-all population of twenty-three million by mid-century. The number grew dramatically—a three-fold increase, to one hundred fifty thousand out of thirty-two million by the Civil War.

As the community attained greater numbers, its composition changed. Already in the eighteenth century, a substantial proportion of the membership of the Sephardic congregations was Ashkenazic. By 1825, the Ashkenazic Jews predominated; by 1850, the Sephardic settlers had become just a small island in an Ashkenazic sea. They were, however, well established economically and looked down upon the poor German Jewish immigrants as social inferiors. The older Jewish families, as well as the new arrivals— at least those who had migrated before 1848—were generally materialistically inclined. They possessed little culture or Jewish knowledge, and their religious observances were of a mechanical nature.

The religious, philanthropic, and social life of American Jewry before the mass German Jewish influx centered about the synagogue, which functioned as a Kehillah. The congregations not only conducted religious services but also maintained schools for the children, where frequently both religious and secular subject matter were taught in the days before free public education. The synagogues also provided for the other religious needs of their members, including kosher meat the year round and *matzot* for the Passover. They owned cemetery grounds, which were commonly purchased as soon as they were required. They also raised the funds for local as well as overseas charities, among them the Palestine institutions.

There were few Jewish communal or noncongregational institutions in operation when the German Jewish mass immigration began. The first such institution, established in 1801, was the Jewish Orphan Home in Charleston. The Hebrew Benevolent Society in New York City was started in 1822, and an orphan asylum was opened ten years later. The German Jews demonstrated a zeal and a talent for organization. Dissatisfied with the narrow scope of synagogue activities, they soon created many philanthropies outside the synagogue: hospitals, lodges, and fraternal orders. These agencies provided a number of much-needed social services for the growing Jewish community. They laid the foundations for the network of Jewish welfare federations and councils in existence today.

12

Reform in America

I. Struggle for Reform

The Charleston Dissenters

IN AMERICA THE FIRST REVOLT against the traditional worship in the synagogue occurred in the old Sephardic congregation, Beth Elohim, in Charleston, South Carolina, some years before the arrival of any of the leaders of Reform from Europe. In 1824, forty-seven members of that synagogue appealed to the trustees to adopt several of the innovations that were in vogue in the Hamburg Temple. They proposed that the service be abbreviated, that some of the Hebrew prayers be translated into English, that the reference to the resurrection of the dead be deleted, and that a regular sermon be delivered in English in connection with the *parsha,* the weekly Scriptural portion read in the synagogue on the Sabbath. Their demands were rejected, and twelve of the petitioners, led by Isaac Harby, a noted journalist and dramatist, seceded from the congregation and founded a new one, which they called the "Reformed Society of Israelites." Within two years, the membership of the new group had grown to over fifty. They introduced instrumental music into their service, worshiped with uncovered heads, and abridged and modified their liturgy.[1] Their attempt, however, foundered; the Reform temple was dissolved in 1833,

285

because of the lack of competent religious direction and guidance.
A Polish-born and German-trained rabbi, Gustav Poznanski
(1805-1879), an advocate of Reform, was called to the pulpit
of Beth Elohim several years later, in 1836. The old synagogue
building, destroyed in the conflagration of 1838, was replaced by
another in which an organ was installed. In his dedication sermon,
delivered in March, 1841, the rabbi declared, in the idiom of the
German Reformers: "This country is our Palestine, this city our
Jerusalem, this house of God our Temple!" The opponents of
Reform withdrew from the congregation and instituted legal proceedings against it, without success. Some formed a new congregation, Shearith Israel. Thus was Reform transplanted to American
soil.

American Reform Congregations

The first Reform congregation to be organized as such in America was the Har Sinai Verein, launched in Baltimore, Maryland,
in 1842, by a group of young people who followed the Hamburg
prayer book in their worship. More than a decade later, in 1855,
they appointed David Einhorn (1809-1879) as their rabbi. Einhorn was an aggressive Reformer, who had previously served as
a rabbi in Germany, and later, in the Reform congregation in
Budapest, Hungary. The second congregation to be organized on
the Reform pattern was Temple Emanuel in New York City, which
held its first service in a private dwelling on the eve of Passover,
1845. Dr. Leo Merzbacher served as the rabbi of this synagogue
until his death in 1855. By then, Temple Emanuel had introduced
a variety of other reforms; it published its own prayer book, employed an organ in the service, inaugurated the confirmation ceremony, discontinued observance of the second days of festivals,
discarded the *talis* (prayer shawl) and the customary headgear
worn by male worshipers.

The Reform movement was making gradual inroads in existing
congregations. In Philadelphia the local *Reform Gesellschaft* united
in 1856 with the congregation Knesseth Israel which had previously
evinced liberal tendencies, and soon the merged group became
Reform. A discontented faction in the membership of the Orthodox
congregation Anshe Maariv in Chicago broke off in 1858 and two

years later established the Sinai congregation, a Reform organiza-
tion. Other synagogues followed a similar pattern of development.
By 1870, a substantial proportion of the two hundred synagogues
throughout the United States had adopted various degrees of
Reform practice; by 1880, most of them could be classed as
Reform.

Isaac Mayer Wise

The outstanding leader, architect, and builder of Reform Judaism in America in the nineteenth century was Isaac Mayer Wise
(1819-1900), whose life spanned more than half a century of
service and achievement on behalf of Reform Judaism. Wise was
a dynamic individual, an impressive orator, a talented organizer,
and a courageous optimist, to whom failure was only a signal for
a renewed and more energetic effort. Before he came upon the
American scene, Reform was merely a prospect in this country; by
the end of his life he had fashioned it into a movement.

Wise had received *Semicha* (traditional ordination) and had
occupied a pulpit for two years at Radnitz, a small town in his
native Bohemia. His congregation was too rigid in its Orthodoxy
to allow him to introduce any reforms. Wise, moreover, was too
rebellious a spirit to accept the indignity of the inferior political
status imposed on the Jews of Bohemia. In fact, he had violated
the local regulation permitting only a few Jewish marriages a year,
in order not to exceed the legal quota of eight thousand six hundred Jewish families in the province. To escape from his oppressive
religious and political environment, he sailed for America in 1846,
together with his wife and infant daughter.

Wise was elected spiritual leader of congregation Beth El in
Albany in 1846, within a few months after his arrival in this
country. The Albany congregation, founded in 1838, was traditionalist in practice and outlook. Though insisting on the strict
observance of the Sabbath, Wise proceeded almost immediately
to inaugurate several reforms: a mixed choir, family pews, and
the confirmation ceremony. In the last innovation, he emulated
the example of his friend, Dr. Max Lilienthal (1815-1882), who
had initiated confirmation exercises earlier in the United Hebrew
Congregations, comprising three synagogues in New York City,

in which he officiated as rabbi. Lilienthal, Wise, and their colleagues were zealous Reformers, who were convinced that the only way to save Judaism was to modify outdated religious usages, attitudes, and doctrines. They aimed to salvage what they regarded as the indestructible core and spirit of Judaism from the mouldiness that they believed had encrusted it in the course of centuries of stagnation. They began with relatively moderate changes in ritual, which were gradually augmented.

In 1850, four years after he had come to Albany, Wise's liberal inclinations were put to a test, when it became known to his congregation that he had openly declared in a debate at the Charleston Reform Synagogue that he did not believe in a personal Messiah or in bodily resurrection. At the following *Rosh Hashana* service, the Orthodox element in his congregation forcibly ejected him from the pulpit. His friends and supporters immediately seceded and organized a Reform congregation, the Anshe Emeth, which became the third Reform synagogue established as such in the United States.

In 1854, Wise left his Reform congregation in Albany to accept the life-long post offered him by B'nai Jeshurun in Cincinnati, which afforded him a broader outlet for his energies and activities, and a greater opportunity to translate his ideas into reality. In his first year in Cincinnati, he attempted to open Zion College, a school which he hoped would train rabbis for American Jewish congregations. It was, however, a short-lived venture. Wise realized that he could not launch such an institution without the cooperation and assistance of the other Reform congregations. That same year, he also started his Anglo-Jewish weekly, *The Israelite,* which was renamed *The American Israelite* in 1874. This publication was intended to be the liberal counterpart of Isaac Leeser's influential traditionalist organ, *The Occident. The Israelite* soon gained prestige and popularity. Since the overwhelming majority of American Jews still spoke German, as did their rabbis, Wise also established a German weekly, *Die Deborah* (The Bee). Until Lilienthal came to Cincinnati a year later, Wise edited and wrote much of his two journals himself.

Wise was a prolific writer. In 1854 he published the first part of his two-volume work, *The History of the Israelitish Nation.*

This volume provoked great controversy because it made no reference to miracles. As an historian, Wise pursued a rationalistic line. He, moreover, attacked the Hebrew monarchy from the viewpoint of a nineteenth-century republican. Yet, his *Pronoas to Holy Writ,* published in 1891, took issue with the Documentary Theory,[2] on the ground that the entire Pentateuch was of Mosaic authorship —a thoroughly conservative view. Both outlooks, the rationalist and the conservative, are commingled in his writings. In that, he appears to resemble Luzzatto.[3] Wise also wrote theological works, several plays, and historical novels, in English and German, as well as numerous essays and articles in various periodicals.

However, Wise did not distinguish himself primarily as a thinker, but as an effective organizer and administrator. His congregation in Cincinnati followed his leadership enthusiastically. Though it was originally an Orthodox congregation, Wise introduced many reforms. He began his notable career at B'nai Jeshurun by eliminating the sale of *Aliyot,* the honor of being called up to the Scriptural reading in the synagogue. He then abbreviated the service, introduced mixed pews, a mixed choir, and later an organ. Wise also discontinued the observance of the second days of the festivals, and finally, in 1873, initiated the practice of worshiping with bare heads. B'nai Jeshurun was regarded as a model by the congregations of the South and West that followed its lead. Wise served his congregation for forty-six years, until his death in 1900.

Minhag America

While in Albany, he joined with several other rabbis in New York City to form a *Bet Din* (religious tribunal), which undertook an ambitious program: the preparation of a text in Jewish history and a catechism for religious schools, as well as a standard ritual for American Jewish worship. Wise was assigned the last project, which was actually the only one that materialized. He called his prayer book, the *Minhag America (American Ritual),* hoping that it would serve as a uniform liturgy for American Jewry. Though he had completed his manuscript some years earlier, he did not publish it until it was approved by a commission of rabbis at the Cleveland rabbinical conference in 1855. Accordingly, the new prayer book took on an intercongregational character, differing in this respect from those prepared by individual rabbis for the use of their own congregations.

The new prayer book, published in 1857 in an English and German edition, omitted the traditional prayers for the return to Zion, the rebuilding of the Holy Temple, the restoration of the sacrifices, the Aaronic priesthood, and the Davidic dynasty. Isaac Leeser,[4] the leader and spokesman for Orthodoxy and Conservatism of the day, expressed shock at the violation of tradition. It was, however, accepted by the Reform congregations in Wise's orbit of influence in the South and West. The prayer book represented the first attempt at a common liturgy for Reform Judaism and was the forerunner of the official Union Prayerbook, issued in 1894.

Revelation and Law

"Judaism teaches no dogmas or mysteries on the belief of which salvation depends,"[5] Wise asserted, implying of course that Judaism was a rational religion. Yet he also declared, "I believe in the revelation of God and the God of revelation."[6] Like Samson Raphael Hirsch,[7] his Neo-Orthodox contemporary, he adopted Judah Halevi's view that the revelation at Sinai was an authentic event, since it was witnessed by a multitude of six hundred thousand (*Ex.* 12:37). This was a rather strange belief for a rationalistic, Reform rabbi, though to Wise it appeared to be a self-evident truth. At Sinai, however, Wise maintained, God revealed only the Decalogue directly to Moses. The remainder of the Pentateuch, described in tradition as *Torath Moshe* (the Law of Moses), is the work of the great legislator and not, as the Orthodox believe, *Min Hashamayim* (from heaven), i.e., of divine origin. This would mean of course that only the Decalogue is eternal and immutable. Those Pentateuchal laws which are embodied in the fundamental ethical principles of the Decalogue take on its character as permanent precepts. The remaining laws of the Torah are, however, of a transitory nature, and have validity only at a particular time and place. The laws of the Talmud, based on the interpretations of the rabbis, are still less authoritative, hence more limited in their binding power, and therefore more subject to change.

Judaism, Wise asserted, is accordingly endowed with the core of a universal religion. Its Decalogue is accepted by Christianity and Islam. All that is necessary to arrive at the permanent basic elements in Judaism, he insisted, is to strip it of its transitory particularistic components—of those of its tenets and practices that were intended only for observance in Palestine in past ages. At the present time, Wise said, Judaism has the potentiality for fulfilling its destiny as the religion of the future.[8] Its universal ethical ingredients, he observed have been incorporated into the constitution, laws, and moral doctrines of the United States and other freedom-loving countries.

Which laws and observances in Judaism have permanent validity and must be preserved, and which are only temporary and may be abrogated? As far as the individual is concerned, Wise suggested that he can determine it for himself as a matter of reason and conscience. This is hardly an adequate answer in a collective discipline such as Judaism. As to which laws may be nullified by the Jewish group as a whole, Wise did not say. He did, however, give a license to cast aside many traditional tenets of the Torah which Jews have regarded as sacred throughout the ages. Wise's theory and approach to Jewish law had overtones of Geiger's, Holdheim's,[9] and Spinoza's viewpoints.

Wise's attitude led him to the conclusion that "legalism is not Judaism . . . Judaism is the fear of the Lord and the love of man, in harmony with the dictates of reason . . ."[10] Wise was bent on eliminating the minute regulations which he felt impeded the progress of Judaism and prevented it from becoming the universal faith. Not only Orthodox Judaism but also fundamentalist Christianity were barriers to the attainment of the aims of Jewish universalism, and both must be overcome. Despite his opposition to Jewish legalism, however, Wise took pride in the fact that some of his reforms could be reconciled with the Halacha. Wise did not seem to take note of the incongruity of his position. If legalism is opposed to the true Judaism; if the law can be modified at will by the authorities in any generation, there seems to be little point in seeking to conform to it. This appears to be only another of Wise's inconsistencies.

Wise and Einhorn

From the beginning of his career in the United States, Wise had identified closely with the country and extolled its ideals of freedom and equality of opportunity. It was his passionate love for his new land that motivated him to master the English language, becoming one of the first German rabbis of his day to do so, after only a decade in the United States. He observed that: "Every German book, every German word reminds him (the German Jewish immigrant) of his old disgrace . . . The Jew must become an American in order to gain the proud self-consciousness of the free-born man." He was convinced that Jews and Judaism could thrive best in democratic America and that, reciprocally, America needed an ethical religion such as Judaism for its growth and development. In his enthusiasm he predicted that Judaism was bound to become the religion of America in the first part of the twentieth century, by reason of its universal, rational, liberal, and humane principles. Christianity, he believed, was unsuitable for **this role because, unlike Judaism, it subscribes to irrational, mystical dogmas.**

In contrast to this view, David Einhorn (1809-1879), a more incisive and radical Reformer than Wise, maintained that the German background of Reform was essential to the movement. It was German philosophy, he explained, that gave Reform Judaism its basic rationale. Kant's stress on the moral foundations of life was in complete harmony with Judaism, which upheld the primacy of ethical law and moral behavior over belief. German idealism and Hegelian thought, with their emphasis on the evolutionary process in all phases of human development, Einhorn pointed out, were the foundations of Reform Judaism. In his monthly, *Sinai,* published in German from 1856 to 1862, Einhorn declared that "the English element under present circumstances is a deterrent to Reform aspirations. German research and science are the heart of the Jewish Reform idea." It might be observed that the German Jewish immigrants were so attached to German culture that they continued to employ the German language in their temples in much the same manner as the immigrant East European Jews used Yiddish.

Of the two, Einhorn and Wise, the former was the more consistent thinker. Einhorn, whose influence extended primarily to Reform congregations in the East, was much more radical than Wise. A follower of Geiger, Einhorn was a Reform extremist and had distinguished himself as such at the Frankfort conference in 1845 and the Breslau conference the following year. He had shown the same tendency in his attitude on the question of slavery in the United States, which was coming to a head in 1861. While Wise opposed abolitionism because it threatened the Union, Einhorn was bold and outspoken in denouncing slavery from his Har Zion pulpit in Baltimore. His pronouncements on this question provoked popular feeling to the point that he was compelled by threats of mob violence to flee secretly to Philadelphia. There he became the rabbi of congregation Knesseth Israel.

In 1856, a year after his arrival in Baltimore, Einhorn published the *Olat Tamid* (*Continual Offering*), a Reform prayer book, because he believed "that the old prayers have become for the most part untruths for present conditions and views." Einhorn's prayer book represented a more extreme departure from tradition than Wise's, for its Hebrew content was very much reduced, and it read from left to right—an arrangement later followed in the Union prayer book. He declared that "like man himself, the child of God, the divine law has a perishable body and an imperishable spirit," implying, as did Geiger, that only the fundamental ethical principles of Judaism were permanent, while its form was changeable and could be accommodated to the thinking of the age.

Einhorn took issue with Wise on other important questions, rejecting the contention that the supernatural Sinaitic revelation was an historical fact. Einhorn did, however, agree with Wise on the supremacy of the Decalogue in Judaism, saying: "The Decalogue is the essence of the covenant between God and man . . . it is therefore binding for all times, places and peoples. . . . All other divine ordinances, on the other hand, are only the signs of the covenant . . . these, from their very nature . . . cannot remain always and everywhere the same." Einhorn, however, accorded a paramount place in Judaism to the teachings of the Hebrew prophets. He did not endorse Wise's belief in the unitary Mosaic authorship of the Pentateuch, regarding it as the product of an evolutionary process.

Unlike Einhorn, Wise was of a temporizing nature. For the sake

of unity with the Orthodox, he sponsored a resolution at the conference held in Cleveland in 1855 to the effect that "The Talmud
contains the traditional, logical exposition of the Biblical laws which
must be expounded and practiced according to the comments of
the Talmud." Einhorn and his supporters protested vehemently
against Wise's statement, since the Reformers had disclaimed the
binding authority of the Talmud. Another example of Wise's readiness to compromise was his solution for the perplexing problem of
attendance at the principal service on Sabbath morning. During the
nineteenth century, it was difficult to abstain from working on the
Sabbath, for the six-day week was the norm, as it still is in most
countries. Wise would not agree to a Sunday worship either in
addition to or instead of that of the Sabbath. In 1886, he introduced the late Friday evening services as a compromise arrangement, which had the advantage of retaining the Sabbath spirit and
atmosphere, while at the same time adjusting to prevailing conditions. The innovation, it may be mentioned, proved so efficacious
that it was later adopted by Conservative congregations and, to a
growing extent, also by Orthodox synagogues.[11]

Einhorn, however, was radical in his approach to the Sabbath
problem as well. To Einhorn, the significance of the seventh-day
Sabbath was only symbolic; *i.e.,* the historical Sabbath day was
merely a symbol which did not affect the spirit or the basic concept
of Sabbath observance. In line with this view, a number of Reform
congregations supplemented or supplanted their Sabbath with
Sunday services, but these attempts met with little success. This
outcome seemed to confirm the wisdom of Wise's late Friday evening worship.

Philadelphia Conference

After almost a quarter of a century of experience with the American Jewish community, Wise came to the conclusion that his efforts
to unify the existing religious parties were in vain. Thereafter, he
concentrated on the consolidation of his own Reform group. He
participated in the conference of exclusively Reform rabbis, convened in Philadelphia by the radical eastern Reformers in 1869.
Only a dozen rabbis attended this first totally Reform rabbinical

gathering; its importance, however, by far exceeded its numbers, for it produced the first collective platform on American Reform. The conclave, dominated by the left wing of American Reform, reflected the liberal ideas and views of Geiger and Holdheim.

A resolution adopted by this conference affirmed the doctrine of the mission of Israel, which held that God had dispersed Israel not as a punishment for its sins, but as a result of the divine purpose —in order to disseminate the teaching of ethical monotheism throughout the world. In regard to Hebrew, the rabbis agreed that though its cultivation was a sacred duty, its use in the synagogue must nonetheless give way "as is advisable under existing circumstances, to the vernacular, so as to make prayer intelligible to the worshiper; for prayer, if not understood is a 'soulless form.' " The idea of resurrection was replaced by that of the immortality of the soul. The distinctions among priests, Levites, and Israelites were abolished, and the references in the liturgy to the priesthood and sacrificial cult were to be regarded as "educational influences of the past," that is, of an historical nature rather than as petitions for their restoration.[12]

The Conference also revised the traditional Jewish marital, divorce, and family laws. The *Yevamah* (*Deut.* 25:7) (widow of a man who died childless) could now marry without going through the rite of *Halitzah,* (removal of the shoe) prescribed in the Bible (*Deut.* 25:9) and still observed by very devout Jews. Moreover, the *Agunah* (fettered woman) whose husband disappeared without leaving any trace or acceptable evidence of his death and who was, therefore, prohibited from marrying by Talmudic law, could now do so if the laws of the state or a civil court permitted it. A civil divorce to which both parties consented was to be fully acceptable to the rabbis; if, however, it was contested by one of the parties, it was to be recognized only if the judicial reasons for granting it had been investigated and found sufficient. The male child of a Jewish mother, like the female, was deemed to be Jewish by descent even if not circumcised. Wise's proposal to waive the requirement of circumcision in the case of a Jewish proselyte was not adopted.

The marriage procedure was also modified to permit an exchange of rings and vows by the two parties, in contrast to Talmudic law, according to which only the groom makes the betrothal declaration and gives the bride the ring. These changes in Jewish law have been adopted in Reform practice.

II. STRUCTURE AND PLATFORM

Intercongregational Cooperation

A SUBSEQUENT CONFERENCE of rabbis, held in 1871, gave impetus to the idea of establishing the first American Jewish intercongregational body, the Union of American Hebrew Congregations, which was formally started in 1873, with a constituency of thirty-four congregations from the South and West, Wise's orbit of influence. Within a few years, however, the leading temples of the East also joined, as did some of the moderate groups. The new central congregational body was not hierarchical in structure, but from its inception served, as it does today, as a coordinating agency in which each affiliated synagogue retains its complete autonomy.

The Board of Delegates of American Israelites, launched in 1859 to defend Jewish rights at home and abroad, merged with the Union in 1879. The Board of Delegates was originally intended as the American counterpart of the British Board of Jewish Deputies, which was founded in 1760 to serve as the spokesman for British Jewry. The creation of the American model followed several abortive attempts by Leeser and Wise to bring the synagogues together into an over-all council. It took the appalling episode of the kidnapping and baptism in 1858 of a Jewish child, Edgar Mortara, in Bologna, Italy, to arouse American Jewry to the need for a central body to initiate concerted action on behalf of the Jewish community in the New World. After its absorption by the Union, the Board of Delegates, functioning as a subsidiary of the latter group, carried on defense activities, aided Jewish immigrants, and performed other services not strictly of a religious nature. In 1925, the Board was dissolved, its work having been assumed by other groups.

The Hebrew Union College

The first objective of the new congregational Union was "to establish a Hebrew Theological College . . . to sustain and govern a seat of learning for Israel's religion and learning." Wise had long

pressed the urgent need for an American institution for the training
of a corps of rabbis reared and schooled in the American democa-
tic environment and tradition. After two years of preparation, the
Hebrew Union College was formally opened on October 3, 1875,
at the Plum Street Temple in Cincinnati, Wise's city, which had
become the acknowledged seat of American Reform. Wise was
elected as the first president of the institution and continued in
this office until his death in 1900. To Wise, the creation of the
College marked the realization of a long-cherished dream. The
school was started with thirteen students and a faculty of three.
The curriculum was based on four years of preparatory study and
a like period of advanced study. The first class of four rabbis was
graduated in 1883. It was intended originally to make the College
a common training school for rabbis for the several religious
alignments, but this plan miscarried.[13]

The financial problems of the institution in its early years were
staggering; separate quarters for the school were not secured until
1881. Before his death, however, Wise succeeded in establishing
the College on a firm foundation. It exerted a strong influence on
the American Reform movement through the spiritual leadership
it provided for its constituent congregations. The College not only
represented an important achievement for liberal Judaism, but also
stimulated the founding of rabbinical seminaries by the other wings
of Judaism.

Central Conference of American Rabbis

Another of Wise's plans, the creation of a rabbinical body to
regulate religious affairs, had to wait for implementation until after
the Hebrew Union College had graduated several classes of rabbis.
Wise then had the nucleus for at least a Reform if not an over-all
rabbinical organization. Some thirty rabbis attended the charter
meeting of the new group in 1889, held in Detroit in conjunction
with the convention of the Union of American Hebrew Congregations. The Reform rabbinical group, which called itself the Central
Conference of American Rabbis, elected Wise as its president,
an office which he held for the remainder of his life. Under his
guidance, the Central Conference grew in prestige and strength.

The rabbinical association adopted a resolution linking itself with the earlier Reform rabbinical conferences in Germany and America. In his message to the Central Conference at its first annual meeting in 1890, Wise insisted that:

> ... The united rabbis have undoubtedly the right also according to Talmudic teachings, to declare and decide ... which of our religious forms, institutions, observances, usages, customs, ordinances, and prescriptions are still living factors in our religious, ethical and intellectual life, and which are so no longer, and ought to be replaced by more adequate means to give expression to the spirit of Judaism and to reveal its character of universal religion. . . .

The traditionalists took exception to the readiness of a handful of Reform rabbis to arrogate to themselves the right to meddle with time-honored practices which had their roots in the sacred texts of Judaism. The Reform rabbis, however, were constrained to follow their principles and anti-nationalistic outlook in shaping the ideology of their movement. In this they were guided largely by the doctrines incorporated in the Pittsburgh Platform, adopted four years before the rabbinical organization was launched.

The Pittsburgh Platform

Alexander Kohut (1842-1894), an outstanding rabbi and Talmudic scholar, had been the vigorous spokesman of moderate Orthodoxy in his native Hungary. His arrival in New York in the spring of 1885 spurred the Reformers to action. His denunciation of Reform as a "deformity" was the signal for the special conference of Reform rabbis convened in Pittsburgh in November 1885 by Kaufmann Kohler, then rabbi of Temple Beth El in New York City. The nineteen rabbis, including several cantor-ministers, who participated in the conference over which Wise presided, adopted a series of principles proposed in the main by Kohler. The program, which came to be known as the Pittsburgh Platform, summarized the position of classical Reform on basic issues. It declared:

> ... *First* ... We recognize in every religion an attempt to grasp the Infinite, and in every mode, source, or book of revelation held sacred in any religious system, the consciousness of the Indwelling of God in man. We hold that Judaism presents the highest conception of the God-idea as taught in our Holy

Scriptures and developed and spiritualized by the Jewish teachers, in accordance with the moral and philosophical progress of their respective ages. We maintain that Judaism preserved and defended, amid continual struggles and trials and under enforced isolation, this God-idea as the central religious truth for the human race.

Second . . . We recognize in the Bible the record of the consecration of the Jewish people to its mission as priest of the One God, and value it as the most potent instrument of religious and moral instruction. We hold that the modern discoveries of scientific researches in the domains of nature and history are not antagonistic to the doctrines of Judaism, the Bible reflecting the primitive ideas of its own age, and at times clothing its conception of divine Providence and Justice dealing with man in miraculous narratives.

Third . . . We recognize in the Mosaic legislation a system of training the Jewish people for its mission during its national life in Palestine, and today we accept as binding only the moral laws, and maintain only such ceremonies as elevate and sanctify our lives, but reject all such as are not adapted to the views and habits of modern civilization.

Fourth . . . We hold that all such Mosaic and Rabbinical laws as regulate diet, priestly purity, and dress, originated in ages and under the influence of ideas altogether foreign to our present mental and spiritual state. They fail to impress the modern Jew with a spirit of priestly holiness; their observance in our day is apt rather to obstruct than to further modern spiritual elevation.

Fifth . . . We recognize in the modern era of universal culture of heart and intellect the approach of the realization of Israel's great Messianic hope for the establishment of the kingdom of truth, justice, and peace among all men. We consider ourselves no longer a nation, but a religious community, and therefore, expect neither a return to Palestine nor a sacrificial worship under the administration of the sons of Aaron, nor the restoration of any of the laws concerning the Jewish state.

Sixth . . . We recognize in Judaism a progressive religion, ever striving to be in accord with the postulates of reason. We are convinced of the utmost necessity of preserving the historical identity with our great past. Christianity and Islam being daughter religions of Judaism, we appreciate their mission to aid in the spreading of monotheistic and moral truth. We acknowledge that the spirit of broad humanity of our age is our ally in the fulfillment of our mission, and therefore, we extend the hand of fellowship to all who cooperate with us in the establishment of the reign of truth and righteousness among men.

Seventh . . . We reassert the doctrine of Judaism that the soul of man is immortal, grounding this belief on the divine nature of the human spirit, which forever finds bliss in righteousness and misery in wickedness. We reject as ideas not rooted in Judaism the belief in bodily resurrection and in Gehenna and Eden (Hell and Paradise) as abodes for everlasting punishment and reward.

Eighth . . . In full accordance with the spirit of Mosaic legislation, which strives to regulate the relation between rich and poor, we deem it our duty to participate in the great task of modern times, to solve, on the basis of justice and righteousness, the problems presented by the contrasts and evils of the present organization of society. . . .

The eight tersely phrased paragraphs became the standard, though not the official, ideology of Reform for the next half century. The Pittsburgh Platform provoked a storm of protest which made it evident that the rift between Reform and traditionalism in American Jewry had become irreparable. Many criticized the platform for its negative stand; it outlined neither an affrmative nor a constructive approach to doctrine or practice.[14] A number of the moderately Reform congregations followed the lead of Rodeph Shalom in Philadelphia and withdrew from the Union of American Hebrew Congregations. Wise's pleas to the effect that the resolutions of nineteen rabbis at the Pittsburgh conference were not binding on the hundred-odd congregations in the Union, or on the Hebrew Union College, were of no avail. The more traditional rabbinical group headed by Dr. Alexander Kohut was now confirmed in its determination to form a movement of its own. The first concrete step in this direction was the establishment of the Jewish Theological Seminary in New York City in 1887, as an institution for the training of rabbis along traditional lines. The opening of the Seminary coincided with the great influx of Orthodox Jewish immigrants from Eastern Europe that was rapidly reshaping the structure and composition of American Jewry.

Reform and Zionism

The definition of the Messianic ideal in universal rather than particularistic terms by the earlier theorists of Reform Judaism had little practical application, except for the deletion of prayers referring to the restoration of the Jewish homeland. However, the situation changed in the 1880's, with the creation of the movement known as the "Lovers of Zion" in Eastern Europe. This organization, comprising a loose federation of Zionist groups, represented a concrete expression of nationalistic sentiment and an effort to translate the idea into a program of action. The anti-nationalistic plank in the Pittsburgh Platform was a response to a specific situation. The issue of Zionism was becoming more and more real and intense.

A small number of Reform rabbis espoused the Zionist cause. Among them were the seventy-five-year-old Bernard Felsenthal (1822-1908) of Sinai and later Zion Congregation in Chicago; his slightly younger colleague Gustav Gottheil (1827-1903) of Temple Emanuel in New York; and Maximilian Heller, later president of the Reform rabbinical conference. However, the majority opposed it. Isaac M. Wise denounced Zionism as a "nationality swindle," explaining that "we are Jews by religion only." Zionism clashed with his idea of Judaism as a universal religion. As such, Judaism could not be linked to any particular political nationalism. Wise, moreover, saw in America, the embodiment of the Messianic ideal which was to usher in an era of brotherhood and equality. To him, as to most Reform Jews of his day, America was Zion and Washington was Jerusalem.

The first World Zionist Congress, convened by Theodor Herzl in Basle, Switzerland, in 1897, appeared as a further step in the realization of the nationalistic objectives of Zionism. This served as a signal for a definite stand by the radical anti-nationalist elements in Reform Judaism. In his presidential address at the Montreal Convention of the Central Conference of American Rabbis, held the same year as the Basle World Zionist Congress, Wise inveighed against Zionism, branding it as the "idiosyncrasy of the . . . late immigrants," alluding of course, to the East European Jewish newcomers to America. The convention followed Wise's lead and adopted a resolution, sustaining the antinationalist viewpoint of the Pittsburgh Platform, and elaborating on it:[15]

> . . . Resolved that we totally disapprove of any attempt for the establishment of a Jewish state. Such attempts show a misunderstanding of Israel's mission, which from the narrow political and national field, has been expanded to the promotion among the whole human race of the broad and universalistic religion first proclaimed by the Jewish prophets. Such attempts do not benefit, but infinitely harm, our Jewish brethren, where they are still persecuted by confirming the assertion of their enemies that they are foreigners in the countries in which they are at home and of which they are everywhere the most loyal and patriotic citizens. . . .

The sentiment expressed in this resolution on Zionism remained the official position of the Reform movement for the next half century.

III. CHANGES IN AMERICAN REFORM

Impact of Events

A GIVEN IDEOLOGY originates as a response to a specific set of conditions or circumstances, and a change in them may produce a shift or even reversal in ideological position. Such a development took place in Reform Judaism in America. The transformation in the Reform pattern of thought may be attributed to a number of historical and sociological factors, principally the rise of anti-Semitism, the collapse of Emancipation, the growth of Zionism and the changed social composition of American Reform. These factors merit examination and review.

Anti-Semitism in Europe

The Jews of Germany and Central Europe attained Emancipation shortly before the Franco-Prussian War (1870-1871), but they were by no means secure in their new status. In 1873, when the false prosperity brought about by the war collapsed, the Jews were blamed as a matter of course. By that time, however, hostility toward the Jews on religious grounds was no longer fashionable. However, the diligent purveyors of hate found a new justification for their animosity in the form of racist theory. The Jews, they claimed, were alien to the German civilization and the German bloodstream, for they were Semites. As such they belonged to an inferior race which sought to dominate the superior Aryan race, to which the Germans belonged. Under these conditions, the Jews could only be considered outcasts, to be alienated from European life. The Jew was again to be regarded, as in medieval times, as a stranger in Europe, though he had lived there for about twenty centuries, longer than most of his neighbors.

The term "anti-Semitism" was first used by a journalist named Wilhelm Marr, said to be of Jewish extraction, in a scurrilous pamphlet against the Jews which he wrote in 1879. Marr warned that the Jews had already gained control over the Germans, and that they were now aspiring to rule the world. He and his cohorts won over to their cause many discontented merchants, frustrated aristocrats, and intellectuals. Among the scholars who supported this doctrine were several pseudo-anthropologists who undertook to "prove" the racial theories. The German historian, Heinrich von Treitschke, a man of mixed German and Slavic extraction, referred to the Jews as "our misfortune." The German composer Richard Wagner, also said to have been of Jewish descent, upheld the superiority of the Aryan race. Though he did not mind receiving aid from Jews, he denounced their influence on German music.

It was Wagner's son-in-law, Houston Stewart Chamberlain, who wrote the most popular "scientific" work in the racist field, which he entitled *The Foundations of the Nineteenth Century*. Chamberlain, the offspring of a British admiral and a German mother, became an ardent German nationalist. He contended that the Jews had contributed nothing of merit to European civilization. Whatever there was of worth in Judaism, Jews had borrowed from other peoples—not even the Bible was theirs. The Jews were physical, mental, and moral degenerates. Jesus, moreover, was actually an Aryan, not a Jew. To retain their genetic advantage, Aryans had to guard their bloodstreams against contamination by Jews. They had to be on the alert to ward off Jewry's influence and not fall prey to its wily scheme. This was the venomous fare fed to the generation that spawned Hitler.

It soon became evident that the leaders and members of these anti-Semitic groups were psychopaths, morally debased individuals, and criminals of all types; so much so that before long, Marr, the "philosopher" of the movement, and others who were misled by its ideas, shunned it. But the movement as a whole continued. Anti-Semitic societies were formed; they instigated wild riots and violence against the Jews, lodging all sorts of accusations against them, including the medieval charge of ritual murder. While Jews could escape religious animosity through baptism, they could not change their genes, and thus had no way of eluding these demonic forces of hate. The anti-Semitic attacks had a dual effect on Jews: they engendered among many a greater sense of Jewish awareness, solidarity, and dignity, but in others they created a feeling of morbid self-depreciation and self-hatred.

In France, the cradle of Jewish Emancipation in Europe a century earlier, the currents of anti-Jewish hostility culminated in the famous Dreyfus affair. In 1894, Captain Alfred Dreyfus, an assimilated Jew, a member of the French General Staff, was accused, court-martialed, and condemned to life imprisonment on Devil's Island on trumped-up charges of selling military secrets to Germany. The French army bureaucracy, the royalists, and the Church opposed all efforts to disprove his guilt and waged a wide campaign to demonstrate that Jews were disloyal and could not be trusted to be faithful citizens. Several years later, in 1899, a Major Esterhazy and a Colonel Henry were proven to be the true culprits, yet the army continued to resist all attempts to vindicate Dreyfus. At his re-trial in 1899, he was again convicted, but now "under extenuating circumstances," and a few days later was pardoned by the French president. But Dreyfus continued to press his innocence, and in 1906, more than a decade after his first trial, he was totally exonerated by the French Supreme Court. The Dreyfus affair had shaken France to its very foundations and resulted in the separation of church and state in that country.

The Zionist Movement

Among the Jews, however, the Dreyfus incident led to another momentous consequence: it became the symbol of the dramatic failure of Emancipation as a means of ameliorating the Jewish situation. This development, together with the virulent anti-Semitic movement that had ripened in Germany and in Central Europe, convinced Theodor Herzl, a brilliant Viennese Jewish journalist, that not assimilation but constructive Jewish nationalism was the antidote to anti-Semitism. In 1897, he convened the first Zionist congress at Basle, which adopted the political Zionist platform. The movement aspired to establish a "publicly recognized and legally secured home for the Jewish people in Palestine."

The Zionist idea soon spread to the United States. It appealed to the East European Orthodox elements who, by 1900, far outnumbered the older German settlers in the American Jewish population, which then totaled a million souls. In 1917, the Federation of American Zionists, established in 1898, was reorganized as the Zionist Organization of America and assumed a broader responsibility and program.

Zionism made considerable progress during the first two decades of its existence. The First World War, however, brought about a sharp improvement in the fortunes of the movement. The war witnessed a rise in the spirit of European nationalism generally and a corresponding decline in internationalist fervor. The Jewish internationalists, who had regarded socialism as a panacea for all world ills, including the problem of the oppression of minorities, were disenchanted by the fact that their comrades in other countries were carried away by nationalist sentiment and participated actively and loyally in their respective war efforts. The Allies on their part contributed to the strengthening of nationalist aspirations by making generous offers to various ethnic groups in Europe to restore their national sovereignties if the Allies should win the war. Zionist leaders were not slow to take advantage of this mood, and they sought concessions that would bring them closer to the realization of their aims.

Legal Sanctions

In England, Dr. Chaim Weizmann, a brilliant chemistry professor and a leading Zionist, won the gratitude of the British government by making an important discovery that was used effectively in their military operations. He succeeded in reaching the ears of highly placed British officials and in enlisting their sympathies for the Zionist cause. His persistent efforts, and those of other Zionist leaders, were rewarded by the historic declaration, issued on November 2, 1917, by Lord Arthur James Balfour, the British Foreign Minister, in the form of a letter addressed to Lord James Rothschild, President of the English Zionist Federation. The Balfour Declaration stated that "His Majesty's Government views with favor the establishment in Palestine of a national home for the Jewish people." Jews throughout the world received the news of the Balfour Declaration with great jubilation. They regarded this pronouncement as the modern counterpart of Cyrus of Persia's ancient pronouncement in 538 B.C.E. permitting the Jews in Babylonia to return to their homeland. At last, eighteen hundred years after the destruction of the Jewish state (70 C.E.), the Jewish hopes of establishing the third Commonwealth seemed to be reaching the point of fruition. In consequence, the membership of the American Zionist Organization soared from twenty thousand in 1914 to one hundred and fifty thousand in 1917. It looked as though the Zionist program would unify the various factions in American Jewish life.

A chain of dramatic events stimulated pro-Zionist sentiment and raised it to a high pitch. On December 11, 1917, the first day of *Hanukkah,* only a few weeks after the issuance of the Balfour Declaration, Field Marshal Edmond H. H. Allenby, the Supreme Commander of the British Expeditionary Forces, bareheaded and on foot, marched into Jerusalem at the head of his troops. The following spring, a Zionist commission, headed by Dr. Chaim Weizmann, came to Palestine to serve in a liaison capacity between the local Jewish community and the British military forces. Some months later, even before the guns were silenced, this commission proceeded to lay the cornerstone of the Hebrew University on Mt. Scopus, a gesture which received the warm acclaim of President Wilson and other allied statesmen. The enthusiasm engendered by these epoch-making and dramatic events stimulated an energetic recruitment campaign for the several Jewish battalions of the British army, which had been created in June 1917 for service in Palestine. This was the first Jewish military unit to fight for the Jewish homeland in eighteen centuries.

The Palestine Refuge

On April 24, 1920, the Supreme Council of European Powers, meeting at San Remo on the Italian Riviera, awarded the Palestine Mandate to Britain. This assignment was confirmed two years later by the Supreme Council of the League of Nations. This Mandate specifically provided that its holder was to help in the creation of a Jewish national home in Palestine. But almost from the start, Britain interfered with this effort. The Mandatory Government proceeded to limit immigration, not in accordance with the absorptive capacity of the country but in order to placate the Arab opponents of a Jewish state. This was, of course, a violation of the mandate. The Jews, in fact, were compelled to cope with both the antagonism of the British administration and that of the Arabs. Despite this they managed to increase the Jewish population in the country from 50,000 in 1920 to some 400,000 in 1935. Immigration to Palestine in the 1930's assumed a double importance: not only was it essential to bring in immigrants to enlarge the Jewish community in Palestine, but every Jewish immigrant from Central and Eastern Europe meant another life saved from the rising menace of Hitler. It seemed incongruous that Jewish refugees, barred from their native lands, should also be denied admission to Palestine by a government that was committed to aid in the upbuilding of the Jewish homeland.

The remarkable achievements in Palestine both in the area of immigration and in the economic field were a source of pride and exultation for Jews throughout the world. Palestine had become not only a refuge for the Jews but also the center of a thriving Jewish culture. Hebrew had been revived as the language of the home, the school, street, press, and theatre. A new art, dance, and song had been created. Palestine, now a centripetal force in Jewish life, acquired a high prestige in the consciousness of Jews which reached out to every sector of American Judaism, including the Reform wing.

Judeophobia in America

The racist theories and the hate propaganda produced in Europe did not reach America in any considerable degree until the period of the First World War. At that time, the disappointment of many Americans with the mad rush of the Allies for power and spoils at Versailles, combined with their discontent with the heavy burdens of war, took on the form of a strong argument for American isolationism. The intense wartime nationalism set in motion a nativist ferment, which assumed the nature of an appeal to preserve the native stock. Racial theories of the mystical superiority of the Nordic people, paralleling those promulgated by Houston Chamberlain, were invoked by writers like William McDougal, Madison Grant, and Lothrop Stoddard. A xenophobia gripped the country. Immigrants, who not long before had been regarded as an economic boon, were now branded a eugenic menace. This agitation was responsible in considerable measure for the Lodge-Johnson Immigration Bill of 1924, which set up discriminatory immigration quotas for Southern and Eastern Europeans, which in effect meant Jews and Italians.

This attitude on the part of many Americans favored the revival of the long dormant Ku Klux Klan, whose membership reached a peak of about four million at that time. Their chief targets of attack were Catholics, Negroes, and Jews. The Red Scare aggravated the situation. The presence of a small minority of Jews among the Communist leaders in Russia gave anti-Jewish groups in the United States a pretext for identifying the Communists with the Jews and the hated "internationalists." Additional fuel to fan the flames of Judeophobia came from the Russian aristocratic emigrés who spread the fantastic canard of a Jewish plot, allegedly revealed in the secret plans of international Jewry, incorporated in the *Protocols of the Elders of Zion*. The *Protocols* had presumably been discovered by the Russian police and published in Russia at the beginning of the current century. The "Elders of Zion" were by innuendo the leaders of world Zionism, who were allegedly scheming to destroy the existing governments in order to replace them with a single world rule of their own, intended to enslave the gentiles. The *Protocols* were translated into many languages, and circulated throughout the world. They were distributed in the United States with the aid of funds provided by Henry Ford, the automobile magnate. The true origin of the *Protocols* was uncovered and disclosed by the London *Times* in August, 1921,[16] but this did not deter Ford from continuing to disseminate his defamatory literature in tens of thousands of copies.[17] He resumed his attacks in a series of articles, published in his *Dearborn Independent,* on "The International Jew," which aimed to prove that the Jews were at the root of all the unrest in the world.[18]

Ford's calumnies were brought to an end abruptly in 1927. An irksome personal libel suit, instituted by Aaron Sapiro, a young midwestern Jewish attorney, seems to have brought Ford to his senses. In the course of the trial, Ford made overtures to Louis Marshall, then president of the American Jewish Committee, to accept a public apology in which he acknowledged that he had been horribly misled and that he was "deeply mortified that his journal had been made the medium for resurrecting exploded fictions." The *Dearborn Independent* was discontinued, but the effect of the poison it left behind could not be eradicated. Some years later, in 1933, Representative MacFadden of Pennsylvania and, in 1939, Thorkelson of Montana alluded to the Jewish conspiracy against world Christendom, "revealed in the *Protocols.*"

There were other evidences of Judeophobia at that time. In 1928, Jews in America were shocked by the recommendation of President A. L. Lowell of Harvard to his Board of Overseers to set up a *numerus clausus,* or Jewish quota, as a solution to the problem of overcrowding, as well as on the ground that "too many Jews at the institution are bound to form an unleavened and unassimilable lump." Though the Board of Overseers rejected the proposal, academic quotas against Jews, covertly applied, became widespread in institutions of higher learning in America. The thought that such a suggestion could be made openly and without embarrassment by the president of a leading American university aroused many Jews out of their complacency.

The Depression of 1929 again proved how easy it is to make the Jew a scapegoat in a period of crisis or tension. Discontented politicians and industrialists who opposed the New Deal branded it as the "Jew Deal." President Franklin D. Roosevelt was the "Jew Rosenfeld," and his braintrusters were "radicals, reds, and Jews." After 1933, anti-Semitism in the United States was no longer of the nativist variety, but largely Nazi-inspired and financed. Numerous anti-Semitic organizations sprang up: the German-American Bund, the Silver Shirts, Khaki Shirts, the Christian Front, and their ilk. There were rabble-rousers among these groups, like Father Charles Coughlin, Joe McWilliams and William Pelley. But among the more cultured who spread the virus of anti-Semitism there were also those like the writer Theodore Dreiser, a national hero of that period, Charles A. Lindbergh, and Senator Burton K. Wheeler.

Though liberals, conscientious individuals, and groups in the clergy and government answered this propaganda, many Jews were frightened and asked uneasily not only "Will it happen here?" but "When will it happen here?" referring, of course, to the Nazi campaign of extermination against the Jews. The Jewish refugees who had at that time escaped from Germany to America were living reminders of what could occur in the wake of anti-Jewish prejudice even in an enlightened country. These conditions stimulated the Jewish consciousness of many who had been drifting away from Judaism. Anti-Semitism proved an effective bar to assimilation; it also exerted a leveling and unifying influence in Jewry, since it did not distinguish between the various classes and alignments in Judaism. The German crusade against the Jews for racial rather than religious reasons, also proved that the world regarded Jews as an ethnic group rather than as only a creedal communion. The majority of Reformers who had previously clung to the latter notion now changed their view and began to consider themselves as a part of a national entity.

Changed Constituency

By the twenties, the offspring of the East European immigrants had made their way into both the pulpits and the pews of Reform temples. The new generation of Reform rabbis was recruited increasingly from Orthodox families, since Reform had failed to reproduce its own spiritual leadership. Reform synagogues welcomed the East Europeans who had attained financial and social position; they needed them to replenish their depleted ranks. Their diminution in numbers was caused by the low birth rate, characteristic of the upper economic strata to which many of the Reform Jews of German origin had belonged, as well as by the defections from Judaism among them.

The newcomers to the Reform congregations, both rabbis and laity, had a nostalgia for the traditional home and synagogue ceremonials to which they had been accustomed; religion was empty for them without these rites. They recognized also that their children needed these rituals to give religion color and substance and make it more vivid and alive. As their numbers and influence grew, the East European elements succeeded in introducing a greater measure of traditional observance into Reform worship. An increasing segment of Reform Jews had become nationalistically inclined, and a sizable portion of both the laity and their spiritual leaders had become Zionists, interested in the rebuilding of the Jewish homeland both as a cultural center and as an asylum for hard-pressed European Jewry. To many of these Jews, Zionism became a substitute for the integration that had failed.

The Columbus Platform

These changing social conditions within the American Reform movement and the rising tide of anti-Semitism in America and Europe combined with the unifying role of Jewish Palestine to bring about a revolutionary change in the basic attitudes and ideology of the Reform movement. For some years rumblings had been heard at the conventions of the Central Conference of American Rabbis to the effect that American Reform had gone too far in its radicalism, that it had to be flexible enough to reconsider its doctrines and practices. At the 1937 conference of Reform rabbis, held in Columbus, Ohio, a commission appointed to study the platform of Reform formally proposed a drastically revised set of guiding principles, which marked a repudiation of the fundamental principles of Reform, which had been incorporated in the Pittsburgh Platform a half century earlier. In a dramatic gesture David Philipson, the only surviving member of the Pittsburgh conference, moved the acceptance of the new program, which was approved

by the overwhelming majority of 101 to 9. The Columbus declaration defined Judaism as the "historical religious experience of the
Jewish people," thus injecting the concept of Jewish peoplehood
into official Reform ideology. The same idea was reiterated in the
fifth principle: "Judaism is the soul of which Israel is the body . . .
Israel has been held together by the ties of common history and
above all, the heritage of faith." The doctrine of Jewish ethnicity
superceded the earlier Reform notion of Jews constituting merely
**"a religious community," to the point of recognizing nonreligious
and secularist Jews as belonging to the House of Israel.**

**The most extreme change in the Columbus Platform was the
resolution in regard to Zionism.** Several years earlier, the Central
Conference had assumed a neutral attitude toward the rebuilding
of the Jewish homeland, but the Guiding Principles of 1937 took
a positive stand, urging all Jews to aid in the "upbuilding of Palestine as a Jewish homeland," by endeavoring to make it "not only a
haven of refuge for the oppressed, but also a center of Jewish
culture and spiritual life." This sharply modified viewpoint reflected not only a change in the rationale of Reform; but also the
vastly different social milieu in which it now functioned.

**The Columbus formulation assumed a considerably more affirm-
ative approach toward traditional observance and practice than the**
Pittsburgh declaration. It called for the "preservation of the Sabbath, festivals and Holy days, the retention and development of
such customs, symbols and ceremonies as possess inspirational
value, the cultivation of distinctive forms of religious art and music
and the use of Hebrew together with the vernacular in our worship
and instruction." It stresses too the need for home rituals.

The statement also differed from the Pittsburgh pronouncement
in its stance on the Bible and Talmud. While the earlier compilation asserted that the Bible was to be regarded as merely "reflecting
the primitive ideas of its own age," and made no mention of the
laws of the Talmud, the Columbus document maintained that "The
Torah, both written and oral, enshrines Israel's ever-growing consciousness of God and of the moral law. It preserves the historical
precedents, sanctions and norms of Jewish life" . . .

Aside from these modifications, the Columbus articles retained
the doctrines of the Pittsburgh program relating to the mission of

Israel, the harmony of Judaism and science, the immortality of the soul and the principles of the progressive revelation and evolution of Judaism. The plank on social justice in the Pittsburgh Platform was rewritten in more elaborate form in the later formulation.

The Union of American Hebrew Congregations, representing the lay membership of Reform temples, adopted a parallel resolution on Palestine at its conference in New Orleans in the same year. Another resolution provided for the restoration of traditional symbols and customs, as well as for the reinstatement of the *hazzan* (cantor) in the synagogue worship. This religious functionary had all but disappeared from Reform synagogues. The blowing of the *Shofar* on *Rosh Hashanah* was also revived. Thus, the over-all lay body in Reform Judaism formally joined its corps of rabbis in reversing Reform's earlier antinationalist and antitraditionalist position. In so doing, they were bringing the Reform movement closer to the other wings in American Judaism.

One Reform leader, Professor Israel Bettan of the Hebrew Union College, explained the new viewpoint in regard to tradition aptly in his epigram to the effect that "the Jew does not pray to a philosophy." A number of traditional rituals were restored to the Union Prayerbook at this time. These included the candle-lighting ceremonial ushering in the Sabbath, a home rite performed by the mother. This ritual was inserted at the beginning of the Sabbath-eve service. The *Kiddush* (sanctification over the wine), a traditional synagogue as well as home rite, was also introduced in the Reform prayer book. The Joint Commission on Ceremonies of the Union of American Hebrew Congregations and the Central Conference of American Rabbis composed new prayers for special occasions, among them the Sabbath nearest Armistice Day, and the Sabbath of *Hanukkah*. *Purim* was also brought back in the Reform synagogue with the reading of an abridged Scroll of Esther in English. A community Seder (order), the festive Passover service and meal, was inaugurated for the second night of Passover, the first being reserved for the home observance.

Several traditional services were modified. A new ritual was adopted for *Simchat Torah* (the Festival of the Rejoicing of the Law). The ritual symbolized the transmission of the Torah to three generations, from grandfather to father to son. The Scriptural reading was introduced into the Friday evening service, which is considerably better attended than the more elaborate Sabbath morning worship, when the Torah portion is traditionally read. The traditional *Bar Mitzvah*[19] for boys was reinstituted in Reform synagogues. An innovation, the *Bat Mitzvah*,[20] was introduced for girls. The latter practice has found its way into congregations belonging to other branches of Judaism.

A wide range of new procedures are now in vogue in Reform congregations. Women have been given equal religious status with men. They sit together; may be called up to the Torah (Meg. 23a); lead the service; and may be counted in a *minyan* or religious quorum of ten, traditionally required for public worship. They are frequently members of synagogue boards and committees. Since 1972 women have been ordained as rabbis and appointed as cantors by Reform synagogues. The officially sanctioned Reform usages are compiled in a special work, though observance is voluntary.[21]

From the start, American Reform was generally more radical in casting off Halachic precepts than the European branch. American Reform Jews observe one day of festivals including Rosh Hashanah, instead of the traditional two. At weddings, neither the *Ketubah,* the marriage document, nor the *Huppah,* the canopy, is required. Nor is it essential to secure a *get* or religious divorce for remarriage. Weddings, moreover, are banned only on the Sabbath and holy days, but not during the traditional days of mourning. The *Shiva* or traditional seven day period of home mourning for the dead is reduced to three days. A mixed choir usually officiates at services, with organ accompaniment. The male worshippers are generally bare-headed and do not wear a *Talith* or *Tefillin* (phylacteries). The dietary regulations too have been dispensed with, together with many others.

Present Status

About 725 synagogues are currently affiliated with the Union of American Hebrew Congregations. This number includes many suburban congregations organized in recent years. The administrative headquarters of the Union was transferred in 1952 from Cincinnati, the original seat of Reform, to New York City, in deference to the fact that the New York metropolis has the largest Jewish population in the United States. An impressive edifice, the "House of Living Judaism," was then erected opposite the sumptuous structure of Temple Emanuel on Fifth Avenue to house the offices of the various departments and services of the Union, its professional organizations, and publications. These take in the Commission on Religious Education, the National Federation of Temple Sisterhoods and the parallel Brotherhood Federation, and the Commission on Social Action. The Union maintains regional offices throughout the country as well. The main office of the Central Conference of American Rabbis is also located in New York City.

The Hebrew Union College, the Reform rabbinical seminary, established in Cincinnati in 1875, merged in 1950 with the Jewish Institute of Religion, which Dr. Stephen S. Wise (1874-1949) founded in New York in 1922. The latter institution was originally launched as a protest against the separatist and anti-Zionist tendencies of the Hebrew Union College, but after the adoption of the Columbus Platform, there was no longer any justification for the continued existence of two independent Reform rabbinical seminaries. The combined seminaries, known as the Hebrew Union College-Jewish Institute of Religion, or College-Institute for short, have four campuses in New York, Cincinnati, Los Angeles, and since 1962 in Jerusalem. The last-named site accommodates the Nelson Glueck post-graduate School of Biblical Archaeology. Rabbinical students are expected to spend their first year of study at the Jerusalem campus.

The College-Institute trains rabbis, cantors, religious school teachers and administrators, music instructors, community workers and archaeologists through its various schools. Aside from its extensive library collections, it maintains a Jewish museum, the American Jewish Archives, and the American Jewish Periodical Center, at one or more of its branches. Dr. Alfred Gottschalk has succeeded the late Nelson Glueck (1900-1971) as president of the overall institution. The New York School is now moving to a site adjacent to the Washington Square Campus of New York University.

The American Council for Judaism

In 1943, the small irreconcilable minority of rabbis and laymen who opposed the pro-Zionism of the Columbus Platform organized the American Council for Judaism. The Council still adheres to the position of classical Reform: it regards Zionism as a secular and political movement, incompatible with Judaism, which, it insists, is purely a religion. Most of the original founders of the Council, particularly the rabbis among them, abandoned it after the state of Israel was established in 1948, recognizing that opposition to Zionism had now lost its meaning. Today the American Council for Judaism exerts virtually no influence in American Jewish life. It has, however, aroused the antagonism of all responsible elements in Jewry.

The New Declaration

The 1976 Convention of the Central Conference of American Rabbis adopted a new set of principles, the first since 1937, which was called the "Centenary Perspective." It recognized that "the Holocaust shattered our easy optimism about humanity and its inevitable progress." It also acknowledged that "the State of Israel . . . raised our sense of Jews as a people to new heights of aspiration and devotion," and that this implied a responsibility to encourage *Aliyah* (immigration to Israel), create strong Jewish communities in the Diaspora, and live intensely Jewish lives to insure Jewish survival. The Reform nationalistic sentiment reached a peak in the establishment of *ARZA,* an acronym meaning "to the land," which stands for "American Reform Zionist Association" and aims to organize *Kibbutzim* in Israel like *Yahel* ("Flashing Light") and to attain recognition of the Reform movement in Israel on a par with that of the Orthodox parties.

The *Shaarei Tefillah* ("Gates of Prayer") published in 1975, as the first revision of the Union Prayer Book issued in 1940, reflects the Reform nationalistic tendencies. Significantly, one of its two editions opens from the Hebrew side. The service for the *Fast of Tisha Be-Av,* the Ninth of Av, is fittingly coupled with that of *Yom Hashoah,* commemorating the contemporary Holocaust. The latter ritual includes the Yiddish Partisan Hymn sung in the Vilna ghetto, exhorting Jews not to despair. The service for the *Yom Ha-Atzmaut* or Israel Independence Day reproduces a stanza of Hannah Senesh's "Blessed is the Match," the last poem of this twenty-three-year-old member of the Palestine Jewish Brigade, written shortly before her execution for parachuting behind German lines in an attempt to rescue Jews. And *mirabile dictu,* the Reform liturgical volume contains the benedictions for putting on the *Talith* and *Tefillin,* the traditional prayer shawl and phylacteries. A guide book, the *Shaarei Habayit* ("Gates of the House"), provides personal prayers to celebrate success, or on suffering disappointment, on entering college, and the like. Explanatory notes, discussions, *Zemirot* or Sabbath hymns are offered in other related manuals to make worship more meaningful and relevant.

13

Conservative Judaism

I. IN THE NINETEENTH CENTURY

Isaac Leeser (1806-1868)

ISAAC LEESER is generally regarded as the principal forerunner of Conservative Judaism in the United States. A native of Westphalia, Leeser acquired his religious and secular education before coming to America in 1824. He settled in Richmond, Virginia, where he was employed for several years in his uncle's business. At the same time, he assisted the *hazzan* (minister) in the religious school of the local Sephardic congregation. During this period, he gained prominence by publishing numerous articles in defense of Jews and Judaism in American and foreign journals. Though an Ashkenazi, Leeser was called to Philadelphia in 1830 to assume the office of *hazzan* of Mikveh Israel, a Sephardic synagogue.

Early in his career at Mikveh Israel, Leeser introduced "external" improvements—English prayers and an English sermon—into the regular Hebrew service. As a consequence of the latter innovation, Leeser became the first Jewish preacher in America. Because of the opposition of a number of his congregants, these changes were not adopted by the congregation formally until 1845,

317

some fifteen years later. In 1850, he resigned his post at Mikveh Israel, because the congregation refused to grant him life tenure. He then became the rabbi of a newly formed synagogue in Philadelphia, Beth El Emeth, which he served until his death in 1868.

Leeser was a creative and dynamic personality in American Jewish life. For almost two centuries before his time, the tiny American Jewish community had been stagnating, bringing forth no scholars, publications, or Jewish institutions worthy of note. But Leeser infused it with new life and activity. In 1843, his remarkable energy and imagination prompted him to launch the first truly national Jewish journal in America, *The Occident and Jewish Advocate,* which he edited himself. His publication appeared as a monthly until his death, except for a brief period when it was issued as a weekly. The volumes of this periodical, a champion of Orthodoxy, present a fascinating panorama of Jewish life in the growing American Jewish community of Leeser's day.

Many other achievements may be credited to Leeser. At his instance, the first American Jewish Publication Society was founded in 1845; unfortunately, it came to an abortive end only six years later, when the building it occupied burned down, together with the plant and stock of the organization.[1] Concerned with the religious training of young and old, he translated, composed, and published a number of children's texts. He also rendered the Sephardic and Ashkenazic prayer books into English to make them more intelligible to the worshipers. His greatest work, however, was his English translation of the Hebrew Scriptures, which appeared in 1853. This volume gave English-speaking Jewry an edition of the Bible in the English language free from the objectionable Christological references and renditions of the King James version. Leeser's English Bible was regarded as the standard Jewish version until 1917, when it was replaced by the Masoretic edition of the Jewish Publication Society, produced by a group of eminent Jewish scholars. Leeser's text, however, continues to be used in synagogues and in Jewish homes to this day.

The interest and insight Leeser displayed in Jewish education embraced all levels. Only a year before his death, he established Maimonides College in Philadelphia, the first rabbinical training school in America. This institution, which also undertook to train cantors and *shochtim* (ritual slaughterers), was closed for lack of funds after only six years of operation, but in the course of its brief existence it turned out several graduates, the first rabbis to be trained in the New World. It also paved the way for the rabbinical seminaries established in subsequent decades.

Leeser's Traditionalism

Leeser deviated only in a small degree from the rigid Sephardic Orthodoxy of his day, and in his viewpoint generally followed the principles outlined by Zacharia Frankel and the Positive Historical School.[2] Orthodoxy, he maintained, "is not that unbending, unyielding, bigoted opposition to improvement which our opponents represent it to be." Yet, he held, it could not yield to "the demands which seekers of innovations may make to render Judaism a thing to accommodate itself to every phase of history. Such a religion would be none at all, as its ground would be constantly shifting." He insisted, however, that "to progress with the age, to adopt all the improvements which have been proved lawful, is perfectly within the limits of Orthodoxy. But," he complained, "the Reformers are not satisfied with this . . . they wish to change, to revolutionize, to alter . . ."[3]

Despite his unrelenting opposition to Reform, Leeser had no intention of creating a separate religious party, for he strongly believed in the need for developing a united American Jewry. He welcomed Isaac Mayer Wise's endorsement of his call, in 1848, for the establishment of an over-all body to bring together the American Jewish congregations. This body, however, did not materialize until 1859, when the Board of Delegates of American Israelites was launched. In his desire to prevent the fragmentation of American Jewry, Leeser called for an "adjectiveless" Judaism, for an indigenous, normative American Judaism which accommodates to honest dissension without separating into a number of factions. Leeser is credited with originating the term *Catholic Israel,* later popularized by Solomon Schechter. The phrase alludes to one of the major principles of the Historical School—the idea of forging a link and an inner identification between the Judaism of the past and present, through a continuous tradition.

Sabbato Morais (1823-1897)

When Leeser left his pulpit at Mikveh Israel in 1850, he was succeeded by Sabbato Morais, a native of Leghorn, Italy, and a disciple of the great Italian Jewish scholar, Samuel David Luzzatto. Morais, unlike Leeser, was a Sephardic Jew. He mastered English while in London, where he served for five years as a teacher at the Orphans School of the local Spanish-Portuguese congregation. A man of unusual mental and spiritual qualities, he possessed great zeal and moral strength. These attributes, combined with his striking physical appearance, impressed his congregation, which prospered under his leadership.

Morais had the courage to take a firm stand in support of a cause in which he believed. A staunch abolitionist, he gave public expression to his views, despite the efforts of some officials of his congregation to silence him. On one occasion, when President Buchanan refused to intercede in the Mortara case,[4] Morais omitted the customary prayer for the head of the government at Sabbath services, despite the protests of the leaders of his congregation.

Like his predecessor Leeser, Morais concerned himself with educational work; he aided Leeser in establishing Maimonides College, continuing to teach there until the institution closed. Later he assisted Isaac Mayer Wise in launching the Hebrew Union College, which he, like others, hoped would be a non-partisan school serving all sectors of American Jewry. Morais, in fact, acted as an official examiner of the College until the adoption of the Pittsburgh Platform in 1885, when he became convinced that a reconciliation of the traditional and Reform tendencies in Judaism was impossible. His hope of bringing about harmony between the two groups prompted him to propose the adoption of a common liturgy, to be composed of the basic prayers prescribed in the Talmud, together with others to be approved by a special conference of the "pious and the erudite," to be convened for this purpose. He was greatly disappointed that his plan did not receive the attention he believed it merited.

Determined to create a new rabbinical seminary, Morais sought the assistance of a dozen colleagues sympathetic to the cause of moderate Orthodoxy and opposed to the extreme radicalism of the Pittsburgh Platform. They followed in varying degrees the doctrines of Frankel's Positive Historical School. Some of their synagogues had family pews, mixed choirs, and organs. The character of their ideological inclinations may be judged from the fact that by the turn of the century, half of them had drifted into the Reform camp. The leading spirits in this group included Benjamin Szold (1829-1902),[5] the veteran rabbi of Oheb Shalom in Baltimore, who had published a prayer book from which he excised the passages relating to the sacrifices, and to which he added other prayers, thereby diverging considerably from the traditional ritual. Another prominent rabbi in this camp was the erudite Marcus Jastrow (1829-1903), the compiler of a Talmudic dictionary, who had arrived in Philadelphia from Warsaw in 1866 to assume the pulpit of Congregation Rodeph Shalom. Jastrow served as vice-president of the infant American Zionist Federation in 1898. Alexander Kohut (1842-1894), scholarly author of another Talmudic dictionary, who at one time was chief spokesman for the Historical School in his native Hungary, was a natural ally of Morais.[6] The main issues that separated the adherents of this trend from the more violent Reformers were the dietary laws, Sabbath observance, Jewish nationalism, and the role of Hebrew in Jewish life.

The Jewish Theological Seminary

Morais was the leading spirit and State Senator Joseph Blumenthal (1834-1901), a devout Jew, was the lay president of the Jewish Theological Seminary Association, which was incorporated in 1886. The purpose of the institution as set forth in its original by-laws was:

> . . . the preservation in America of the knowledge and practice of historical Judaism as ordained in the Law of Moses (Torath Moshe) and expounded by the prophets (Nebiim) and sages (Hakamim) of Israel in Biblical and Talmudical writings, through the establishment and maintenance of a Jewish Theological Seminary for the training of rabbis and teachers; (and) the attainment of such cognate purposes as may be deemed appropriate . . .

The Seminary[7] was opened in 1887 at the Shearith Israel Synagogue in New York, with a class of eight students. Sabbato Morais, its dedicated founder, assumed the office of president of the faculty and served in this capacity until his death. During his administration, he led the Seminary in the spirit of his fervent Sephardic Orthodoxy.

The Seminary Constituency

Around the turn of the century, the Seminary represented a relatively small and unstable constituency consisting of a dozen synagogues in New York City, Philadelphia, and Baltimore. These synagogues veered between Orthodoxy and Reform. They differed from Orthodoxy in that their prayer books deviated from the traditional norm; moreover, they had family pews and in some instances also organs. Yet they had departed from tradition to a lesser extent than the Reformers. These congregations were not sufficiently united in ideology or purpose to support a rabbinical seminary, nor did the size of the group warrant a separate rabbinical school.

However, the composition of American Jewry at this time was undergoing a radical change. The enactment in Russia of the infamous May Laws of 1882[8] was the climax of a horrible series of pogroms and persecutions, which spread across the Jewish Pale of Settlement. The disabilities and violence to which the Jews were exposed drove thousands of them from Russia to America. Restrictions and oppressions in other East European countries added to the vast number fleeing to America. In the two decades between 1880 and 1900, American Jewry increased from two hundred fifty thousand to a million. While the older settlers had been mainly of German origin and of predominantly Reform tendencies, the bulk of the new arrivals adhered to the intense East European type of Orthodoxy. The wave of newcomers with their vast numbers soon overwhelmed the tiny, indigenous, and staid American Orthodoxy. This was the potential clientele of the Seminary. However, it was not the first generation of these immigrants, but their better established and more acculturated offspring, that founded or joined the less traditionalist Conservative synagogues. The Seminary before long became the spiritual center and rallying point of the Conservative congregations throughout the country.

The Seminary Crisis

After Morais' death (1897) an attempt was made to enlist the support of the East European Orthodox elements on behalf of the Seminary. Until then, only the few older Orthodox congregations were identified with this institution. The following year, Henry Pereira Mendes (1852-1937), minister of the Sephardic Shearith Israel congregation in New York, led an effort to create a central Orthodox congregational body, the Union of Orthodox Jewish Congregations, in order to give the Seminary a broader congregational base. However, at its second conference in 1898, this federation voted to endorse only the Orthodox institution, the Rabbi Isaac Elchanan Yeshiva, founded in 1896, thereby repudiating an earlier resolution to support the Seminary as well. The Orthodox congregational organization, dominated by a leadership with an East European background, could not approve of a school with modernist leanings, which was so far removed from them in spirit and outlook. As a result, the Seminary sponsorship became convinced that there was no alternative but to steer an independent course.

The Seminary had been struggling financially since its inception, but Morais' death left it orphaned to the point of crisis. For a while it looked as if it would meet the same ill fate as Leeser's Maimonides College had suffered some thirty-five years earlier. This was fortunately averted by one of Morais' devoted pupils in Philadelphia, Cyrus Adler (1863-1940), a young man who had gained prominence in traditionalist Jewish circles.[9] Determined that the work of his revered teacher must not come to naught, Adler enlisted the interest of Jacob H. Schiff (1847-1920), a Jewish leader and philanthropist, in the plight of the Seminary. Schiff, a Reform Jew, was a descendant of a rabbinic family and had acquired a thorough Jewish education at Samson Raphael Hirsch's day school in Frankfort.[10] It was a point of pride with him that one of his progenitors, the *Mahram* Schiff (1605-1641), was the author of an important and popular Talmudic commentary.

With the aid of his Reform friends, including the Guggenheims, the Lehmans, the Lewisohns, and Louis Marshall (1856-1929), Schiff raised half a million dollars to reorganize the Seminary and place it on a firm financial footing. They joined the board of the institution, limiting their concern to fiscal matters and leaving educational policy to the faculty. To this group of Jewish leaders, the Seminary was the medium by which the older segment in American Jewry would help their East European coreligionists achieve their own synthesis of tradition and modernism, as they, the earlier settlers, had made theirs. It was clear to them that the graduates of the Hebrew Union College were culturally, socially, and religiously far too distant from the East European Jews to serve as their spiritual guides.

It was Cyrus Adler, too, who in 1902 induced the reconstituted board of the Seminary to bring Solomon Schechter from England to assume the presidency of the institution. Schechter was exceptionally well suited for this post. His East European background coupled with his Western training qualified him to mediate between the Orthodox faculty he organized and the Reform members of the Seminary board. Schechter occupied the office of president for thirteen years, until his death in 1915. During his incumbency, the Seminary experienced a period of vital growth and expansion which made it an outstanding and world-renowned academy of higher Jewish learning. Schechter also played a major role in shaping the ideology and structure of the Conservative movement.

II. In the Twentieth Century

Solomon Schechter (1847-1915)

In the Yeshivot of his native Rumania and in Lemberg (Lwow), Solomon Schechter, a young *illuy* (prodigy), acquired a thorough Talmudic training. His family, famed for its piety and learning, belonged to the *Habad*,[11] a group which espoused an intellectualized form of Hassidism. Schechter's earliest contact with Western culture dated from 1871, when, at the age of twenty-four, he went off to study at the *Beth Hamidrash* (lit. House of Learning) in Vienna. This school, a relatively modern institution of advanced Jewish learning, afforded him a glimpse into the methodology of the Science of Judaism and prepared him, in addition, for his rabbinic ordination. In his fourth year in Vienna, Schechter enrolled at the local university. From there he went to Berlin, where he continued his Jewish studies at several of the higher Jewish academies while pursuing his general studies in the faculty of philosophy at the University of Berlin. In the German capital, he became the tutor in rabbinics of Claude Montefiore, scion of one of the leading Jewish families of England, who induced Schechter to accompany him to London.

Schechter's arrival in England was a turning point in his career. He quickly mastered the English language and developed an elegant written style. His scholarly articles, which have since been published in his *Studies in Judaism,* attracted considerable attention and, in 1890, won him a post at Cambridge. He began as a lecturer in rabbinics and several years later was advanced to Cambridge's equivalent of professorial rank. In the spring of 1902, at the age of fifty-five, Schechter accepted the presidency of the Jewish Theological Seminary of America.

Schechter's Genizah Discoveries

Schechter was a follower of Frankel's Historical School. He had gained great prominence as a result of his discoveries in the *Genizah*[12] of the Fostat (old Cairo) synagogue. In one of his essays, Schechter described the *Genizah* as a "cemetery" of discarded books and documents, a "limbo to which were consigned remnants of good books to be preserved from harm and bad books to be preserved from doing harm."[13] Schechter went to the old synagogue in Cairo, ransacked the *Genizah,* and brought back with him a miscellany of a hundred thousand manuscripts, including letters, legal records,and official documents. The manuscripts contained a sensational find—a copy of an old Hebrew edition of the *Book of Ben Sira* (Ecclesiasticus) that he had been seeking. The original Hebrew text of· this volume, which forms a part of the Apocrypha,[14] had been lost for centuries and was known mainly from quotations in the Talmud, and from the Greek and other translations.

In the valuable source[15] materials which Schechter had uncovered there was much that illuminated Jewish life in the Diaspora from the eighth to the fourteenth centuries. For his great contribution to Hebraic scholarship, Cambridge University awarded him an honorary doctorate. Later, in 1903, he was elected an Honorary and Advisory member of the New York University Senate. In 1911, Harvard bestowed upon him an honorary doctorate. Schechter's achievements and fame added significantly to the prestige of the Seminary.

Reorganization of the Seminary

One of Schechter's first tasks upon coming to the Seminary was to assemble a faculty consisting of promising young scholars. In his first report to his board, he deplored the fact that the Seminary had been designed as a rabbinical training school, rather than as an institution to foster Jewish learning for its own sake, in the tradition of the European Yeshivot. "We live now in an age of specialization," he said facetiously, "when funerals and burials have been raised to the dignity of a fine art, and praying has become a closed profession." Traditionally, Schechter explained, the rabbi was a scholar, not a cleric, always *primus inter pares* (first among equals)—a man distinguished for his learning in a community in which learning prevailed. "I consider it not without danger to create a religious aristocracy which might soon claim the King . . . and crowd the rest of us out from his Divine Presence," he wittily wrote in his biennial report.[16] The primary role of the rabbi (master, or learned authority) was to teach and interpret the law, not to serve as parson, preacher, rector, or priest. The change in the function of the rabbi, Schechter stated, reflected the fact that Jews were themselves no longer versed in the Torah and were "in need of artificial support, like other denominations."

Together with a colleague, Professor Alexander Marx, Schechter undertook to build up an extensive Jewish library. Judge Mayer Sulzberger of Philadelphia, a brilliant Jewish scholar, donated his own large collection of Judaica. In 1909, aided by a gift from Jacob H. Schiff, the Seminary opened the Teachers' Institute, of which Mordecai M. Kaplan was appointed principal.[17]

The American Jewish Scene (1900-1920)

A glimpse at the American Jewish scene during the early decades of the current century offers an insight into the social milieu in which the Conservative movement was fostered. Through immigration and natural increase, the American Jewish population grew from about one million at the turn of the century to more than double this figure by the end of the first decade. The avalanche of immigration continued; it was interrupted during the four years of the First World War, but it was resumed soon afterwards. By 1920, the Jewish population of America is estimated to have reached three million five hundred thousand, the majority of whom had entered the country as immigrants. The newcomers were divided into a variety of groupings; there were among them secularists and religionists, Zionists and anti-Zionists, Orthodox and liberals of various shadings. They tended to join congregations composed in the main of their own countrymen, often of people from the same city or town from which they had originated, thereby accentuating their different backgrounds. They regarded themselves as Austrian, Lithuanian, Rumanian, Ukrainian, or other types of hyphenated Jews, with little to integrate them into the common body of American Jewry.

The social, cultural, and economic configuration of the American Jewish community was now in flux. The leading Jews in political and civic affairs and in Jewish philanthropy were the descendants of the earlier German Jewish immigrants, but the children of the East European settlers had now begun to come to the fore. They had taken advantage of their freedom and educational opportunities in America and had risen quickly, entering the liberal professions, business, and industry, and generally striking roots in the American economy. These younger people abandoned the crowded city slums and ghetto neighborhoods of their childhood and moved to better homes in other areas. The cultural differences among their parents were dissolved in the common American environment in which they were reared.

This generation proved fertile soil for the cultivation of Conservative Judaism, for they desired to maintain the religious customs of their fathers in a modernized context, in conformity with American standards of behavior. A growing number of the synagogues they established in their new neighborhoods turned to Conservatism, which was now taking definite form as another religious tendency in American Judaism. The new movement no longer depended for its leadership and sponsorship on elements in the older Orthodox synagogues; it was now developing its own leadership and rapidly becoming an independent force in American Jewry.

The United Synagogue

The Seminary represented the first phase in the institutionalization of Conservatism. The next step in this process was the establishment in 1913, two years before Schechter's death, of the Conservative congregational organization, the United Synagogue. Sixteen synagogues responded to Dr. Schechter's call to form this new body which adopted the same name used by the central congregational federation of English Jewry.[18] As the Conservative counterpart of the Union of Orthodox Jewish Congregations and the Reform Union of American Hebrew Congregations, the United Synagogue became the lay arm of the Conservative movement. Schechter was elected president of the United Synagogue, the aims of which were outlined in the preamble to its constitution:

> . . . The advancement of the cause of Judaism in America and the maintenance of Jewish tradition and its historical continuity,
>
> To assert and establish loyalty to the Torah and its historical exposition;
>
> To further the observance of the Sabbath and dietary laws;
>
> To preserve in the service the reference to Israel's past and the hopes for Israel's restoration;
>
> To maintain the traditional character of the liturgy with Hebrew as the language of prayer;
>
> To foster Jewish religious life in the home, as expressed in traditional observances;
>
> To encourage the establishment of Jewish religious schools, in the curricula of which the study of the Hebrew language and literature shall be given a prominent place, both as the key to the true understanding of Judaism, and as a bond holding together the scattered communities of Israel throughout the world.
>
> It shall be the aim of the United Synagogue of America, while not endorsing the innovations introduced by any of its

constituent bodies, to embrace all elements essentially loyal to traditional Judaism and in sympathy with the purposes outlined above. . . .

Gradually other congregations, led in the main by graduates of the Seminary, joined the United Synagogue, and in 1918, its Women's League was organized.

The Rabbinical Assembly of America

By 1919, the Seminary Alumni Association, founded in 1901, had grown to about one hundred members. It was decided to broaden its scope by converting it into a general Conservative rabbinical organization to which qualified nongraduates of the Seminary would also be admitted. The name of the association was therefore changed to the Rabbinical Assembly, and the latter became the third institutional arm of the Conservative movement, corresponding to the Orthodox rabbinical groups and the Reform movement's Central Conference of American Rabbis. The Rabbinical Assembly assumed the task of interpreting the doctrines and practices of Judaism in accordance with the Conservative viewpoint.

Growth of Conservatism

Schechter had laid the ideological and structural foundation of Conservative Judaism in America. In the years following his death, the movement grew rapidly, attracting the first and second generations of East European Jews who found Orthodoxy too rigid and Reform too lax for the expression and satisfaction of their religious interests. Though in the later twenties and thirties, an increasing number of the children of East European immigrants joined Reform temples, a considerably larger portion was drawn to Conservative congregations, as they did not find the Reform synagogue socially congenial. Each of the three major institutions in Conservatism, the Seminary, the United Synagogue, and the Rabbinical Assembly, reflected in its development the growth of the movement as a whole.

In the ensuing decades, Conservatism grew beyond expectation. By 1960, the American Jewish population, now largely middle-class and prosperous, had attained a figure of approximately five and a half million. The country as a whole was in the throes of what has been described as a religious revival, marked by great increases in church affiliation, particularly in the mushrooming suburban areas. Judaism, along with other religious denominations, experienced its share of the general expansion. By that time, too, the Jewish working class with its antireligious, cosmopolitan, and secularist element had undergone a marked decline. The Conservative United Synagogue, embracing some 830 affiliated congregations, now forms the largest branch of American religious Jewry. Like those of the other religious parties, the Conservative congregations are diversified in their respective practices and observances; they are spread widely over an ideological spectrum extending from left-wing Orthodoxy to right-wing Reform.

Expanded Program

Cyrus Adler, a native American, followed Schechter in 1916 as acting president; in 1924 as president of the Seminary, holding the latter office until his death in 1940. Adler's successor, Louis Finkelstein, an outstanding Jewish scholar and a former member of the Seminary faculty, served as the Seminary's first Chancellor. The institution expanded greatly under his administration. Aside from the Rabbinical School, it maintains a Teachers Institute to prepare instructors for religious schools, a school for cantors and the study of Jewish music, a College of Jewish Studies, an extensive library with a most significant collection of Jewish manuscripts, and a Jewish museum. Its popular Eternal Light radio and television program, produced in cooperation with the National Broadcasting Corporation, reaches vast audiences.

In March 1965, the Seminary launched the Schocken Institute for Jewish Research in Jerusalem. The following year, it opened the American Student Center in Jerusalem to accommodate and provide instruction for its students spending a year in Israel. The Seminary also operates the Institute for Religious and Social Studies for the discussion of problems confronting religion on a nondenominational basis. Among its other vital activities are the Ramah summer camps and Leaders Training Fellowship. The Seminary's Institute for Religious and Social Studies discusses problems confronting religion on a nondenominational basis.

In 1969 the Seminary opened its Institute for Advanced Studies in the Humanities on a graduate level. Dr. Gerson D. Cohen succeeded Dr. Finkelstein as Chancellor in 1972.

The University of Judaism, the West Coast branch of the Seminary, located in Los Angeles, California, prepares teachers for Jewish schools and serves as a center for graduate study and research. It aims to equip both the professional and lay leadership of the various Jewish community agencies, as well as Jewish intellectuals and the general public, with a knowledge and appreciation of the tenets and values of Judaism. The University renders a sorely needed and vital service to the vast Jewish community in and around Los Angeles.

The United Synagogue, too, has broadened its program immeasurably in recent decades. Its Commission on Jewish Education publishes brochures, textbooks, and a variety of teaching aids. Among the organizations sponsored by this body are the National Academy for Adult Jewish Studies and the Federation of Jewish Mens' Clubs. The United Synagogue maintains a center in Jerusalem and sponsors other activities throughout Israel.

III. Schechter's Doctrines

Schechter's Rationalism

Schechter was the principal ideologist of the Conservative movement. Though a rationalist in his approach to scholarship, Schechter appears to have found it difficult to accept the view of revelation in purely natural terms. He indicated that the Historical School has equated revelation with history "and when Revelation or the Written Word is reduced to the level of history, there is no inherent difficulty in elevating history in its aspect of tradition to the rank of Scripture, for both have then the same human or divine origin

. . . and emanate from the same authority."[19] But he admitted that occasionally he could not but "rebel against this new rival of Revelation in the shape of history."[20] Its scientific function notwithstanding, he attributed to the Historical School generally, "an enlightened scepticism combined with a staunch conservatism which is not wholly devoid of a certain mystical touch."[21]

Significantly, Schechter saw mystical overtones even in the Halacha and found that "the sea of the Talmud has also its gulf stream of mysticism which runs through the wide ocean of Jewish thought, constantly commingling with the icy waters of legalism and increasingly washing the desolate shores of an apparently meaningless ceremonialism."[22] There is nothing sacrosanct about the rationalism of the age as evidenced in the approach of the Historical School, Schechter observed. It, too, may be an intellectual fad in this generation just as philosophical speculation has characterized other eras in Judaism. In this and in other instances, Schechter was too much the mystic to be a consistent thinker. It may even be said of him that in his approach to religion he erected a wall separating his religious beliefs from his scientific outlook.

That Schechter did not regard Judaism as a purely rationalistic religion is further confirmed by his attitude toward dogma. He took exception to Moses Mendelssohn's contention in his *Jerusalem* that Judaism is based entirely on reason and that it possesses no dogma. Schechter conceded that Judaism does not ascribe any saving power to dogma, but he held that nonetheless it "regulates not only our actions but also our thoughts." Judaism, moreover, embraces life, but "a life without guiding principles and thoughts is not worth living." Schechter also took issue with Mendelssohn on the Biblical attitude toward belief. The latter claimed that the first Commandment does not purport to direct us to believe; Schechter[23] on the other hand argued that Jewish scholars, including Maimonides, Judah Halevi, and Nachmanides, did interpret the Commandment, "I am the Lord thy God . . ." as a prescript enjoining belief in the existence of God.[24]

Catholic Israel

In Schechter's opinion, the Historical School regarded as primary not the Bible of revelation but rather the Bible as interpreted by tradition. This evolving Jewish tradition, the product of Scriptural interpretation, Schechter called the Secondary Meaning of the Bible. The Secondary Meaning is incorporated in the rabbinic works, the Talmud, and later authoritative texts. Thus, the center of authority is transferred by the Historical School to the "collective conscience of Catholic Israel as embodied in the Universal Synagogue,"[25] which for more than twenty-three centuries has carried on a persistent search for God, through the activities of saints, scholars, martyrs, sages, philosophers, and mystics. The efforts of Catholic Israel in this direction can serve as a true guide for the present and future.

A corollary to this view of the role of Catholic Israel is that "neither Scripture nor primitive Judaism, but general custom forms the real rule of practice" that is applied by the teachers and sages in every age, so that "the norm as well as the sanction of Judaism is the practice actually in vogue."[26] The prevailing religious customs and rituals are consecrated by the fact that they are observed by Catholic Israel—the unique and holy people that assumed the sacred task of fostering the religious tradition rather than the converse, as one might normally believe.

Catholic Israel, or the Universal Synagogue, as envisaged by Schechter, transcends both geographical and temporal boundaries. It applies not to a single community, but to all of Israel in time and place. For this reason, Schechter objected to the suggestion of Kaufman Kohler (1843-1926), then president of the Hebrew Union College, that American Judaism should be moulded into a local synthesis which would represent the spiritual creation of the oldest people as influenced by the cultural climate of the youngest, the American nation. Schechter felt that this kind of territorial limitation violated the cardinal principle of Catholic Israel in which the past is a factor to be consecrated. Similarly, too, in Schechter's conception of Catholic Israel, the present is only as a link in the chain of continuity, a part of the long process of Jewish development, for "unless it is a present which forms a link between two eternities, representing an answer of Amen to the past and an opening prayer to the future, it will be a very petty present, indeed, while its so-called needs will often be a caprice of the mob or a whim of fashion or the hobby of some wilful individual sure to disappear when viewed *sub specie aeternitatis.*"[27]

It was this conception, too, that provoked Schechter to protest against Isaac Mayer Wise's proposal to create a synod which would strive "to renew and establish Judaism as a form worthy of continuance as a living force"—in other words, to reformulate the tenets of Judaism. The idea was dormant for a while, but it was resuscitated after Wise's death. It was not consonant, however, with the principle of Catholic Israel as the only force that could and should shape Judaism. There is no sacerdotalism in Judaism, Schechter explained, no clergy that has the authority to standardize its principles and precepts, for "religion is a matter of the heart" and "no man is capable of representing other men in matters spiritual." Not the rabbi, but the Torah is the source of authority. The rabbi is merely a teacher or interpreter of Torah. A synod might, Schechter feared, become hierarchical in character and promulgate doctrines that would produce a schism in Judaism, thereby destroying its unity and its sense of continuity with the past and future.[28]

Jewish Nationalism

The Palestine colonization effort sponsored by the Lovers of Zion movement of the 1880's was supported by some of the leaders of the Historical School for humanitarian, if not for nationalistic, reasons. However, other members of the Historical School had their reservations about Theodor Herzl's political Zionism. They either believed that Zionism was merely a romantic dream, or they feared it as a grossly secular, rather than a religious, ideology. Zionist aspirations divorced from religious ideas might, they felt, develop into a chauvinistic nationalism which could become a menace to Judaism.

The kind of Jewish homeland that Schechter and many of his colleagues envisioned was to be a spiritual center, one that would "produce Isaiahs" rather than merely serve, as the early Zionists had planned, as a haven for persecuted Jewry. Schechter's position on this issue coincided with that of Ahad Ha-Am (1856-1927), the father of Spiritual or Cultural Zionism. However, while the latter conceived of Judaism primarily as a humanistic and ethical system, to Schechter, the Jewish religion and Jewish nationalism were an indivisible unity. In 1905, Schechter formally joined the Zionist movement. He took this step because he felt that Palestine as the Holy Land occupied a vital role in Judaism; moreover, it was intimately associated with the principle of Jewish peoplehood, the core of his doctrine of Catholic Israel. Schechter also saw in Zionism a bulwark against assimilation—a means of rousing the Jewish consciousness of the secularists whose return to religious Judaism might be brought about through the path of nationalism.

Schechter, like many other intellectual Zionists, was an "affirmer of the Diaspora" and, like Ahad Ha-Am, was convinced that a spiritually regenerated Palestine would serve as the spiritual center of Judaism and as a source of cultural and religious creativity and vitality for the Jews in the periphery. But the periphery, too, he felt, must continue as a fountain of Jewish creativity. Schechter forged a link between Conservatism and Zionism which still holds firm. The key word in Ahad Ha-Am's idea of cultural Zionism, *Mercaz,* standing for *Mercaz Ruhani* (spiritual center), the acronym of the Movement for the Reaffirmation of Conservative Zionism, is the official name of the new Conservative Zionist organization. It was launched at the 1978 Conference of the Rabbinical Assembly, despite the rejection of a similar move by the United Synagogue.

Hebrew

The followers of the Historical School also regarded Hebrew as essential to Jewish life. Schechter declared that "a nationality without an historical language, without a sacred literature, is a mere gypsy camp." He therefore denounced as a tragedy the gradual exclusion of Hebrew from the synagogue and the prevailing ignorance of the Hebrew tongue. "This may not be the *Galuth* (Exile) of the Jews, but it is the *Galuth* of Judaism, or as certain mystics expressed it . . . the *Galuth* of the Jewish soul, wasting away before our eyes."[29] In 1913, Schechter was elected honorary president of the Congress of Hebrew Culture, held in Vienna.

Attitude Toward Reform

The Historical School objected to Orthodoxy, regarding it as too static and too rigid for conditions in the modern world; it rejected Reform because of its recurrent abrogations of Jewish

doctrine and practice, which Schechter referred to as "amputa-
tions." Schechter characterized the aim of the Reformers to "de-
orientalize" Judaism as "a piece of theological anti-Semitism which
thoughtless boys copied from Christian theologians, for the West
is predominantly secular and has not shown any genius for religion
as did the East."[30] Moreover, he felt, the fact that Judaism is an
expression of the ethical ideals of the Hebrew prophets does not
justify the repudiation of ritual and practice, for "man cannot live
on oxygen alone."

Judaism, Schechter further urged, will best be understood by
Judaism and not by foreign parallels—a thought reminiscent of the
criticism of Samuel David Luzzatto and Samson Raphael Hirsch.
If reform is needed, it must be in conformity with the Torah and
Jewish doctrine, which Schechter insisted is flexible enough for all
reasonable purposes. Reforms are not acceptable if they are not
within the framework of Jewish tradition or if enacted by a rabbinical body that repudiates the binding authority of the Mosaic or
rabbinic law. "Judaism," he said in another context, "is absolutely
incompatible with the abandonment of the Torah . . . The assertion
that the destruction of the Law is its fulfillment is a mere paradox
and recalls strongly the epigram of Sir Boyle Rocne . . . that he
would give up a part, and if necessary, the whole of the constitution to preserve the remainder."[31]

Jewish Legalism

In the second of his four *Epistles to the Jews,* which he wrote
in 1901 as a sort of farewell message to the Jews of England,
Schechter derided the Reformers who, as Westerners, upheld the
ethical spirituality of Judaism as opposed to the legalism of the
East European Jewish traditionalists. He repeated a discussion that
he had on this question with an East European Jew, a mere tradesman, but a learned man. The latter reminded him that the three
last great leaders of Judaism, the Baal Shem, Rabbi Elijah of
Vilna, and Krochmal, were not mere aesthetes but great spiritual
figures; moreover, they were all East Europeans. The East European Jew had this to say on the matter of spirituality and legalism:[32]

. . . You incessantly prate about a spiritual religion whilst we

insist on spiritual *men* . . . You proceed to blame religion
for its lack of spirituality . . . Instead of blaming religion, we
reproach ourselves. It is not that which comes from the
Torah which defiles. It is the things which proceed out of
the man, his mental attitude during the performance of the
Divine Commandment, his purpose in fulfilling it, which may
leave a defiling effect even on things heavenly and pure . . .
Man has thus to furnish the Law with wings of love and awe
to make it return to God Who gave it, and it is his fault if,
instead of this, he becomes a dead weight to the Law, drag-
ging it down to the earth, and to things earthly against its
real nature . . . Now having recognized how great the proper
performance of a Mitzvah is dependent on the nature of the
performers and that it is the man who becomes a burden to
the Law, not the Law a burden to man, we left religion undisturbed and set to work upon man . . .

Mission Theory

Schechter regarded the traditional Messianic hope as a paramount ideal in Judaism, in its particularistic as well as its universalistic connotations. To Schechter this aspiration implied the restoration of Israel to Zion, where the Universal Kingdom of One
God would be established for all mankind.

Like Luzzatto and other opponents of Reform, Schechter ridiculed the mission theory of the Reformers. The idea of a mission,
he contended, presupposes a group of zealous missionaries endowed with a burning faith, which is hardly to be found among the
Reformers ,who make a virtue of adapting to and compromising
with their environment. Missionaries are made of sterner stuff.
"They convert the world, but do not allow the world to convert
them." The phrase "intellectual missionaries" or "passive missionaries," which the Reformers sometimes used to describe their
attitude toward the mission theory, Schechter insisted, is self-
contradictory and has no real meaning. It would be a different
matter if the Reformers were to demonstrate a zeal in the observance of Jewish institutions like the Sabbath, even at the risk of
material loss.[33] They would then be much closer to the missionary
spirit.

IV. CONSERVATIVE IDEOLOGY

The Conservative Approach

THE TERM "CONSERVATIVE" had been attached to the moderates by the Reformers because the moderates had branded them as radicals. This name hardly describes the movement aptly. Conservative Judaism, as previously noted, is the American version of the principles of Positive Historical Judaism. The Conservatives accept the findings of modern scholarship that Judaism is the product of a long period of growth and evolution. However, this process did not result in broken or inconsistent lines of development; quite the contrary, the major currents of Judaism run consistently through the extensive literature of the Jewish people, created in successive ages. These currents are discernible as a continuous strand in the progressive stages of development in Judaism, in the sense that "the boy is father to the man." The same idea was expressed in the remark of Leopold Zunz, a leader of the Science of Judaism movement in Germany, to the effect that "prophecy and the psalms are again revived in the hymnology of the Middle Ages."[34]

The evolutionary principle, however, contradicts the belief in divine revelation; the one is a naturalistic concept, while the other is a supernatural doctrine. Those members of the Historical School who clung to tradition attempted to reconcile the two ideas by reinterpreting the doctrine of revelation in rationalistic terms. They explained it as a metaphor, a subjective experience, an inspired thought, or even as divine guidance in historic destiny. The Conservatives have followed a similar pattern.[35] Conservative rabbis, in the main, do not subscribe to a literal divine revelation, but rationalize it in a naturalistic manner.[36]

Tradition and Change

The traditionalists who uphold the Sinaitic revelation insist on a divine sanction for the rules and regulations specified in the Biblical and rabbinic texts—all of which are essential links in that revelation. They see in the *Shulchan Aruch* and legal compilations of a similar nature the only authentic and authoritative guides for the conduct of the Jew. This notion would deny any one the right to modify or innovate religious doctrine or practice. This, however, is not the position of the Historical School or of the Conservative movement. While accepting the authority of tradition, they also support the idea that change is an essential feature of religion, as of any other living institution. But changes are to be instituted only by the masters of Jewish learning, with due regard for the attitude of the masses toward a given reform or innovation and for the place of a given usage or observance in Jewish history and tradition.[37]

In the Conservative view, therefore, Judaism is not to be thought of as an heirloom, to be preserved intact for future generations, but rather as a living organism which must adapt itself to its era and surroundings in order to survive. But such an adjustment, Conservatism insists, must be made within the framework of Jewish tradition. In 1937, Professor Louis Finkelstein enunciated the position of Conservative Judaism on this question. In his address to the Rabbinical Assembly on the occasion of the fiftieth anniversary of the Seminary, he declared: "Jewish law is . . . not frozen or ossified; it possesses resiliency. The code of Hammurabi can rest unchanged in the Louvre. The Torah endures in human life and must partake of the vitality, the adaptability and the fluidity of all organisms." [38]

A decade earlier, Dr. Finkelstein had stressed the need for change and adjustment in bold and cogent terms:

> . . . If a breach is to be made in the levee, it is better to make it deliberately, thoughtfully, intentionally and intelligently, so that we may control the water . . . Such voluntary breaches in the wall of Judaism have been made heretofore . . . After all, Resh Lakish did say, 'Sometimes the transgression of part of the law is the saving of the whole of it.' . . . Still it cannot be denied that the attitude of permitting changes in the usage of Israel by individual congregations and rabbis is untraditional and revolutionary. Revolutions can be justified in only one way—by being successful. It was revolutionary for the Babylonian Amoraim to set themselves up as judges and rabbis without the traditional Palestinian *Semicha;* it was revolutionary for Rabbi Gershom to gather a synod for the purpose of making new enactments . . . All

these changes were justified by the fact that they helped to save Judaism in crucial periods. The necessity was recognized by *Kelal Yisroel,* and what had been a break with tradition became itself tradition. The American Declaration of Independence was adopted in violation of the established political order, but that did not prevent it from becoming the basis of a new order in whose tradition it is the most precious document. The will of the American people made regular what was essentially irregular and so, the living will of the Jewish people has often made proper what was at first and in essence improperly done.

If the shifting of values and the introduction of new devices will actually bring Jews back to God, to the Torah and to the synagogue, they will doubtless be accepted. They will then take their place beside the Maccabean innovation which permitted war in self-defense on the Sabbath day; beside the Tosafistic leniencies in regard to the wine of Gentiles;[39] beside R. Isaac Elhanan's new interpretation permitting the remarriage of a woman whose husband was drowned at sea.[40] ...

Ideological Vagueness

Notwithstanding this statement, which represents the ideological viewpoint of Conservatism, the movement has hesitated to define its position on Jewish practice, ritual, and usage. A proposal to do so was adopted by the United Synagogue a half century ago. In 1917, a committee headed by Professor Louis Ginzberg of the Seminary faculty recommended the formation of an authoritative council for the interpretation of Jewish law and practice as a guide for Conservative congregations. This proved to be a sterile gesture, as were subsequent attempts in this direction. One of the grounds for the continued reluctance to undertake such a task is the fear that it may appear to many as a design to revise the traditional *Shulchan Aruch* or to supersede it. As a result, the ideology of Conservatism has remained vague and indefinite.[41]

This vagueness in Conservative ideology has often resulted in considerable disagreement between the spiritual and lay leadership on the fundamental principles and practices of Conservatism. There are those who believe that it should be "adjectiveless," that is, that it should not appear as one faction within a divided Jewry but rather as the emerging, normative, and all-encompassing form of American Judaism. Hence, they do not recognize a need for clarifying their basic orientation, particularly since Judaism, they argue, is essentially a praxis stressing conduct, in which belief and creed are subordinated. Others contend that the designation "Conservative" is fitting and significant, since it well describes the primary goal of this branch of American Judaism—to conserve Jewish values and traditions.

Those within the Conservative camp who decry the indefiniteness of its ideology claim that a clearly defined position will help in the orientation of Judaism to a changing environment. Others support the *status quo* and make a virtue of inexplicitness. They regard the absence of a specific rationale as advantageous, since it permits flexibility and allows for a certain eclecticism, that is, for the selection of the best elements in the other branches of Judaism. Conservatism, they urge, should be experimental and pragmatic and cope with each situation as it arises. Elasticity in doctrine makes for an umbrella-type, all-embracing movement, while a definite ideological commitment may foster exclusiveness.

This attitude, of course, represents an attempt to capitalize on a perplexing dilemma. It has accordingly, been said that the growth of Conservatism can be ascribed more to its perceptive psychology than its amorphous philosophy.

The Rabbis' Dilemma

Inasmuch as all elements in Conservatism regard Judaism as evolving or changing, the problem becomes one of deciding what changes may be instituted. The Rabbinical Assembly is faced with the formidable task of adapting the Halacha to the prevailing conditions in American Jewish life. Though Conservatism has managed in some measure to agree on its basic tenets, it has found greater difficulty in applying them in actual practice. In view of this, there is a contingent in the Conservative rabbinical organization which advocates a policy of inaction. They fear that tampering with the Halacha may engender more problems than it will solve; it may provoke disputes and create simmering controversies which will result in cleavages in the ranks. They trust that life will bring about its own solutions.

Opposed to this group are those who insist on taking concrete steps in the interpretation of Halacha. Some who uphold this view tend toward a strict construction which would discourage excessive change. On the other hand, the radical Reconstructionist wing demands a broad interpretation and, if necessary, even the adoption of *Takkanot* (new enactments and new rules) to suit modern conditions. The proponents of this view, however, have to chart a course somewhat between the Scylla of the Seminary faculty who favor fidelity to tradition and the Charybdis of the left wing, particularly among the laity, who have relatively little regard for the Halacha. Many of the latter criticize the Conservatives for *"davening* (praying) Orthodox and thinking Reform."

The Committee on Jewish Law and Standards of the Rabbinical Assembly is charged with the responsibility for recommending revisions in religious practice on the basis of Halachic interpretation.[42] This committee, it should be noted, was substantially enlarged in 1948 to make it more representative of the divergent opinions prevailing in the Assembly. The issues it deals with are presented in the form of rabbinic questions and responsa. Unanimous decisions of the Law Committee are submitted to the entire Assembly for approval, so that these decisions may have official sanction; in case of dissent, however, both conclusions—that of the majority and that of the minority—are promulgated by the Law Committee. A divided opinion of the Law Committee is not even voted upon by the Assembly, on the theory that it represents the views of the individuals who advance it. In practice, however, there is little difference between the two types of opinions, for neither is binding on the Conservative constituency. Thus, the Assembly's determinations can exert only a moral influence.[43]

Aside from the legal decisions of the Rabbinical Assembly, there are innovations that have been approved as a matter of consensus in Conservative Judaism, without recourse to the Halachic analysis or scrutiny. Among these are the late Friday evening services, mixed pews, confirmation exercises, and *Bat Mitzvah.* Similarly, Conservative Jews have tacitly abandoned a number of Biblical prohibitions, such as that against shaving the beard (*Lev.*

19:27) forbidding *Shatnez,* the wearing of garments made of a mixture of cotton and wool (*Lev.* 19:19, *Deut.* 22:11) or barring the marriage of a *Kohen,* (one of priestly descent) to a divorcee (*Lev.* 21:7) or the laws in reference to levirate marriage (*Deut.* 25:5). The same is true of a number of rabbinical ordinances including those concerning the prescribed monthly ritual bathing of women for purification. Conservative synagogues generally do not frown on automobile travel to services. The traditional service, too, has been modified; it contains English elements, though in the main, its Hebrew structure has been preserved. The men worship with covered heads. Conservatism, moreover, expects adherence to the dietary laws, especially in Jewish group functions. In 1969, the observance of the second day of festivals was made optional, except for Rosh Hashanah.

Conservative Prayerbooks

In 1946, after years of effort, the Rabbinical Assembly and the United Synagogue published jointly the first standard *Sabbath and Festival Prayer Book.* Subsequently in 1961, the Assembly issued its *Weekday Prayer Book.* These liturgical texts provide a translation, notes, and supplementary readings to the prayers. Some negative expressions in the preliminary benedictions of the *Shachrit* or morning service were reworded as affirmatives. Thus, instead of the male worshiper blessing God for "not making me a woman," he now does so for making me "in Thine image." The phrase "for not making me a slave" reads "for making me free." Similarly, the idiom "for not making me a heathen" was altered to "for making me an Israelite." Moreover, the passages dealing with animal sacrifices intended as study material in the old liturgy were deleted. The reference to the resurrection of the dead in the *Amidah,* the silent prayer, was replaced with the concept of immortality. The petition for the restoration of animal sacrifices in the Sabbath *Musaf* (supplementary service) was converted through a modification in the verb tense to an historical memory—a stage in Jewish worship, and not a hope for the future. However, the beliefs in the Chosen People and in a personal Messiah were retained for their spiritual implications.

The Rabbinical Assembly's *Mahzor for Rosh Hashanah and Yom Kippur* (1972) suggests for Yom Kippur afternoon a reading of an

ethical nature (Lev. 19:18) in place of the traditional one outlining
the laws of sexual purity (Lev. 18). It includes a memorial tribute
to the countless Holocaust victims, which is appropriately linked to
the dirges for the Ten Martyrs of Roman times in the traditional
Musaf. An amended mourners' *Kaddish* or sanctification which
recalls Hitler's murder sites brings a shudder to the worshiper:
"*Yitgadal*—Kishinev; *Veyitkadash*—Warsaw; *Shmei Rabba*—Ausch-
witz," and thus through the long list of Nazi death camps and
pits of hell.

The *Neilah,* the closing Yom Kippur twilight service, induces a
solemn mood: "The sun is low, the hour is late, let us enter thy
gates," runs a popular *Neilah* hymn. The worshiper has much to
contemplate at this time, when according to the metaphor of
tradition, the fate of all humans is sealed. A newly added medita-
tion by the late Rabbi Milton Steinberg (1903-1950) clothes this
concept with profound meaning.

V. THE FEMINIST PROBLEM

The Agunah

The Bible permits only the husband to initiate a divorce (Dt.
24:1). If then he abandons his wife, or refuses her a *get* (Jewish
divorce), or vanishes and no Halachically acceptable proof of his
death is adduced, the wife is not considered a widow and is unable
to remarry in a religious ceremony. Jewish law has no presumption
of death after the lapse of a period of years, as is true of civil law.
The wife then becomes an *Agunah,* and remains "fettered" to her
previous marriage. An unscrupulous husband could even make
extortionate demands as a condition for a *get.* The *Agunah* problem had reached inordinate proportions in the wake of the Nazi
murders and dislocations during World War II. To Reform rabbis
this was not an issue, because they follow the civil law in these
instances. Orthodox and Conservative rabbis, however, will not
perform a marriage of an *Agunah.*

To alleviate the tragic plight of the *Agunah,* a joint commission
of the Seminary faculty and the Rabbinical Assembly enacted a
Takkanah in 1954 which provided for the addition of a condition
in the *Ketubah* or "marriage writ" to compel a recalcitrant civilly

divorced husband to grant his wife a *get*. The condition was believed to be enforceable in civil courts, but it later turned out not to be so. The idea, however, aroused intense opposition and controversy on the part of the Orthodox. The Conservative Law Commission eventually had to resort to the *Hafkaat Kidushin,* a rarely used annulment procedure, to free the *Agunah* from her marriage. This action implied, however, that the *Halacha* was too rigid to solve the *Agunah* problem.

Religious Equality

To overcome a form of sex discrimination in the Conservative synagogue, a 1955 responsum permits women an *Aliyah,* the honor of "ascending" the reading platform to recite the blessings over a portion of the Torah reading. This practice is anomalously both permitted and discouraged in the same Talmudic passage (Meg. 23a). Because the Rabbinical Assembly's Law Committee was divided on the question, the final determination was left to the individual rabbi or synagogue. Since then, the struggle for equal women's rights in the Conservative movement had gained momentum. At the 1972 Rabbinical Assembly convention a group of cultured and Jewishly oriented young women who grew up in Conservative institutions, staged a demonstration and demanded sweeping changes in Conservative Halachic practice to raise women to a level of Halachic equality both as synagogue functionaries and in other capacities with the men. The United Synagogue had endorsed these demands earlier.

On the issue of counting women in a *minyan,* the quorum of ten required for public worship, the majority of the Law Committee in 1973 approved Rabbi Philip R. Sigal's responsum which required public worship as obligatory for women as for men. Accordingly women should be included in a *minyan*. Rabbi David M. Feldman opposed the *Takkanah* embodying this viewpoint as catering to a passing fad. The Jewish woman's natural role, he maintained, is in the home and consequently she has no obligation to join in public worship and should not be counted in a *minyan*. This question was also left to the *mara d'atra* or local rabbi and congregation since the Law Committee's decision on it was split.

The problem of the ordination of Conservative women rabbis

346   *Modern Jewish Religious Movements*

was discussed at the 1977 rabbinical convention. The late Henrietta Szold, founder of Hadassah, had been permitted to attend the Jewish Theological Seminary in 1903 on condition that "she would not use the knowledge she gained to seek ordination." The matter, however, remained dormant in the ensuing seven decades. Shortly before the 1977 rabbinical conference, sex qualifications for membership in the Rabbinical Assembly were eliminated from its constitution. This meant that a woman ordained by a recognized rabbinical school could theoretically join the Assembly. In opposing the measure, Rabbi David M. Feldman stressed that his attitude was not due to male chauvinism, but to his idea of natural predisposition. A woman should do her share for Jewish survival at home. Moreover, it was pointed out, a male rabbi is to be preferred because, as in the case of the Deity, a reference to a "He" is more strengthening than to a "She." But advocates of women's ordination challenged: "How many gifted spiritual leaders has the Jewish people done without, because one half of the Jewish population is biologically ineligible?" The debate culminated in an agreement to suspend further action to allow the question to be studied for two years. The majority of the study commission recently approved the measure, though its opponents warned that it is likely to cause an internal rift in the Conservative ranks. The Seminary faculty on its part, may refuse to admit women for ordination, thereby leaving the issue unresolved.

14

Reconstructionism

I. HISTORY AND APPROACH

The Movement

A SIGNIFICANT FACTION in the Conservative movement maintains that Conservatism should have a very clear and precise ideology. One of the most influential proponents of this point of view is Mordecai M. Kaplan, who has expounded an indigenous philosophy of American Judaism, known as Reconstructionism, which reckons with the conditions prevailing in American Jewish life.

Actually, Reconstructionism represents a fourth alignment in American Judaism, alongside Orthodoxy, Reform, and Conservatism. Officially, however, Kaplan and his chief disciples among the Conservative rabbis have retained their original affiliation with the Rabbinical Assembly. The Reconstructionists themselves maintain that they are a school of thought concerned with evolving a philosophy which will cut across partisan lines, rather than with forming a new religious party. The influence of the Reconstructionist minority in the Rabbinical Assembly far surpasses its small numbers; it has served as a catalyst in the thinking of many rabbis both within and outside the organization. Many Jewish functionaries, teachers in Jewish schools, social and community workers,

347

as well as a core of widely scattered laymen throughout the country, have been influenced in varying degrees by Kaplan's principles and ideas.

Mordecai M. Kaplan

The founder of Reconstructionism, Professor Mordecai M. Kaplan, is regarded by many as the most creative contemporary philosopher in American Jewish life. A native of Lithuania, he came to America in 1889 as a child of eight. He received his education at the College of the City of New York, Columbia University, and the Jewish Theological Seminary. After graduating from the Seminary, he occupied several pulpits in New York City. Because of his liberal ideas, he clashed with the rigidly Orthodox sector in these congregations. In 1922, he resigned as rabbi of the Jewish Center on West 86th Street to found the Society for the Advancement of Judaism, which undertook to disseminate his principles. This institution served as the laboratory for his ideas and experiments in ritual and liturgy. Among the activities of his synagogue, he stressed and stimulated group study and discussion as an expression of the ideal of Torah in Jewish life. This idea, together with others, was emulated by congregations throughout the land.

For some forty years, Kaplan served as professor of homiletics and Midrash at the Seminary and also as head of its Teachers' Institute. He also taught at Columbia Teachers College, at the now defunct Graduate School for Jewish Social Work, and at the Hebrew University in Jerusalem. A versatile scholar, an intrepid, lucid, and incisive thinker, Kaplan has written many articles and a number of books elucidating his Reconstructionist theory. The first full exposition of his philosophy was published in 1934, in his *Judaism as a Civilization.* In the same year, he started a bimonthly periodical, *The Reconstructionist;* in 1940, he established the Reconstructionist Foundation, which maintains its own press. The Foundation aims to advance the Reconstructionist doctrines. Kaplan retired in 1963 and now resides in Jerusalem.

The Problem

In his *Judaism as a Civilization* which caused a great stir in Jewish circles, Kaplan explained that the purpose of his new approach was to come to grips with the problem of disintegration in

Jewish life. He saw an urgent need to reinterpret Judaism in a way that would meet the challenge of rationalism and modernism —the trends which are bringing about a progressive desertion of the synagogue and defection from Judaism. Kaplan sees a dark future ahead for American Judaism unless this tendency is curbed.

The various ideological movements in American Jewry, according to Kaplan, have failed to offer the modern Jew sufficient justification for identification with Judaism. Nor have they provided an affirmative basis for unity among those who sincerely wish to maintain their Jewishness. Reform, at least in its classical version, is inadequate for this purpose, because it has repudiated the idea of Jewish peoplehood and whittled down the law in Judaism to a mere abstraction of ethical teachings. Nor does Neo-Orthodoxy meet these needs, because its supernatural outlook clashes with the rationalistic views of the contemporary Jew; moreover, it subordinates or rejects the principle of Jewish nationalism and, like Reform, has replaced it with the vacuous doctrines of a Jewish mission. Because it is too rigid to allow for change, it cannot become an effective force in the modern world. Conservatism, essentially a compromise between Reform and Orthodoxy, is too vague and amorphous ideologically for the searching Jew. Finally, secular nationalism, which ignores the religious aspect of Judaism, presents a distorted image of Judaism that is repugnant to the synagogue Jew. The answer, Kaplan concluded, lies in the planned reconstruction and reformation of the underlying philosophical foundations of Judaism, as a result of a carefully devised program of action, rather than through a process of pragmatic adjustment.

Taking into account the fact that there are both religious and secularist Jews in America today, and believing that the conception and scope of Judaism must be broad enough to include both, Kaplan defined Judaism as an all-embracing, evolving religious civilization in which are included a variety of religious and non-religious or secular cultural components. Such a view of Judaism can be translated into practical terms through the medium of an organic Jewish community represented by a single, over-all leadership. Thus the agencies of the all-encompassing Jewish community would give expression to all facets of Jewish life: religious, cultural, social, and aesthetic. In this, Kaplan adapted Simon Dubnow's *Diaspora Nationalism,* which called for cultural autonomy for the Jewish minorities in East European nations before World War II.

The Reconstructionist has no quarrel with the Orthodox Jew, or, for that matter, with the adherent of any other wing in Judaism who can conscientiously subscribe to its doctrines and practices. Kaplan, himself an observant Jew, expounded his theory for the benefit of those who require a prop for their weakening faith; for them his movement offers a "formula for the social strategy best suited to advance Jewish life." Though his ideology has many opponents in all religious groupings, it has attracted a number of followers from the Conservative and Reform contingents, as well as from among the secular nationalists whose spiritual interests cannot be satisfied by Jewish nationalism and culture alone.

II. JUDAISM AS A CIVILIZATION

A Religious Civilization

KAPLAN regards Judaism as "something far more comprehensive than the Jewish religion. It includes that nexus of a history, literature, language, social organization, folk sanctions, ethics, social and spiritual ideals, esthetic interests which in their totality form a civilization."[1] Only in Israel, the center and spiritual reservoir of Judaism, is it primary; everywhere else it is supplementary. Only in Israel, where the Jewish civilization predominates, can the Jew live a complete Jewish life; outside of the Jewish state he shares the common civilization of the country in which he lives. In America, for example, he pursues the common ideals, mores, and culture of his fellow Americans and is loyal to American institutions, but in addition, he participates actively with other Jews in all phases of the Jewish civilization, which, though subordinate to the prevailing American culture, informs part of his consciousness. Though the American Jew finds his principal expression in the American civilization, he should also foster and further that in him which is distinctively Jewish, both for the sake of his people's survival and as a way of achieving maximum spiritual satisfaction. Thus, the American Jew is committed to the lofty ideals of both Judaism and American democracy, which fortunately, are not only compatible but harmonious.

The foremost aim of Reconstructionism, in the words of its founder, is "to find an affirmative basis for unity among all who want to remain Jews." Its program, as represented in its wheel-shaped emblem, places Israel, the Jewish homeland, at the hub and "center of the Jewish civilization, from which all dynamic forces of Judaism radiate." The land of Israel is vital to the Jewish civilization, for "What soil is to the life of a tree, a land is to the civilization of a people."[2] The principles of Reconstructionism have been succinctly outlined by Professor Kaplan as follows:[3]

1. JUDAISM AS AN EVOLVING RELIGIOUS CIVILIZATION
   Judaism, or that which has united the successive generations of Jews into one people, is not only a religion; it is an evolving religious civilization. In the course of its evolution, Judaism has passed through three distinct stages, each reflecting the conditions under which it functioned.

2. WHAT THE PRESENT STATE CALLS FOR
   During those stages the Jews constituted a people apart. Now, the Jewish People, like every other, must learn to live both in its own historic civilization and in the civilization of its environment. That will usher in the democratic stage of Judaism during which the reconstitution of the Jewish People, the revitalization of its religion, and the replenishment of its culture will be achieved.

3. UNITY IN DIVERSITY
   Jewish unity should transcend the diversity among Jews, which is the result of geographical dispersion and of differences in cultural background and in world outlook.

4. THE RENEWAL OF THE ANCIENT COVENANT
   Jews the world over should renew their historic covenant binding themselves into one transnational People, with the Jewish community in Israel, henceforth to be known as "Zion," as its core.

5. ERETZ YISRAEL THE SPIRITUAL HOMELAND OF WORLD JEWRY

Eretz Yisrael should be recognized as the home of the historic Jewish civilization.

6. OUTSIDE ISRAEL, THE FOUNDATION OF ORGANIC COMMUNITIES
Outside Israel, Jewish peoplehood should lead to the establishment of organic communities. All activities and institutions conducted by Jews for Jews should be interactive and should give primacy to the fostering of Jewish peoplehood, religion and culture.

7. PREREQUISITES TO THE REVITALIZATION OF RELIGION
The revitalization of religion can best be achieved through the study of it in the spirit of free inquiry and through the separation of church and state.

8. HOW THE BELIEF IN GOD IS TO BE INTERPRETED
The revitalization of the Jewish religion requires that the belief in God be interpreted in terms of universally human, as well as specifically Jewish, experience.

9. WHAT GIVES CONTINUITY TO A RELIGION
The continuity of a religion through different stages, and its identity amid diversity of belief and practice, are sustained by its *sancta*. These are the heroes, events, texts, places and seasons, which that religion signalizes as furthering the fulfillment of human destiny.

10. TORAH AS SYNONYMOUS WITH ONGOING JEWISH CULTURE
The traditional concept of Torah should be understood as synonymous with Jewish religious civilization and should, therefore, embrace all the ongoing ethical, cultural and spiritual experiences of the Jewish People.

Components of Jewish Civilization

The wheel in the emblem of Reconstructionism may be said to represent the dynamic, evolving, and ongoing Jewish civilization, which undergoes continual change in its course through history. The Jews are not merely a religious denomination; they have produced a civilization. "Religion," according to Kaplan, "is a quality inherent in the very substance of a civilization" and can no more be separated from it than "whiteness from snow, or redness from blood." A civilization however, has nonreligious ingredients, such as law, language, literature, art, history, and folk traditions—all of which add to its uniqueness. Both the religious rituals and the distinguishing secular elements in Judaism are vital inasmuch as they are the symbols by which the Jew expresses his identification with the Jewish group and its civilization. The study of the Hebrew language is essential to the Jewish civilization because it is the key to its literature. It is the vernacular used in the State of Israel today and serves as an important link between Jews all over the world.

Ritual and Folkways

In Kaplan's rationalistic formulation of Judaism, Jewish rituals and usages should be regarded as *minhagim* (customs or folkways) rather than *mitzvot* (divine commandments). These folkways, Kaplan explains, "are the social practices by which a people externalizes the reality of its collective being."[4] They serve as exhilarating "religious poetry in action," expressing a mood or an idea and establishing a bond between the individual and his people. They do not possess magic power, but they may help an individual to enter into communion with God. These observances will impress those who practice them, and add interest, character, and zest to their lives. Kaplan believes that where the traditional religious procedures are seen in these terms, "there need not be the feeling of sin in case of occasional remissness nor the self-complacency which results from scrupulous observance."[5] The dietary regulations, for example, have endowed the physical act of eating with spirituality and contributed substantially to the Jewish atmosphere in the home. Inasmuch, however, as they are not immutable laws but merely folkways, it is not essential to adhere to them rigidly outside the home, nor should they subject one to social segregation. Orthodox Jews who wish to adhere rigidly to the *Shulchan Aruch* and traditional codes may do so, but other groups in Judaism who do not consider these laws to be of divine origin may take steps to revise them. The latter should set up criteria by which to determine which usages are to be retained as significant and vital and which may be modified as lacking in meaning. They may also find a need for the introduction of new customs and folkways to reflect new values. The Reconstructionist Guide to Religious Observance sees it as a matter of self-fulfillment, not Halachic mandate. One need not sacrifice a career in order to keep the Sabbath. This attitude may tend to make Judaism a religion of convenience.

Apart from religious folkways such as the Sabbath, the prescribed festivals and worship, there are also others which reflect the consciousness of the group. Dr. Kaplan makes several interesting suggestions in this regard. He proposes the use of Jewish names as a way of showing one's Jewish identity. The first names of Jews in the Diaspora should be distinctively Jewish, he suggests, while family names should resemble the names used by the general community, thereby indicating the fact that Jews live in two civilizations, the over-all American and the supplementary Hebraic milieu. Kaplan also recommends a change in the traditional Jewish calendar used in fixing the dates of religious occasions. Instead of numbering the Jewish year from Creation, which is without reasonable basis in the light of our current astronomical and geological knowledge, Jews should count the years from the destruction of the Second Temple[6] (70 C.E). This historic event, a turning point in Jewish history, reminds the Jew of his present plight in the world. These and other new customs,[7] Kaplan believes, would help to strengthen Jewish sentiment and awareness among Diaspora Jewry. It will not do, he urges, to wait for an authoritative religious body to be created in the chain of religious tradition for the purpose of modifying Jewish ritual and practice as the Orthodox insist. Groups of scholars and rabbis should collaborate in drawing up a guide for ritual, which in time, Kaplan assumes, would take root and become standard. Such an enterprise, moreover, should be democratic. Exponents of modernism as well as proponents of tradition and also the Jewish secularists should be represented. Thus the present and the past will each have a voice. The conception of Judaism as a civilization which permits for diversity of belief and practice, will provide the rationale for such a plan.[8]

Ideological Influences

Kaplan has borrowed some of his basic attitudes toward Judaism from Ahad Ha-Am[9] (1856-1927), the originator of the doctrine of spiritual or cultural nationalism. "The salvation of Israel," Ahad

Ha-Am said, "will be brought about by prophets not diplomats." He envisaged the self-governing Jewish community in the Jewish homeland as the instrumentality and prelude for the resuscitation of the Jewish spirit, which is to serve as a beacon light for the entire Jewish world. Ahad Ha-Am was an "affirmer of the Diaspora" and espoused the spiritual regeneration also of the Jewish periphery, the communities outside the Jewish state, through a process of nationalistic education designed to awaken the Jewish consciousness. In the United States, Jewish survival can be assured, Kaplan believes, by means of the Reconstructionist program. Kaplan has also been influenced in his blueprint for the organic Jewish community in America by the principles of Diaspora Nationalism, promulgated by Simon Dubnow (1860-1941), the renowned Jewish historian, who called for the establishment of autonomous Jewish cultural communities in East European countries having sufficient Jewish populations.

Kaplan closely follows the leading American pragmatist, John Dewey (1859-1952), who perceived reality as constantly changing and developing—hence the need for reconsidering and reconstructing prevailing opinions and outlooks. The first task of religion is, accordingly, to make life more meaningful and to raise the individual and his group to a higher spiritual level. But this cannot be accomplished in this day and, Kaplan asserts, by means of the doctrine of revelation and the idea of a supernatural divinity. Instead of these beliefs, he posits the God of experience, in a naturalistic[10] approach to religion. This conception has its social implications; for, as the correlative term "teacher" implies "student," so Kaplan's notion of God is associated with humanity. Accordingly, he says, "Godhood can have no meaning for us apart from human ideals of truth, goodness and beauty interwoven in a pattern of holiness."[11]

Kaplan's sociological views, which occupy a pivotal place in his thinking, may be attributed largely to the social theories of Emile Durkheim (1858-1917), the great French-Jewish sociologist. As a result of his investigation of the relatively static society of savage tribes, Durkheim found that primitive people were controlled by the "collective consciousness of the tribe." He concluded therefore that the individual's mental life, his religious experience, and ex-

- MMK most infl. by those 4 who came of age when he was born

pression were conditioned chiefly by his social environment. Religion accordingly embraces the cherished values, interests, beliefs, and aspirations of tribal society. It sanctifies those ideas and institutions it considers important, as a means of preserving them. These become the *sancta* of the group; they are evolved in the will glorify Him," (*Ex.* 15:2; *Shab.* 133b) was interpreted as calling for the enhancement of "the beauty of the *Mitzvah*", (the religious precept). Accordingly, ceremonial articles, among them the wine cup and the Menorah, the Torah scroll, the Holy Ark, the Scroll of Esther, and numerous other ritual objects were decorated, ornamented, or illuminated in a variety of ways.[12] As for literature, the Bible, the Apocrypha, and later medieval works attest to a highly developed Hebraic literary tradition. Sculpture, Kaplan observes, was the only form of aesthetic expression not cultivated in Judaism, mainly because of the prohibition against the making of graven images (*Ex.* 20: 4); however, today the traditional interdict against this type of art lacks a rational foundation since there is no longer any fear of idolatry.

Because architecture is an index of civilization, synagogue buildings and other Jewish institutional structures should have a distinctly Jewish character. Jewish art and Jewish books can add to the Jewish atmosphere of the home. In Jewish worship, poetry, music, song, drama, and the dance should be employed in order to raise its aesthetic level. "If formerly religion spoke in the language of art, the present tendency is to raise art to a religion."[13]

The Synagogue Center

As early as 1908, while he was rabbi of Congregation Kehilath Jeshurun in New York City, and long before he evolved the Reconstructionist viewpoint, Kaplan proposed a comprehensive synagogue program combining religious, cultural, social, and recreational activities, thus expanding the Jewish house of worship into a true *Bet Knesset* (a Place of Assembly). Such an institution had been initiated earlier by a group of American churches and was subsequently emulated by several Reform rabbis; it was Kaplan, however, who gave the idea of the synagogue center its rationale. In 1918, he organized the Jewish Center in Manhattan along the lines he advocated. A decade later, Dr. Israel H. Levinthal did likewise at the Brooklyn Jewish Center, which he headed. Soon similar programs were started across the country. Today, however, the synagogue center is quite a common institutional pattern throughout the country.

The Organic Community

The social entity which can best represent and maintain the multifaceted Jewish civilization, Kaplan advocates, is not the congregational unit, which deals primarily with the religious aspect of Jewish life, but a democratic Jewish community organization which would encompass the whole gamut of Jewish interests, activities, and needs. This Jewish community, Kaplan believes, should operate through a coordinating body, the community council, which should administer all religious, educational, philanthropic, and social institutions. Special attention is to be given to Jewish religious and educational agencies, since they form the core of Jewish life. Jewish institutions, such as exist today, are to carry on welfare, recreational, social, and guidance services in the name and on behalf of the over-all community. One advantage of this kind of organization would be the elimination of the wasteful duplication and reckless rivalry that so often plagues the Jewish community. To make for greater effectiveness, the community structure would function on several levels, local, regional, and national.

Membership in the consolidated Jewish community would be open to all affirming Jews who wish to identify themselves with their people. The individual Jew would derive from this affiliation a sense of participation and status in the Jewish entity. The central community, which would replace the synagogue as the primary institution in Jewish life, would extend its influence to a larger area of the individual's life than the synagogue. It would register marriages, divorces, and deaths; it would be concerned with the economic welfare of the Jew, the defense of his civil rights, and similar functions. Such a community organization would serve as a concrete expression of the idea of Jewish peoplehood.

A body of this kind is not new to Jewish history. The European Kahal was the result of coercion imposed from without by the segregationist policies of the host people among whom the Jews lived, but the proposed community pattern is to represent the voluntary interest of Jews in their collective existence and survival. Nor is such a form of minority organization new to American life; the Roman Catholic Church furnishes a model for the projected Jewish community framework, with one major distinction. The voluntary Jewish community must be democratic and not authoritarian or hierarchical in structure. The Jewish community would exercise a degree of control, but it would give full freedom of expression to its diverse ideological groups.[14] The over-all community, moreover, and not its individual agencies or synagogues would pay the salaries of its employees, though the selection of personnel would be left to the respective services. As a result, each worker would be responsible in a substantial degree to the total community.

The idea underlying the total community would have particular significance in the area of Jewish education. Each school would be a subsidiary of the community, not merely a part of a single congregation. The school would, accordingly, imbue its pupils with a feeling of loyalty to *Kelal Yisrael* (the totality of Israel) rather than to a particular synagogue, denomination, or ideological sector as is frequently the case today. The organic community would thus become a strong force for Jewish unity. Despite the interest aroused by this proposal, it proved little more than an alluring theory. Attempts to launch a number of such community organizations proved abortive.

The Covenant of Unity

The idea of the organic Jewish community is based on the concept of *Kelal Yisrael,* but this doctrine implies a sense of identification not only with the local or even the nationwide community, but with the whole of Jewry. Emancipation and the creation of the State of Israel have wrought vast changes in the interrelationships of world Jewry. The citizens of the Jewish homeland today constitute a nation. The Jews outside the State of Israel, on the other hand, no longer regard themselves as being in exile, but are fully integrated culturally, politically, economically, and socially in their countries. Nor does traditional Judaism, founded on revelation, any longer constitute a binding spiritual tie among the Jewries of the world. Their unity requires a redefinition and a reformulation in a new "covenant." The "covenant" idea is a new folkway which Kaplan has designed, based on the many precedents in Jewish history, for initiating a new epoch in Jewish life with a formal covenant. The Israelites entered into a covenant at Sinai (*Ex.* 24: 8); they did so also when they completed their journey in the wilderness (*Deut.* 28:69); again when Josiah inaugurated his religious revival (2*K.* 23:3); also in the days of Ezra and Nehemiah (*Neh.* 10:1) and on other momentous occasions.

A new covenant, Kaplan suggests, should be inaugurated by a Covenant Assembly to be held in Jerusalem, in which every segment of world Jewry would be represented. It should formally recognize that a new stage in Jewish life has begun with the establishment of the Jewish state. The covenant should serve as a stimulus for the extension of the Zionist ideal into a "Greater Zionism," based on the concept of a "transnational" Jewish community, whose core is in Eretz Israel, the birthplace and center of the Jewish civilization, but whose branches extend throughout the globe. Though owing their undivided political allegiance to the countries of which they are citizens, Jews the world over would forge moral and spiritual links with the Jews of Israel and with each other, "through a reaffirmation of the covenant which has kept them united hitherto." The covenant would thus create a common bond among all sections of Jewry, regardless of their brand of Judaism.

The covenant, as a new creative symbol in Judaism, might give rise, too, to a new ritual of initiation into the Jewish community. Every Jew, upon attaining full maturity, would go through a ceremonial in which the ideal of *Kelal Yisrael* and the unity and mutual responsibility of all Jews would be celebrated. The induction ceremony would take place on a special day which would be observed each year as Jewish Unity Day, "the day when Israel shall have become an *Am Berit*, or 'Covenant People'." Such a ritual could, Kaplan believes, become a powerful force in Jewish life.[15]

III. DOCTRINAL INTERPRETATION

God and Revelation

IN A NUMBER OF RESPECTS, the fundamental doctrines of Reconstructionism are even more radical than the prevailing Reform viewpoint. Perhaps the most outstanding example of the extreme rationalism of Reconstructionism is the God idea it propounds. Kaplan defines his concept of the Deity as the "cosmic process that makes for man's life abundant or salvation,"[16] or as "the source of our will-to-salvation."[17] He envisages God in broad pragmatic terms as the "Power both in and beyond nature which moves men to seek value and meaning in life;"[18] that aspect of reality or existence "which elicits the most serviceable traits, the traits that enhance individual human worth and further social unity." For Kaplan, the term "salvation" connotes a striving in the context of one's culture for the fulfillment of human destiny[19]—a naturalistic idea without supernatural or other-worldly overtones. The knowledge that man requires in order to attain salvation "in whatever way communicated to man, constitutes divine revelation." The Reconstructionist prayer book declares, moreover, that "not God revealed the Torah to Israel, but the Torah revealed God to Israel",[20] implying thereby that the Torah is the source of the Jewish conception of God rather than that God is the source of the Torah. This view is in line with liberal Conservative thought, and Reconstructionism ventured to expound it in bold and explicit terms.

Good and Evil In Kaplan's Philosophy

Kaplan, like Dewey, sees evil in its functional rather than theoretic aspect. The Mishnaic exhortation to bless God for evil as for good (M. Ber. 9:5) means to Kaplan that the evil in life should not negate our faith in God as the source of the good. Evil is, as in Hassidism, not a reality in itself, but, like darkness, merely an interruption in the flow of the light, which dispels it. God, the creative Force in the universe, waits for man to join Him in recreating the world by transforming evil, or transcending it, if as in the phenomenon of death, it is beyond human control.

This optimistic Jewish view is the antithesis of the Greek, which regards life as "a huge spiderweb, at the center of which Fate, or Necessity, like a great spider, feeds on the victims in the filaments of the web."[21] Judaism, however, regards man as being tried and challenged in his faith in God, and in his ability to endure his trial to the point of ultimate release or redemption from evil. The path to this goal is delineated in the Hebrew Scriptures.

Prayer and Worship

What is the role of prayer in Reconstructionist thought? Of what use is prayer to a process, power, or tendency that is not personal in essence? What response can one elicit or expect from a deity in the Reconstructionist mode of thought? Kaplan attempts to provide a naturalistic answer to these vital religious questions.

Worship, Kaplan maintains, is necessary for subjective reasons. Prayer is essential as an outpouring of one's emotions. Through it, we become aware of the force that functions within us, in our inner consciousness, in our human relationships, and in our environment, and such awareness makes that force more effective. In prayer too, a man gives expression to his ideas or to the spiritual goals of his group, the fulfillment of which constitutes salvation. In this manner, the petitioner is bound to gain faith and strength in time of crisis and release from tension, sorrow, and fear. Prayer will thus have considerable psychological benefit and a cathartic effect on the worshiper, strengthening his ideals. Its dialogical aspect may be achieved by means of "reification," a process which treats the abstract as real and concretizes the imaginary. It is a method used in poetic metaphor, where the poet addresses an intangible concept such as virtue or love.

But aside from the question as to the place of prayer in Reconstructionism, there is also the liturgical problem posed by the traditional petitions for the restoration of the sacrificial cult, entrenched in Orthodox Judaism. The Pentateuch and Talmud deal with animal sacrifice extensively, and its cessation as a consequence of the destruction of the Holy Temple was lamented by Jews for centuries. In modern times, of course, these prayers have become obsolete and inapplicable, yet they are retained in their entirety in the Orthodox prayer book, and in modified form in the Conservative.[22] The Reformers took a clear stand on this question in the Pittsburgh Platform (1885) and declared that they did not expect "a return to a sacrificial worship under the administration of the sons of Aaron," and, therefore, omitted these passages[23] from their liturgy. The Reconstructionists have taken a similar position, thereby displaying more courage and clarity than the Conservatives who, in order to remain loyal to tradition, merely modified the wording and verb tenses in these prayers, referring to them as memories of the past. However, both the Reconstructionist and Conservative liturgies allude to the spirit of sacrificial devotion implicit in the ancient sacrificial service in the Holy Sanctuary.

The Avodah

This ideal is reflected in the traditional *Avodah* (worship ritual) incorporated in the Yom Kippur *Musaf* (additional) service. The passages describing the solemn sacrificial procedures are followed immediately by the dirge for the Ten Martyrs who, during the Hadrianic persecutions (132-135 C.E.), violated the Roman decree forbidding the teaching of the Torah, and suffered death for their defiance. The Reconstructionist liturgy links with the elegy for the martyrs of old, the tragic and horrifying episode of the Ninety-Three Maidens of the Holocaust in contemporary times. These ninety-three were students and teachers at the Orthodox Beth Jacob Girls School in Poland who resisted in the only way they could the Gestapo orders to receive and entertain German soldiers. They joined in a suicide pact, recited the *Vidduy* (the last confession of the dying), swallowed poison, and died together —*Al Kiddush Hashem,* hallowing the Divine Name.

Doctrine of the Chosen People

The Conservative prayer book alludes to the doctrine of the election of Israel, explaining it as a spiritual selection, implying the dedication of the Jewish people to a spiritual purpose. This concept should not be excluded from the prayers merely because "it has been vulgarized and misunderstood in some circles," the compilers of this prayer book insist. In fact, they add a caution that the omission of this doctrine from the liturgy might be construed as an admission that the objections to it are justified. The Orthodox and Reform liturgy also affirm this belief. The latter, however, together with the Neo-Orthodox, interpret it in terms of the mission theory, maintaining that God has chosen Israel to spread the teachings of ethical monotheism.[24]

To Kaplan, the idea of the chosen people is a supernatural one— a "futile compensatory mechanism of imagined superiority," that is, a psychological means of maintaining a sense of self-worth in the face of the hostility suffered by Jews throughout the ages. The Reconstructionists have, therefore, deleted all references to the chosen people from their worship, on the ground that it makes "invidious comparisons between Israel and other nations." Kaplan concedes that this belief alludes to the ideal of the dedication of the Jew to a lofty, ethical objective—to advance the moral state of mankind; but he cannot condone its inherent overtones of superiority. The Reconstructionists have found a substitute for this doctrine in the moderate conception of the idea of vocation, which maintains that all civilizations are called upon "to foster their freedom and responsibility in such a way as to become as fully human as their potentialities warrant." In this manner, all peoples can make their contributions to human progress; none are singled out as superior or chosen.[25]

Religion of Democracy

Religion, Kaplan points out, is concerned not only with theology, but, like democracy, represents an attempt to enhance human progress. Democracy, like religion, implies a faith in the possibility of human betterment. The two concepts may, therefore, be said to represent systems of salvation that incorporate a belief in a power that makes for salvation. Because the religion of democracy lacks theistic tenets or dogma, it may be accorded a place in the public schools, thereby solving the perplexing problem of teaching religion in the state schools. Education in democracy might well make of the American people "an instrument of divine revelation," as Kaplan sees it. Democracy offers America a common religion which would help to inculcate in Americans a spirit of love and loyalty, fervor and zeal toward its lofty principles.

Religious Equality

Democracy has its place also in the synagogue, the Reconstructionists maintain, particularly as it relates to the role of women. The Reconstructionists lean toward the Reform group in this regard. They have adopted the *Bat Mitzvah* ceremonial for girls, on a par with the *Bar Mitzvah* for boys. The same ritual procedures, including the reading from the prophets, are followed for both girls and boys. In most Conservative synagogues, however, a different

ritual procedure has been introduced for the *Bat Mitzvah* to distinguish it from the traditional *Bar Mitzvah*.

The Reconstructionists have also accorded women the honor of
an *Aliyah* (being called up for the recitation of a benediction over
the Scriptural reading) on an equal basis with the men, as do
Reform synagogues.[26] Like the Reformers, too, the Reconstructionists accept women in the rabbinate.

IV. CRITIQUE AND EVALUATION

The Naturalistic Approach

THE RECONSTRUCTIONIST TENETS have evoked a good deal of censure from various quarters. Kaplan's naturalistic approach has been
a special target of attack. The critics of Reconstructionism insist that
there is nothing distinctively Jewish about its God ideas. The abstract deity envisaged by Kaplan, they say, may satisfy the philosophical qualms of a few intellectuals, but it cannot have any
appeal for the average worshiper. Few, if any, can pray with fervor
to a remote, detached power, process, or force and expect to
derive therefrom the faith, courage, and comfort to live meaning-
fully and overcome obstacles.

One of Kaplan's most ardent disciples, the late Milton Steinberg
(1903-1950), a leading Conservative rabbi, attacked his teacher's
basic theological views. "Is God an actuality or merely an aspect
of reality—a functional concept, the product of Dewey's philosophy
of instrumentalism?" Steinberg challenged. The latter philosophy,
directed toward helping humanity in adjusting to its natural environment and solving some of its fundamental problems, doubtlessly has its value, Steinberg implied. It cannot, however, he indicated, be permitted to take the essential place of faith in man's
spiritual life. Kaplan's notion of God, Steinberg felt, can hardly
generate a spirit of piety and devotion, for it is devoid of the feeling of reliance, the poetry and sense of mystery that one commonly

associates with the idea of the Supreme Being. Intellectuality too, it must be recognized, has its limits and limitations.

Tradition

The readiness of Reconstructionism to depart from tradition has been another ground for opposition. In this regard, Schechter's quip about Reform—that men do not live by oxygen alone—can be applied to Reconstructionism. That tradition occupies a hallowed place in religious consciousness and cannot be readily dispensed with was evidenced by the reaction to an early liturgical experiment attempted by Kaplan. In the synagogue of the Society for the Advancement of Judaism in New York, of which Kaplan was the spiritual leader, he eliminated the *Kol Nidre,* the traditional liturgical formula annulling religious vows,[27] which is recited at the beginning of the *Yom Kippur* eve service. He did so on the rational ground that it had been a source of misunderstanding between Jews and non-Jews for centuries and had, in fact, provided a pretext for the enactment of the medieval Jewish oath. The soul-stirring Psalm 130, which begins with the verse "Out of the depths have I called Thee, O Lord" chanted to the haunting and captivating traditional *Kol Nidre* melody, was to replace the latter liturgical passage. However, there was an overwhelming protest to this innovation and, at the insistence of the worshipers, the *Kol Nidre* was restored to the Reconstructionist ritual with only minor changes. The emotional appeal of the traditional *Kol Nidre* as the opening portion of the liturgy of the solemn fast overcame by far the possible objections to its content, even in the sentiments of as liberal a congregation as Kaplan's.

Other Doctrines

The Reconstructionist philosophy has been denounced as being atheistic, as secularizing Judaism and enthroning the Jewish people as the principal factor in the Jewish civilization. It has been accused of displacing the Torah and the God of Israel, and of leaving little room for a personal relationship between God and the individual, as taught by traditional Judaism and other religions. It has also been charged with having constructed Judaism into a sociological mould, thereby depriving it of its essential religious character and motivation.

The idea of the organic community has also been criticized on the ground that such an over-all body may readily emerge as a bureaucracy and may fail to reach the individual as effectively as the present-day smaller unit. An absorption of the Jewish spiritual leadership in the general structure of the Jewish community might also, it is claimed, lead to the neglect of the basic spiritual values so essential to Jewish survival. To some, the all-embracing community appears to be a ghetto or a state within a state, having no place in a democracy. Kaplan, however, points to the precedent of the Catholic Church in support of his proposal, particularly since the Church exerts a far greater control over the individual's life than he envisages in his plan for a democratic Jewish community. In the main, however, Kaplan's scheme of the coordinated community has been endorsed by many who reject his theological doctrines.

Kaplan's Influence

Reconstructionism marks a radical extension of the rationalistic currents in Conservative Judaism. Kaplan has carried them to a point to which none of his colleagues had previously ventured. His critics are legion, but though they do not favor his remedies, few disagree with his keen analysis of the ills and problems facing the Jews of America. If Kaplan has done little else, he has at least succeeded in arousing the professional and lay Jewish leadership to the need of rethinking and reconstructing their approach to the grave issues confronting American Judaism. The movement scored a crowning achievement in 1968 when it opened the Reconstructionist Rabbinical College to train men and women as rabbis and leaders "who will be devoted to the idea of the on-going organic Jewish community and a reconstructed Jewish civilization." Rabbi Ira Eisenstein is its first president. The College, like the Reconstructionist movement, has been hindered in its growth by a lack of funds. It has, however, helped to strengthen the Reconstructionist wing of American Judaism.[28]

15

Orthodoxy in America

I. Before 1882

Iberian Refugees

THE SECOND OF AUGUST, 1492, was a fateful day both in the history of the world and in Jewish history. On that day Columbus started out on his momentous voyage of discovery. By coincidence that day was the Ninth of Ab, a day of lamentation in the Hebrew calendar—a day of mourning for the destruction of the Holy Temple and the ancient Jewish state. As Columbus noted in his diary, his little fleet sailed past the gloomy ships carrying thousands of Jewish exiles, who had been banished from Ferdinand's and Isabella's Christian kingdom in Spain. These exiles were leaving their native Spain forever, after they and their forebears had lived there for some fifteen centuries and contributed liberally to its welfare, its wealth, and its culture. Little could Columbus have anticipated then that he would discover a territory where the descendants of the same exiles would ultimately find peace and freedom.

No accurate figures are available for the great number of Spanish Jews who were banished from their homes. The estimates vary from 150,000 to several times that figure. About a hundred thousand found a temporary refuge in Portugal for which they paid heavily. By 1497, the Jews were expelled from Portugal—but before then, all under twenty-five were baptized by force. Thus the Iberian peninsula became *Judenrein*. The remaining Jews had been converted to Christianity. Many of these converts, however, became Marranos, who practiced their Jewish rites in secret and sought an opportunity to flee to other lands where they could live in greater freedom. Some Spanish Marranos later found a haven in the Spanish settlements in Mexico,[1] but there too the arm of the dreaded Inquisition reached them. Marranos from Portugal settled in Brazil, which had been colonized by the Portuguese.

In 1631, the Dutch wrested Recife (now Pernambuco), then the capital of Brazil, from the Portuguese. For almost a quarter of a century, the Marranos in Recife enjoyed religious liberty and could observe the tenets of Judaism without restraint. The Jewish community in that settlement grew considerably with reinforcements from many sources, particularly from Amsterdam. They formed their own congregation, which they called Kahal Kodesh (Holy Congregation); they prospered and rejoiced in their freedom. All this, however, came to a disastrous end in 1654, when the Portuguese, in their continuous war against Holland, laid siege to Recife and captured it. The Jews were forced to leave the town, some returning to Holland, others going to other Dutch colonies.

Congregation Shearith Israel

One band of twenty-three men, women, and children braved the perils of the seas and made their way to North America, to the Dutch colony of New Amsterdam. After an adventurous journey they reached their destination in September, 1654. Peter Stuyvesant, the governor of the colony, tried to exclude them, but their coreligionists in the Dutch West India Company in Amsterdam interceded in their behalf, and they were permitted to remain, but only under various restrictions.

In its second year in the Colony, the small group of Jewish settlers was permitted to purchase a plot of land for a *Bet Hayyim* (a House of Life, as a cemetery is euphemistically called in Hebrew). Evidently, it was needed at the time. However, permission was not granted to open a regular synagogue until after the settlement had been under British rule for over half a century. Until then, the Jewish congregation worshiped in makeshift or rented quarters. In 1728, the settlers erected their synagogue on Mill Street on lower Broadway—the first Jewish house of worship in North America—which they called Shearith Israel (Remnant of Israel). Its constituency, largely Sephardic, adhered to the Sephardic ritual. Shearith Israel still exists today and is widely known as the Spanish-Portuguese synagogue.

The Newport Synagogue

In 1658, fifteen Jewish families from Holland founded the second Sephardic Jewish congregation in America in Newport, Rhode Island, which they called Jeshuat Israel (Salvation of Israel). It was natural for Jews to settle in Rhode Island, the colony established by Roger Williams, who granted religious freedom to all. The Jewish community of Newport grew and, in 1687, acquired a burial ground. In 1763, more than a century after the congregation was established, it built its own synagogue edifice—a beautiful, colonial structure.

Newport at the time was a prosperous commercial center, and its Jewish community, said to have numbered twelve hundred souls, was thriving. But not long afterwards, in 1776, the city was occupied by the British and Hessians, and the congregation dispersed. It was re-established after the Revolution, but by that time Newport had surrendered its commercial supremacy to New York and other ports. The Jews left the town, and the synagogue was closed for almost a century. It is now the oldest synagogue structure in America.[2] In 1946, it was proclaimed a national shrine, and was dedicated as such on August 31, 1947.

The historic founders of the Jewish community of Newport were not forgotten, however. Their memory was enshrined and immortalized by Henry Wadsworth Longfellow (1807-1882), in his long poem, *The Jewish Cemetery in Newport*.[3] Several verses will give the flavor of the poem:

How strange it seems! These Hebrews in their graves,
   Close by the street of this fair seaport town,
Silent beside the never silent waves,
   At rest in all this moving up and down!

How came they here? What burst of Christian hate,
   What persecution, merciless and blind,
Drove o'er the sea—that desert desolate—
   These Ishmaels and Hagars of mankind?

They lived in narrow streets and lanes obscure,
   Ghetto and Judenstrasse, in mirk and mire;
Taught in the school of patience to endure
   The life of anguish and the death of fire.

All their lives long, with the unleavened bread
   And bitter herbs of exile and its fears,
The wasting famine of the heart they fed,
   And slaked its thirst with the marah of their tears.

And thus forever with reverted look
   The mystic volume of the world they read,
Spelling it backward, like a Hebrew book
   Till life became a Legend of the Dead.

Colonial Synagogues

In 1733, soon after James Oglethorpe, a wealthy Englishman possessed of "a strong benevolence of soul," began to settle Georgia as a philanthropic venture for the rehabilitation of unfortunate debtors, Jews came to Savannah. Though the trustees of the settlement objected to the admission of Jews, Oglethorpe permitted them to stay. That same year, they organized the third synagogue in America—Mikveh Israel (Hope of Israel) which like its predecessors was Sephardic in ritual. The following year, a group of German Jews arrived in Savannah and joined the congregation. But they left it after a few years to create their own synagogue—the fourth in North America and the first to be founded by Ashkenazic Jews.

Around 1745, the fifth Jewish congregation on American soil, also named Mikveh Israel was launched in Philadelphia. Pennsylvania offered a congenial atmosphere for the Jewish colonists because its charter guaranteed religious freedom not only to Christians of all denominations, but to everyone who "acknowledged One Almighty and Eternal God." A synagogue building was constructed in 1782, when the Philadelphia congregation was enlarged by the influx of Jewish patriots from New York and other areas occupied by the British.

The Fundamental Constitution of Carolina, drawn up in 1669 by John Locke, a liberal English philosopher, offered religious tolerance "to Jews, heathens and other dissenters." The constitution was abandoned, but its principle of religious toleration survived and attracted an increasing number of Jews to the settlement. By 1750, the Jewish community of Charleston, South Carolina, attained sufficient numbers to organize the sixth synagogue in the American colonies. They called it Kahal Kodesh Beth Elohim Unveh Shalom (Holy Congregation, House of God and Mansion of Peace). Three quarters of a century later, the first attempt at Reform in America originated in this congregation.[4]

Ashkenazim in America

There were other Ashkenazic Jews in colonial America,[5] aside from the small concentration in Savannah. A few had come to America even before the first Jewish settlement was started in New Amsterdam. Some Polish Jews had fled their homes and escaped to America during the Cossack uprising of 1648.[6] Their escape route led through Germany, Holland, and England,[7] and surreptitiously through France, which had not officially admitted Jews since 1394. Because the suffering of the Polish Jews did not abate in the ensuing century, their small but steady westward migration continued, and was augmented by Jews from Central Europe and Germany. Grinding poverty, low status, persecution, threatened expulsion, impossible taxes and restrictions motivated some of the more venturesome to seek to improve their lot in the New World.

The flow of Ashkenazic Jews to America, only a trickle in the seventeenth century, became a more steady stream in the eighteenth, swelling the Jewish population in the New World from only a few hundred in 1700 to approximately three thousand by 1800.

It is possible that the Ashkenazic Jews were in the majority in several of the American colonies by the end of the Revolutionary War; yet even so, they were probably satisfied to remain in the established Sephardic congregations. No doubt a portion of them were absorbed by the Sephardim, who were on a higher social level than the Ashkenazim. Toward the closing decades of the eighteenth century, the names of several prominent Polish Jews appear in the records of the Sephardic synagogues, notably Hayim Salomon (1740-1785) of Philadelphia, who advanced money to George Washington for the maintenance of his army. The religious school of Shearith Israel of New York is still known as the Polonies Talmud Torah, in honor of Meyer Polony, a Polish Jew who, upon his death in 1801, left the school an endowment of $800, a fair sum for those days. Isaac M. Wise stated in his memoirs that when he landed in New York in 1846, the oldest congregation was Sephardic, but its oldest member was a Polish Jew.

While the post-Napoleonic migration from Germany of both Jews and non-Jews was in progress, a far smaller but no less constant outflow of Jews from Russia had begun. The movement gained impetus from the cruel and barbaric cantonization system introduced by Czar Nicholas I in 1827. A universal conscription law required twenty-five years of military service, beginning at the age of eighteen, for all. But the Jews were compelled to serve as "cantonists" for a preparatory term of six years, which began at the tender age of twelve. To supply these cantonists, or, more correctly put, the victims, the Jewish communities were allotted quotas. To meet these quotas, the communities had to employ "catchers" to kidnap boys even younger than twelve from their parents. The children were sent away to distant parts of the country. Only a few survived the brutalities, rigors, and hardships of cantonization. The ostensible purpose of this legalized kidnap system was Russification; actually it was designed as a means of forced baptism.

Jews continued to leave Russia in the course of the century.

The extension of the military draft to the Jews of Russian Poland in 1845 precipitated an emigration of Jews from that region. These Jews strongly resented the fact that they had not been granted citizenship in return for their military service. Rumanian Jews, also victims of relentless persecution, began to come to America in a discernible movement in the latter 1860's. However, not all the Ashkenazim came to America in order to escape oppression. Some came to improve their economic conditions or to seek their fortunes in the New World. In fact, among the several thousand Jews who joined the gold rush to California in 1849 and the period following, there was a group of Jewish immigrants from Eastern Europe.

Early Ashkenazic Synagogues

More than half a century elapsed from the time the Sephardic Mikveh Israel congregation was established in Philadelphia until an Ashkenazic synagogue, Rodeph Shalom, was launched in that city. Though it was not formally organized until 1802, Rodeph Shalom had started as early as 1795 as a *minyan*.[8] Unlike other Ashkenazic congregations, it did not originate from a split in an older congregation, but it grew out of the natural desire of the Ashkenazim to worship in accordance with their own ritual, rather than to follow the Sephardic ritual of Mikveh Israel. The founders of the new synagogue were Dutch, German, and Polish Jews.

In New York City, the first Ashkenazic synagogue, Bnai Jeshurun, was formed in 1825, two centuries after the establishment of the Sephardic Shearith Israel. The new congregation was founded mainly by English, German, Polish, and a few Dutch Jews, who withdrew from the earlier Sephardic congregation in protest against policies and practices they deemed objectionable. Once a precedent of secession was created, it continued. In 1828, congregation Anshe Chesed was launched by a group that left Bnai Jeshurun. In 1839, a contingent of Polish Jews seceded from both Bnai Jeshurun and Anshe Chesed to form a new congregation, Sharey Zedek. This process of proliferation was a result both of the increase in Jewish population in the city and of the difference in background of the immigrants, who felt more comfortable among their own countrymen. A similar pattern was followed in other cities.

The first synagogue in New York City to be organized predominantly by Russian and Polish Jews was the Bet Hamidrash (house of study),[9] launched in 1852. It was the forerunner of the Bet Hamidrash Hagadol, still located on the East Side of Manhattan. There were several rabbis among the twelve founders of the congregation. One of them, Abraham Joseph Ash, acted as a volunteer rabbi until 1860, when he was paid two dollars per week. He occupied this pulpit with several interruptions until his death. During these intervals, Ash made futile attempts to enter business and become financially independent, so as to serve as rabbi without compensation, as he had done during the first eight years of his incumbency.

Rabbi Ash, the first qualified rabbi of an East European congregation in the New World, was an outstanding Talmudic scholar who had received *Semicha* (ordination) from famous European rabbis. Orthodox Jewry at the time was plagued by many unauthorized religious functionaries, freelancers and self-styled "reverends," who undertook to carry on rabbinical duties for which they were not properly prepared.[10] Rabbi Ash is credited with having established the precedent permitting the conversion of a Protestant church building into a synagogue, on the ground that Protestant houses of worship, unlike the Catholic, do not have ikons or images and, therefore, do not come under the prohibition of the first Commandment. This decision was of considerable importance, since many church structures during this and subsequent periods were transformed into synagogues. The Bet Hamidrash Hagadol served as a model for later congregations formed by Jews of East European origin.

Attempts at Union

As the number of Orthodox congregations grew, it became increasingly evident that some form of cooperation and concerted effort among them was essential. In Eastern Europe, the synagogues were subject to the control of the over-all community governing body; in America, there was no such central organization, and each synagogue was independent and supreme in its own right. The absence of organization was marked by a chaotic lack of standards in the various phases of religious life, including the supervision of *Kashruth,* the observance of dietary and ritual slaughter practices by meat producers and tradesmen. The failure of Orthodoxy to handle its religious affairs in a dignified manner, and the consequent commercialization of religious functions, led many Jews, particularly among the more cultured, to lose respect for Judaism and, more particularly, for Orthodoxy.

To remedy the situation, fifteen of the principal Orthodox congregations in New York created the Board of Delegates of Orthodox Hebrew Congregations in 1879, for the prime purpose of appointing a chief rabbi to supervise and regulate religious matters in the growing Orthodox Jewish community. The new rabbinical office was to be supported by means of the *Karobka* (tax on kosher meat) which was the method employed for the maintenance of the Jewish communal institutions in Eastern Europe. Jewish leaders in the other wings of Judaism warned against this manner of financing the new venture and pointed out that it was both impractical as well as unbecoming, but to no avail. After nine years of negotiation with various European rabbis, the united Orthodox congregations induced Rabbi Jacob Joseph of Vilna (1848-1902) to accept the post of chief rabbi. The project, as many expected, was a fiasco, for people refused to pay a higher price for kosher meat, which was relatively expensive to start with. Moreover the rabbis of the various synagogues declined to recognize the authority of the new chief rabbi or submit to his discipline. The organization soon collapsed, and its rabbi was disgracefully abandoned and left to his own resources. Subsequent attempts of this nature in other cities, notably Chicago, also failed. Orthodoxy during this period was a whirlpool of controversy; it had not yet reached sufficient maturity for effective cooperation and joint effort.

II. AFTER 1882

East European Persecutions

AFTER 1882, East European immigration poured out as a tidal wave, the result largely of the reactionary policies of Alexander III of Russia (1881-1894), who succeeded his father after the latter's assassination. The young sovereign was determined to follow the plan for the solution of the Jewish problem in Russia proposed by his chief adviser, Pobiedonostzev, the Procurator of the Holy Synod of the Greek Orthodox Church. Pobiedonostzev advocated that a third of the country's five million Jews should emigrate; another third should be baptized; and the remainder, starved.

The Russian government did not hesitate to adopt this cruel and cynical program. The new policy was appropriately inaugurated by a series of pogroms. The ignorant masses, particularly the peasants, roused by vicious anti-Jewish propaganda, attacked over a hundred and sixty Jewish communities, slaying hundreds, wounding many more, and looting thousands of Jewish homes and properties. Shocked by these atrocities, the governments of many European countries and of the United States protested to the despotic Russian oligarchy, which finally yielded to public opinion and stopped the savage riots. Instead of taking punitive measures against the perpetrators, however, the Russian government charged that the victims themselves were responsible for the outrages—presumably by provoking the population, although the government never explained how. This wave of violence was followed by the *May Laws* of 1882, so named after the month of their enactment.

The *May Laws* were designed to strangle the Jews economically and intellectually. The Pale of Settlement, the territory in which Jews were permitted to reside, was substantially reduced. Thousands were driven out, often at twenty-four hours' notice, from the rural areas and cities in which they had been living, into the already overcongested Pale. The Jewish district could not support its original population with its inordinate number of craftsmen and shopkeepers, and the influx of newcomers in the same occupations taxed the economy of the Pale to the breaking point. The resulting misery and poverty were beyond description. In addition to these repressions, the *numerus clausus,* the quota of the Jewish students in secondary schools and universities, was reduced. Thus, the Jews of Russia were under heavy attack politically and economically.

The condition of the two hundred and fifty thousand Jews of Rumania was no better. Jewish settlements had existed in that country before its conquest by the Romans (107 C.E.). Through trickery and chicanery, however, only an infinitesimal number of Jews were granted the right of citizenship which had been guaranteed them by the Rumanian government in the Treaty of Berlin, signed in 1878. Far from emancipating its Jews, the government expelled them from town and village, refused them admittance to colleges and universities, and barred them from numerous vocations. The protests of other countries, including the United States, were of no avail. In the Polish province of Galicia, where anti-Semitism was rampant, the condition of the Jews was equally hopeless.

The Jews of Eastern Europe were thus left with no alternative but to starve or migrate, and naturally, those who could chose the latter course. The resulting exodus brought six hundred thousand Jews from these lands to America in the period between 1882 and 1900. The influx continued without interruption until the First World War. From 1900 to 1920, a million Jews entered the United States, swelling its Jewish population to an estimated three million, a twelvefold increase over that of 1880.

Adjustment

There was a wide gulf between the backgrounds of the swarm of East European immigrants and their American coreligionists. The former spoke Yiddish; they were poor, crude in manner, and lacking in refinement, having emerged from medieval ghetto conditions in their native lands. They found an America which was the product of four centuries of social, political, and industrial progress. Since their home countries were extremely backward in these respects, they were compelled to make a leap of several centuries from an almost medieval society to a modern one. They lacked worldly knowledge. On their arrival, they flocked to the squalid tenements in the crowded slum areas of the big cities, where their kinsmen and townsmen had settled. Many found employment in the needle trades and toiled long hours in sweatshops under inhuman conditions for a pittance. Soon problems of employer-employee relations widened the already great social and economic distance between them and their well-established German Jewish bosses who had preceded them to these shores.

In their homelands, the East European Jews had known only

one type of Judaism—Orthodoxy, for in that region the more liberal religious movements, Reform and the more moderate viewpoint of the Historical School, or even Samson Raphael Hirsch's Neo-Orthodoxy, had failed to make any inroads. Toward Jewish nationalism most of the newcomers entertained warm sentiments. Steeped in Jewish learning and religious observance, many of the erudite and pious found the secular environment of America alien to their temperaments. They looked back with yearning and nostalgia to the spiritual and religious life they had led in their native towns, a life which revolved about the synagogue and its *Bet Hamidrash* and which drew its inspiration from the Sabbath and the festivals. Those immigrants who felt the lack of this zeal and fervor in the American milieu found adjustment to the New World particularly difficult. Not all the new settlers of this era, however, were Orthodox, or even religiously disposed. There was a substantial contingent of secularists who were indifferent or opposed to religion of any kind. This group included the Jewish socialists and assimilationists who believed that the situation of Jews everywhere would improve when the condition of people generally and of the proletariat in particular was ameliorated.

The Yeshiva Rabbi Isaac Elchanan

Because Orthodoxy fosters intense Jewish piety and observance, it depends for its survival on a well-trained rabbinic and lay leadership. The traditional medium for the training of this kind of personnel in Europe was the Yeshiva, an advanced institution of Talmudic learning.[11] The first American school of this level, the Yeshiva Rabbi Isaac Elchanan, founded on the lower East Side in New York City in 1896, was named for the great Talmudic sage of Kovno, Lithuania, Isaac Elchanan Spector, who died shortly before the institution was opened. Like its European prototype, the American academy undertook to prepare students for *Semicha,* as well as to train *Talmidei Chachamim* (disciples of the wise) or scholars, on the principle of *Torah Lishmah* (the acquisition of learning for its own sake). In 1908, the students of the Isaac Elchanan Yeshiva insisted on being permitted to engage in secular studies while attending the Yeshiva. After considerable discussion and negotiation, their demand was granted. This innovation, which represented a departure from the educational pattern of the East European Yeshivot, set the school on a more liberal path than it might otherwise have followed. It enabled those desiring collegiate preparation for professional or commercial careers to acquire a sound Talmudic background as well.

In 1915, Dr. Bernard Revel (1885-1940), a brilliant Jewish scholar and prosperous businessman, accepted the invitation to assume the presidency of the Yeshiva. He proceeded to enlarge his institution by attaching to it a preparatory department, the Yeshiva Etz Chaim, a secondary Jewish day school on the lower East Side, which offered a combined program of secular and Jewish instruction. Later, in 1921, the Mizrachi Teachers Training School, founded several years earlier, was incorporated as a division of the Yeshiva. In order to spare students the trouble and strain of attending two separate schools, and also to provide an atmosphere "harmonizing the age-old truths and ideals of faith and culture with the fruits of modern knowledge," Dr. Revel, in 1928, created as part of the Yeshiva a liberal arts college with the authority to grant baccalaureate degrees. A year later, the expanded school moved from the East Side to a new campus in upper Manhattan. The union of a secular college with a traditional Yeshiva was a landmark in both American and Jewish education, and represents an embodiment of the Neo-Orthodox ideals of Samson Raphael Hirsch.

In 1943, several years after Dr. Revel's death, Dr. Samuel Belkin, formerly Dean of the Yeshiva Rabbinical Seminary, was elected president of the over-all institution. Two years later, Yeshiva College was accredited as a university, empowered to confer additional degrees, including the doctorate. Yeshiva University has been immeasurably enlarged. It is a nonsectarian institution with seven graduate and five undergraduate schools at four centers in Manhattan and the Bronx, and an affiliate, the West Coast Hebrew Teachers College in Los Angeles. It also maintains two high schools for boys and two for girls. The extensive network of liberal arts, science, mathematics, and other academic programs offered by Yeshiva are served by well-equipped libraries and laboratories. The university operates a museum and archive. A peak achievement was the opening of the Albert Einstein College of Medicine in 1955, which event was paralleled in 1976 by the opening of the Benjamin N. Cardozo School of Law. Yeshiva also sponsors the Wurzweiler School of Social Work, a cantorial training program, as well as numerous auxiliary projects, including the publication of scholarly journals in Hebrew and in English and a series of Jewish scholarly monographs. In April, 1978, the institution announced the opening of the Simon Wiesenthal Center for Holocaust Studies in Los Angeles as a major repository in America for books and records on the Holocaust.

Union of Orthodox Jewish Congregations

With the growth of Orthodox Jewry in America, the need for a central body to speak for it and guide it became more pronounced. The attempt to organize it, however, was impeded by several factors. The Orthodox Jewish immigrants came from a widely diversified background; there were among them Russian, Polish, Rumanian, Lithuanian, Austrian, Hungarian, Galician, and West European Jews. They were, moreover, spread over a wide ideological spectrum representing varying shades of piety. The Orthodox synagogues were poor and constantly struggling financially. They were, moreover, unaccustomed to cooperation and discipline. Despite these formidable difficulties, a group of leaders from among the native core of American Orthodoxy, by dint of a determined effort, succeeded in establishing an over-all Orthodox congregational body. This was accomplished in 1898, only a decade after the collapse of the Board of Delegates of the Orthodox Congregations, on the initiative of Henry Pereira Mendes, minister of the Sephardic congregation Shearith Israel.

The new federation of congregations was named the Union of Orthodox Congregations. From its beginnings, it represented modern Orthodoxy. The preamble to its original constitution committed its affiliates to accept as binding "the authoritative interpretation of our Rabbis as contained in the Talmud and Codes." Though this body has as yet failed to achieve the strength and prestige of the central congregational agencies of the other wings of Judaism, its record is by no means unimpressive.

One of its principal attainments lies in the regulation of *Kashruth,* which it wrested from irresponsible elements who exploited it for their own profit. The Union presently uses the encircled *U* to label and certify as kosher some one thousand seven hundred items of food, produced by several hundred manufacturers. It also publishes a considerable amount of literature on the meaning of the dietary laws and other traditional practices. The actual supervision of *Kashruth* is carried on by the Rabbinical Council of America, the rabbinical arm of the Union. The manufacturers themselves absorb the expense involved in the supervisory operation, so that there is no extra cost to the consumer for the approved product.

For many years, the Union sponsored the Jewish Sabbath Alliance, which conducted an employment bureau as a means of encouraging Sabbath observance. This service was subsequently taken over by the National Council of Young Israel, although with the five-day week now prevailing, it is less needed than formerly, when a six-day week was common. The Union has also played a role in the field of Jewish education. It has continuously cooperated with the Rabbi Isaac Elchanan Yeshiva and Yeshiva College as its educational hub. Its Women's Branch established the Hebrew Teachers Training School for Girls in 1928, which merged with Yeshiva University in 1953. Aside from its women's division, the Union assists several auxiliary groups, including a national youth organization, the Yavne National Religious Jewish Students' Association, the Association of Orthodox Jewish Scientists, as well as other agencies and commissions. It produces educational materials for these groups and issues several periodicals and publications, including a popular bimonthly, *Jewish Life*. The Union is the recognized voice of American Orthodoxy, although only the larger and more influential of the estimated one thousand seven hundred Orthodox synagogues are formally affiliated with it.[12] These range ideologically from liberal congregations with mixed seating to the ultratraditionalist, *i.e.* from those bordering on Conservatism to extreme Orthodoxy. The current trend is toward the right.

The Orthodox Rabbinical Organizations

While there is only one central rabbinical body in each of the other alignments in American Judaism, there are a number of such organizations in American Orthodoxy. The differences in background among the various rabbinic groups and the number of rabbinical schools representing varying shades of Orthodoxy account for the existence of separate associations. The oldest among them, the *Agudath Ha-Rabbanim,* known by its English name also as "The Union of Orthodox Rabbis of the United States and Canada," was founded in 1902 by a core of fifty rabbis who had been ordained in Eastern Europe. For many years it was directed by Israel Rosenberg, a prominent Orthodox rabbi and a founder of the Isaac Elchanan Yeshiva. This association with a membership of six hundred, aims to strengthen every phase of traditional Jewish life: *Kashruth,* Sabbath observance, religious education, greater adherence to the Orthodox marriage and divorce procedures, and other traditional practices. The Union also endeavors to maintain dignified standards in the Orthodox rabbinate.

During the First World War, this rabbinical body participated in the creation of the *Ezrath Torah* (Aid to Torah) Fund, which it has since sponsored. This agency has rendered various forms of aid to needy rabbis, scholars, and Yeshivot in Eastern Europe. After the outbreak of World War II, the Orthodox rabbinical Union established the *Vaad Hatzala* (Committee for Rescue), which assisted refugee rabbis and Talmudic scholars in war-torn Europe, helping in their rescue and rehabilitation. The *Vaad* played an active role in the transfer of Yeshivot from Poland and Lithuania to Palestine and the United States. In 1964 the Union led in the campaign for the adoption of the New York State Sabbath Closing Law, permitting Sabbath observers to keep their business establishments open on Sunday instead of on the Sabbath. The organization inclines to the right in its religious orientation. Though its membership represents the highest level of Talmudic scholarship, the organization has declined considerably in prestige and has yielded much of its ground to the younger rabbinic groups with an American-trained constituency and outlook.

The graduates of the Rabbi Isaac Elchanan Rabbinical Seminary and of several institutions founded later differed considerably in their rearing and training from the majority of the membership of the Union of Orthodox Rabbis. The latter, educated in Europe, generally spoke Yiddish, while the former were at home in English and usually held college degrees, which the European-trained rabbis lacked. Because of this difference in orientation, the graduates of the Rabbi Isaac Elchanan Yeshiva created their own Rabbinical Alumni Association in 1924. At about the same time, the Rabbinical Council of the Union of Orthodox Jewish Congregations was formed to serve as the rabbinical authority of this congregational body. In view of the identity of a large part of the membership of the two rabbinical groups, arrangements were made in 1930 for their merger. The new organization was named the Rabbinical Council of America. In 1942, the Council absorbed the Rabbinical Association of the Hebrew Theological College in Chicago,[13] and later also the graduates of Ner Israel Rabbinical College in Baltimore. The Rabbinical Council also admits qualified rabbis who are privately ordained in accordance with traditional Jewish practice. It serves as the rabbinical arm of the Union of Orthodox Jewish Congregations.

The Rabbinical Council of America, with its membership of over eight hundred, is the largest and most influential Orthodox rabbinical organization. It publishes a splendid scholarly quarterly, *Tradition,* and a Hebrew Halachic journal, *HaDorom,* a bulletin, *The RCA Record,* and other publications. It has recently created a *Bet Din* to deal with family problems and to decide complex cases involving religious law. Its program also includes welfare activities on behalf of its membership, as well as projects in Israel.[14]

Aside from these major rabbinical associations in American Orthodoxy there are several smaller ones. The Rabbinical Alliance of America is a rightist group, consisting of a meager membership drawn in the main from among the graduates of the Yeshiva Torah Vodaath and Mesivta Chaim Berlin and other *Yeshivot Gedolot* (advanced Talmudic academies granting *Semicha*). The *Hithachduth Ha-Rabbanim,* which refers to itself as the Central Rabbinical Congress of the United States and Canada, is composed largely of Hassidic rabbis.

Young Israel

In 1912, a band of young men and women living on the lower East Side of Manhattan founded a cultural organization which aimed to foster Orthodoxy among American Jewish youth. Several years later this group, known as Young Israel, established a model synagogue which attempted to make the traditional worship services more decorous and aesthetic than those commonly conducted in East European synagogues. The founders of Young Israel maintained that a dignified and interesting religious worship would attract the American Jewish youth and keep them in the Orthodox fold. To further this goal, they introduced congregational singing and eliminated the sale of religious honors and other forms of commercialism from the services. The organization soon branched out to other parts of the New York metropolis and to other cities as well, and by 1922, the National Council of Young Israel was launched to coordinate the burgeoning movement.

Young Israel has since become a movement of national scope with some one hundred branches and approximately twenty-five thousand affiliated families in the United States and Canada. It carries on a varied program of religious, cultural, and social activities designed to "awaken a love for Orthodox Judaism and the Jewish people within the hearts of American Jewish youth." It helps Jewish soldiers in the American armed forces to abide by traditional observances. It organizes teen-agers and college students, maintaining for the latter an Intercollegiate Council of Young Adults. The Young Israel Employment Bureau aids applicants in finding employment in which they can observe the Sabbath and the Jewish festivals. An Eretz Israel Committee, functioning since 1926, stimulates the membership of the organization to participate in nonpolitical projects for the benefit of the Jewish community in Israel. The Young Israel Institute of Jewish Studies, in existence since 1947, provides courses centrally and encourages the local organization to open adult classes in various areas of Jewish study. It publishes the *Young Israel Viewpoint*.

The founders of Young Israel were originally inspired and guided by two members of the Conservative Jewish Theological Seminary faculty, the late Professor Israel Friedlander and Professor Mordecai M. Kaplan, who evidently projected it as a Conservative organization. However it shifted to Orthodoxy, though it has been relatively liberal in its Orthodoxy. It did, however, insist that its officers should be Sabbath observers. There has been a swing to the right in recent decades, largely because of the change in the character of its leadership. Until the Second World War Young Israel was dominated by a lay leadership, but it has since been increasingly influenced by its Council of Young Israel Rabbis, who occupy the pulpits of Young Israel congregations. These rabbis generally tend toward a more intense Orthodoxy. The merger of the two Israeli religious political parties in 1957 into the National Labor Party (*Mafdal*) led to the merger of their American ideological counterparts as the Religious Zionists of America (RZA). RZA resembles Young Israel in aim, program, and constituency.

Agudath Israel in America

While Young Israel and the Union of Orthodox Jewish Congregations view Judaism as a synthesis of religion and nationalism, the more pietistic *Agudath Israel* conceives of Judaism exclusively in religious terms. *Agudath Israel* (Union of Israel), founded in 1912 as a worldwide Orthodox movement, did not succeed in creating an adult branch of its organization in the United States for several decades. The American wing of *Agudath Israel* grew out of the *Zeirei Agudath Israel,* a youth organization launched in 1923 by a small band of observant young people on the lower East Side of Manhattan. Similar Orthodox groups soon appeared, recruiting their membership chiefly from among the first generation of Polish, Galician, and Hungarian immigrants.

By the end of the decade, the various units functioning throughout the city organized themselves into a loosely knit coordinating council. In 1929, the council set up a national office charged with the task of building up a countrywide association. At that time, the movement comprised only one thousand five hundred adults and a thousand juniors, the latter consisting of children's, youth, and adolescent groups. The adult American Section of the movement was organized in 1939. During the war and postwar years, the central office of *Agudath Israel* in America carried on activities embracing overseas relief, immigration, educational work and a public relations program. Since 1952, the *Agudah* has published a Yiddish monthly, *Das Yiddishe Vort,* and an English monthly, *The Jewish Observer.* The membership in all age groups had reportedly reached ten thousand by mid-century and is said to have increased since. Its recent growth may be attributed largely to the influx of extreme religious elements among the post-World War II immigrants, who introduced a more rigorous standard of pietism into the movement. *Agudath Israel* is a separatist group in traditional Judaism in America.

Separatism

The Orthodox community of Frankfort, Germany, maintained its separate existence since 1849, when it seceded from the main community in accordance with a policy of *Trennungs Orthodoxie*.[15] In 1940, a number of Orthodox immigrants from Frankfort and other parts of Germany who had come to New York during the Nazi period and settled in the Washington Heights area, established the congregation K'hal Adath Yeshurun along the lines of the Frankfort community. They follow the isolationist tendencies pursued by their community in Frankfort. They conduct their independent educational institutions, supervise with considerable zeal their own kosher food shops, maintain their own separate *mikvah* (ritual bath) and other religious institutions, without recourse to the larger Jewish community. They are members of *Agudath Israel,* whose antinationalist outlook they share. Unlike the East European sector of the *Agudah,* they patronize secular learning.

The policy of separation is based on the view that rigid religiosity is of far greater importance than Jewish unity. They regard the Jewish people as a unique, supernatural entity existing for one major purpose—the observance of Jewish law. This, they believe, is a divine trust, which permits them no leeway or compromise. Accordingly, they can see no reason for joining with any other body that does not share their practices.

In 1955, eleven prominent *Roshei Yeshivah,* heads of distinguished Yeshivot and leaders of the *Agudah* transplanted in America from various parts of Europe, took a formal step to approve this separatism. They issued an *issur* (prohibition) against the participation of Orthodox rabbis in non-Orthodox rabbinical organizations and activities. This was clearly directed at the Synagogue Council of America and the New York Board of Rabbis, both coordinating bodies which include synagogues and rabbis of all wings of Judaism. The *issur* signified the nonrecognition of other than Orthodox rabbis or their institutions as a matter of Jewish law.

The doctrine of separatism had already disrupted the unity in American Orthodoxy. It has been a major cause for the existence of several Orthodox rabbinical organizations. This idea has penetrated the ranks of the Rabbinical Council and the Union of Orthodox Hebrew Congregations. The majority in these organizations resist the demand for separatism on the practical ground that their withdrawal from the coordinating organizations will deprive the latter of the vital moderating and restraining influence that the Orthodox presently exercise. The principle of separatism in Jewish Orthodoxy theatens to create a schism and sectarianism in Judaism.

Orthodox Ideology and Observance

While each of the other two alignments in American Judaism maintains a single theological school, Orthodoxy has over thirty.[16] Ideologically, the schools may be distinguished largely by their attitudes toward secular education. The Rabbi Isaac Elchanan Theological Seminary is the archetype of the rabbinical training institution that expects its graduates to acquire a collegiate training, in addition to their Jewish studies. It embraces, generally speaking, the nationalistic religious viewpoint of the *Mizrachi,* which assumes the Neo-Orthodox and modernist outlook on general culture. This liberal tendency is shared by a small portion of the *Yeshivot Gdolot,* chiefly the Hebrew Theological College in Chicago and the Ner Israel Rabbinical College in Baltimore.

Most of the other higher Yeshivot in the United States take a doctrinal position to the right of the Rabbi Isaac Elchanan Seminary. The archetypes of the latter category are the Yeshiva and Mesivta Torah Vodaath and the Yeshiva and Mesivta Chaim Berlin, both in Brooklyn. These two institutions conduct departments extending from kindergarten through the seminary level. In fact, each maintains a *kolel* (postgraduate department); the former in Monsey, New York, and the latter in New York City. The bulk of the *Yeshivot Gdolot* were transferred from Eastern Europe.[17] Like their East European antecedents, they frown on a liberal arts education, but make a concession in the case of professional training, since it is a means of earning a livelihood. However, they do not regard collegiate study as essential for the rabbinate.

It is simpler to explain the religious outlooks of the Orthodox Yeshivot than of sections of the Orthodox constituency. Membership in a traditional synagogue is not necessarily conclusive evidence of Orthodox leanings, for there are many instances of nonobservant Jews joining or continuing their membership in Orthodox synagogues for other reasons. There are Orthodox congregations in which few except the rabbi adhere to the rigid requirements of Orthodox practice, though the official stamp, tenor, policy, and affiliation of the group is traditionalist. Some join these congregations as a matter of sentiment, because their parents have been members or founders. This is particularly true in the smaller communities, where individuals not infrequently retain an inactive association with an Orthodox synagogue and a more active affiliation with a liberal congregation at the same time.

In the larger Jewish communities, Orthodoxy is stronger, though even there, many identify themselves with it only on sad family occasions, and less frequently in connection with marital celebrations or other joyous functions. It would seem then that the question of who is an Orthodox Jew in America is, practically speaking, a moot one. Theoretically, of course, the answer is relatively simple, for Orthodoxy requires fidelity to the regulations set down in the *Shulchan Aruch,* the traditional code of Jewish Law,[18] and a nonobservant Orthodox Jew is virtually an anomaly[19] and a contradiction in terms. Such a designation connotes an inconsistency between one's commitment and one's practice.[20]

The Halachist's Viewpoint

Dr. Joseph Soloveitchik, who succeeded his father as Professor of Talmud and Religious Philosophy at Yeshiva University's Rabbi Isaac Elchanan Theological Seminary, is a towering Jewish scholar and interpreter of the Halacha. He has served as Chairman of the Halacha Commission of the Rabbinical Council of America, the largest Orthodox rabbinical body, for over a decade. His distinction as an authority on the Halacha led to his having been invited in 1960 to accept the chief rabbinate of the Jewish community of Israel, but he declined the offer. Dr. Soloveitchik, often referred to as The Rav (rabbi) by his disciples, exerts a marked influence on the students and on the rabbinic alumni of the Yeshiva with his erudite, illuminating, and brilliant expositions of the Halacha, emerging from a rich background of Jewish and secular training.

Dr. Soloveitchik was born in Poland in 1903, the heir to a family tradition of outstanding Talmudic learning. He embarked on his Jewish studies at an early age, and also acquired a general education, which prepared him for matriculation in the Faculty of Philosophy at the University of Berlin, where he developed a deep interest in Neo-Kantian thought.[21] He received his doctorate in 1931 on the basis of a dissertation on the philosophy of Hermann Cohen.[22] A year later he came to America and settled in Boston, where he accepted a rabbinical post which he has held ever since.

True religion, Rabbi Soloveitchik maintains with other Jewish and Christian theologians, is neither an opiate nor a leap to peace of mind and contentment. The path leading to the green pastures and still waters of spiritual peace is not a smooth one. Though many have been shaken by the "great and strong wind" described in the vision of Elijah (*IK.* 19:11) which "rends mountains and shatters the rocks," few have heard God's "still, small voice." The attainment of genuine religion is the product of an inner spiritual conflict and tension, a wrestling with doubt and contradiction, a state described by the Psalmist in the verse: "Out of the depths have I called Thee, O Lord" (*Ps.* 130). Only as the outcome of a depressing sense of loneliness, as suggested by Kierkegaard, can one genuinely cry unto the Lord and enter into close communion with Him.

The genuine religionist differs in his outlook from that of the cognitive personality, the scientist and investigator, whose function is to seek knowledge. The latter attempts to understand the workings of the natural laws that make for order in the universe; he strives to remove the veil that enshrouds them. The truly religious individual, however, is obsessed primarily with the *mysterium tremendum.*[23] In fact, the more of nature's processes that are unravelled, the greater the religionist's wonder at the underlying miracle of the cosmos and the divine force behind it. He cannot but concede with Job (42:3) that the ultimate answers to the cosmic riddle are beyond his comprehension. Maimonides evidently recognized the two types of insight as may be judged from his dual approach to the perception of God. In his *Mishne Torah,* the Halachic code, he asserts that the prime precept in the Torah is to attain a knowledge of God.[24] However, in his philosophical work, the *Guide to the Perplexed,* Maimonides expounded the doctrine of negative attributes,[25] which is based on the premise that God's essence is unknown and unknowable to man. This, Rabbi Soloveitchik implies, exemplifies the dichotomy between the two modes of perception. The abstract metaphysical aspects of the universe are beyond the ken of cognition; they merely serve as an area of speculation for the religionist. Only the world of causality, of time and place, is within man's province. The latter, too, is within the precincts of Halacha.

Religion and Halacha

Pure religion, Dr. Soloveitchik goes on to explain, tends towards the transcendental. While the religionist may turn to asceticism and withdraws from life, the Halachist is within its hub and center. The Halachic individual resolves his dilemma between cognition and pure religion by means of the *a priori,* God-given Torah with its norms, standards and precepts, which chart the secure path he pursues in the world. By means of his deeds, directed towards a spiritual life, he achieves sanctity. Time provides the fervent follower of the Halacha with recurrent cues for the performance of the regimen of *mitzvot* (precepts) which permeate every avenue of his existence. That the Halacha is rooted in the here and now, may be seen from the law regarding death as ritually contaminating (*Num.* 19:11) and the grave as a source of ritual uncleanliness, in contrast to other religions that revere the dead and sanctify the tomb as the threshold of the beyond. This viewpoint is evidenced also in the Mishnaic dictum, "Better is one hour of repentance and good deeds in this world than a whole life in the world to come" (*Abot* 4:22). The same attitude toward life gave rise to the Halachic principle that the "saving of human life supercedes the Sabbath," and to other teachings of this nature.

The Halachist pursues an opposite course from that of the religionist, for he aims to bring heaven down to earth; the *Shechinah* into space and time. Thus he bestows sanctity upon the sanctuary he builds, thereby infusing the spirit of the infinite into finite existence. The religionist, of course, attempts the reverse; he translates the finite into infinity; he longs to lift the lower world to the upper. The Halachist, too, sets up in his divine, *a priori* laws a blueprint for the ideal life, recognizing that it represents an abstract Utopian state of existence, unattainable by flesh and blood. To this end, he investigates and studies not only the laws that function in life, but also those which are not actually in operation and which serve merely to outline or delineate the abstract, ideal, optimum society. He is like the mathematician who recognizes that no earthly geometric figure is as perfect as a theoretic one, yet knows that from the latter, the pure form of mathematics, physicists and other scientists derive the laws they require in their respective disciplines.

The Halacha sets down specific and positive standards and guidelines. There is little qualitative difference in the precepts of the Halacha. They are all to be performed with equal deference, reverence and solemnity, since, directly or indirectly, they have all emanated from the Sinaitic Revelation. The ritual act of the sounding of the *Shofar* on *Rosh Hashanah,* the Jewish New Year, a solemn day of prayer and penitence, should accordingly evoke no greater awe or emotion than the *Lulav* (palm ceremony) on Succoth, the harvest festival, which is a joyous day of Thanksgiving.

Worship and penitence are prime religious obligations for the Jew. To be meaningful, these acts must be the result of spiritual tension and a deeply felt need to come closer to God. Both are to bring about self-scrutiny and self-recreation—a new heart and new strivings. Sincere penitence is not to be related merely to the dead past, but should reckon with a living present that merges into a future in which meritorious deeds take the place of unworthy ones. The ultimate goal of loyal adherence to the precepts of the Halacha is the attainment of the state of godliness which leads to the highest spiritual plane envisaged in Judaism—that of prophecy.

One could not help but wonder if Dr. Soloveitchik has not over-idealized the Halacha. No doubt his purpose is to justify its rigid observance. He overlooks, however, the danger, that a too literal application of the Halacha may defeat its underlying spirit. The view that Halacha is an *a priori* system of revealed law has, for example, prompted Dr. Soloveitchik to advise a Jew whose town's only synagogue has mixed seating, which is Biblically prohibited as an "unseemly thing" (Dt. 23:15), that he will do better to worship at home on *Rosh Hashanah* than to enter the synagogue, even for the brief period of the solemn rite of *Shofar* blowing, let alone for the entire service. Dr. Soloveitchik evidently fails to realize that such intransigence may lead to the violation of some vital principles, values, and the spirit of Judaism, which may be of greater moment than Halachic consistency. Inflexibility and undeviating conformity to the Halacha may at times be a doubtful virtue.

III. THE NEW IMMIGRATION

The Nazi Beginnings

THE EMIGRATION of Jews from Germany had practically ceased in 1871, when the Jews were legally enfranchised in that country. Their new status, however, continued for only sixty years, until the rise of Nazism. The Nazis declared the Jews to be the enemies of Germany and the world and made no secret of plans to annihilate them. The Nazis' marching song proclaimed their determination to crush Jewish skulls; they declared that they would triumph only when their swords were drenched with Jewish blood. Neither the liberal world nor German Jewry believed that this could happen in the land of Goethe and Schiller—but it did.

The Nazi action against the German Jews began with a government-sponsored nationwide boycott against Jewish business, launched on April 1, 1933, a few months after Hitler had assumed the office of Chancellor of the Reich. While the police watched, Nazi storm troopers standing outside Jewish stores blocked customers from entering. The boycott was soon followed by an order excluding Jews from civil service and other phases of public life. On May 10, 1933, medieval book burnings were re-enacted. In huge midnight bonfires in Berlin and other cities, some twenty thousand books "not in the Nazi spirit" or written by German Jewish authors were consumed in the flames; nor were the Jews spared physical violence. The world was taken by surprise; but the Germans submitted to the Nazi dictatorship with considerable equanimity. The majority of Germans were not unduly disturbed by these events, nor by the suppression of their political, religious, or cultural freedoms. "What really aroused the Germans in the thirties," wrote William L. Shirer, "were the glittering successes of Hitler in providing jobs, creating prosperity, restoring Germany's military might and moving from one triumph to another in his foreign policy."[26]

Flight from Terror

The Jews in Germany were now frightened. Thousands fled in panic. The majority sought refuge in European lands, hoping that before long they would be able to return home. Of those who went overseas, about three thousand five hundred came to America in the years 1933-1935. A greater number made their way to Palestine. An interval of relative calm ensued in the next few years, which led many, including the Jews of Germany, to believe that the first onslaughts were only a passing storm. But in September, 1935, at the rally of the Nazi party in Nuremberg, the promulgation of the so-called Nuremberg Laws was the signal for a campaign of violence and the renewal of atrocities against German Jews.

The new edicts deprived the German Jews of citizenship, subjected them to forced labor, and compelled them to wear the medieval yellow badge. These laws applied not only to born Jews, but even to baptized Jews who had one Jewish grandparent. The new anti-Jewish measures produced another tide of emigration, this time with a changed destination, few going to European countries. Most went to Palestine, but some twenty-two thousand landed on American shores during the next three years. When the Nazis overran Austria in March, 1938, and unleashed their terror against that country's Jews, the flow of emigrants from Central Europe was swelled still further.

Then came the *crystal night* pogrom staged throughout Germany on November 10, 1938. Two hundred synagogues were destroyed, and thousands of Jewish shops and homes looted. Murder and assault, pillage and arson were the order of the day, and some twenty thousand Jews were sent to concentration camps.* The Jews of Germany now recognized their desperate plight.

Through his strategy of terror, Hitler succeeded in annexing Austria in March, 1938. In October he marched into the Sudetenland, which belonged to Czechoslovakia. The latter territory was ceded to Germany as a result of the infamous Munich Pact, by which Neville Chamberlain of England and Edouard Daladier of France shamefully betrayed Czechoslovakia. This "peace with honor," as Chamberlain hypocritically called it, shocked the liberal world. Eduard Benes, the Czechoslovak president, was forced to resign and leave his country. The twenty-five thousand Jews of the Sudetenland fled to Czechoslovakia. But Hitler, intoxicated with victory, could not be curbed. The following March, he called the new Czech president to Berlin and forced him to agree to make Czechoslovakia a Reich Protectorate. Only thirty-five thousand of the one hundred and seventy-seven thousand Jews of that country managed to escape before the outbreak of the Second World War in September, 1939.

It is estimated that of the five hundred and eighty thousand immigrants to the United States between 1933 and 1942, "a maximum of one hundred and sixty thousand Jewish refugees were admitted . . . and all within the framework of the existing immigration laws."[27] These refugees included many Jewish professionals and intellectuals: scientists, writers, physicians, university professors, some of whom enjoyed worldwide fame. Among the new arrivals were a sizeable number of intensely Orthodox Jews. They gave considerable impetus to the unprecedented growth of the Jewish day school movement in America in the following decade. This pattern of intensive Jewish schooling combined with secular studies had been fostered among the Orthodox by Samson Raphael Hirsch. With this wave of immigration also came a group of East

---

* The assassination of a minor official in the German embassy in Paris by Hershel Grynspan, a Polish Jewish youth, served as the pretext for the riots. The assailant had been thrown into a mood of despondency when he learned that his father had been among the thousands of Polish Jews deported from Germany and stranded in a no-man's land on the Polish-German frontier, where they suffered exposure and starvation. Young Grynspan's purpose was to call the attention of the world to the German atrocities against the Jews. Only one foreign statesman, President Franklin D. Roosevelt, made a strong gesture of protest against the German outrages, recalling the American ambassador from Berlin.

European Orthodox rabbis and scholars who transplanted their higher Yeshivot to the New World.[28]

A distinguished Talmudical scholar and Orthodox leader, Rabbi Ahron Kotler (1892-1962), a *Rosh Yeshivah* in Polish Lithuania, established the first *Kolel* or post-graduate non-professional Talmudical Institute in 1943. It is called the Beth Medrosh Govoha (Higher Academy), and is located in Lakewood, N.J., away from the distractions of Manhattan. Here married men, ordained rabbis and others devote themselves to Talmudic learning, the Yiddish concept of "lernen" as a way of life. A modest stipend is provided for those requiring it. The following year another *Kolel,* the Beth Medrosh Elyon, was founded by Rabbi Shragai Medelowitz at Monsey, N.Y. Similar ventures followed.

Hassidic Orthodoxy and the Williamsburg Hassidim

Towards the close of the First World War, a writer[29] on Hassidism stated that in America, at the time, "Chassidism is placed in the very queer position of having four Zadikim without Chassidim, and thirty thousand Chassidim without a single Zadik." The same writer deemed it doubtful that the Hassidim could gain a foothold in the American milieu. The true Hassid, he explained, remained in Europe, and those who came to this country compromised too quickly with the American environment to retain their own tradition and mode of life. However, that writer did not reckon with the vagaries of history.

In 1918, in the lower Williamsburg section of Brooklyn, a group of Polish Hassidim established an ultrapietist Yeshiva, which they called Torah Vodaath (Torah and Knowledge). This school attracted around it a colony of Hassidim, disciples of several *rebbes* who had settled in the neighborhood. In the twenties and thirties, a small coterie of other Hassidic *rebbes* migrated from Poland and Galicia to the United States but, like their predecessors, their influence was limited to their own small circles.

After World War II, the Hassidic community in Williamsburg was reinforced by the young survivors of the Nazi concentration camps who came to this country in the hope of reviving and resuming the Hassidic life they had led in their native lands.[30] They were accompanied by several of their own prominent *rebbes,* who set up synagogues and homes in large dwellings in the area. Thus, over the years, Williamsburg has become a center of Hassidic Orthodoxy.

The Lubavitcher Hassidim

The headquarters of the Lubavitcher Hassidim is located several miles away from the Williamsburg Hassidic center. The movement began in 1940 when the late Rabbi Joseph Isaac Schneerson, better known as the *Lubavitcher Rebbe,* arrived here with his entourage. He came to America from his native Russia to escape Communist persecution. His forceful propaganda and educational activities soon made an impact on the American Jewish community. Rabbi Schneerson, together with his followers, represented the *Habad,* the intellectual wing of Hassidism. His organization has established a network of elementary and higher Yeshivot in communities throughout the land. In these schools the traditional and Hassidic texts are taught in accordance with the *Habad* program. Rabbi Joseph Schneerson's successor, Rabbi Menachem Mendel, like several other leading figures in his group, is equipped with a good secular education in addition to his rabbinic and Hassidic training.

The Lubavitcher Hassidim differ from other Hassidic groups in their zeal in reaching out beyond their own camp. Every Jew in their eyes is worth cultivating, for he possesses a *Nitzotz* (spark) which can be fanned into a flame of Jewish piety. This attitude motivates the Lubavitcher Hassidim to seek support and recruits in the Jewish community at large. The same idea prompted them to sponsor the released-time program for religious instruction permitted by the New York City and other public school systems. The Lubavitcher Hassidim organized released-time classes for Jewish elementary school children in the hope of influencing them to greater religious observance and study and eventually to attract them to their ranks. They also maintain a press, which publishes various types of religious and educational literature.

Hassidic Piety

Their traditions, customs, dress, and practices pervade every aspect of the daily life of the Hassidim. Under guidance of their religious leaders, they lead an isolated, cloistered existence, which may be compared in a large degree to that of the Amish and similar Christian sects. The Hassidim, in contradistinction to most of the earlier Jewish immigrants to America, have never wanted to cast off the peculiar practices, values, and norms which they brought with them. In fact, they are determined to cultivate them more intensely in their new surroundings. They cherish their American citizenship because it affords them the freedom to remain an island unto themselves.

The Hassidim generally wear beards. Their younger sons wear long earlocks, and their married women shave their heads and don *sheitels* (wigs). On the Sabbath, many of. the men dress in long caftans, fur hats, slippers, and long white stockings reaching to the knees, regardless of the season of the year.[31] Their children attend their own day schools from morning to night, their sons and daughters going to separate schools. The youngsters receive a secular education in deference to the state requirements, though many of the parents regard mundane culture as heretical. An important institution among the Hassidim is the *Mikvah* (ritual bath) used for the purpose of maintaining ritual cleanliness. The Hassidim shun mixed dancing, radio, television, and worldly literature. They endeavor to perform their religious obligations in the spirit of joy which is a vital principle in Hassidism.

The Hassidim have introduced a new mode in American Orthodoxy—*glatt kosher* (perfectly kosher) meat. Meat about which there is any question, though approved as kosher by competent authority, is excluded from this category. The Hassidim have also employed the *Shatnez* laboratory, a scientific facility, to test their garments to determine whether or not they contain a mixture of wool and linen prohibited by Biblical law (Lev. 19:19; Dt. 22:11). This is a curious instance of the use of science in aid of a ritualistic tradition.

Though a number of Hasidic groups have started settlements in Israel, some regard the Jewish secular state and its government as sinful. The *Satmar Rebbe,* Rabbi Joel Teitelbaum, who is the leader of a major Hungarian Hassidic dynasty and was ironically saved from the Nazis by the Zionists, sees the Holocaust as God's punishment for the sin of Zionism and the creation of the secular State of Israel. He leads the anti-Israel sector

among the Hassidim. This group regards Hebrew as too sacred a
language for ordinary use, to which it is put in Israel. Their own
vernacular is Yiddish. They collaborate with the *Neturei Karta*
(guardians of the city), the small but articulate ultrareligious anti-
Israel faction in Jerusalem. They persistently and vociferously protest against the religious persecutions and discriminations allegedly
suffered at the hands of the Israel government by the *Neturei Karta*
and their confederates in Israel. The antinationalist minority exerts
little if any influence on the American Jewish scene.

New Centers

The Hassidic core in the main has been a vitalizing force in
Orthodoxy. Though Williamsburg is the principal center of Hassidism in America, the movement has enclaves in other Jewish communities. Many of the original residents of Hassidic Williamsburg,
who have attained a better financial status, have moved out of that
area to better sections, only to be replaced by newcomers. The
Hassidic population of Williamsburg is estimated to be between
twelve thousand and fifteen thousand. One group, the *Skwerer*
Hassidim, has left Williamsburg and established a suburban, self-
contained settlement in Rockland County, about twenty miles from
New York City, which they named Squaretown. Special busses,
which by an Act of the Legislature are permitted segregated seating for women and which are equipped with *mehizot* (partitions)
for this purpose, are like rolling synagogues in which prayer
services are conducted on the way to city work and on the way
home in the evenings. The Satmar and other Hassidim have built
similar suburban villages. The new, semirural semiurban surroundings contrast sharply with those of Williamsburg. The long established Yeshivot were forced to move from their old areas to better
and more fashionable neighborhoods. The largest, the Yeshiva
Torah Vedaath, as well as the Mesivta Yeshiva Rabbi Chaim
Berlin, moved to the Flatbush section of Brooklyn; the Bobover
relocated in Borough Park; while several others went to Long
Island. Tifereth Jerusalem on the lower East Side built an additional campus on Staten Island.

A Changed Image

The National Jewish Population Study estimated the Orthodox constituency (1970) at 209,000 or 11% of the total 1,190,000 Jewish householders in the United States. Of these 209,000 householders, 4.2% under age 30 represent the core of the future. A study of eight Young Israel synagogues indicates that the average modern Orthodox family has 2.5 children, slightly above the overall Jewish birthrate of 2.2. The extreme Orthodox and Hassidic families show a higher birthrate of from three to six children.

Contemporary Orthodoxy offers a different image from that of the earlier immigrant generation. The present one is predominantly native-born, secularly educated, and at home in the American environment in which it was reared. Some 20% of the respondents in the Young Israel study hold Masters degrees, while another 3% have attained their doctorates or are working for them. As many as 63% in this group are professionals. American Jewish Orthodoxy is now largely middle class in composition and life style, the mother often pursuing her own career, while sending her children to a Jewish day school. This contributed to the unparalleled increase in this type of school. The 60 Orthodox elementary and secondary day schools in the United States, with a total enrollment of 10,200 in 1945, grew to 92,000 students in over 500 elementary and high schools in 1979. These figures attest to the confidence of Jewish parents in their day schools, which they no longer regard as parochial but rather as private schools affording a plus over the public schools in terms of intensive Jewish schooling.

Orthodoxy too has developed a greater visibility. *Kippot* (skull caps) associated with Orthodox dress are fairly common on the campus. So is the provision there for kosher food. Hassidic records, religious articles, as well as Orthodox publications and organizations have achieved a good market. The Association of Orthodox Scientists has doubled its membership in the last decade to 1,000. The newly created American Jewish College Faculty Association embraces several hundred members while over 6,000 Jewish public school teachers are affiliated with the New York City Orthodox Jewish Teachers Association. The resurgence of Orthodoxy may be credited to the spiritual hunger of an expanding segment of the Jewish youth, including *Baalei Teshuvah* or non-religious "returnees," who find fulfillment in traditional Jewish values. Prominent among them is the ideal of *Lomdut* or Jewish learning fostered by the Yeshivot.

IV. WHAT OF THE FUTURE?
(*Postscript*)

"Since the Holy Temple was destroyed," Rabbi Yochanon said, "the gift of prophecy had been taken from the prophets and given to fools and children." Despite this, it may be useful to project future trends and developments in the several branches of American Judaism in the light of the present.

The National Jewish Population Study estimates that 82% of the approximately 1,900,000 Jewish householders in the United States (1970) identify with a particular religious orientation. A meager 1.4% regard themselves as "agnostics and atheists," and 2.5% as "not Jewish." Of those 1,900,000 some 40.5% consider themselves Conservative Jews, 30% Reform, 11.4% Orthodox, while 12.2%, including secularist Jews, say they are "just Jewish." Only 44% of those belonging to a particular religious movement are members of a synagogue, but as few as 8% attend religious services every Sabbath or more often. As many as 27% do not attend them at all, while 28% go less than four times a year, evidently only on the High Holy Days and on *Yahrzeit,* the anniversary of the death of a parent or close relative. Thus in his "seventh day absenteeism" the American Jew emulates the poor example of the Protestant majority.

In addition to synagogue attendance, the compliance with traditional dietary practices is a major index of religious piety, at least among the Orthodox (11%) and Conservatives (40%) who officially expect adherence to them. But of this minimum potential of 51% only 28% abide by *Kashruth,* and of those 53% are foreign born. These figures suggest that the next generation of American Jews will reduce its observance of these rituals. The low ratios of synagogue attendance and *kashruth* observance justify the conclusion that traditional Jewish religious life in America is like Mark Twain's river—"a mile wide and an inch deep."

Orthodox Jewry is bound to remain distinct from the other religious alignments, because of its loyalty to Halacha. However, the homogenizing influence of the American environment, the shared interest of all Jews in the State of Israel, as well as the conspicuous return of the Reform movement to Jewish tradition, are factors that will narrow the ideological gap between Conservativism and Reform. This may lead to a common agreement between them along specific lines such as a joint religious calendar which would provide for the celebration of one day of major Jewish festivals by the Conservatives and two days of *Rosh Hashanah* by the Reformers—or similar compromises. Nevertheless the vested institutional interests of the two divisions would most likely keep them apart. As for the Reconstructionists, it would seem that their separate and independent rabbinical school would induce them to continue their own federation within Conservativism as at present.

The most crucial problem facing all shades of American Judaism is the demographic one. The fear of adding to the world's population explosion has resulted in an inordinate number of childless marriages among Jews which, together with the ominously low Jewish birthrate of 2.1 as compared to 2.8 for the Protestants and 3.2 for the Catholics, is a very serious threat to Jewish survival. The Jewish group is consequently aging rapidly with 43% over 50 as against 39% for the general American population; and a median of 36.7 years for the Jews and 30.7 for Americans as a whole. The decline in the level of fertility will reduce not only Jewish school enrollment but also congregational affiliation, for many couples join a synagogue in order to send their children to its school. Since parents often maintain a Jewish home for the sake of the children, this may also affect the Jewish character of the home. These conditions may cumulatively prove catastrophic for a small people like ours which has already lost six million in the Holocaust; and, unless curbed, could bring about a self-inflicted genocide.

A bright spot in this bleak picture is, however, the phenomenal growth of full time Jewish education in America. Its 600 Jewish day schools provide a combined program of Jewish and secular studies to some 100,000 children and teenagers, or 26% of the

Jewish school population. Originally these day schools were a monopoly of the Orthodox, but they now include a network of fifty Conservative Solomon Schechter schools with an attendance of 9,000 pupils and a nucleus of seven Reform day schools with some 750 students. It is noteworthy that about 12% of these schools are on the secondary level. Though part time Jewish schooling is declining, other forms of Jewish education are coming into their own. Among these are the collegiate courses in Judaica, adult study groups, Jewishly motivated summer programs, youth and adults visiting and studying in Israel, and similar projects. These are bound to produce a more Jewishly enlightened leadership that will raise the quality of American Jewish life.

We must, however, bear in mind that demographically we are an endangered species. To cope with this peril, American Jewry should launch a crusade to impress upon its young people the importance of raising families of sufficient size as essential to their own happiness as well as for Jewish survival. We must also exert every effort to convert the losses from the rising tide of inter-marriage, to plusses. We should, moreover, approach these tasks with confidence and an abiding faith in the Jewish future. The traditional symbol of Jewish existence is the frail "*Sukkah* (booth) of David" always falling, yet never collapsing, despite the storms and winds assailing it. As Samuel of old had said: "The Eternal of Israel will not belie it." (I Sam. 15:29)

NOTES

PART ONE

NOTES TO CHAPTER ONE

[1] The great Russian writer Dostoievski once said that if Jesus had returned to earth during the Middle Ages, he would have recoiled with horror at the treatment of his people that he would have witnessed.

[2] In Chaucer's ballad *The Prioress's Tale,* little Hugh of Lincoln (1255) "was laid low by cursed Jews." Eighteen Jews were executed on a charge of ritual murder in that episode.

[3] In 1928, in Massena, New York, a rabbi was questioned on this charge by the state police. Fortunately, the child involved in this incident was found alive.

[4] The term *Kahal* frequently refers to the administrative council of the community.

[5] A *Takkanah* is an enactment promulgated by a rabbinic authority for the public welfare or for the purpose of religious or moral improvement.

[6] There were, *e.g.,* poll taxes, protection and community assessments, fees on marriage, burial, renewal of charter, coronation, and accession of a new pope. Some enactments had ridiculous or humiliating names, as New Year money, the Martinmas goose payment, ale-house imposts, money used to purchase fish for the priests for fast days and pike for the university president during Passion Week. See Ismar Elbogen, *History of the Jews,* p. 141.

[7] Russia's Pale of Settlement was an overcrowded district in Imperial Russia, where Jews were permitted the right of permanent residence. The Jews were hemmed in in the cities and towns of only ten provinces in Poland and fifteen in Russia. The edict creating the Pale dates back to the *Ukaze* (decree) of 1791, issued by Empress Catherine.

[8] Some believe it is a corruption of *Giudecca,* Italian for *Judaica,* while others think that it is related to the Hebrew word, *get* (divorce or separation)—a rather far-fetched notion.

[9] The vital meaning that the Sabbath had acquired in Jewish life led a contemporary Jewish thinker, Ahad Ha-am (1856-1927), to comment that "more than Israel had kept the Sabbath, the Sabbath had kept Israel."

[10] There is some opinion to the effect that because of its educational character, the synagogue was referred to in medieval Germany as the *shule,* from the German *schule* (school). Similarly in Italy, it was called *scuola,* and in Southern France, the *eccolo.* However, others believed that this term

403

is derived from the Latin *schola,* which Italian Jews used to designate their community. This term is used in the sense of "school of thought." According to Dr. Moritz Guideman, the term was borrowed from Christian usage, which avoided calling the synagogue a church.

11 During the Second World War, Hitler revived the ghetto in Poland and other east European countries, but he used it merely as a way station on the road to the extermination centers.

NOTES TO CHAPTER TWO

1 See Charles Singer, "The Nature of Jewish Thought," in Edwyn R. Bevan, *The Legacy of Israel,* p. 173 ff.

2 In England, the need for Hebraic learning was brought to the fore by the controversy on the validity of Henry VIII's (1491-1547) marriage to Catherine of Aragon, who had been espoused earlier to Henry's deceased brother. The dispute revolved about the seemingly contradictory provisions in the Old Testament: one passage (*Lev.* 18:16) apparently prohibiting wedlock between the widow and her deceased husband's brother, another (*Deut.* 25:5) mandating it, if the brother died childless, in order that the deceased's name "be not blotted out from among Israel." If the Levitical law were to prevail, Henry's union with Catherine was improper *ab initio* and could, therefore, be annulled; if the Deuteronomic principle applied, the marriage to Catherine was valid and also permanent, because the New Testament forbade divorce and remarriage. To secure an authoritative interpretation of the meaning of the Biblical passages, Henry VIII turned to Jewish scholars abroad, as there were few, if any, Jews in England after their expulsion in 1290. This situation led Henry to establish a chair of Hebrew at Cambridge in 1540, at the height of the controversy.

3 Werner Sombart, the eminent German economic historian, author of *The Jews and Modern Capitalism* (London: 1913), who adopted a Marxian approach to his analysis of capitalism, regarded it as a Jewish creation. There is little doubt that the Jews played an important role in capitalism, but Sombart viewed their role with a jaundiced eye. He saw an affinity between Judaism and capitalism in its concept of sin and "in its rationalization of life." He attributed its evils to the opportunistic and hostile attitude of the Jews towards the Christians. Little wonder that in the thirties Sombart became a Nazi.

4 Samuel Oppenheimer attained fame as the initiator of the Hebrew collection at the Bodelian Library at Oxford.

5 Of interest also is another argument that the Amsterdam rabbi advanced for the return of the Jews. He had a curious but fervent belief that the Messiah would come if the Jews were dispersed throughout all lands. He saw their continued exclusion from England as a deterrent to the realization of this hope.

6 This eminent family derived its name from the red shield on its home in the Frankfort *Judengasse.*

NOTES TO CHAPTER THREE

[1] He also referred to himself in his Hebrew correspondence as Moses Dessau, after the name of his native city.

[2] The concluding sentence of Kant's *Critique of Practical Reason* may be apropos here: "Two things fill the mind with ever new and increasing admiration and awe, the oftener and the more steadily we reflect on them; the starry heavens above and the moral law within . . . The former begins from the place I occupy in the eternal world of sense and enlarges my connection therein to an unbounded extent with world upon world and system upon system and, moreover, into the limitless times of their periodic motion, its beginnings and continuance. The second begins from my invisible self, my personality, and exhibits me in the world which has true infinity . . . The former view of a countless multitude of worlds annihilates as it were, my importance . . . The second, on the contrary, infinitely elevates my worth as an intelligence by my personality . . . at least as far as may be inferred from the destination assigned to my existence, by this law, a destination not restricted to conditions and limits of this life, but reaching into the infinite."

[3] See Alexander Carlbach, "Autonomy, Heteronomy and Theonomy," *Jewish Life*, Vol. IV, No. 1, Fall 1963, p. 5 ff.

[4] These laws, applicable to pre-Noahides and non-Jews proscribe: 1) idolatry; 2) blasphemy; 3) murder; 4) incest; 5) robbery; 6) lawlessness; 7) eating flesh from a living animal.

[5] The statistics of the period translated Dohm's statement in terms of figures. Of the estimated figure of 300,000 Jews in Germany at the time, about two-thirds were engaged in petty trade and peddling, 10 per cent were domestics, 8 per cent were handworkers, and the remaining 15 per cent in other occupations.

[6] The specification of these three fundamental beliefs evidences the deistic influence in Mendelssohn's thinking. Deism was a school of religious thought popular in seventeenth and eighteenth century England. The deists generally believed in natural rather than supernatural or revealed religion, in providence and in immortality, though not all deists accepted the last-named doctrine. In a later period, deists believed in a deity apart from the world, who left its workings to natural laws. Deism influenced Voltaire, Thomas Paine, Benjamin Franklin, and Thomas Jefferson, among others.

[7] There is a dispute in rabbinic literature as to whether the first verse in the Decalogue (*Ex.* 20:2), beginning with the phrase "I am the Lord thy God," is a precept enjoining belief in God or is an identifying reference, merely indicating the source and the authority for the Decalogue. According to one Talmudic opinion, the initial verse of the Ten Commandments implies an imperative to believe (*Mak.* 23b, 24a). Some medieval scholars, including Maimonides (*Book of Commandments* 1) endorsed this view. On the other hand, there is a Talmudic statement to the effect that the Decalogue begins with the third verse, "Thou shalt have no other gods before Me," and accordingly, the first verse is only of an introductory nature and not a commandment (*Horayoth* 8b). Hasdai Crescas in his *Light of the Lord* (ch. 1) accepts the latter opinion.

⁸ See footnote 4.

⁹ See Chap. 4, p. 87 ff.

¹⁰ This freedom of thought and opinion is demonstrated in the statement in the Talmud (*M. Yevamoth* 1:4 and *Eduyot* 4:8) to the effect that though the schools of Hillel and Shammai disagreed on their interpretations of various phases of the law of marriage and divorce, the members of each school did not hesitate to marry women of the other school whose marital status was determined according to the viewpoint of their opponents.

¹¹ Professor Mordecai M. Kaplan, in speaking of the meaning of dogma says, "When traditional beliefs carry with them the authority of the group which insists that they be accepted as a sign of loyalty and obedience, they acquire the connotation, and nowadays also the odium which is associated with the term, dogma." "On Creeds and Wants" in Leo Schwartz ed. *The Menorah Treasury*, JPS 1964, p. 141.

¹² See Chap. 6, fn. 23.

¹³ The Catholic Herald defended President de Valera's act in sending condolences to the German government on the death of Hitler, in the following terms: "Not only was Mr. de Valera logically and technically correct, but as head of a Christian State he behaved in a perfectly Christian —one might say Christ-like way . . . Hitler was a very wicked and misguided man, but he was not anti-Christ." (Catholic Herald, June 1945, quoted in Isidore Epstein, *The Faith of Judaism*, London: Soncino Press 1960, p. 73)

¹⁴ This is exemplified by Jehoshaphat's exhortation: "Believe in the Lord your God, so that ye shall be established; believe in His prophets and ye will prosper" (II *Chr.* 20:20). It is interesting to note that the same root (*Amn*) is used for the verb "believe" as for "established," showing that the basic meaning of this verb is not *belief* in the creedal sense, but in the sense of "confirmed." The term *Amen* is derived from the same root, and implies a truth confirmed or established. The root, *Amn* and derivative verbs are used in the same sense in other places in Hebrew Scriptures.

There is a difference of opinion in rabbinic literature as to whether the reliance on the Deity is to be the result of a knowledge of Him or merely of tradition (cabbala) a faith or belief transmitted from one generation to another. Characteristically, the Hebrew Bible generally encourages the *knowledge* of God and does not mention belief as such. Moses pleaded with God, "Show me Thy ways, that I may *know* Thee," (*Ex.* 33:13), or "*Know* this day and lay it to thy heart, that the Lord, He is God in heaven above and upon the earth beneath; there is none else" (*Deut.* 4:39). Isaiah speaks of "the *knowledge* of the Lord, as the waters cover the seas" (*Is.* 11:9); Jeremiah envisages God as saying "but let him that glorieth, glory in this that he understandeth and knoweth Me" (*Jer.* 9:23). A knowledge or understanding of God is, of course, the result of an intellectual or rational process rather than the outcome of a creedal faith. In fact, a medieval philosopher, Bachya (ca. 1050) stated that "He who can investigate the subject of God's existence and unity through reason, is obligated to do so, as far as his mental powers permit" (*Duties of the Heart*, Gate of Unity, Chap. 3). Maimonides suggested that those who cannot arrive at an understanding of the Deity through a rational process must do so through *cabbala*, that is the acceptance of doctrines or teachings transmitted by earlier generations (*Guide* 1:33). Some medieval sages such as Judah Halevi maintained, however, that tradition is more desirable in this regard than reason (*Kuzari* 5:21).

[15] cf. Albo *Sefer Ha-Ikkarim* 1:4 ff.

[16] Some scholars like Leopold Low (1811-75), Solomon Schechter (1850-1915), and Kaufman Kohler (1843-1926) opposed Mendelssohn's view on the question of dogmas in Judaism. In his essay on this subject (*Studies in Judaism,* pp. 180-181) Schechter insisted that, "Judaism regulates not only our actions but also our thoughts. We usually urge that in Judaism, religion means life, but we forget that a life without guiding principles or thoughts is not worth living." Schechter conceded, however, that Judaism does not ascribe any saving power to belief in these dogmas (p. 147). Are these dogmas, then, in the Christian sense of the term? The answer would appear to be in the negative.

[16a] See chap. V p. 107.

[17] The Jewish idea of the hereafter is very vague. In general, it is the opposite of the concept of "this world." See George Foote Moore, *Judaism,* Vol. II, page 389.

[18] There is some opinion to the effect that the phrase, "is not derived from the Torah," is an interpolation. In this form it could be used as a weighty argument against the Sadducees who did not subscribe to this doctrine of resurrection. The rabbis who held that it originated in the Torah base their claim on *Deuteronomy* 32:39 which represents God as saying, "I shall kill and make alive." This phrase, however, is generally assumed to be an allusion to God's power of life and death over his creatures, rather than the doctrine of resurrection. Actually, the only clear Biblical assertion of this doctrine is in *Daniel* 12:2 which is ascribed to the Maccabean period (ca. 165 B.C.E.). See also Soncino Talmud, *Sanhedrin,* Vol. II, p. 604. note 12.

[18a] The twelfth article dealing with the Messianic expectation became especially popular in recent decades because it represented the death song sung by Jewish martyrs in the Nazi extermination camps, as they were led to the gas chambers and crematoria. It is a remarkable commentary on the invincible spirit of the Jew that these victims of cruelty and barbarism found the courage to proclaim an abiding faith and hope for the improvement of a humanity that failed them, rather than seek comfort in the hope of a more blissful after-life, represented in the last of Maimonides' Thirteen Articles of Faith.

[19] From the first fundamental, the existence of God, is derived the notion of His unity, incorporeality, eternity and freedom from defect. The second principle, revelation, implies the belief in the omniscience of God, the selection of the prophets as His media for revelation and the truth of their utterances. The third doctrine, retribution, is the source of the belief in Providence. From the *Sharashim* or roots emerge six *Anafim* or branch doctrines, viz., creation ex nihilo, the supremacy of Moses' prophecy, the immutability of the Mosaic law, the observance of the commandments, resurrection and the coming of the Messiah.

[20] See Chapter 5. p. 109ff.

[21] *Sefer Ha-Ikkarim* 3:20, 23.

22 The Sephardim maintained a combined curriculum in the school they established and conducted in Amsterdam a century earlier.

23 It is said that when the deadline for registration of Jewish family names arrived, those who had not selected one themselves were given names of birds, minerals, flowers. That is said to account for some curious family names among Jews. The Jews were prohibited from assuming Christian names.

24 Not until 1848 were the Austrian Jews again granted a substantial number of civic rights, and not until 1866 did they attain legal equality.

25 Mendelssohn once said humorously that, as a Jew, on crossing into Dresden he had to pay a *Leibzoll* (body tax) which "appraised a German philosopher at the same value as a Polish cow."

26 He had also translated Menasseh ben Israel's appeal to Cromwell into German.

27 One of Mendelssohn's grandsons was the noted composer, Felix Mendelssohn-Bartholdy.

28 The mourner's prayer of "sanctification" recited in the synagogue.

29 Typical is the case of the two daughters of the wealthy Jew, Moses Isaacs of Berlin (d. 1776), who were cut off in his will if they married non-Jews. They did so after his death and contested the will on the ground that in converting to Christianity they did not repudiate God or religion; that Christianity is an ethical and moral faith; and that their father the testator could, therefore, not have intended to exclude them from their inheritance for joining the church.

30 See Chap. 8.

NOTES TO CHAPTER FOUR

1 See Chapter 3, p. 57.

2 See p. 112ff.

3 It is of interest to note that the French representative encountered opposition to his mission to win civic equality for the Jews not only on the part of the Dutch elements, but also from Jewish leaders, who feared that complete emancipation would draw Jews away from their religious life.

4 In Portugal, the Inquisition had been overthrown earlier, in 1820, when several thousand Marranos openly returned to Judaism, after their families had been practicing their religion in secret for about three centuries.

5 The questions were:

    1. Are Jews permitted to marry several wives?

    2. Does the Jewish law permit divorce? Is such divorce recognized if received without civil sanction or if obtained by laws which are in opposition to the French code?

    3. May a Jew or Jewess marry a Christian or does Jewish law restrict marriage only between Jews?

    4. Do the Jewish people consider the French their brothers, or aliens?

    5. In either case, what are the obligations of the Jews towards Frenchmen of other faiths?

6. Do the native Jews of France who are regarded as French citizens by French law regard France as their Fatherland? Do they regard themselves as obligated to defend it? Are they obliged to obey the laws and the requirements of the Civil Code?

7. Who appoints the rabbis?

8. What judicial powers do the rabbis exercise over the Jews, and with what authority do they do so?

9. Does their authority rest upon written laws or upon tradition?

10. Are there any vocations prohibited to the Jews by their religion?

11. Does their law forbid the exaction of usury from other Jews?

12. Does this law forbid the exaction of usury from their non-Jewish fellow citizens?

⁶ *Pesach* (Passover), a spring festival, is linked with the liberation of the Israelites from Egyptian bondage. *Shavuoth* (the Feast of Weeks, the Day of First Ripe Fruit) is also identified with the giving of the Torah to Israel. *Succoth* (the Festival of Booths) is observed as the autumn harvest festival, but it commemorates, too, the sojourn of the Hebrews in the wilderness. The minor religious holidays are associated primarily with historic events, also reflecting the close tie between the Jewish group and its faith.

⁷ The Jewish group may be presently described as a nation, or a political polity, only in the State of Israel.

⁸ The sentiments that Jews entertain for their fellow Jews in other lands can perhaps be better understood by our generation than it could have a century or more ago, for our horizons today are international in scope and no longer circumscribed by a narrow brand of nationalism.

⁹ Despite this, Reform Judaism in France made little headway in the preceding or even the current century. Traditional Judaism, however, also lost ground among the native French Jews. This may be due in a degree to the fact that religion generally had lost its hold in France.

¹⁰ The major faiths, it might be observed, similarly interdict a marital union with one belonging to another religion. The Roman Emperor from the fourth century on, and Christian Church councils from the sixth to the thirteenth century have repeatedly prohibited mixed marriages. Since the nineteenth century, however, most European countries and all of the American states make provision for such marriages.

¹¹ After 1831, the state took over this expense.

¹² The voluntary Consistoire Central is made up of local consistories throughout France and formerly also in Algeria. Moderate traditionalism prevails; the sexes are separated but organ music and mixed choirs are common. The rigidly Orthodox element is outside the Consistory, though it maintains good relations with it. The Reform movement is very small. There is, however, a sharp cleavage between the Sephardic Algerian Orthodoxy and the Ashkenazic French Jewry, due to different background and customs. With the influx of over a quarter of a million Jews from Algeria, there are now about half a million Jews in France; about 60% Ashkenazic and 40% Sephardic. See *American Jewish Year Book* vol. 66 (1965) p. 374 ff.

PART TWO

NOTE TO PRELUDE

[1] It should be borne in mind that aside from the religious, there is a nonreligious culturist or secular viewpoint in Jewish life which came to the fore at about the same time as the major religious opinions. It was Moses Hess (1812-1878) who first expounded the theory of Jewish secular nationalism in his *Rome and Jerusalem,* published in German. It may be noted parenthetically that this was the same year that Rabbi Zevi Hirsch Kalisher (1795-1874) wrote his *Derishat Zion,* espousing what might be described as the idea of religious nationalism.

Hess was a socialist who had broken with his friend Karl Marx on the issue of dialectical materialism. In its place Hess advocated his own theory of spiritual and ethical socialism, which omitted the principle of the class war, so prominent in Marx's thinking. Hess maintained that the Jews were a nation who should return to their ancestral soil and create there the ideal socialist state as a model to the world. In Jewish nationalism, Hess saw the promise of Jewish survival and the regeneration of the Jewish homeland as a refuge from both physical and spiritual oppression. Hess saw Judaism as a *culture* rather than as a religion, for Judaism possesses humanistic values, a great ethical literature, a language and history, folklore—in sum, the makings of a distinct culture. He saw this civilization as the product of the creative genius of the Jewish people, among whom it forms an indissoluble bond.

Hess's nationalistic ideas, as that of a contemporary, Peretz Smolenskin, (1842-1880), were influenced by the general nationalistic climate permeating Europe in their days. Smolenskin had left his native Lithuania and settled in Vienna, a center of numerous nationalist groups. He incorporated his ideas in his *Am Olam* (Eternal People) which became a classic of Jewish nationalism in Eastern Europe. Despite the secular character of Jewish nationalism, it made an impact on various Jewish groups. This viewpoint persists today among a substantial segment of Jewry.

NOTES TO CHAPTER FIVE

[1] Leo Jung, "Major Aspects of Judaism" in Leo Jung ed. *Judaism in a Changing World,* pp. 3-4.

[2] The term *Torah* is sometimes used in its broadest sense to include the entire range of religious literature to the present day.

[3] The Scribes were the expositors of the Torah in the Babylonian exile (586-536 B.C.E.) and subsequently after the restoration in Palestine as well. They were the forerunners of the rabbis.

[4] The Biblical verse, "Hear O Israel, the Lord our God, the Lord is One!" (*Deut.* 6:4), has been the epitome of Judaism through the ages.

[5] The phrase "command you" was said to be an allusion to the oral law.

[6] This is said to be derived from the verse "And thou shalt show them the way wherein they shall walk" (*Ex.* 18:20).

7 The *Mishna* is not the only collection of laws incorporating the discussions of the laws in the Palestinian *Yeshivot* (academies). There are other collections scattered in various works made by younger colleagues or contemporaries of Rabbi Judah (d.ca. 217). Among them are the compilations of Rabbi Nathan Bar Kappara and Rabbi Hiyya, which contain laws omitted by Rabbi Judah. Prominent among them are the *Braitha* (external laws) and the *Tosefta* (additional laws).

8 The collections of *responsa* in post-Geonic times are generally divided into two stages. The first one, extending from the eleventh to the end of the fourteenth century—a time which roughly coincides with the invention of printing—is referred to as the period of the *Rishonim* (earlier scholars). The second, running from the fifteenth century to our own period, is described as the period of the *Aharonim* (later scholars). Many hundreds of thousands of *responsa* have been collected during these centuries. See Solomon B. Freehof, *The Responsa Literature,* JPS, 1955.

9 His Hebrew name was Moshe ben Maimon.

10 The letters of the Hebrew alphabet have numerical values. Thus, *Aleph* is 1, *Bet* is 2, *Gimel* 3, *Daled* 4, etc. The letter *Yud* represents ten, and *Yud Daled* or 10 and 4 signify 14.

11 However, in his philosophical work, *The Guide to the Perplexed* (III:32), Maimonides pointed out that the sacrificial cult in ancient Judaism was mainly a concession to the mores of the times, to keep the Jews from resorting to pagan worship. The explanation for this inconsistency may be that Maimonides felt that he should include all the laws of the Torah in his code, since he intended the *Yad* as a popular text for the rank and file in Jewry, who would not understand the omission of what they regarded as part of the Mosaic law. In his *Guide to the Perplexed,* which was designed for the intellectual elite, Maimonides did not hesitate to speak his rationalistic mind more candidly.

12 *Mishneh Torah: The Book of Judges* Treatise V, 12:5.

13 *Berlin Monatschrift,* Vol. XXV, p. 530, quoted by H. D. Schmidt in "The Terms of the Emancipation 1781-1812," in Yearbook I, *Leo Baeck Institute,* 1956, p. 30. However, it has been generally assumed that this term was first used by Furtado, president of the Assembly of Notables, at the sessions of the Assembly in 1806.

14 David de Sola Pool "Judaism and the Synagogue" in Oscar Janowsky ed. *The American Jew,* p. 35.

15 Many Protestant denominations including the Archbishop of Canterbury, and the Free Church Council, representing the other denominations, denounced this dogma, as being without Scriptural basis or without any foundation in the ecumenical creeds.

16 Catholic Encyclopedia, Vol. III, p. 752, New York, 1908.

17 See *Mishneh Torah: Hilkot Melachim* 11:4 (unexpurgated edition based on Roman Ms.) Jerusalem, Mossad Harav Kook, 1955.

18 The cases of Spinoza and da Costa were exceptional situations. The Jewish community in Amsterdam, established only some decades earlier, feared that unless they took definitive steps to show their displeasure with those not abiding by the tenets of Judaism, they would be suspected of harboring atheists in their midst. Such a charge, they believed, might endanger the status of tolerance they enjoyed.

19 Dr. Israel H. Levinthal, a leading Conservative rabbi and outstanding homiletist, points out that the *Tannaim* used the word "syag" or "hedge," rather than "geder" meaning fence. A fence around a garden, he explains, protects it, but the fence also obstructs the view. A hedge, however, not only protects the garden but adorns it. Dr. Levinthal criticizes the Reformers for discarding all hedges and abandoning the "garden of Jewish life for all to tread upon it as they will," thereby destroying the garden. The Orthodox, on the other hand, he points out, propose the erection of higher fences, not realizing that in this manner they "conceal the charm of the garden from the sight of the viewer." Moreover, a high fence may defeat its purpose, for as one ancient sage warns, it may "fall and destroy the very plants which it was supposed to protect." Israel H. Levinthal, *Point of View,* An Analysis of American Judaism, New York: Abelard-Schuman, 1958, pp. 53-54.

20 The official chain of *Semicha* or ordination was abolished ca. 350. It could be reinstated, according to Maimonides, by the unanimous agreement of all scholars in the Jewish homeland. The restoration of the formal traditional *Semicha* would endow its recipients with the right not only to interpret the Halacha, but also to mould it, as the rabbis of the Talmud did. The only attempt to re-establish formal ordination was made by Jacob Berab (1474-1546) an older contemporary of Caro in Safed, but this was not successful.

21 *Sepharad* is mentioned in *Obadiah* (1:20) as a place name. Actually Sardis in Asia Minor is meant. There is an allusion to *Ashkenaz* in *Genesis* (10:3) as the grandson of Japhet, supposedly the ancestor of the Ashkenazim. In *Jeremiah* (51:27), *Ashkenaz* is the name of a region. The name *Sepharad* has been used for Spain since Geonic times. *Ashkenaz* has been used for Germany since the Crusades.

22 It has been suggested that *Sepharad* might have been associated with Hesperia which bears a sound resemblance to Iberia or to Bosporus. The latter, of course, could not be Spain. Similarly, *Ashkenaz* might be related to Saxony, as a common name for all of Germany. See Salo W. Baron, *A Social and Religious History of the Jews,* Vol. IV, JPS 1957, pp. 3-4.

23 Modern Hebrew as spoken in the State of Israel employs the Sephardic pronunciation which had been preserved in the Holy Land by the oriental communities that had continued there for centuries. The Ashkenazic Jews who came to Israel adopted this pronunciation.

NOTES TO CHAPTER SIX

1 The term *Cabbala* (reception) refers to the body of mystical thought and interpretation of the Scriptures, developed since the seventh century. It suggests that the esoteric teachings had been received and transmitted from ancient sources.

Its chief work, the *Zohar,* probably compiled by Moses ben Shem Tov Leon (ca. 1250-1305), was attributed by him to Rabbi Simon ben Yochai who lived in the second century.

2 Some prefer to translate it as the "Master of the Good Name."

3 Literally "room," the school usually occupying a room in the teacher's home.

⁴ This is one of the reasons that the historicity of the Besht, like that of Moses, Jesus, Buddha, and other religious leaders has been doubted. (See e.g. Ephraim Deinard, *Alatah*, (Darkness) New Orleans, 1930). There seems, however, to be little ground for any such opinion, particularly in the case of the Besht.

⁵ A *Tzaddik* (righteous) is a term used to denote a charismatic Hassidic leader. See p. 129ff.

⁶ The Cabbalistic symbol of sin is the *Kelipah* (shell) which should be cast away.

⁷ In Hebrew, the letters *Tzadi* and *Zayin* are frequently interchangeable.

⁸ Judah Leib Peretz, "If not Higher," in *Stories and Pictures,* translated by Helena Frank, JPS 1936.

⁹ He later adopted the family name, Schneerson. His descendants still bear this name.

¹⁰ Translated by Nissan Mindel, New York: Kehot Publication Society, 1962.

¹¹ *Ari* means lion. Initials of name stand for Ashkenazi Rabbi Isaac (Luria) (1534-1572), who introduced special preliminary prayers and *Kavanoth* (concentrations or meditations) deemed to be effective in bringing about the Messianic redemption.

¹¹ᵃ A similar supererogation may be discerned in the title of *Tzaddik,* which they bestowed on their leaders.This term reflects an extraordinary degree of piety, ethical merit and spiritual attainment.

¹² The date of his release, the nineteenth of *Kislev,* is still observed as a holiday by the Lubavitcher Hassidim, as the *Habad* Hassidim are now known.

¹³ Buber regarded Christianity in its early stages as a Jewish ideology, which was later corrupted through the intrusion of alien elements.

¹⁴ In a limited sense, this concept may be applied to art or nature. One may be struck with awe by a landscape and give vent to the feelings it arouses within him. The landscape may be said to be speaking to him metaphorically. It merely affords him an experience, which though living and impressive, is only passive. It is the individual who projects his feelings to the object; but there is no active response or address on its part, and the bond is thus not complete.

¹⁵ From *Kivun,* (intention, direction, or concentration). Kierkegaard, for example, advocated a complete abandonment to the Absolute, a doctrine which led him to the logical necessity of breaking off his engagement with the girl he loved. As a result, he was pursued by a sense of guilt throughout the last decade and a half of his short life.

¹⁶ Martin Buber, *Hassidism and Modern Man,* ed. and trans. by Maurice Friedman, New York: Horizon Press, 1958, p. 233.

¹⁷ Cf. *I John* 4:20.

¹⁸ Martin Buber, *Hassidism,* New York: Philosophical Library, 1948, pp. 168-175.

¹⁹ Martin Buber, *Two Types of Faith,* pp. 157-158.

²⁰ Martin Buber, "The Faith of Judaism" in *Israel and the World,* 1948. p. 17.

²¹ Martin Buber, *Hassidism,* New York: Philosophical Library, 1948, p. 96.

22 Martin Buber, *Two Types of Faith,* p. 57ff.
23 "A man is not justified by the works of the Law, but by the faith of Jesus Christ." (*Gal.* 2:16). Note the numerous passages in the New Testament disparaging the law, such as *Gal.* 2:4, 21; *Rom.* 10:4. Paul maintained the law, is intended chiefly for criminals and sinners (*I Tim.* 1:8ff).
24 Buber, *op. cit.,* fn. 22, pp. 7-12, pp. 57ff.
25 Ernst Simon, *Martin Buber;* in Jewish Frontier XV, Feb. 1948, p. 26.
26 Buber, *op. cit.,* fn. 22, p. 96ff.
27 Martin Buber, "Religion and Ethics" in *Eclipse of God,* tr. by Maurice S. Friedman et al. New York: Harper Torchbooks, 1959, p. 126.
28 Hess in his *Rome and Jerusalem* (Tenth Letter) has alluded to this trait in Judaism. Samson Raphael Hirsch also confirmed this characteristic in Judaism when he referred to the Jewish calendar as the religion of the Jew. This quality has been illustrated by the example of the Jew living in a cold northern climate, building even there a *Succah* (booth) in commemoration of the sojourn of his ancestors in the desert over three thousand years ago. Thus, a Jew hallows time.

NOTES TO CHAPTER SEVEN

1 See Chapter 3, fn. 6.
2 Some regarded Friedlander's idea as an attempt to "Judaize the Church." What he may have had in mind was the creation of a Jewish sect in Christianity, which if it materialized might have been more injurious to Judaism than total apostasy.
3 A leading Protestant theologian of the time, Friedrich Schleiermacher (1768-1834), entered the discussion with a brochure in which he contended that it was actually impossible for the would-be proselytes to become wholehearted Christians. Aside from their religious attachments, their ethnic or nationalistic differences were bound to prove an insurmountable barrier to complete absorption by the Christian majority.
4 Traditionally the rabbis had preached in the synagogue only twice a year: on *Shabbath Shuva,* (Sabbath of Repentance), immediately preceding *Yom Kippur,* (The Day of Atonement), and on the *Great Sabbath* which comes directly before the beginning of the Passover festival. These semiannual sermons were devoted primarily to discourses on religious law and observance rather than to the kind of ethical exhortations that formed the content of the church sermons, which Jacobson emulated. Sermons outside the regular service were delivered by *Magidim* (preachers).
5 See Chap. 4, p. 91.
6 By the Edict of March 11, 1812, the Jewish religion in Prussia was merely to be tolerated and not officially recognized. This, of course, applied to the Jewish religious functionaries as well.
7 See Chapter 9, fn. 3; also p. 219.
8 The name was derived from a phrase in *Isaiah* 62:1.
9 It has been said that Liebermann later converted and entered the service of Pope Pius IX, to whom he was of great value because of his Talmudic erudition. There is, however, reason to believe that this Eliezer Liebermann was confused with one Jacob Lieberman, who, like Eliezer, was a rabbi's

son. (See Joseph Klausner, *Historia Shel Hasifrut Haivrit Hahadasha,* Second Ed., Vol. II, Jerusalem 1952, p. 111, note 4.) Jacob Lieberman was canonized by the Church in 1919. Of Lieberman the apostate, it is told that when his brother, a rabbi, observed the traditional period of mourning customarily kept by the family of an apostate, the convert came to pay him a condolence call. The latter has also been said to have intervened with the Vatican at various times on behalf of his former coreligionists—a mode of conduct which is not at all typical of apostates in Jewish history.

10 A reference to *Deut.* 28:69.

11 Known as the *Hatam-Sofer* after the title of his major work. In his volume of *responsa,* he conceded that there is no distinct prohibition in Jewish law against worshipping with uncovered head. This is merely an age-old custom which he believed should be respected and followed as such. See also Chap. 9, fn. 21.

12 Reference to *Lev.* 26:25.

13 Reference to *Ecc.* 3:7.

14 See p. 365.

15 Actually, the first halting steps in this direction were taken not in Germany but in Amsterdam, where in 1796, a new congregation was founded which omitted from the prayer book the numerous and involved *piyutim,* the medieval liturgical poems superimposed on the basic structure of the service. At that time, Holland was under French control and influence.

16 See Chap. 8, p. 202ff.

17 S. Holdheim *Über die Autonomie der Rabbinen und das Prinzip der Jüdischen Ehe.* Schwerin 1843, *Vorwort* p. 7.

18 At the Breslau rabbinical conference (1846), Holdheim resorted to another farfetched analogy to find support for his transfer of the principal service from the Sabbath to Sunday. He cited the Biblical verse (*Nu.* 9:10) which permits one who was "unclean" or "on a far journey" to defer the Passover offering, as the precedent on which he relied (*Protokolle der* 3 *Rabbinische Konferenz,* pp. 70-73). Holdheim later held both Sabbath and Sunday services.

19 *Maamar Al Dvar Halshut,* Berlin: 1861, p. 21.

20 See Chap. 4. p. 85.

21 Until the middle of the fourth century C.E., the beginning of the Jewish month was fixed on the testimony of witnesses who observed the phases of the moon, since the Jewish calendar is a lunar one. Though the beginning of the Jewish month has since been determined on the basis of mathematical computations, the custom of observing two days of a festival, based on the earlier pattern, continued as a tradition in the Diaspora.

22 David Philipson, *The Reform Movement in Judaism,* New York, Macmillan, 1931.

23 *Ibid.* p. 430.

NOTES TO CHAPTER EIGHT

1 The slogan of the Crusades, "Hep-Hep," probably stood for "Hieroso-lyma est perdita!" (Jerusalem is destroyed!)

2 Zunz soon had further occasion to use his research talents for practical purposes. The Prussian government enacted a law to restrict the Jews to their old traditional names, as a means of enabling the authorities to iden-tify them easily as Jews. Traditional names, the government claimed, were in line with common Jewish usage. Zunz's work on Jewish names, published in 1837, proved that Jews had always borrowed their names from the people among whom they lived and that the use of other non-Jewish names is not a deviation from Jewish practice, as the edict assumed. As a result of this study, the Prussian law was modified to prohibit Jews from using purely Christian names like Peter, Christian, and the like, but they were permitted to employ other names. At the time, also, of the blood libel in Damascus in 1840, Zunz refuted the contention that the Talmud permitted the use of blood by the Jews.

3 The medieval liturgical poetry added to the basic structure of the service.

4 *More Nebuchei Hazman*, Warsaw, ed. 1894, (Gate 13) p. 201.

5 The Orthodox rabbis objected to Frankel's assertion that the oft-quoted Talmudic phrase, *Halacha L'Moshe M'Sinai* (law received from Moses at Sinai) refers to ancient regulations, some even antedating the Theophany,—whose origin had been forgotten. For this reason, they were credited to the Sinaitic revelation, though they were not actually a part of it. The Orthodox insisted, of course, on a literal rather than a liberal interpretation of this, as of other, traditions. They adhered to the dictum (*Meg.* 19b) that "God showed Moses the inferences of the Torah and the inferences of the Scribes and the innovations which were to be introduced (in the future) by the Scribes." A similar statement appears in the Jerusa-lem Talmud (*Peah.* 6a) to the effect that "even what a competent student is bound to innovate was already said at Sinai."

6 The *Monatschrift* continued almost until the Second World War.

7 With some variations, the Jews' oath was administered throughout Germany in the synagogue in the presence of a tribunal of three, or a *minyan* (quorum of ten male Jews required for public worship). The de-ponent was required to wear a *talis* (prayer shawl) and *tephillin* (phylac-teries) and sometimes even shrouds, and invoke upon himself the curses of *Lev.* 26:16ff. and *Deut.* 27:13ff. the ten plagues of Egypt, as well as the leprosy of Naaman (2*K.* 5:27) and similar imprecations.

8 The Mishna (*Yoma.* 8:9) specifically declares that for transgressions between man and God, the Day of Atonement effects atonement, but for transgressions between man and his fellow man, the Day of Atonement effects atonement *only if one has appeased his fellow man.* Accordingly, the *Kol Nidre* cancels only religious, not civil, obligations. There was, therefore, no valid ground for this oath.

9 An example of customary law is the common-law symbolic transfer of the physical possession or ownership of real property known as *livery of seisin.* The seller—either actually on the land or in sight of it—delivers a twig or clod to the purchaser as a token of sale. This is suggestive of the

ancient method of transferring title to a field by the removal of a shoe, described in the Bible (*Ruth* 4:7, 8). After this latter practice fell into disuse, a kerchief passed from the seller to the purchaser became the token of a completed transaction in the sale of real or personal property. This custom is still practiced today among pious Jews.

10 Schechter explained his terms *Tradition* and *Secondary Meaning* of the Scriptures in the following passage: "Jewish tradition or . . . the Oral Law, or as we may term it, (in consideration of its claims to represent an interpretation of the Bible,) the Secondary Meaning of the Scriptures, is mainly embodied in the works of the Rabbis and their subsequent followers during the Middle Ages." (*Studies in Judaism*, First Series, Introduction, p. XV).

11 The scribes were the early interpreters of the Torah from Ezra (ca. 450 B.C.E.) until the Tannaitic teachers recorded in the Mishna.

12 *Studies in Judaism*, First Series, Introduction, pp. XVII-XIX.

13 Essay on Zacharia Frankel in *Students, Scholars and Saints*, JPS, 1945, pp. 206-207.

14 Actually the original dictum may have been intended literally to indicate that dispersion made it impossible to annihilate Jewry, for while one Jewish center was destroyed, another may have flourished. The Reform interpretation of this dictum diverged from the simple textual meaning.

15 *Literaturblatt des Orients* (1842), p. 363.

16 The viewpoint of the liberal Gabriel Riesser (1806-1863), who hoped to gain Jewish emancipation as part of the general struggle for political democracy, was more frank and logical. He did not associate the struggle for Jewish emancipation with Jewish nationalism but simply indicated that since German Jews generally gave up their Jewish national interests, there was little point in praying for the return to Zion. He insisted, however, that there was nothing contradictory in such a prayer with the ideals of German patriotism. So long as one was a German citizen, he owed his complete allegiance to Germany, but if he wished to leave his native land and adopt another, it was proper for him to relinquish his citizenship there and transfer his loyalty to another state.

17 In one of his letters in *Tzir Neaman*, Prague, 1830, p. 14.

18 Essay on *Lo Zeh Ha-Derech* (1889) in *Al Parashat Drachim*, Vol. I, Berlin: Juedischer Verlag, 1921; Leon Simon trans., "The Wrong Way" in *Ten Essays on Judaism and Zionism*, London, Routledge, 1922.

19 See Bernfeld, *Toldot HaReformazion B'Yisroel*, Warsaw, 1908, p. 169.

20 *Op.cit.*, fn. 17.

21 Graetz, *History of the Jews*, JPS, 1895, Vol. V, pp. 682-683.

22 It may be of interest to note that in denouncing the Berlin temple's adoption of the Sunday service, the traditionalists pointed to the fact that the Christians in the early centuries had taken a similar step in order to distinguish themselves from practicing Jews. A critic of the Berlin temple, Moses Mendelssohn of Hamburg, ridiculed the substitution of Sunday for the Sabbath worship in a parody he based on Alkabetz's liturgical poem, the *L'cho Dodi*, recited at the traditional Sabbath eve service:

> Come my beloved, with chorus of praise
> Welcome Bride Sunday, (Sabbath) the Queen of Days.

23 The Berlin congregation remained the only congregation in Germany that followed so extreme a course.

24 *E.g.* "And thou shalt be buried at a ripe old age" (*Gen.* 15:15)) was translated, "Thou shalt be *supported* in ripe old age." . . . See also Jacob Gorov in *Hadoar,* Vol. 43, No. 12 (Jan. 18, 1963) p. 192 for a reference to other errors.

25 David Philipson, *Reform Movement in Judaism,* p. 255.

26 See Chap. 5, p. 101.

27 *Megillat Taanit,* M. 10.

28 Often referred to by the initials of his Hebrew name as *Shir.*

29 See Chap. 5, p. 105.

30 Literally, "generations."

31 A quotation from *Isaiah* 3:12.

32 An allusion to observances which Reform had discarded.

33 A sect in Judaism that was founded by or came into prominence with the publication of Anan ben David's (d.ca. 800) *Book of Precepts.* This sect adhered to the Bible only and repudiated the Talmud. There are still a scattered few survivors of the group, mainly in Russia and Turkey.

34 The Samaritans were perhaps the first dissenting sect in Israel, having separated completely from Jews and Judaism around the fifth century B.C.E. when they built their own temple on Mt. Gerisim. They accepted only the Pentateuch from among the books of the Hebrew Bible. A meager remnant of several hundred still survives, most of whom reside in or around Nablus, near their sacred mountain, the ancient center of their history.

35 At the Frankfort Conference, Geiger, who presided, referred to Rapoport's letters to the Conference, but did not read them, ostensibly because they were written in Hebrew. Geiger announced that they would be made available to those who wished to read them, but this did not occur.

NOTES TO CHAPTER NINE

1 The extreme pietists still object to a secular training for their sons, since they regard general culture as Judah Halevi (1085-1140) described it, "only as an ornament, not fruit but flowers." Some ultra-Orthodox Jews even today allow only their daughters but not their sons to engage in secular study, insisting that their sons must not waste precious time on such frills, but should devote themselves to Jewish learning exclusively.

2 He was popularly known as the *Hatam Sofer,* a name derived from the phrase in *Daniel* 12:4, the initial letters of which stand for the Hebrew title of his major work, *Hidushei Teshuvot Mosheh Sofer,* (*The Novellae and Responsa of Moses Sofer*). See Eliezer Katz, *Ha-Hatam Sofer,* Jerusalem; Mosad Harav Kook, 1960, p. 131ff.

3 Bernays generally used the Sephardic title of *Chacham* (sage) rather than the Ashkenazic *rabbi* (master) as a means of pointing up his secular educational attainments, which distinguished him from the typical rabbi of his day.

4 West European and American Orthodoxy today generally subscribe to this Neo-Orthodoxy.

5 See Chap. 7, p. 159.

6 See fn. 1.

7 See Chap. 7, p. 173ff.

8 It might be noted in passing that Abraham Geiger urged that as soon as a group of Reform Jews agreed to throw off the yoke of Talmudic Judaism, they should petition the government for permission to form a separate community. Thus Geiger also appears to have been opposed to state-enforced membership in the Jewish community. (Geiger, *Posthumous Writings,* Vol. 2, p. 55.)

9 *Chukim* have been defined as laws not grounded in reason, and *Mishpatim,* as those which are so grounded.

10 For a bibliography of his writings, see S. R. Hirsch, *Judaism Eternal,* Vol. I, tr. by Dr. I. Grunfeld, London: Soncino Press, 1956, pp. XLIX ff.

11 *Horeb*: 7:34. This statement is reminiscent of a similar one in Judah Halevi's *Kuzari* 1:86. Since *Ex.* 12:37 refers to six hundred thousand men, Hirsch calculated an average of three more persons in each family, or about two and a half million souls.

12 S. R. Hirsch, *Nineteen Letters of Ben Uziel,* tr. by Bernard Drachman, New York; Funk and Wagnalls, fn. p. 19. This method is reminiscent of some of Philo's allegorizations of Biblical names, *e.g. Israel* refers to the "man who saw God" (*Ish raah el*).

13 Grunfeld, *Horeb,* (English translation) Vol. I, London: Soncino Press, 1962, p. LVIII.

14 "Hebrew Instruction as General Education" in Grunfeld, tr., *op. cit.,* fn. 10, p. 195.

15 In applying this technique, Philo employed the system used by the Stoics in their attempt to harmonize the Homeric myths with the doctrines of philosophy.

16 See *e.g. Judaism Eternal,* Vol. I, *op. cit.,* 108ff.

17 *Horeb*:68:454. Maimonides maintained that the purpose of the dietary laws is to curb the appetite of man as a disciplinary measure.

18 *Ibid.,* 57:409.

19 Josephus believed that the prohibition of cross-breeding was a means of discouraging moral perversion among human beings.

20 Maimonides classified the laws prohibiting shaving of the beard under the heading of idolatrous worship; those against *Shatnez* as designed to avoid emulating the practices of the Amorites; those against a man's wearing a woman's garments as aiming to prevent improper sex conduct.

21 *Horeb* 69:458, 461. It may be of interest to note that an outstanding rabbinic authority, Solomon Luria (1510-1573), held that though we may pray bareheaded, he would refrain from doing so *mipnei marit ayin* (*i.e.* for appearance sake) out of consideration for others who might be offended because they believe it to be a violation. In Jewish tradition, it should be indicated that a custom assumes the force of law. (Freehof, *The Responsa Literature,* JPS, 1955, p. 129; also by the same author, *A Treasury of Responsa,* JPS, 1963, p. 183.) The Talmudic authorities on this question are reviewed in these sources. According to Lauterbach (*CCAR Journal,* Vol. 38, p. 589 ff.) Elijah, Gaon of Vilna, concurred in this view.

22 The attitude of Rashi towards the rite of the red heifer (*Nu.* 19) is indicative of the devout Jew's approach to ritual practices generally. According to Rashi, God presumably says, "It is an enactment before Me and you have no right to reflect on it." In other words, there is no need for justifying God's commandments.

[23] Grunfeld, tr., *Horeh, op. cit.* fn. 13, Introduction, p. LXXX.

[24] S. R. Hirsch, *The Nineteen Letters of Ben Uziel,* tr. by Bernard Drachman, New York: Funk and Wagnalls, 1898, pp. 18-20.

[25] *Ibid.,* p. 22.

[26] *Ibid.,* p. 29.

[27] Grunfeld, tr., *Horeb, op. cit.,* fn. 13, 75:491.

[28] *Nineteen Letters,* pp. 66-67.

[29] Grunfeld, tr., *Horeb, op. cit.,* fn. 13, 113:714.

[30] In his *Horeb* (30:220), Hirsch paraphrased "In the wilderness prepare the way of the Lord," (*Is.* 40:3) as referring to Israel's dispersion and mission in the Diaspora, though it is traditionally explained as referring to Israel's return from the Diaspora to Zion—a meaning which is the reverse of that of Hirsch.

[31] The Talmudic basis for this statement is "The Holy One, blessed be He, exiled Israel among the nations only that proselytes might join them" (*Pes.* 87b). Also p. 178, Chap. 7.

[32] *Nineteen Letters,* pp. 161-162; Grunfeld (tr.) *Horeb,* London: Soncino Press, 96:608.

[33] For this reason, Hirsch attacked Frankel's view that the oral law represented a later stage of development than the written.

[34] From *Collected Writings* excerpted in Jacob Breuer, ed. *Fundamentals of Judaism,* New York: Philip Feldheim, 1949, p. 128.

[35] Quoted in Grunfeld *op. cit.,* fn. 16., p. XXVII. See also *Nineteen Letters,* p. 148.

[36] *Nineteen Letters,* pp. 167-168.

[37] *Ibid.,* p. 167.

[38] *Ibid.,* p. 155.

[39] *Ibid.,* p. 156-157.

[40] *Ibid.,* p. 171.

[41] Quoted in S. R. Hirsch, *Jewish Learning in Practical Life,* in I. Grunfeld, *Judaism Eternal,* Vol. II, London: Soncino Press, 1956, p. 287.

[42] *Horeb,* 98:618; *Nineteen Letters,* p. 127 ff.

[43] Rabbi Levi, an *Amora* of the third century, is cited as saying that the oaths implied in the verse: "I adjure you, O daughters of Jerusalem" (*Can.* 2:7) include three: "not to make public the end (of *Galut*), nor force it, nor reveal the secret to the gentiles" (*Ket.* 111a).

[44] *Horeb,* 96:608.

[45] *Ibid.* 33:237.

[46] *Ibid.* 96:609.

[47] "*Av*" in Grunfeld, *op. cit.,* fn. 10. Vol. I, p. 128 ff.

[48] "Religious Instruction" in Grunfeld, *op. cit.,* fn. 10, Vol. I, 160ff

[49] *Ibid.,* p. 171 ff. It should be remembered that Hirsch here was speaking of first generation German immigrants to America, who arrived in the 1840's.

[50] He formulated his theory of cultural pluralism in these words: "The pure bright light beam is a fusion of seven colors; it is not monotone and uniformity which produce the finest tones and colors, but the unity and harmony of diverse elements." *Ibid.,* p. 190.

[51] *Ibid.,* p. 218.

[52] *Ibid.,* p. 119.

[53] *Ibid.,* pp. 183-184.

[54] See Chap. 12, p. 316.

⁵⁵ In large Jewish communities in Poland, it had been customary for Hassidic families to give their sons a thorough Jewish education, and train them in the ways of the pious. Their daughters, however, were sent to general Polish schools where they acquired a secular schooling mainly. As a result, the girls lived in a world totally at variance with that of their brothers. When these girls later married the sons of Hassidic families, there was a wide gulf between the backgrounds of the wives and husbands. The Beth Jacob Schools were intended to remedy these conditions by providing an intensive Jewish education for girls from Orthodox Jewish homes.

⁵⁶ See Joseph S. Bentwich, *Education in Israel,* JPS, 1965. pp. 108-109.

⁵⁷ cf. Hirsch's view, p. 239, *Horeb* 96:608.

⁵⁸ In America, the adult men's organization merged with the Hapoel Hamizrachi to form the Religious Zionists of America.

NOTES TO CHAPTER TEN

¹ *Kuzari* IV:13, 15, 16.

² It is told of the elder Luzzatto that in order to avoid the penalty for violating this injunction, he wrote a letter to his son urging him to take up a vocation. The father was said to have arranged to take a copy of this letter with him to the grave to serve as proof in the next world of his good intentions.

³ The portion of the Prophets read in the synagogue at the Sabbath and holy day morning services as a sequel to the Pentateuchal portion.

⁴ *Shadal* is an anagram which stands for the Hebrew initials of his name.

⁵ For a list of his works, see the article by Max Seligson in *Jewish Encyclopedia.* Vol. VIII, pp. 225-226. Also the excellent monograph in Hebrew by Joseph Klausner in *Historia shel Hasifrut Haivrit Hahadasha,* Vol. II (Second Ed.) Jerusalem: Ahiasof, 1952, is provided with a comprehensive bibliography (p. 47 ff, 78 ff).

⁶ See Chap. 8, p. 194ff.

⁷ *Epistolaria* II, pp. 922-923.

⁸ These diacritical marks, consisting of accents and vowels appearing in Hebrew Biblical books mostly below but also above the letters of the words, have been devised to fix the accepted Masoretic, *i.e.,* "handed down" or traditional reading and pronunciation of the Hebrew texts. This system is essential, because the words in the traditional Bible scroll consist only of consonants that may lend themselves to various readings. The Hebrew letters HMR, for example, form a noun which may mean either "clay," "wine," "donkey," or "donkey-driver." Originally, the correct readings were transmitted by word of mouth from teacher to pupil, but this, of course, was an unreliable method. For several generations, the so-called Masoretic School of Tiberius, Palestine, worked on this system of vocalization, which was completed by the tenth century. Aside from the vowels, the Masorites invented a system of *neginot,* (notes for cantillation) which are used also as accents and as punctuation marks to indicate pauses at the ends of phrases or clauses in the Bible. The Masorites, moreover, compiled footnotes to correct the words in the Biblical text that have been corrupted through error in the course of the centuries. To further ensure the trans-

mission of the accurate text, the Masorites counted the number of letters and words in the individual books of the Bible. Another system of vowels, discovered in the nineteenth century, originated in Babylonia at about the same time as the one in Palestine, but the latter system is preferred, both because it is more efficient and also because of its long usage.

9 *Iggrot Shadal* VI, p. 780.

10 *Ibid.,* Vol. I, p. 72 ff.

11 *Loc. cit.*

12 *Lexioni di Teologia Deogmatica Israelitica,* Trieste, 1864, p. 15 ff.

13 *Mehkrei Hayahadut,* Vol. I, pp. 117-240.

14 *Ozar Nehmad* I, p. 82 ff.

15 The Talmud in another passage (BB 15a) gives later dates, ranging from the time of the Judges and the Babylonian exile to the period of Ahasuerus (fifth century C.E.). R. Samuel ben Nachmani also disputed the Mosaic authorship of the Book of Job, maintaining that it was only a parable (BB 15a). Hai Gaon (939-1038) agreed with this view.

16 *Mehkrei Hayahadut* I, p. 59 ff.

17 *I Kuzari*: 81, 83, 86, 87.

18 As proof of the supernatural origin of the Torah, Luzzatto argued naively that writing was not widespread in Mosaic times.

19 "Our law as a whole is divided among the emotions of fear, love and joy, through each of which one can approach God. Thy contrition on a fast day brings one no nearer to God than joy on the Sabbath and Holy Days . . . If thy joy lead thee so far as to sing and dance, it becomes worship and a bond between thee and the Divine." Judah Halevi, *Kuzari* 2:50.

20 The Hebrew root *rachem* (pity) is associated with *rechem* (womb) and thus, implies maternal tenderness and love. This derivation probably had no bearing on Spinoza's classification of this emotion as a feminine virtue, but it suggests a striking coincidence.

21 The year his son was born (1829) Luzzatto completed a work by that name, dealing with the *Targum Onkelos,* an Aramaic commentary on the Pentateuch. Onkelos was a *Tanna* (Mishnaic teacher) of the second century who was confused with Aquila, the *Ger* (stranger, or proselyte) who lived in the same century and composed a Greek translation of the Bible that has since been lost. *Ohev Ger,* (lover of the proselyte) is Philoxenus in Greek.

22 *Ozar Nehmad* II, p. 103 ff, p. 131; *Kinor Naim* p. 283 ff

23 *Mehkrei Hayahadut* II, p. 244ff, *Iggrot Shadal* V, pp. 704-780.

24 Maimonidies, *Hilchot Deot.* 1:7.

25 Shadal was said to have been challenged by a colleague on the ground that he, like Ibn Ezra, proposed emendations to the Bibilcal text. "But mine are not emendations but the correct text," Shadal countered.

26 *Tanakh* stands for the Hebrew initials of *Torah, Neviim, Ketubim* (the Law, the Prophets, and the Writings) which comprise the Hebrew Scriptures. Here Luzzatto reversed the order of the name Kant, to produce *Tanakh*. See also *Peninei Shadal,* p. 115.

27 This contradicts Locke's *Tabula rasa* concept and the theories of the sensationalists. In refutation of the notion of innate ideas, one could ask

why God did not implant the innate idea of God more firmly in the minds of the skeptics and atheists, so that they, too, would accept Him.

28 *Iggrot* 1405.

29 *Kuzari* II; 36.

30 He also published Judah Halevi's religious poetry in the *Divan*, (1864). See p. 251.

31 *Kinor Naim* 374-480.

32 *Guide III*: pp. 32, 46.

33 *Guide III*: 32.

34 *Mehkrei Hayahadut* I: 40, 45.

35 *Guide III*: 43.

36 This thought is reminiscent of Ahad Ha'Am's views in his essay *Slavery and Freedom*, written in 1904.

37 *Iggrot* V, p. 660.

38 *Kinor Naim*, p. 429.

39 *Mehkrei Hayahadut* II, p. 164.

40 *Kerem Hemed* IV, pp. 119ff.

41 *Iggrot* V, p. 701.

42 *Discorsi storico-religiosi, agli studenti Israeliti*, pp. 114 ff.

43 *Kerem Hemed*, pp. 132 ff. Luzzatto retorted cynically that had he assailed Moses ben Amram, the *Maskilim* would have commended him; but for criticizing Moses ben Maimon, they had denounced him.

44 See Chap. 7, p. 161.

45 A reference to *Deut.* 13:14 ff.

46 *Iggrot* VIII, p. 1246.

47 *Ibid.*, p. 1139, *Epistolario* II, p. 819.

48 *Hapardes* III, p. 120.

49 *Iggrot* VIII, p. 1249.

50 *Ibid.*, I, p. 143 ff.

51 *Hapardes* III, p. 119.

52 *Iggrot* VII, p. 1071.

53 See his essay, "The Spiritual Revival," in Leon Simon's *Selected Essays by Ahad Ha'am*, JPS, 1912, pp. 253 ff.

PART THREE

NOTES TO CHAPTER ELEVEN

1 See fn. 1, Chap. 8.

2 This rise may be attributed to many causes. In general, living conditions were better in the nineteenth century; the advances in medicine had cut down infant mortality and increased longevity, while the birthrate remained high. The industrial revolution, too, enabled larger numbers of people to become self-supporting and to marry at an earlier age. Improved nourishment, due to the ability to transport foods from America and other distant lands in greater quantities, may have also been a factor contributing to the longer lifespan.

3 Because the name Jew had ghetto associations, Reformers frequently referred to themselves as Israelites and were also called so by their liberal

countrymen. Gabriel Riesser, a militant fighter for Jewish rights, published a journal in 1832 which he called *Der Jude*. He was offered a substantial sum to help him in his new venture if he would agree to change the name of his publication to the *Israelite*. He refused, explaining that the old Jewish custom of changing the name of a dangerously ill person to another one so as to make it difficult for the Angel of Death to find him is generally not an effective device. The same is true of the foes of the Jews, against whom a change in name is a futile gesture.

⁴ He was famed for his abortive attempt to establish Ararat (1825) as a settlement for Jews, on Grand Island in the Niagara River, as a preliminary to their return to Palestine.

⁵ In 1844, Mordecai M. Noah delivered an address before a Protestant congregation in Philadelphia, pleading for a Jewish national restoration in Palestine. The address was published and widely distributed under the title *Discourse on the Restoration of the Jews*. Earlier in 1818, President John Adams had written to Noah, "I really wish the Jews again in Palestine as an independent nation."

NOTES TO CHAPTER TWELVE

¹ The Reformers adopted Ten Articles of Faith, in a creed modelled after that of Maimonides. They subscribed to a belief in universal monotheism, the Decalogue, and immortality, among others.

² The Documentary Theory assumes that the Pentateuch is not of Mosaic authorship, but is a composite of independent writings produced by various writers in different periods.

³ See Chap. 10, p. 252ff.

⁴ See Chap. 13, p. 317ff.

⁵ *Essence of Judaism,* Cincinnati: Bloch Publishing Co., 1868, p. 8.

⁶ Dena Wilansky, *Sinai to Cincinnati,* New York: 1937, p. 178.

⁷ See Chap. 9, p. 226.

⁸ *Op. cit.,* note 6, p. 33.

⁹ See Chap. 7. p. 180.

¹⁰ *Op. cit.* note 6, p. 30.

¹¹ These Conservative and Orthodox congregations often hold an early service on Friday at sunset in addition to the later worship, which includes a sermon or lecture.

¹² The interpretation given in the Sabbath and Festival Prayerbook issued by the Rabbinical Assembly of America (Conservative) conforms to this idea. See Sabbath Prayerbook, Foreword, p. X, also p. 141.

¹³ This result is attributed at least in part to a curious and untoward incident. A group of Cincinnati businessmen tendered a dinner at the Highland House Hotel on July 11, 1883, in honor of the first graduating class of the Hebrew Union College. Though a Jewish caterer had been engaged, the first course served at the dinner was shrimp. A number of the delegates were gravely offended by this *trefa* (lit. "torn," *i.e.* non-kosher) banquet, and they left the dinner hall in angry protest. The occurrence highlighted to the Orthodox the need for a traditional rabbinical seminary. See John J. Appel, "The Trefa Banquet," *Commentary,* Vol. 41, No. 2. (Feb. 1966), p. 75.

¹⁴ The dangers inherent in such a break with tradition as a result of extreme rationalism have been poignantly demonstrated in a number of instances involving Reform rabbis. One example is that of Felix Adler (1851-1933), the son of Samuel Adler (1809-1891), a rabbi of Temple Emanuel in New York. The son had been sent by his father's congregation to Germany to study in the secular and rabbinical institutions there in order to prepare to become his father's associate and eventually his successor. Shortly after he returned home in 1873, he repudiated the rabbinate, maintaining that there was no room in the modern world for separate religions. The "Mosaic religion," he declared, was a "religious mosaic." This, of course, was a reference to the so-called Documentary Theory of Biblical critics and scholars, to the effect that the Pentateuch and the former Prophets consist of a merger of various narratives and codes, produced by different authors in different ages. The Pentateuch, is, accordingly, not the product of a single revelation. Felix Adler insisted that neither Judaism nor any other religion could be the final arbiter of the moral law, and he gave expression to this view in the Ethical Culture movement which he founded in 1876.

The reactions of two other leading rabbis in Boston were similar. Solomon Schindler, a prominent Boston Reform rabbi left the rabbinate in 1893, after almost two decades of service, to become an advocate of Bellamy's doctrines of social reform. A successor of Schindler in the Boston pulpit, Charles Fleischer left it some thirty years later to establish a community church in that city. These instances may well have been exceptions, but they indicate the extent to which an exaggerated rationalism in religion may lead. It was one thing for Reform to attempt to improve the synagogue service or its decorum, but to apply the yardstick of philosophy or logic for determining which tradition to retain and which to cast out might well result in "throwing out the baby with the bath." If Judaism is to be equated with ethical humanism, why Judaism as a separate religion—or why any denominational religion? Reform Judaism, if merely an ethical creed, differs little from Christianity and might consistently merge with it, unless particularistic factors of religion, doctrine, history, tradition, symbolism, ritual, literature, and similar elements are brought into play.

¹⁵ CCAR Year Book, (1898) XLI.

¹⁶ In France, the cosmetic manufacturer Coty did likewise.

¹⁷ Philip P. Graves, the Constantinople correspondent of the London *Times* found that the *Protocols* were plagiarized from Maurice Joly's anonymous work entitled *La Dialogue aux Enfers entre Machiavel et Montesquieu (Dialogue in Hell between Montesquieu and Machiavelli)* which appeared in Brussels in 1864. In this volume, the author, a non-Jew, charged Napoleon III with plotting against the safety of the rest of Europe. In 1865, the author was arrested, fined, and imprisoned. (London *Times*, August 16-21, 1921). Forgeries of this type were not entirely unknown in attempts to rouse antagonism against a group. In 1890, the American Protective Association (APA) "discovered" the *Instructions to Catholics*, in which Cardinal Gibbons allegedly attacked the spread of education and ordered the exclusion of heretics from employment, their places to be taken by Catholics. The APA also circulated widely the forged "Encyclical" of Pope Leo XIII, calling upon Catholics to exterminate all heretics in the

United States on or about the Feast of Loyola, 1893. (Humphrey J. Desmond, *The APA Movement,* Washington: New Century Press, 1912, pp. 19-25).

[18] In 1935, a court in Berne, Switzerland, in convicting two Nazis for circulating the *Protocols,* found them to be a rank forgery on the basis of the evidence of distinguished and expert witnesses.

[19] This means "a son of the commandments" and marks the celebration of the attainment of the age of thirteen by a Jewish boy, at which time he is considered mature from the religious viewpoint.

[20] Jewish religious law regards a girl as maturing a year earlier than the boy. Accordingly, she attains her *Bat Mitzvah,* the stage of "a daughter of the commandments" at the age of twelve.

[21] Solomon Freehof, *Reform Jewish Practice,* Vols. I and II, Cincinnati: The Hebrew Union College Press, 1944, 1952.

NOTES TO CHAPTER THIRTEEN

[1] The presently existing Jewish Publication Society was established in Philadelphia in 1888.

[2] See Chap. 8.

[3] Quoted in Mordecai Waxman, ed. *Tradition and Change,* New York: The Burning Bush Press, 1958, p. 53.

[4] See Chap. 12, p. 296.

[5] He was the father of Henrietta Szold, founder of Hadassah, the women's Zionist organization.

[6] See Chap. 12, p. 298.

[7] The American institution adopted the same name as that created by Zacharia Frankel in 1854, thus demonstrating its affinity for the European institution.

[8] See Chap. 15, p. 376ff.

[9] Among the other pupils trained and inspired by Morais who became leaders in American Jewish life were Isaac Husik (1876-1939), an outstanding authority on medieval Jewish philosophy, Mayer Sulzberger (1843-1929), an eminent Hebrew scholar and jurist, and the philanthropists, Hyman Gratz (1776-1856) and Moses Aaron Dropsie (1821-1905). The last named endowed the institution of higher Jewish learning in Philadelphia which bears his name.

[10] See Chap. 8.

[11] See Chap. 6.

[12] The word *Genizah* means a repository or storage place. In ancient synagogues, in particular, it was the place where old and discarded books and manuscripts were kept.

[13] "A Hoard of Hebrew Manuscripts," in Solomon Schechter, *Studies in Judaism,* Second Series, 1908.

[14] A collection of ancient literature not included in the Hebrew canon.

[15] Of particular significance today is another volume Schechter extricated from the debris, containing the teachings of the pre-Christian Zadokites, a sect governed by rules markedly similar to those in the Manual of Discipline subsequently found in 1947 at Qaumran among the Dead Sea Scrolls.

[16] *Jewish Theological Seminary Biennial Report,* 1902-1904, pp. 98-99.

[17] See Chap. 14, p. 347.

[18] Though the influential minister of the Sephardic Shearith Israel congregation, H. Pereira Mendes had proposed the creation of this organization as early as 1912, his congregation did not join it because, as he explained, the trustees "were hesitant to join a body in which there were representatives of those who, congregationally or individually, commit themselves to what is not Orthodox Judaism."

[19] *Studies in Judaism,* First Series, *op. cit.* p. XV.

[20] *Ibid.,* p. XXI.

[21] *Ibid.,* p. XVII.

[22] *Ibid.,* p. XXIII.

[23] Schechter, "The Dogmas of Judaism" in *Studies in Judaism,* Second Series, JPS, 1911, p. 180.

[24] Dr. Israel Levinthal quotes his late father, Rabbi Bernard L. Levinthal, who used the symbol of the tephillin, or phylacteries, to illustrate the emphasis of Judaism on action. The phylactery placed on the forehead has four compartments, in which the Biblical passages are inserted, while the phylactery on the arm has only a single compartment. This suggests that concerning particulars of the creed there may be a multitude of opinions, but in the matter of the code of action, there must be unity. (Israel H. Levinthal, "Point of View" Abelard Schuman, New York, 1958, p. 57.)

[25] Schechter developed the concept of the Universal Synagogue from Adolph Jellinek's principle of *Knesset Israel*—the *ecclesia* of Israel.

[26] *Op. cit.* note 19, p. XIX.

[27] Solomon Schechter, Seminary Addresses, New York: Burning Bush Press 1959, p. 45.

[28] The Conservatives, like their forerunners in the Historical School, have interpreted "Catholic Israel" in practical terms as referring to committed Jews, not to those who may be ignorant or indifferent to the values of Judaism. See Chapter 8, p. 214. Also, Waxman, *op. cit.,* p. 89.

[29] *Op. cit.* note 27, p. 97.

[30] *Ibid.,* p. 22.

[31] *Ibid.,* p. 22.

[32] *Op. cit.,* note 23, pp. 189-190.

[33] Solomon Schechter, "Abraham Geiger," *Studies in Judaism,* Third Series, JPS, 1924, pp. 79-80.

[34] Quoted in Solomon Schechter, *Studies in Judaism,* First Series, 1911, Introduction, p. xxix.

[35] In 1945, Joseph Zeitlin published a doctoral study (*Disciples of the Wise,* Teachers College, Columbia University,) in which he reported that in 1937, eighty-one percent of the Conservative rabbis and eighty percent of the Reform rabbis in his sample entertained a naturalistic rather than a supernaturalistic outlook on religion.

[36] In 1947, Mordecai M. Kaplan in summarizing the beliefs of the various alignments in Conservatism declared that the center group no longer believes in divine revelation as an historical event, but only as a theological concept. Revelation as an historical event, Kaplan explained, implies a supernatural communication occurring at a specific time and place, but as a theological concept, it refers to "the natural experience of the human

mind which reacts to anything as opening new vistas of meaning and holiness." (Mordecai M. Kaplan, "Unity and Diversity in the Conservative Movement," in Mordecai Waxman, *op. cit.*, p. 221.)

37 See Chap. 8, p. 209ff.

38 Louis Finkelstein, "Tradition in the Making" in Waxman, *op. cit.*, p. 194.

39 Rabbi Samuel ben Isaac of Troyes known as *Rashi* (1040-1105), famous Biblical commentator, ruled that Christians were not idolators, hence they are not banned by Talmudic law from handling the production or distribution of wine, prohibited to idolators.

40 Louis Finkelstein, "The Things that Unite Us" (Address, 1927)quoted in Waxman, *op. cit.* pp. 313, 318, 319.

41 The vague platform espoused by Conservatism has aroused criticism in Conservative circles. It curbs initiative in effecting change, since nothing is to be done until the people as a whole takes a position. Professor Mordecai Kaplan considers such an approach impractical "as a compromise between wishing to stand still and being afraid to go forward." Mordecai M. Kaplan, *The Future of the American Jew*, p. 387.

42 One such question in recent years has been whether the use of electricity on the Sabbath is a violation of the prohibition against kindling a fire on the Holy Day (*Ex.* 35:3); another was the problem of riding to services on the Sabbath which is also based on the Biblical Sabbath law (*Ex.* 31:12ff).

43 The extent to which the *status quo* is upheld may be seen from the decisions of the Law Committee on the use of the organ. In 1948, that Committee opposed its use at synagogue services. In 1963, it permitted the use of the organ as legitimate "under existing circumstances;" However, the opinion of the Law Committee calls attention to certain "hazards" inherent in its use and appears to discourage it. See Herbert Parzen, *Architects of Conservative Judaism,* New York: Jonathan David, 1964, pp. 217-218.

44 The traditional Aramaic version is signed only by the witnesses, not the bride and bridegroom. The latter merely sign the English translation of the *Ketubah*.

45 A wife must accept a divorce, in accordance with the *Takkanah* of Rabbi Gershom of Mayence (ca. 1000).

NOTES TO CHAPTER FOURTEEN

1 Mordecai M. Kaplan, *Judaism as a Civilization* (2nd Printing) New York: The Reconstructionist Press, 1957, p. 178.

2 *Ibid,* p. 186.

3 *The Reconstructionist,* Vol No. 17. (Dec. 25, 1964) p. 32.

4 Kaplan, *op. cit.,* note 1, p. 432.

5 *Ibid.,* p. 441.

6 Jews have not always counted the years from creation but from important events such as the reigns of kings (*IK* 15:1, 16:8, 22:41) and other major occurrences (*IK.* 6:1; *Ezek.* 1:2; 40:1; *Ezra* 3:8). The year of the destruction of the Temple was employed by the rabbis for several centuries,

and medieval documents have been found bearing such dates. See *Avodah Zarah* 8b-9a. See also Rashi's note on p. 8b in this Tractate: "He who counts the succession and life of the sages or the years of documents of indebtedness may count from the Destruction." See also notes in I. Epstein ed., *Tractate Avodah Zarah,* London: Soncino (English) ed., 1935, pp. 42-43.

7 Kaplan, *op. cit.,* note 1, p. 454-455.

8 *Ibid.,* p. 222.

9 See p. 381.

10 Matthew Arnold's naturalistic outlook on religion influenced Kaplan. See Norman Flinker, "Matthew Arnold and Mordecai Kaplan, *The Reconstructionist* Vol. XXXI No. 14, Nov. 1965, p. 7 ff.

11 Mordecai M. Kaplan, *Meaning of God in Modern Jewish Religion;* New York; Behrman's Jewish Bookshop, 1937, p. 26.

12 *Op. cit.* note 1, p. 205.

13 *Ibid.,* p. 455.

14 The overall Jewish welfare organizations today are generally not representative of the entire community. Their directorates are usually self-perpetuating,and the Jewish public has little, if any, voice in its affairs. Under the community plan, however, these agencies would be democratic in structure and administration.

15 Mordecai M. Kaplan, "Toward the Formulation of Guiding Principles for the Conservative Movement," address before the Rabbinical Assembly, 1949, in Mordecai M. Waxman, ed., *Tradition and Change, op. cit.* pp. 304 ff.

16 *The Future of the American Jew,* New York: Macmillan Co., 1948, p. 183 ff.

17 *Sabbath Prayer Book,* New York: Reconstructionist Foundation, 1945, Introduction p. xx, *Ibid,* p. 173.

18 *Ibid.,* p. XIX.

19 *Op. cit.* (note 16) p. 172.

20 *Op. cit.* p. XXV.

21 *Op. cit.* (note 11) p. 65.

22 The Conservative *Sabbath and Festival Prayer Book,* (New York: Joint Prayer Book Commission of Rabbinical Assembly and United Synagogue of America, p. IX, p. 141, and elsewhere) refers to "the (animal) sacrifices which they (our ancestors) have performed." The traditional *Siddur* (order of prayers) includes a petition for the restoration of the. sacrifices. The Conservative prayer book omits the Talmudic passages relating to the Temple procedure in offering up the sacrifices, which are included in the traditional *Siddur* as a prelude to the morning service.

23 *Op. cit.* Sabbath Prayer Book, p. xxvii.

24 See p. 233, p. 178 *supra.*

25 *Op. cit.* note 16, pp. 79, 211ff, 228.

26 The practice of calling women for an *Aliyah* is discouraged in the same passage in *Meg.* 23a which sanctions it, because of the "dignity of the community." Evidently, it was regarded as being more in keeping with the dignity of the congregation to call up only men.

27 Reform congregations had introduced this change in their liturgy earlier. See Chap. 8, note 8.

NOTES TO CHAPTER FIFTEEN

[1] There still exists a synagogue of Indian Jews, who are believed to be descendants of the Marranos. The synagogue is presently located in Calle Caruzo on the outskirts of Mexico City. See Norman Fendell, "Mexico's Indian Jews" in Bernard Postal and David H. White, ed., *The Best of Ten Years* (a *Jewish Digest* compilation) Houston, Tex.: D. H. White & Co., p. 113.

[2] It is now known as the Touro Synagogue in honor of Judah and Abraham Touro, sons of Isaac Touro, who donated funds for the preservation of this synagogue. Isaac Touro arrived from Jamaica in 1790, to serve as the minister of Jeshuat Israel.

[3] An American Jewish poet, Emma Lazarus (1849-1883), a younger contemporary of Longfellow, also memorialized this colonial congregation in a poem, *The Jewish Synagogue of Newport,* in lines which recall the mood and sentiment expressed by the older poet in his verses on the Newport Jewish cemetery. It will be of interest to reproduce several stanzas:

> Here, where the noises of the busy town,
>   The ocean's plunge and roar can enter not,
> We stand and gaze around with tearful awe,
>   And muse upon the consecrated spot.
>
> What prayers were in this temple offered up,
>   Wrung from sad hearts that knew no joy on earth,
> By these lone exiles of a thousand years,
>   From their fair sunrise land that gave them birth!
>
> Nonetheless the sacred shrine is holy yet
>   With its lone floors where reverent feet once trod.
> Take off your shoes as by the burning bush
>   Before the mystery of death and God.

[4] See p. 285.

[5] Another Ashkenazic synagogue, Beth Sholom, was known to be in existence in Richmond, Virginia in 1790, but it was undoubtedly organized after the Revolution.

[6] See Chap. 6, p. 116ff.

[7] In 1655, after Cromwell's talks with Menasseh ben Israel, Jews were tacitly though not officially permitted to enter England. The legal barriers were not formally removed until the last decade of the seventeenth century.

[8] This term is also used to denote an informal group, which gathers together for worship.

[9] Strictly speaking, the *Bet Hamidrash* is the chapel which is supplied with religious texts used for study, but the term refers also to the synagogue. Hence, Bet Hamidrash Hagadol means "Great Synagogue."

[10] Ash was violently opposed to the attempt of Reform rabbis to preach or lecture in Orthodox congregations; he formulated his objections in a document which he pointedly titled in idiomatic Talmudic phraseology: "What authority has the offending ox to poach on the premises of the injured (offended) party?"

[11] These higher Talmudic institutions are sometimes referred to as

Yeshivot Gdolot (higher Yeshivot) to differentiate them from the *Yeshivot Ktanot* (elementary Yeshivot), the Jewish day schools in America which offer a combined program of Jewish and secular training.

[12] Charles S. Liebman, "Orthodoxy in American Jewish Life" in *American Jewish Yearbook,* Vol. 66, p. 55.

[13] Now part of the recently created Jewish University of America.

[14] Liebman, *op. cit.* note 12, p. 51ff.

[15] *Ibid.* p. 53.

[16] Liebman, *op. cit.* fn 12 p. 92 ff.

[17] *Loc. cit.*

[18] *The Riverton Study,* published in 1957 by the American Jewish Committee, based on interviews of a sample of several hundred families in an industrial town in the East with a Jewish population of eight thousand five hundred, is revealing. The proportion of those labeling themselves as Conservatives was forty-three percent; the Orthodox constituted sixteen percent; both groups thus formed fifty-nine percent of the total sample. Only thirty-one percent, however, of the individuals interviewed observed some of the dietary laws; they bought kosher meat, but only eight percent had two sets of dishes; thirty-one percent light candles on Sabbath eve; a mere twenty-two percent attended synagogue on other than the High Holy Days. The members of both wings in Judaism are normally expected to adhere strictly to all the observances referred to, yet actually a relatively small percentage do so.

[19] Seldom is an Orthodox synagogue established in the suburbs; the first synagogue launched is generally Conservative; the next one, if the community is of sufficient size to support an additional synagogue, is usually Reform. Albert I. Gordon, *Jews in Suburbia,* Boston: Beacon Press, 1959, pp. 97 ff. Also, Judith Kramer and Seymour Leventman, *Children of the Gilded Ghetto,* New Haven: Yale University Press, 1963, pp. 153-161.

[20] Liebman, *op. cit.* fn. 12 pp. 34 ff.

[21] The Neo-Kantian school regarded pure mathematics and the laws of pure science as the foundation of reality.

[22] Hermann Cohen (1842-1918), a former professor of philosophy at the University of Marburg, was the founder of the so-called Neo-Kantian Marburg School, which applied Kant's method of critical idealism to religion, science, and other branches of culture. Following Kant's principle of the "autonomy of reason" as the source of all ethics, Cohen maintained the independence of philosophical cognition as a purely logical process of thought, separated from experience. He regarded the Hebrew prophetic ideal of justice as central in Judaism and as the basis of social morality. Messianism, to Cohen, represented the goal of continuous human advancement. The Utopia for which we are to aspire should therefore always be posited in the future. Hermann Cohen was vehemently opposed to Zionism, because he believed that Jews would be defeating their universal Messianic aims if they established their own political state. Accordingly, unlike the classical Reformers, he regarded the Jews as a nationality—a people, united by historical bonds, the Hebrew language as a sacred tongue, and other ties—and not merely a religious communion.

[23] See his Hebrew essay "Ish Hahalacha" (Man of the Halacha) in *Talpioth,* 1944, pp. 651 ff. See also "The Lonely Man of Faith" in Tradition, Vol. 7, No. 2, Summer 1965.

[24] Hilchot Yesodei Hatorah 7:1.

[25] This doctrine suggests that we can know more about what God is not, than what He is, for our human perceptions are limited, whereas God is Infinite and Perfect. Thus, terms such as living, wise, or good are too narrow to apply to God. Our notions of God's attributes may be more correctly expressed in broad negative concepts—that God is not dead, not unwise, not unknowing and the like. God exists, Maimonides declared, "without possessing the attributes of existence." (Guide I:56ff).

[26] William L. Shirer, *The Rise and Fall of the Third Reich,* Conn. (Crest Reprint) Fawcett Publications; p. 333.

[27] Ilya M. Dijour, "The Refugee Problem," *American Jewish Yearbook,* Vol. 46, (1944-1945), p. 307.

[28] Accurate figures are not available, since immigration authorities did not classify the immigrants by religion after 1943.

[29] Isaac Even, "Chassidism in the New World," in *Jewish Communal Register* 1917-18, New York: Kehillah (1918), p. 341.

[30] George Kranzler, *Williamsburg, A Jewish Community in Transition,* New York: Philip Feldheim, 1961. Also Solomon Poll, *The Hassidic Community,* New York: Free Press of Glencoe; (Crowell-Collier Publishing Co.) 1962.

[31] This was originally the festive attire of the Polish aristocracy two centuries ago, when Hassidism was founded. The Hassidim have made this *Malbush* (garb) a part of their tradition.

[32] The federal government, according to the Constitution, operated on the basis of powers delegated to it by the states. That Constitution abolished any religious test as a qualification for federal office, but the states could establish such a test. Moreover, according to the Federal Constitution, only those who were qualified to vote in the "election of the most numerous branch of the State Legislature," could vote for members of the House of Representatives. These disabilities were subsequently abolished. In 1780, South Carolina and Pennsylvania removed them; Delaware did so in 1792; Maryland in 1825; Rhode Island in 1842; North Carolina in 1868; and New Hampshire as late as 1876. The new states, however, admitted under the Ordinance of 1787, were required to grant equal civic and religious rights to all.

[33] In a recent study of the Jewry of a Midwestern city (Minneapolis), only five percent of the sample studied indicated that members chose a specific synagogue as a matter of religious conviction; sixteen percent did so for social reasons and the "remainder" in order to enroll their children in the school. Kramer and Leventman, *op. cit.* note 19, p. 157.

[34] See p. 289.

ABBREVIATIONS

B.B. — *Baba Bathra* — Last of Three Treatises on *Nezikin* (Damages)

A.Z. — Tractate *Avodah Zarah, B.T.*

b.— born

B.C.E. — Before Common Era

Ber. — Tractate *Berachot, B.T.*

B.M. — *Baba Metzia*, Middle Tractate of Three Treatises on *Nezikin* (Damages), B.T.

B.T. — Babylonian Talmud

Can. — Canticles or Song of Songs

C.E. — Common Era

cf. — compare

ca. — circa, around, about

Chr., Chron. — Book of Chronicles

ch., chap. — chapter

d. — died

Dt., Deut. — Book of Deuteronomy

Ecc. — Book of Ecclesiastes (Koheleth)

ed. — edited by, editor

e.g. — for example

Ex. — Book of Exodus

ff. — pages or passages following

fn. — footnote or note

Gal. — Galatians

Gen. — Book of Genesis

Gr. — Greek

Guide — *Guide to the Perplexed* (Maimonides)

Hab. — Habakkuk

Hag. — Tractate *Hagigah, B.T.*

ibid. — ibidem — (in the work cited) in fn. next above

i.e. — that is

Is., Isa. — Book of Isaiah

Jer. — Book of Jeremiah

J.P.S. — Jewish Publication Society of America, Philadelphia, Pa.

Jer., J.T. — Jerusalem (Palestinian) Talmud

Ket. — Tractate *Ketubot,* B.T.
Kid. — Tractate *Kiddushin,* B.T.
K. — Book of Kings
Lat. — Latin
Lev. — Book of Leviticus
Matt., Mt. — Matthew
Lit. — literally
loc. cit. — loco citato, (in the same place) cited in fn. next above
M. — Mishna
Mak. — Tractate *Makkoth,* B.T.
Meg. — Tractate *Megillah,* B.T.
Ned. — Tractate *Nedarim,* B.T.
Neh. — Book of Nehemiah
Nu., Num. — Book of Numbers
op. cit. — opere citato(in author's work cited previously)
Pes. — Tractate *Pesachim,* B.T.
Pr., Prov. — Book of Proverbs
Ps. — Book of Psalms
R. — *Rabbah,* (Midrash *Rabbah*)
Rom. — Romans
R.H. — Tractate *Rosh Hashanah,* B.T.
San. — Tractate *Sanhedrin,* B.T.
Shab. — Tractate *Shabbat,* B.T.
Tim. — Timothy
tr. — translator, translated by
viz. — namely
Zech. — Book of Zechariah

SUGGESTED READINGS AND REFERENCES

GENERAL WORKS

(Only works in English are cited.)

Agus, J. B.—*Evolution of Jewish Thought,* New York: Abelard Shuman 1959

American Jewish Yearbook—1899-1979 (JPS),* issued annually by the American Jewish Committee. vol. 50 (1948-9), p. 867ff., contains index of special articles and statistics in vols. 1-30; p. 661ff., contains subsequent index in vols. 51-78 (1951-1978)

Bamberger, Bernard O.—*Story of Judaism,* New York: Union of American Hebrew Congregations 1957

Baron, Salo W.—*A Social and Religious History of the Jews,* 16 vols., New York: Columbia University 1958

Davis, Moshe—"Jewish Religious Life and Institutions in America," in Louis Finkelstein, ed. *The Jews, Their History, Culture and Religion,* (4 vols. JPS 1949) vol. I

Epstein, Isidore—*Faith of Judaism,* London: Soncino Press 1960
—*Judaism,* Baltimore: Penguin 1960

Feingold, Henry L.—"The Conditions of American Jewry in Historical Perspective: A Bicentennial Assessment," in *AJYB,* vol. 76, (1976), p. 3ff.

Finkelstein, Louis, ed.—*The Jews, Their History, Culture and Religion,* 4 vols. JPS 1949

Grayzel, Solomon—*A History of the Jews,* JPS 1965 (16th reprint)
—*A History of the Contemporary Jews,* JPS and Meridian 1960

Graetz, Heinrich—*History of the Jews,* 6 vols. JPS 1926

Guttmann, Julius—*Philosophy of Judaism,* tr. David W. Silverman, New York: Holt, Rinehart and Winston 1964

Jacobs, Louis—*A Jewish Theology,* New York: Behrman House 1973

The Jewish People, Past and Present, 4 vols. Central Yiddish Cultural Organization, New York: Martin Press 1946 and subsequent years

* JPS—*Jewish Publication Society of America*—Philadelphia, Pa.

435

Kaplan, Mordecai M.—*The Greater Judaism in the Making,* New York: Reconstructionist Press 1960

Landman, I. ed.—*Universal Jewish Encyclopedia,* 10 vols. New York: Universal Jewish Encyclopedia Publishing Co. 1939-1943

Learsi, Rufus—*Israel: A History of the Jewish People,* Cleveland: World Publishing Co. 1949

Levinthal, Israel H.—*Point of View,* London and New York: Abelard Schuman 1958

Millgram, Abraham E.—*Great Jewish Ideas,* Washington, D. C., B'nai B'rith Department of Adult Jewish Education, 1964
—*Jewish Worship,* JPS 1971

Publications of American Jewish Historical Society 1893-1966

Roth, Cecil, ed.—*Encyclopedia Judaica,* 16 vols., Jerusalem: Keter 1972

Sachar, Howard—*The Course of Modern Jewish History,* Cleveland: World Publishing Co. 1958

Schechter, S.—*Studies in Judaism,* 3 vols. JPS 1896, 1908, 1924

Schwartz, Leo, ed.—*Great Ages and Ideas of Jewish People,* New York: Random House 1956

Simon, Maurice—*Jewish Religious Conflicts,* London: Hutchinson's University Library 1950

Singer, I., ed.—*Jewish Encyclopedia,* 12 vols., Funk & Wagnalls 1902-1905

Waxman, M.—*A History of Jewish Literature,* New York and London: Thomas Yoseloff (Second Edition) 1960

CHAPTER ONE

IN GOD'S NAME

Abrahams, Israel—*Jewish Life in the Middle Ages,* JPS 1920

Baer, Itzhak—*A History of the Jews in Christian Spain,* 2 vols., JPS 1966

Baron, Salo W.—*The Jewish Community,* 3 vols., JPS 1942

Ehrman, Albert—"The Origins of the Ritual Murder Accusation and Blood Libel," in *Tradition,* vol. 15 no. 4 (Spring 1976)

Ehrman, Ruth—*Jewish Life in the Middle Ages,* London: Edward Goldston, 1932

Finkelstein, Louis—*Jewish Self Government in the Middle Ages,* New York: The Jewish Theological Seminary of America, 1924

Flannery, Edward H.—*The Anguish of the Jews,* New York: Macmillan Co. 1964

Grayzel, Solomon—*The Church and the Jews in the Thirteenth Century,* New York: Hermon Press 1966

Hay, John—*Foot of Pride,* Boston: Beacon Press 1950
Liebeschutz, Hans—"Relevance of the Middle Ages for an Understanding of Contemporary Jewish History," in *Year Book XVIII, Leo Baeck Institute,* London: Secker and Warburg 1973
Lowenthal, Marvin—*Jews of Germany,* JPS 1938
—*A World Passed by,* New York: Behrman's 1938
Marcus, Jacob P.—*The Jew in the Medieval World* (A Source Book, 315-1791), New York: Meridian Books JPS 1960
Morton, Frederic—*The Rothschilds,* New York: Atheneum 1962

CHAPTER TWO

THE ROAD TO EMANCIPATION

Baron, Salo W.—"Ghetto and Emancipation," *Menorah Journal,* June 1928
Box, D. G. H.—"Hebrew Studies in the Reformation Period and After," in Edwyn R. Bevan, and Charles Singer, eds., *The Legacy of Israel,* Oxford: Clarendon Press 1927
Carsten, F. L.—"The Court Jews, A Prelude to Emancipation," in *Yearbook III, Leo Baeck Institute,* London: East and West Library 1958
Glatzer, Nahum N.—*The Dynamics of Emancipation,* Boston: Beacon Press 1968
Greenberg, Hayym—"The Myth of Jewish Parasitism," in *The Inner Eye,* New York: Jewish Frontier Publishing Co. 1953
Parkes, James—*Conflict of Church and Synagogue,* Cleveland: World Publishing Co. and JPS, Meridian 1961
—*The Jew in the Medieval Community,* London: 1938
Patinkin, Don—"Mercantilism and the Renaissance of the Jews in England," *Jewish Social Studies,* July 1946
Philipson, David—*Old European Jewries,* JPS 1943
Roth, Cecil—*Jews in Italy,* JPS 1946
—*A Life of Menasseh ben Israel,* JPS 1945
—*A History of the Jews in England,* Oxford: Clarendon Press 1941
—*The Magnificent Rothschilds,* London: 1939
—*The Jews in the Renaissance,* JPS 1959
Rudavsky, David—"Hebraic Studies in Colleges and Universities," *Religious Education,* July-Aug. 1964
Shohet, D. M.—*The Jewish Court in the Middle Ages,* New York: 1931
Strauss, Raphael—"The Jews in the Economic Evolution of Central Europe," *Jewish Social Studies,* January 1941
Wirth, Louis—*The Ghetto,* Chicago: University of Chicago Press, (Phoenix Books) 1958

CHAPTER THREE

THE ENLIGHTENMENT

Arendt, Hannah—"Privileged Jews," *Jewish Social Studies,* January 1946

Atlas, Samuel—"Solomon Maimon," in *Historia Judaica,* vol. XIII (1951), p. 109ff.

Herz, Henrietta—"A Salonist Remembers," in Leo W. Schwartz, ed. *Memoirs of My People,* JPS 1943

Jospe, Alfred—"Moses Mendelssohn," in Simon Noveck, ed. *Great Jewish Personalities in Modern Times,* Washington, D.C.: B'nai B'rith, Department of Adult Jewish Education 1960

Kopald, J.—"Friendship of Lessing and Mendelssohn," *Yearbook of the Central Conference of American Rabbis,* vol. 39, New York: 1929

Kupferberg, Herbert—*The Mendelsohns: Three Generations of Genius,* New York: Scribners 1972

Levy, Felix A.—"Moses Mendelssohn's Ideals of Religion and Their Relation to Reform Judaism," *Yearbook of the Central Conference of American Rabbis,* vol. 39, 1929

Lowenthal, Marvin—*The Jews of Germany,* JPS 1938

Marcus, Jacob R.—"Israel Jacobson," in *Yearbook of the Central Conference of American Rabbis,* vol. 38, pp. 386-498, 1928

Ozer, Charles L.—"Jewish Education in the Transition from Ghetto to Emancipation," *Historia Judaica,* vol. IX p. 75ff. 1947

Patterson, David—"Moses Mendelssohn's Conception of Tolerance," in *Between East and West,* (Essays in memory of Bela Horowitz) London 1958

Rothman, Walter—"Mendelssohn's Character and Philosophy of Religion," *Yearbook of the Central Conference of American Rabbis,* vol. 39, 1929

Schechter, Solomon—"The Dogmas of Judaism," in *Studies of Judaism,* First Series, JPS 1911

Untermeyer, Louis—*Heinrich Heine, Paradox and Poet:* 2 volumes, New York: 1937

CHAPTER FOUR

EMANCIPATION AND ITS AFTERMATH

Baron, Salo W.—"The Modern Age," in Schwarz, Leo, ed., *Great Ages and Ideas of the Jewish People,* New York: Modern Library, 1956

Kober, Adolph—"The French Revolution and the Jews in Germany," *Jewish Social Studies,* October 1945
Liptzin, Solomon—*Germany's Stepchildren,* JPS 1944
Lowenthal, Marvin—*The Jews of Germany,* JPS 1938
Posener, S.—"The Immediate Economic and Social Effect of the Emancipation of the Jews in France," *Jewish Social Studies,* July 1939
—"The Social Life of the Jewish Communities in France in the Eighteenth Century," *Jewish Social Studies,* July 1945
Schmidt, H. D.—"The Terms of the Emancipation, 1781-82," in *Yearbook I, Leo Baeck Institute,* London: East and West Library 1956
Szajkowski, Zosa—*The Economic Status of the Jews in Alsace, Metz and Lorraine* 1648-1789, New York: 1954
Waldman, Mark—*Goethe and the Jews,* New York: Putnam's 1934

CHAPTER FIVE

NATURE OF TRADITIONAL JUDAISM

Albo, Joseph—*Sefer Ha-Ikkarim (Book of Principles)* tr. Isaac Husik, 4 vols., JPS 1946
Appel, Gersion—*A Philosophy of Mitzvot,* New York: Ktav 1975
Belkin, Samuel—*Essays in Traditional Jewish Thought,* New York: Philosophical Library 1950
—*In His Image.* New York: Abelard Schuman 1960
Berkowitz, Eliezer—*God, Man and History,* New York: Jonathan David 1961
—*Man and God: Studies in Biblical Theology,* Detroit: Wayne State University Press 1969
—*Major Themes in Modern Philosophy of Judaism,* New York: Ktav 1974
Cohen, A., ed.—*The Soncino Books of the Bible* (14 volumes), London 1947 and subsequently
Daiches, Salis—"Dogma in Judaism," in Leo Jung, ed. *The Jewish Library Series II* New York: Bloch 1930
Danby, H.—*The Mishnah,* tr. from the Hebrew with introduction and brief explanatory notes. London: Oxford University Press, 1933
—*The Faith of Judaism,* London: Soncino Press, 1960
Epstein, Isidore, ed.—*The Babylonian Talmud with Introduction and Commentary,* London: Soncino Press, vol. 1-36, 1935-1952
—ed. *Maimonides, VIII Centenary Memorial Volume,* London: Soncino Press 1935-1952

—*Hasidism,* tr., by Dr. Greta Hort and others, New York: Philosophical Library 1948

—*I and Thou,* tr. by Ronald Gregor Smith, Second edition, New York: Charles Scribner's Sons 1958

—*Israel and The World,* New York: Schocken Books 1948

—*Tales of the Hasidim, The Early Masters,* tr. by Olga Marx, New York: Schocken Books 1947

—*Tales of the Hasidim, The Later Masters,* tr. by Olga Marx, New York: Schocken Books 1948

—*Ten Rungs: Hasidic Sayings,* tr. by Olga Marx, New York: Schocken Books 1947

—*Jewish Mysticism and the Legends of the Baal Shem,* tr. by Lucy Cohen, London: Dent 1931

Diamond, Malcolm L.—*Martin Buber: Jewish Existentialist,* New York: Oxford Press 1960

Dresner, Samuel H.—*The Zaddik,* New York: Abelard Schuman 1960

Dubnow, Simon—*History of the Jews in Russia and Poland,* vols. 1 and 2, JPS 1946 (reprinted)

Friedman, Maurice S.—*Martin Buber: The Life of Dialogue,* Chicago: University of Chicago Press 1955

—"Martin Buber" in Simon Noveck ed. *Great Jewish Thinkers of the Twentieth Century,* Washington, D. C.: B'nai B'rith Department of Adult Education 1963

Ginzberg, Louis—"The Cabbala" in *Jewish Law and Lore,* JPS 1955

Greenstone, Julius H.—*The Messiah Idea in Jewish History,* JPS 1943

Grossman, Mordecai—"A Mystical Approach to Judaism," *Menorah Journal,* vol. 16, p. 97ff, February 1929

Herberg, Will—*The Writings of Martin Buber,* New York: Meridian Press 1956

Jacobs, Louis—*Hassidic Prayer,* New York: Schocken Press 1973

Judaism—A Quarterly Journal, New York: vol. 9, Summer 1960 (Issue devoted to Hassidism)

Klausner, Joseph—*Messianic Idea in Israel from Its Beginning to the Completion of the Mishna,* tr. William F. Stinespring, New York: Macmillan Co. 1955

Levin, Meyer—*The Golden Mountain,* New York: Jonathan Cape and Robert Ballou 1932

Minkin, Jacob S.—*The Romance of Hassidim,* New York: Thomas Yoseloff (new edition) 1955

Mintz, Jerome R.—*Legends of the Hassidim,* Chicago: University of Chicago Press 1974

Muller, Ernest—*History of Jewish Mysticism,* Oxford: East and West Library 1946

Newman, Louis I.—*Hasidic Anthology,* New York: Bloch Publishing Co. 1944

—and Samuel Spitz—*Maggidim and Hasidim* (anthology), New York: Bloch Publishing Co. 1962

Freedman, H. and Maurice Simon, ed.—*Midrash Rabbah,* translated with brief notes, vols. 1-10, London: Soncino Press, 1939

Freehof, Solomon B.—*Responsa Literature,* JPS 1955
—*A Treasury of Responsa,* JPS 1963

Ginzberg, L.—*On Jewish Law and Lore* (Essay: 'Introduction to the Babylonian Talmud') JPS 1955

Ganzfried, Solomon—*Code of Jewish Law,* tr. Herman Golden, New York: Hebrew Publishing Co., 1927

Halevi, Judah—*Book of Kuzari,* tr. Hartwig Hirschfeld, New York: Pardes 1946
—*The Kuzari,* ed. by I. Heinemann, London: East and West Library 1947

Klapperman, Gilbert—*The Story of Yeshiva University,* New York: Yeshiva Univ. Press 1969

Lamm, Norman—*Faith and Doubt,* New York: Ktav 1972

Lauterbach, J. Z.—*Mekilta,* 3 vols. JPS 1941
—*Midrash and Mishnah,* JPS 1941

Liebman, Charles S.—"Orthodoxy in American Jewish Life," in *AJYB* vol. 66 (1965), p. 21

Pool, David de Sola, ed.—*The Traditional Prayer Book* (prepared under the direction of Rabbinical Council of America), New York: Behrman House Inc. 1960

Rackman, Emanuel—*One Man's Judaism,* New York: Philosophical Library 1970

Rothkoff, Aaron—*Bernard Revel,* JPS 1972

Strack, H. L.—*Introduction to the Talmud and Midrash,* JPS 1931

Waxman, Meyer—*Judaism, Religion and Ethics,* New York: Thomas Yoseloff 1958

Wouk, Herman—*This is My God,* New York: Doubleday and Co. (paperback) 1960

Zimmels, H. J.—*Ashkenazim and Sephardim,* New York: Oxford University Press 1958

CHAPTER SIX

HASSIDISM AND NEO-HASSIDISM

Buber, Martin—*The Tales of Rabbi Nachman,* tr. Maurice Friedman, New York: Horizon Press 1958

—*Hasidism and Modern Man* ed. and tr. by Maurice Friedman, New York: Horizon Press 1958

—*For the Sake of Heaven,* tr. from the German by Ludwig Lewison JPS 1945. Second edition with new foreword. New York: Harper & Bros. 1953, Meridian, JPS (paperback) 1958

Poll, Solomon—*The Hassidic Community of Williamsburg,* Glencoe: The Free Press, Inc. 1962

Raisin, M.—*The Haskallah Movement in Russia,* JPS 1913

Rubinstein, Aryeh—*Hassidism,* New York and Paris: Leon Amiel 1975

Schneerson, Joseph I.—*Some Aspects of Chabad Chassidim,* Brooklyn, New York: Machne Israel (770 Eastern Parkway) 1961

Schilpp, Paul A. and Friedman, Maurice—"The Philosophy of Martin Buber," in *Library of Living Philosophers,* vol. 12, London: Cambridge University Press 1967

Scholem, Gershon—*Major Trends in Jewish Mysticism,* New York: Schocken (seventh printing) 1973

—*Sabbetai Zevi,* Princeton: Princeton University Press 1975

Simon, Ernest—"Martin Buber and German Judaism," in *Leo Baeck Institute Yearbook III,* London: East and West Library 1958

Silver, Abba Hillel—*A History of Messianic Speculation in Israel,* Boston: Beacon Press 1959

Sperling, Henry and Maurice Simon, and P. Levertoff tr.—*The Zohar,* 5 vols. London: Soncino Press 1931-1934

Schneur Zalman of Liadi—*Tanya,* tr. Misan Mindel, Brooklyn, New York: Kehot Publication Society 1962

Urbach, E. E. et al eds.—"Studies in Mysticism and Religion," presented to Gershom G. Scholem, Jerusalem: Hebrew University Magnes Press 1967

Weiner, Herbert—*9½ Mystics: The Kabbala Today,* New York: Holt, Rinehart and Winston 1969

Wiesel, Elie—*Souls on Fire,* tr. Marion Wiesel, New York: Random House 1972

CHAPTER SEVEN

THE STRUGGLE FOR REFORM JUDAISM IN GERMANY

Freehof, Solomon—*Reform Jewish Practice and Its Rabbinic Background,* Cincinnati: Hebrew Union College 1952

Katsh, Abraham I.—"Nachman Krochmal and the German Idealists," *Jewish Social Studies* April 1946

Landsberg, Max—"The Reform Movement after Abraham Gelger," *Yearbook of the Central Conference of American Rabbis*, vol. 20, 1910

Morgenstern, Julian—*As a Mighty Stream*, JPS 1949

Nussbaum, Max—"Nachman Krochmal," *American Jewish Yearbook*, vol. 44, JPS 1942

Petuchowski, J. J.—*Prayerbook Reform in Europe*, New York: Union of American Hebrew Congregations 1968

Philipson, David—*Reform Movement in Judaism*, New York: Macmillan 1931

Plaut, W. Gunther—*The Rise of Reform Judaism*, New York: 1963
—*Growth of Reform Judaism*, New York: 1965

Raisin, Jacob S.—"The Reform Movement before Geiger," *Yearbook of the Central Conference of American Rabbis*, vol. 20, 1910

Schechter, Solomon—"Abraham Geiger," in *Studies in Judaism* (third series) JPS 1924

Schwartzman, Sylvan—*The Story of Reform Judaism*, New York: Union of American Hebrew Congregations 1953

Schorsch, Ismar—"The Philosophy of History of Nachman Krochmal," *Judaism*, vol. 10, No. 3 (Summer) 1961

Weiner, Max—"Abraham Geiger and the Science of Judaism," *Judaism* vol. II, No. 1, January 1953
—*Abraham Geiger and Liberal Judaism*, tr. Ernest J. Schlochauer, JPS 1962

CHAPTER EIGHT

THE HISTORICAL SCHOOL

Bamberger, Bernard—"Beginnings of Modern Jewish Scholarship," *Yearbook of the Central Conference of American Rabbis*, vol. 42, 1932

Bamberger, F.—"Zunz's Conception of History," in *Proceedings of the American Academy for Jewish Research*, vol. 12, 1941

Frankel, Zacharia—"On Changes in Judaism," in Mordecai Waxman, ed. *Tradition and Change*, New York: Burning Bush Press 1958

Ginzberg, Louis—"Zechariah Frankel," in *Students, Scholars and Saints* (reprinted) JPS 1945

Reissner, H. G.—"Rebellious Dilemma—The Case Histories of Eduard Gans and Some of His Partisans," in *Yearbook II, Leo Baeck Institute*, London: East and West Library 1957

Rudavsky, David—"The Historical School of Zecharia Frankel," in *Journal of Jewish Sociology;* vol. V, no. 2 (Dec. 1963), p. 12ff.

Schechler, Solomon—"Leopold Zunz," in *Studies in Judaism,* Third
    Series, JPS 1924
    —"Historical Judaism," in Mordecai Waxman, ed. *Tradition and
    Change,* New York: Burning Bush Press 1958
Wallech, L.—"Beginnings of Science of Judaism," *Historia Judaica,*
    April 1946
Wolf, Immanuel—"On the Concept of a Science of Judaism," (1822)
    in *Yearbook II, Leo Baeck Institute,* London: East and West
    Library 1957

CHAPTER NINE

NEO-ORTHODOXY IN GERMANY

Breuer, Jacob, ed.—*Fundamentals of Judaism,* New York: Phillip
    Feldheim 1949
Hirsch, Samson R.—*Introduction to Commentary on Torah,* tr. Joseph
    Breuer, New York: Phillip Feldheim 1948
    —*Nineteen Letters of Ben Uziel,* tr. Bernard Drachman, New
    York: Funk and Wagnalls 1899
    —*Judaism Eternal* (selected essays), tr. L. Grunfeld, 2 vols.
    London: Soncino Press 1956
    —*Horeb,* tr. I. Grunfeld, 2 vols., London: Soncino Press 1962
    —*The Pentateuch,* commentary tr. by Isaac Levy, New York:
    Bloch Publishing Co. 1956-1962
    —*The Psalms,* commentary tr. by Gertrude Hirschler, New York:
    Phillip Feldheim 1960
Jelenko, Edward W.—"Samson Raphael Hirsch," in Simon Noveck,
    ed. *Great Jewish Personalities in Modern Times,* Washington,
    D.C. B'nai B'rith Department of Adult Education 1960
Jung, Leo—"Samson Raphael Hirsch," in *Guardians of Our Heritage,*
    New York: Bloch Publishing Co. 1958
Rosenbloom, Noah H.—*Tradition in an Age of Reform: The Religious
    Philosophy of Samson Raphael Hirsch,* JPS 1976
Schwab, Herman—*History of Orthodox Jewry in Germany,* tr. Irene
    R. Birnbaum, London: Mitre Press 1950
Wolfsberg, Y.—"Popular Orthodoxy" in *Yearbook I, Leo Baeck In-
    stitute,* London: East and West Library 1956

CHAPTER TEN

LUZZATTO'S NEO-ORTHODOXY

Morais, Sabbato—"Samuel David Luzzatto," in *Italian Hebrew Literature*, New York: Jewish Theological Seminary 1926
Newman, Aryeh—"Luzzatto—Centenary of a Modern Traditionalist," in *American Zionist*, vol. 56, no. 3, December 1965
Rosenbloom, Noah H.—*Luzzatto's Ethics—Psychological Interpretation of Judaism: A Study in the Religious Philosophy of Samuel David Luzatto*, New York: Yeshiva University 1965
Rudavsky, David—"S. D. Luzzatto's Jewish Nationalism," *Herzl Yearbook*, vol. 6, New York: Herzl Press 1964-5
—"Samuel Luzzatto and Neo-Orthodoxy," *Tradition*, vol. VII, no. 3, Fall 1965

CHAPTER ELEVEN

ON TO AMERICA!

Baron, Salo W.—"The Impact of the Revolution of 1848 on Jewish Emancipation," *Jewish Social Studies*, July 1949
Glanz, Rudolph—"The Immigration of German Jews up to 1880," *YIVO Annual of Jewish Social Science*, vol. 2-3, 1947-48
—"Source Materials on the History of Jewish Immigration to the U.S. 1800-1880," *YIVO Annual of Jewish Social Science*, vol. 6, 1951
Glanz, Rudolf—"German Jews in New York City in the Nineteenth Century," in *YIVO Annual of Jewish Social Science*, Vol. 11, 1956-7
Kisch, Guido—*In Search of Freedom*, London: Edward Goldson and Son 1949
Kober, Adolph—"Jews in the Revolution of 1848 in Germany," *Jewish Social Studies*, April 1948
Kohler, Max—"Jewish Rights at the Congress of Vienna (1814-15) and Aix-la-chapelle," *Publications of the American Jewish Historical Society*, vol. 21, 1918
Wischnitzer, Mark—*To Dwell in Safety*, JPS 1949

CHAPTER TWELVE

REFORM JUDAISM IN AMERICA

Borowitz, Eugene B.—"Reform Judaism in America," *Judaism*, vol. 3, no. 4, Fall 1954

CCAR Journal—A Commentary on "Reform Judaism—A Centenary Perspective," (Special Issue) vol. XXIV, no. 2, Spring 1977

The Centennial of Reform Judaism in America, Publication of the American Jewish Historical Society, vol. LXIII, no. 2, December 1973

Cohon, Samuel M.—"Kaufmann Kohler, the Reformer," in *Mordecai Kaplan Jubilee Volume*, Jewish Theological Seminary, New York: 1953

——"Reform Judaism in America," *Judaism*, vol. 3, no. 4, Fall 1954

——"Kaufman Kohler," in Simon Noveck, ed. *Great Jewish Thinkers of the Twentieth Century*, Washington, D.C.: B'nai B'rith Department of Adult Education 1963

Freehof, Solomon—*Reform Responsa*, Cincinnati: Hebrew Union College Press 1960

Glatzer, Nathan—*American Judaism*, Chicago: University of Chicago Press 1959

Heller, Joseph—*The Zionist Idea*, New York: Schocken 1949

Hirschler, Eric E. ed.—*Jews from Germany in the U.S.*, New York: 1955

Hyamson, A. M.—*Palestine under the Mandata 1920-1948*, London: 1950

Knox, Israel—"Isaac Mayer Wise" in Simon Noveck ed., *Great Jewish Personalities in Modern Times*, Washington, D.C.: B'nai B'rith Department of Adult Education 1960

——*Rabbi in America* (Story of Isaac M. Wise) Boston: Little, Brown and Co. 1959

Lauterbach, Jacob Z.—*Rabbinic Essays*, Cincinnati: Hebrew Union College 1951

Learsi, Rufus—*Jews in America*, with epilogue by Abraham J. Karp, 1954-1971, New York: Ktav 1972

Levy, Beryl—*Reform Judaism in America*, New York: 1933

Levy, Felix A.—"Reform Judaism in America," *Judaism* vol. 1, no. 4, October 1952

Marcus, Jacob Rader—*American Jewry: Documents, Eighteenth Century*, Cincinnati: Hebrew Union College 1959

Morgenstern, Julian—*As A Mighty Stream*, JPS 1949

Neuman, J. H.—"Jewish Battalion and the Palestine Campaign," *American Jewish Yearbook*, vol. 21, 1919

Petuchowski, Jacob J.—"Bookbinder to the Rescue," *Conservative Judaism*, vol. XXX, no. 1, Fall 1975, p. 7ff.

Philipson, David—*Max Lilienthal, American Rabbi,* New York: Bloch 1915
—*My Life as an American and a Jew,* Cincinnati: J. G. Kidd & Son 1941
—*The Reform Movement in Judaism,* New York: Macmillan Co. 1931
Reform Judaism—Essays by Alumni of Hebrew Union College, Cincinnati: Hebrew Union College Press 1949
Schappes, Morris U.—*Documentary History of the Jews in the United States,* (revised ed.) New York: Citadel Press 1952
Schwartz, Jacob D., ed.—*Responsa* of the Central Conference of American Rabbis, contained in Yearbooks 1-50, New York: Union of American Hebrew Congregations 1954 (mimeographed)
Schwartzman, Sylvan D.—*The Story of Reform Judaism,* New York: Union of American Hebrew Congregations 1953
Stein, Leo—*The Racial Thinking of Richard Wagner,* New York: Philosophical Library 1950
Temkin, Sefton—"New Reform Liturgy," *Conservative Judaism,* vol. XXX, no. 1 (Fall 1975), p. 16ff.
—"A Century of Reform Judaism in America, *AJYB,* vol. 74 (1973-74), pp. 3ff.
Weitzman, Chaim—*Trial and Error,* JPS 1949
Wilansky, Dena—*Sinai to Cincinnati,* New York Renaissance Book Co. 1939
Yearbook of the Central Conference of American Rabbis from 1890 to date.

CHAPTER THIRTEEN

CONSERVATIVE JUDAISM

Adler, Cyrus—*I Have Considered the Days,* JPS 1945
—*Jacob Henry Schiff, His Life and Letters,* 2 vols. New York: 1928
—"Louis Marshall," *American Jewish Yearbook,* vol. 32 JPS 1930
—ed.—Semi-Centennial Volume, New York: The Jewish Theological Seminary of America 1939
Bentwich, Norman—*Solomon Schechter,* JPS 1948
Davis, Moshe—*The Emergence of Conservative Judaism,* JPS 1962
Dorff, Eliot M.—*Conservative Judaism,* New York: United Synagogue of America 1977
Friedman, Theodore—"Jewish Tradition in Twentieth Century America: The Conservative Approach," in *Judaism,* vol. 3, no. 4 (Fall) 1954

Gordis, Robert, ed.—"Conservative Judaism on its Ninetieth Birthday (symposium view from the right and left) in *Judaism,* vol. 26, no. 3 (Summer 1977)

Kaplan, Lawrence J.—"Dilemma of Conservative Judaism," *Commentary,* vol. 62 no. 5, (November 1976) p. 44

Karp, Abraham J.—*A History of the United Synagogue of America 1913-1963,* New York: United Synagogue of America 1964

Leeser, Isaac—*Discourses in the Jewish Religion,* 10 vols. Philadelphia: 1844-1867

Lerner, Anne Lapidus—"Who Hast Not Made Me A Man," The Movement for Equal Rights in American Jewry, *AJYB,* vol. 77 (1977), p. 3ff

Neuman, Abraham A.—"Cyrus Adler," *American Jewish Yearbook,* vol. 42, JPS 1940

Novak, David—*Law and Theology in Judaism,* New York: Ktav 1974

Parzen, Herbert—*Architects of Conservative Judaism,* New York: Jonathan David 1964

Schechter, Solomon—*Seminary Address and Other Papers,* New York: Burning Bush Press (paperback edition) 1959
—*Some Aspects of Rabbinic Theology,* New York: Schocken Press (paperback edition) 1961
—*Studies in Judaism,* JPS First Series (1896)—Second Series (1908)—Third Series (1924)

Siegel, Seymour, ed.—*Conservative Judaism and Jewish Law,* New York: Rabbinical Assembly 1977

Sklare, Marshall—*Conservative Judaism,* Glencoe, Illinois: Glencoe Free Press 1955

Waxman, Mordecai ed.—*Tradition and Change,* New York: Burning Bush Press 1958

Zeitlin, Joseph—*Disciples of the Wise,* New York: Teachers College Press, Columbia University 1945

CHAPTER FOURTEEN

RECONSTRUCTIONISM

Agus, Jacob—"Law as Standards," *Conservative Judaism,* vol. 6 no. 4, (May 1950)
—*Modern Philosophy of Judaism,* New York: Behrman House 1970

Cohen, Jack J.—*The Case for Religious Naturalism,* New York: Reconstructionist Press 1958

Eisenstein, Ira—*Creative Judaism,* New York: Behrman's 1936
—*Judaism Without Supernaturalism,* New York: Reconstructionist Press 1958
—"Mordecai M. Kaplan" in Simon Noveck, ed. *Great Jewish Thinkers of the Twentieth Century,* Washington, D.C.: B'nai B'rith Department of Adult Education 1963
Kaplan, Mordecai M.—*The Greater Judaism in the Making,* New York: Reconstructionist Press 1960
—*The Purpose and Meaning of Jewish Existence,* JPS 1964
—*Judaism as a Civilization,* New York: Reconstructionist Press (reprint) 1957
—*Future of the American Jew,* New York: Macmillan 1948
—*The Meaning of God in Modern Jewish Religion,* New York: Behrman's 1937
—*Judaism in Transition,* New York: Covici Friede 1936
—*The Religion of Ethical Nationhood,* New York: Macmillan 1970
—"Unity in Diversity in the Conservative Movement," in Mordecai Waxman, ed. *Tradition and Change,* New York: Burning Bush Press 1958
—"Toward the Formation of Guiding Principles for the Conservative Movement," in Mordecai Waxman, ed. *Tradition and Change,* New York: Burning Bush Press 1958
Liebman, Charles S.—"Reconstruction in American Jewish Life," *AJYB,* vol. 71 (1970), p. 318ff.
Martin, Bernard—"Conservative Judaism and Reconstructionism in the Last Three Decades," *Journal of Reform Judaism* (formerly CCAR Journal) vol. XXV, no. 2 (Spring 1978), p. 95ff.
Steinberg, Milton—"Reconstructionism—A Creative Program" in Mordecai Waxman, ed. *Tradition and Change,* New York: Burning Bush Press 1958
—*Anatomy of a Faith,* New York: Harcourt, Brace and Co. 1960

CHAPTER FIFTEEN

ORTHODOXY IN AMERICA

Baron, Salo W.—*The Russian Jew Under Tsars and Soviets,* New York: Macmillan 1976
Belkin, Samuel—*Essays in Traditional Jewish Thought,* New York: Abelard Schuman 1956

Dresner, Samuel H.—*Levi Yithak of Berditschev,* New York: Hartmore House 1974

Goodman, Abraham Vasser—*American Overture,* JPS 1947

Greenberg, Louis—*The Jews in Russia,* 2 vols. New Haven: Yale University Press 1944

Grimstein, Herman—*The Rise of the Jewish Community of New York 1654-1860,* JPS 1945

Horowitz, George—*Spirit of Jewish Law,* New York: Central Book Co. 1963

Karp, Abraham J.—"New York Chooses a Chief Rabbi," *Publications of the American Jewish Historical Society,* vol. 44, March 1955

Kranzler, George—*Williamsburg—A Jewish Community in Transition,* New York: Phillip Feldheim 1961

Lamm, Norman—*Faith and Doubt: Studies in Traditional Jewish Thought,* New York: Ktav 1972

Learsi, Rufus—*The Jews in America: A History,* Cleveland: World Publishing Co. 1954

Lichtenstein, Ahron—"Joseph Soloveitchik" in Simon Noveck, ed. *Great Jewish Thinkers of the Twentieth Century,* Washington, D.C.: B'nai B'rith Department of Jewish Education 1963

Liebman, Charles S.—"Orthodoxy in American Jewish Life," in *American Jewish Yearbook,* vol. 66, JPS 1965
—*The Ambivalent American Jew: Politics, Religion and Family in American Jewish Life,* JPS 1973

Marcus, Jacob R.—*Early American Jewry,* 2 vols. JPS 1951

Poll, Solomon—*The Hassidic Community of Williamsburg,* Glencoe, Ill.: Glencoe Free Press 1961

Rackman, Emanuel—"American Orthodoxy, Retrospect and Prospect," in *Judaism,* vol. 3, no. 4 (Fall 1954)
—*One Man's Judaism,* New York: Philosophical Library 1970

Rothkoff, Aaron—*Bernard Revel,* JPS 1972

Rubin, Israel—*Satmar, An Island in the City,* New York: Quadrangle Books 1972

Schappes, Morris—*A Documentary History of the Jews in the United States 1654-1875,* New York: Citadel Press 1952

Shapiro, David S.—*Studies in Jewish Thought,* New York: Yeshiva University Press 1975

Soloveitchik, Joseph B.—"The Lonely Man of Faith," *Tradition,* vol. 7, no. 2 (Summer 1965), p. 5ff.

Starr, Joshua—"Jewish Citizenship in Roumania 1878-1940," *Jewish Social Studies,* January 1941

Tscherikower, E.—"Jewish Immigrants to the United States 1881-1900," *YIVO Annual,* vol. 6, 1951

Whiteman, Maxwell—*A History of the Jews in Philadelphia,* JPS 1957

Wischnitzer, Mark—*To Dwell in Safety,* JPS 1948

INDEX

Aaron of Lincoln, 22
Abbé Gregoire, 81
Abelard, Peter, 35-36
Abrahamism, 258-260, 264
Abravanel, Isaac, 68
Adler, Cyrus, 323-324, 330
Aggada, 103, 105
Agudat Ha-Rabbanim 382ff., and Kaplan, 360
Agudath Israel, 96, 244ff., 385ff.
Ahad Ha-Am, 140, 270, 334ff., 353ff.
Akiva, Rabbi, 101
Albo, Joseph, 60, 68, 255
Alexander III, 375
Alien Status, 23, 24, 26, 30, 95; compulsory ghetto, 27; in Germany, 93
America, Jewry in: 58, 271-273, 282ff.; Judeophobia, 308ff.; Reform Movement, 166, 285ff., and Zionism, 301ff., changes, 309ff., in early 1900's, 325-327; Conservative Movement, 317ff., Orthodoxy, 376ff.
American Council for Judaism, 245, 315-316, 401
American Zionist Federation, 321
Anti-Semitism, in Europe, 303ff, in America, 308ff.
Apostasy, 74-76, 157
Aquinas, Thomas, 35
Arabs, 34-36; philosophical and scientific knowledge, 36; cultural interests, 114; and Palestine, 307; see Islam
Arbaah Turim, 108
Aristotle, 63, 67, 107, 133; Aristotelian thought, 35, 37, 195, 252, 259, 266
Ash, Abraham Joseph, 374
Ashkenazim, 80-81, 96, 108, 112-115, 160, 272, 284, 318, 371ff.
Assembly of Notables, see France
Association for the Interests of Orthodox Judaism, 244
Atticism, 258-260, 265
Baal Shem Tov, Israel, see Besht
Bachya ibn Pakuda, 66
Bacon, Roger, 36
Baeck, Leo, 141
Baer, Dov of Meseritz, 131, 137
Balfour Declaration, 273, 306
Bamberger, Seligman Ber, 224
Bar Kochba, 102
Bassevi, Jacob, 45
Behrend, Bernard, 281
Beilis, Mendel, 21
Belkin, Samuel, 379
Ben Asher, Jacob, 108
Ben David, Abraham of Posquieres, 111
Berlin Temple, 159, 179
Berlin Temple Verein, 206
Berliner, Nachman, 165
Bernard of Clairvaux, 20
Bernays, Isaac, 160ff., 201-202, 219-220
Bernhard, Isaac, 51
Berr, Berr Isaac, 82, 84
Berr, Cerf, 80
Besht, 121ff.; his teachings, 123; his disciples, 123; 336
Bet Din, 287, 344, 383
Beth Elohim, Charleston, 285
Biur, 69, 71
Black Death, 22
Blood Libel, 20ff.
Blumenthal, Joseph, 321
Board of Delegates of American Israelites, 296, 319
Board of Delegates of Orthodox Hebrew Congregations, 375

Boccaccio, Giovanni, 37
Borne, Ludwig, 280
Brandeis, Louis Dembitz, 282
Brazil, 47
Breslau, Mayer Israel, 165
Breslau, Mendel, 70
Brit Emet, 164
Buber, Martin, 96, 139ff.; biographical, 140-141; Zionism, 142-143; dialogue relationship, 144ff.; influence on others, 153-155
Cabbala; and Christian doctrines, 39; in Hassidism, 118-119, 129, 133, 146
Capital and Capitalism, 44ff., 48
Caro, Joseph, 108
Catherine of Russia, 52
Catholic Israel, 319, 332ff.
Central Conference of American Rabbis, 297-298, 302
Chamberlain, Houston Stewart, 303, 308
Chorin, Aaron, 161, 205
Chmielnicki, Bogdan, 116-117
Chosen People, Doctrine of, 92, 362
Christian IV, 46
Christian Advocates of Religious Freedom, 18
Christian Hebraists, 39-41
Christian State, Doctrine of, 92, 279
Christianity: 68, 110, 113, 114, 121, 124, 148; universal goal, 62; creed, 66, 109, Roman Catholic dogma, 110; Buber's impact on, 153-155; 214, 291, 300; in Germany, 276ff.
Christ-killers, 22
Church and Jews, 19, 42
Church and State: Mendelssohn's views, 59-60; place of law, 62; *assignats,* 84
Cohen, Nehemia, 119
Collegio Rabbinico, 251
Columbus, Christopher, 43, 367
Columbus Platform, 273, 311ff., 400
Commentary on the Mishnah, see Maimonides
Commerce, Jews in, see Occupations, Jewish

Commercial Revolution, 43ff.
Condillac, Etienne, 253-254
Congress of Hebrew Culture, 335
Congress of Vienna, 187, 263, 274-275
Coronel, Nachman Nathan, 269
Conrad III, Emperor, 20
Conrad IV, 22
Conservativism: 77, 184; Schechter's and Ginzberg's views, 199-200; see America, Jewry in:
Copernicus, 36
Cossack Uprising, 116-117
Council of Nicea, 66
Council of the Four Lands, 26
Council of Trent, 42
Counter - Reformation, 30, 42
Crémieux, Adolphe, 281
Crescas, Hasdai, 68, 255
Critique of Pure Reason, see Kant, Immanuel
Cromwell, 46, 58
Crusades, The, 17, 20, 23, 34, 43, 47, 113-114
Cultural Zionism, see Ahad Ha-Am
da Gama, Vasco, 43
Darkei Hamishna, see F r a n k e l, Zacharia
d'Asniers, 93
Declaration of the Rights of Man, see France
Deism and Deists; 55, 60, 70; and natural religion, 63; 156
Denmark, 46
De Pintos, 47
Derishat Zion, 247
Descartes, René, 260ff.
Desecration of the Host, 21
Devotional Addresses of the Jews, see Zunz, Leopold
Dewey, John, 354
Die Deborah, see Wise, Isaac Mayer
Die Welt, see Buber, Martin
Dohm, Christian Wilhelm von, 57-58, 72, 80-81
Dreyfus, Alfred, 304-305
Dubnow, Simon, 354
Durkheim, Emile, 354
Dutch Guiana, 47
Edict of 1812, 204

Edict of Toleration, 72-73
Edward III, 44
Eger, Rabbi Akiva, 163-164
Einhorn, David, 283, 286, 292ff.
Eisenmenger, Johann Andreas, 40-41
Eleh Divrei Habrit, 163
Elijah of Vilna, 137ff., 336
Elimelech, Rabbi of Lizensk, 126
Emancipation, 17, 18, 47, 49, 58, 69, 76; price of, 62; Mendelssohn's impact upon, 74; in France, 82-83; in Germany, 91, 93; in Europe, 93; 178, 235; Luzzatto's views, 265-267
Emerson, Ralph Waldo, 255
Encyclopedists, 17, 18
Enfranchisement: 88; of European Jewry, 83
England, 46
Enlightenment, General, 17, 56, 60
Enlightenment, Jewish; see *Haskalah*
Entdecktes Judenthum, see Eisenmenger, Johann
Epistles to the Jews, see Schechter, Solomon
Erasmus, 38
Essay Concerning Human Understanding, 37
Essay on Compensation, 255
Euchel, Isaac, 70
Ewald, John, 277
Excommunication, see *Herem*
Expulsion: from England, 23; from Spain, 23; from France, 23; averted in Antwerp, 45; and in Venice, 45; and in Bordeaux and Hamburg, 46
Faith and Works: in Judaism, 63; in Christianity, 64
Familienten Gesetz, 29-30
Felsenthal, Bernard, 283
Festival Prayer Book, see Kaplan, Mordecai M.
Feudalism, 23; religiously dominated system, 23; Jew as middleman, 23; as moneylender, 24
Fichte, 92
Financiers, Jewish, 45ff., 80
Finkelstein, Louis, 330, 339
France, Jews in: 46, 48, 79-91; National Assembly, 81-82; Declaration of the Rights of Man, 81, 91; civic equality for Jews, 81-82; Cult of Reason, 83; Temple of Reason, 83; reaction to Emancipation, 83; the Directorate, 84; Alsatian Jews, 84-85; Assembly of Notables, 85-90; Grand Sanhedrin, 89-90; Infamous Decrees, 90-91; *Organic Regulation on the Mosaic Religion,* 91; Consistory, 91; assimilation, 91; Dreyfus affair, 304-305
Frank, Jacob, 121, 125
Frank L. Weil Institute, 315
Frankel, David, 50
Frankel, Zacharia, 174, 189, 192ff., 270, 319
Frankfort Conference, 179, 206ff., 216
Frankfort Reform Society, 268
Frederick II, 27, 93
Frederick the Great, 47
Frederick William II, 74
Frederick William IV, 280
French National Assembly, see France
French Revolution, 33, 42, 74, 79-80, 91, 276
Friedlander, David, 72, 156
Fries, Wilhelm, 276-277
Furtado, Abraham, 86
Galen, 36
Gans, Eduard, 187-188
Ganzfried, Shlomo, 108
Geiger, Abraham, 167; 172ff.; 189, 208, 220; scholarly research, 174-175; theories, 175-178; 291
Gemara, 103, 111
Genizah, 325
Geonim, 105, 215, 252-253
Germany, 46-49; and Jewish Enlightenment, 50-78; and Reform Judaism, 156ff.; Historical School, 192ff.; see also Violence, Nazi
Gershom, Rabbenu of Mayence, 25, 105
Gersonides, 255
Ghetto, 18, 27ff., 69, 95; self-segregation, 27; compulsory ghetto, 27;

in Italy, 27; in Germany, 27-28, 29; in Poland, 28, 29; in France, 28; origin of name, 28; walled area, 28; restrictions, 29; cultural and spiritual life, 30-31; economic life, 31-32; effect on the Jew, 32; jargons, 33; abolition, 33, 83; 275, 240-241

Ginzberg, Asher, see Ahad Ha-Am

Ginzberg, Louis, 340, 360

Giyur, Rite of, 65

Goethe, 33, 75, 92, 264

Gottheil, Gustave, 301

Graetz, Heinrich, 189, 266

Grotius, Hugo, 195

Guide for the Perplexed of the Time, 169

Guilds, Craft 23, 24, 44; as religious fraternities, 23

Gutenberg, John, 38

Habad, 96, 132-135, 324, 396

Hacohen, Jacob Joseph, see Besht, disciples of

Halacha, 65, 101, 106, 139; Frankel's interest, 193; 341ff.; 388ff.

Halevi, Abraham Eliezer, 163, 267

Halevi, Judah, 169, 249, 251, 255, 263, 290, 332

Halutzim, 142-143

Hamburg Temple, 159-160; dispute, 201

Ha-Meassef, 70-71

Hammarskjold, Dag, 154

Harby, Isaac, 285

Hardenberg, Prince, 277

Har Sinai Verein, 286

Haskalah, 17, 71, 73, 95; inroads of, 139

Hassidism, 96; conditions giving rise to, 116-121; how founded, 121-123; principal doctrines: God, 125-126; Good and Evil, 126-127; Prayer, 127-128; Joy, 129; *Tzaddik,* 129-132; *Habad* School, 132-135; opposition to, 135-139; 273

Hazakkah, 25; *Jus Cazaka,* 25

Hebrew, 70; in the Renaissance period, 38; rabbinic literature and Christianity, 38-41; Christian Hebraists, 38, 40; texts, 49; in

France, 88; in the service, 96; literature (Golden Age in Spain), 114; in Hamburg Temple, 159-160; Geiger's view, 178-179; issue at Frankfort Conference, 207ff.; Hirsch's view, 238, 242; and Luzzatto, 268-269; in American Reform, 295, in Palestine, 307 Schechter's view, 335

Hebrew Benevolent Society, 284

Hebrew Melodies, see Heine, Heinrich

Hebrew Union College, 296ff., 315, 324

Hegel, George Wilhelm, 167-168, 188, 190, 292

Heine, Heinrich, 75-76, 188, 280

Hellenism, 66

Heller, Maximilian, 301

Henry II of England, 22

Herem, 24-25; exercised by the Kahal, 24-25; and intermarriage, 89; 360

Herz, Henriette and Marcus, 75, 190

Herzl, Theodor, 301, 305, 334

Hess, Mendel, 165

Hess, Moses, 238

Hevrat Dorshei Lashon Eber, 70

High Holy Day Prayer Book, 360

Hillel, 101, 211

Hippocrates, 36

Hirsch, Samson Raphael, 72, 173, 210, 219ff.; writings 225ff.; concepts of religion, 226-239; and education, 240-243; 250, 270, 290, 336

Hirch, Samuel, 167

Historical School (Jewish), 77, 96,-97, 186ff.; 192ff.; Schechter's views, 199-200; significance, 214; 319, 321, 331ff.

Historische Rechtschule, 196-197

History of the Israelitish Nation, see Wise, Isaac Mayer

Hithachduth Ha-Rabbanim, 383

Hochstraten, Jacob von, 39

Hofjuden, 45

Holdheim, Samuel, 179ff.; 291

Holland, 46-47, 115; spirit of tolerance, 43; Batavian puppet republic, 83
Holy Alliance, 275
Horeb, see Hirsch, Samson Raphael
"House of Living Judaism", 314-315
Humanities, 37-38; Humanist movement, 35; and tolerance, 38; in Judaism, 180
Humboldt, William, 277
Hundt, Hartwig, 277
I and Thou, see Buber, Martin
Ibn Ezra, 259-260
Iggrot Shadal, see Luzzatto, Samuel David
Imperial Serfs, see *Servae Camerae*
Infamous Decrees, see France
Inquisition, The, 46, 83, 114
Irredentist movement, 263
Isaac, Rabbi Levi of Berdichev, 128
Islam, 34-35, 110, 113, 121, 291, 300
Israel, State of 112, 115, 154, 349, 358, 398
Isserles, Moses, 108
Italy; Orthodoxy in, 250ff.; struggle for unification, 263
Jacobson, Israel, 157ff.; Berlin Temple, 159; 159ff.
Jastrow, Marcus, 321
Jerusalem, see Mendelssohn, Moses
Jesus, 64, 68, 147, 150-151; proof of divinity, 39
Jewish Institute of Religion, 315
Jewish Publication Society of America, 318
Jewish Orphan Home, 284
Jewish Science, Movement for, see Science of Judaism.
Jewish Theological Seminary, 301, 321ff.; expanded program, 330-331
Jewish Theological Seminary in Breslau, 193-194
Joseph, Rabbi Jacob, 375
Joseph II, Emperor, 72-73
Judah the Prince, 101-102
Judaism: Mendelssohn's concept, 60; and Reason, 60-61; dogma and doctrine, 61, 63, 65, 98, 109ff.; creed, 62, 65, 89; ethnic factor, 87-89; unique concept, 88; *mitz-*

vot, 109; idea of God, 152; ethnic factor, 177, 180; a creed, 182; effect of German Reform, 184; Frankel's definition, 198-199; Luzzatto's view of Scripture and ethics, 255-258; as a civilization, 348ff.; covenant of unity, 358ff.
Judaism as a Civilization, see Kaplan, Mordecai M.
Judengasse, 28, 29
Judenspiegel, 277
Juedische Freischule, 72-73
Kahal: institutions, 24; functions, 24; government and judicial authority, 25; taxation, 25; corporate autonomy, 26; officials, 26; in Poland, 117, 119; 223-224; 357; 400
Kaidonover, Hirsch, 120
Kalischer, Zevi Hirsch, 238, 246
Kant, Immanuel, 51-53, 63, 134, 168, 231, 292
Kaplan, Mordecai M., 326, 346ff.; see Reconstructionism
Kav Hayashar, see Kaidonover, Zevi Hirsch
Kehillah, see *Kahal*
Kelal Israel, 197, 340, 358
Kepler, 36
Kierkegaard, Soren, 142, 145, 389
Kinaat Haemet, see Chorin, Aaron
Kley, Edward, 159, 220
Knesset Israel, 245
Koheleth Mussar, 70
Kohler, Kaufmann, 298
Kohut, Alexander, 300, 321
Kompert, Leopold, 282
Kossuth, Louis, 280
Krochmal, Nachman, 78, 169ff.; 197, 215; his interpretation of Judaism, 171ff.; 266, 270, 336
Kunitzer, Moses, 161
Ladino, 32-33, 113
Lasker, Edward, 223
Lateran Council: Third, 24, 27; Fourth, 21, 27
Lavater, Johan Casper, 54-55
Leeser, Isaac, 288, 296, 317ff.
Leibnitz, 49, 60, 70
Lessing, Gotthold Ephraim, 56
Levin, Rahel, 75

Levinthal, Israel H., 356
Levita, Elijah, 252
Levy, Samuel, 82
Lichtfreudliche Gemeinden, 206
Liebermann, Eliezer, 161ff., 267
Lilienthal, Max, 283, 287-288
Lithuania, 118
Locke, John, 37, 253-254, 371
Lodge-Johnson Immigration Bill, 308
Lombards, 24
London Polyglot, 40
Longfellow, Henry Wadsworth, 369
Louis XIV, 79
Louis XV, 80
Louis XVI, 74, 80
Louis Philippe I, 279
"Lovers of Zion," 301
Lubavitcher Hassidim, 396
Luria, Isaac, 68
Luther, Martin, 39, 41; and the Jews, 41-42
Luzzatto, Ephraim, 250
Luzzatto, Hezekiah, 250
Luzzatto, Moses Hayim, 250
Luzzatto, Samuel David, 78, 97, 234, 249-270, 289, Scriptural truth and ethics, 255-258; and Spinoza, 260 ff.; views on nationalism and emancipation, 263-267; 320, 336, 337
Magyars, 280
Maimonides, 35, 50, 62-63, 66, 105-106, 110; *Thirteen Articles of Faith*, 47; *Mishneh Torah*, 106; *Yad Hachazakah*, 107; *Sefer Hamitzvot*, 107; creed, 111; 228, 234, 255, 259-260, 264-266, 389ff.
Maimonides College, 318, 320
Malshin, 25
Manzoni, Alessandro, 252
Mappa, see Isserles
Marr, Wilhelm, 303
Marranos, 43, 46, 79, 86, 114-115, 368
Marriage and Divorce, 86-87, 89; intermarriage, 89, 92, 181; revisions of Philadelphia Conference, 295-296
Marshall, Louis, 323
Marx, Alexander, 326

Maximilian, Emperor 39
May Laws of 1882, 272, 322, 376
Medicine, Jews in, 31-32, 49
Meisels, Mordecai, 22-23
Memorbuch, 22
Menasseh ben Israel, 46, 58
Mendel, Menachem, 396
Mendel, Rabbi, 150
Mendelssohn, Dorothea, 75
Mendelssohn, Moses, 18, 49-78, 80, 109; writings, 51-52, 58-59, 69-71; influenced by Kant, 52-53; ethical viewpoint, 53; and Lavater, 54-55; attitude to Christianity, 54-57; friendship with Lessing, 56-57; and von Dohm, 57-58; views on Church and State, 59-60; concept of Judaism, 60-62; and revival of Hebrew, 69-81; and Enlightenment, 73; 255, 268, 332
Mendes, Henry Pereira, 323, 380
Mercantilism, 44-45
Merzbacher, Leo, 283, 286
Messianism, 96, 107, 124, 148, 151; Pseudo-Messianism, 118, 121, 178; Frankel's belief, 202, 209; Frankfort Conference, 209; Rapoport and, 216; 268; and Reform, 301; 337
Metternich, 274
Midrash, 104
Milim Leloha, 49
Military s e r v i c e , Jews and: in France, 83-84, 87, 91
Minhag America, 289
Mirabeau, Count, 18, 75, 81
Mishna, 101-103, 111
Mishneh Torah, see Maimonides
Mission Theory, 172, 177-178, 232ff., Luzzatto's views, 268; 295; 312-313, 337
Mithnagdim, 135ff., 138
Mizrachi, 96, 244ff.
Mohammed, 68
Mole, Commissioner, 86
Monatschrift für Geschichte und Wissenschaft des Judenthums, see Frankel, Zacharia
Moneylending, 23-24; 45-47, 80, 84, 87, 90; position of Jew, 24; Chris-

tian prohibition, 24
Montefiore, Claude, 324
Montefiore, Moses, 281
Montesquieu, 18
Morais, Sabbato, 320ff.
Mortara, Edgar, 296, 320
Moser, Moses, 188
Moses, 61, 99, 110; Mendelssohn and Mosaic Law, 59, 252, 255, 289-290
Moslems, see Islam
Munk, Salomon, 184
Mussar literature, 120
Napoleon Bonaparte, 83, 89-90, 93; and Assembly of Notables, 85; 158-159, 263, 274
Nathan the Wise, see Lessing, Gotthold Ephraim
Nationalism, Jewish, 77, 204, 238ff., 272, Luzzatto's Particularism, 263 ff.; Schechter's views, 334ff.
Neo-Hassidism, 96ff.
Neo-Orthodoxy, 97, 210; in Germany, 218ff.; Luzzatto's 249ff.
Netivoth Shalom, 69
Neturei Karta, 398
Neuer Israelitische Tempel Verein, 220
New Testament, 64, 175
Newton, 36-37
New York Board of Rabbis, 386
Nicholas I, 372
Noah, Mordecai Manuel, 281
Nogah Hatzedek, see Liebermann, Eliezer
Numerus Clausus, 309, 376
Occupations, Jewish: in Palestine, 23; under feudal system, 23; in medieval economy, 24; in the ghetto, 30-31; in commerce, 44-48, 79; after Edict of Toleration, 72; in Alsace-Lorraine, 80; and Assembly of Notables, 87; prohibition under Infamous Decrees, 90; 276
Oglethorpe, James, 370
Olat Tamid, 293
On the Civic Improvement of the Conditions of the Jews, see Dohm, Christian Wilhelm von

Oppenheimer, Samuel, 45
Or Adonai, see Crescas, Hasdai
Organic Regulation on the Mosaic Religion, 90-91
Orthodox and Orthodoxy, 96, 98, 109-111, reaction to Mendelssohn, 77; opposition to Buber, 154; opposition to Jacobson, 158; opposition to Reform Temples, 165; effect of Reform upon, 184-185; and Neo-Orthodoxy in Germany, 218ff. in Italy, 249ff.; see also America, Jewry in
Palestine, see Zion and Zionism
Pascal, Blaise, 252
Paul of Tarsus, 124, 147, 149, 151
Peninei Shadal, 251
Petrarch, Francesco, 37
Pfefferkorn, John, 38; controversy, 39-40
Phaedon, see Mendelssohn, Moses
Philadelphia Conference, 294-295
Philip the Fair, 23
Philipson, David, 182, 184, 311
Philipson, Ludwig, 206
Philo, 66, 208
Philoxenus, 258
Pilpulism, 32, 137, 139,234
Pittsburgh Platform, 272, 298ff.; 320, 361, 400
Pobiedonostzev, 376
Poland, Jewry in, 116ff.
Polony, Meyer, 372
Portugal, 46
Positive Historical School, see Historical School (Jewish)
Poznanski, Gustav, 286
Preliminary Studies of the Septuagint, see Frankel, Zacharia
Principles of Jewish Matrimonial Law, see Holdheim, Samuel
Prophets, 65, 88, 177, 242, 293
Prosbul, see Hillel
Protestantism, 41-42; Reformation, 30, 39-41, 206, 214
Protocols of the Elders of Zion, 272, 308-309
Prussian Emancipation Act, 276
Rabbi Isaac Elchanan Yeshiva, 323, 378ff.

Rabbinate; 110, 112; combined with medical profession, 31; opposition to secular learning, 49; criticism of Mendelssohn, 55; reduction of authority in France, 87; under consistorial organization, 91; and Hassidism, 119, 136-137; new type, 166; Reform, 283; Schechter's view, 334

Rabbinical Assembly, 341ff.

Rabbinical Council of America, 381, 387.

Rapoport, Solomon Judah, 215ff.

Rashi, 105, 266

Rationalism, 156-157, 195; of Schechter, 331; of Kaplan, 359ff.; see also Reason

Reason, 35, 37, 95; Kant's views, 53; and dogmas, 61, 63, 67; Cult of, see France; Temple of, see France; Age of, 109;

Rebbe, see *Tzaddik*

Recanati, Jacob Hai, 161

Reconstructionism, 346ff.; aims, 350ff., principles, 351ff.; doctrinal interpretations, 359ff.

Reconstructionist Foundation, 347

Reform Movement: 96-97, 109; religious ferment, 161ff.; growth of movement, 166ff.; Krochmal's impact, 172; decline, 183; influence, 184-185; Frankel's attitude, 202-203; *Reform Vereine,* 283; rabbinical leadership, 283; see also America, Jewry in:

Reformation, The, see Protestantism

Reines, Isaac Jacob, 247

Religionsgesellchaft, 222

Renaissance, The, 17, 35-38, 42, 190

Residence Restrictions, 72; under Infamous Decrees, 90

Responsa, 71, 105-106; Anti-Reform, 163ff.

Reuchlin, Johan Van, 38-39

Revel, Bernard, 379

Revelation: 53; Revealed Legislation, 61; Geiger's views, 175; Frankel's views, 214; Wise's view, 290, 390

Riesser, Gabriel, 279, 281

Rights of Residence, 23, 25, 48

Rindfleisch, 21

Ritual Murder Charge, in Damascus, 281; see Blood Libel

Romanticism, 190, 219; influence on Frankel, 194ff., influence on Luzzatto, 252ff., German, 276

Rosenberg, Israel, 382

Rosenzweig, Franz, 141

Rothschild, Amschel, 47, 281

Rousseau, 17, 48, 252-253, 259

Rudimenta Hebraica, see Johan Reuchlin

Rudolph II of Austria, 22

Ruhs, Friedrich, 276

Saadya, 60, 66-67, 255

Sabbath: in ghetto life, 30; Holdheim's view, 181, Ginzberg's view, 200; Reform views, 294

Sabbath Prayer Book, see Kaplan, Mordecai M.

Sadducees, 211

Salomon, Hayim, 372

Salon Jewesses, 75

Salvation, Essentials for: Mendelssohn's views, 61; in Christianity, 64; in Judaism, 110

Sanhedrin, Grand, see France

San Remo Conference, 307

Satmar Rebbe, 397-398

Schechter, Solomon, 67, 197, 199-200, 319, 324ff.; doctrines of, 331ff.

Schiff, Jacob H., 323, 326

Schiller, 264

Schlegel, Friedrich von, 75

Schleiermacher, 75

Schneerson, Joseph Isaac, 396

Schnierer, Sarah, 246

Scholasticism, 35

Schutzgeld, 47

Schutzjuden, 47-48, 51, 92

Science of Judaism, 77-78, 167; motivating factors, 189ff.; and Frankel, 193; and Hirsch, 237-238; 267, 270, 324

Secular Learning: in the 18th century, 48-49; in Germany, 72-73; in France, 81, 84; in Jacobson's

school, 157; in Hirsch, 223, 224, 240ff.
Sefer Ha-Ikkarim, 68
Sefer Hamitzvot, see Maimonides
Sephardim, 81, 96, 112-115, 160, 272, 284-285, 318, 372
Servi Camerae, 22; protection, 23
Seven Laws of Noah, 55, 62
Shadal, see Luzzatto, Samuel David
Shearith Israel, 369
Shechinah, Concept of, 125-127, 142, 145-146, 154
Shem Tov of Leghorn, 161
Shneur Zalman, of Ladi, 132ff 135, see also Habad
Shochet, Alexander, see Besht, disciples of
Shulchan Aruch, see Caro, Joseph; also, 112, 162, 337, 340, 388
Sic et Non, see Abelard, Peter
Sinzheim, David, 86, 90
Skwerer Hassidim, 398
Smith, Adam, 57-58
Smolenskin, Peretz, 77
Society for Culture and Science of Judaism, 280-281
Society for the Advancement of Judaism, 347
Sofer, Rabbi Moshe, 163, 218-219.
Solomon, Gotthold, 204-205
Soloveitchik, Joseph, 388ff.
Spinoza, Benedict, 134, 251, 260ff., 291
Spiritual Zionism, see Ahad Ha-Am
Steinberg, Milton, 364ff.
Sulzberger, Mayer, 326
Summa Theologica, see Aquinas, Thomas
Symbolik, 227
Synagogue: in ghetto life, 31; as Kehillah, 284; in Eastern Europe, 378
Synagogue Council of America, 386
Szold, Benjamin, 321
Takkanah, 25, 26, 342
Tam, Rabbenu, 105
Tanya, see Shneur Zalman, of Ladi
Taxation, 22-23, 57, 72, 74, 80; fiscal responsibility of *Kahal,* 25-26
Theobald of Cambridge, 21

Thirteen Articles of Faith, 255; criticized by Crescas, 68, see Maimonides
Tiktin, Solomon, 173-174
Tillich, Paul, 154
Tonnerre, Count Clermont, 81
Torah: Mendelssohn's views, 61, 99; *Torah Shebichtav,* 99; *Torah Shebal Peh,* 99; rabbinic interpretation, 100; exposition and interpretation, 100-101, 112; in Hassidism, 136; to Buber, 148ff.; Frankel's beliefs, 198-199; Hirsch's views, 226ff., 233ff.
Torah im Derech Eretz, 223, 240
Tracte des Sensations, 254
Tradition: Schecter's views, 199-200; in Reconstructionism, 365
Traditional Judaism and Traditionalists, 77, 96, 98-99
Transubstantiation, see Desecration of the Host
Treaty of Westphalia, 80
Treitschke, Heinrich von, 303
Trennungs Orthodoxie, 224, 386
Tzaddik, 124, 128-136
Union for Jewish Culture and Science, 188
Union of American Hebrew Congregations, 296, 313ff.
Union of Orthodox Jewish Congregations, 323, 380ff., 387.
Union Prayerbook, 290
United Synagogue, 328ff.
University of Judaism, 331
Vico, Giovanni Battista, 171
Victor Emanuel II, 33
Vindiciae Judeorum, see Menasseh ben Israel
Violence, Anti-Jewish, 19ff.; against Alsatian Jewry, 80; in Spain, 114; Nazi persecutions, 273, 393ff., East European persecutions, 375.
Volksgeist, 196-197
Voltaire, 33, 48, 252
Wagenseil, Johann, 40
Wagner, Richard, 303
Wealth of Nations, see Smith, Adam
Wenceslaus IV, 23
Weizmann, Chaim, 306

Wertheimer, Samson, 45
Wessely, Naphtali Herz, 71, 72
William of Norwich, 21
Williamsburg, Hassidim, 395
    ings 288-290; 320
Wise, Stephen S., 315
Wissenschaft des Judentums, see
    Science of Judaism
World Zionist Congress, 244, 301-
    302, 335
Worship Addresses, see Holdheim,
    Samuel
Yellow Badge, 27, 30
Yeshiva Torah Vodaath, 345, 398
Yeshiva University, 248, 379ff.
Yeshivot: in ghetto, 31; 383, 387-
    388
Yiddish, 32, 48, 69-70, 113, 272,
    385

Yigdal, 62
Yisroel Mensch, 226, 243
Young Germany Movement, 279
Young Israel 381, 383ff.
Zevi, Shabbetai, 118-119
Zeitgeist, 211, 233-234
Zion and Zionism; of Martin Buber,
    141ff., Frankel's idea, 203ff.;
    Hirsch's attitude, 238ff., 244ff.;
    269-270; precursors, 281; Reform
    view, 301ff.; Movement, 305ff.;
    334
Zionist Organization of America,
    305
Zohar, 118, 121, 199
Zunz, Leopold, 169, 186-192, 338,
    339
Zusya, Rabbi, 144